THE AMERICAN
OCCUPATION OF JAPAN

THE AMERICAN OCCUPATION OF JAPAN

The Origins of the Cold War in Asia

MICHAEL SCHALLER

New York   Oxford
OXFORD UNIVERSITY PRESS

Oxford University Press

Oxford   New York   Toronto
Delhi   Bombay   Calcutta   Madras   Karachi
Petaling Jaya   Singapore   Hong Kong   Tokyo
Nairobi   Dar es Salaam   Cape Town
Melbourne   Auckland

and associated companies in
Beirut   Berlin   Ibadan   Nicosia

Library of Congress Cataloging in Publication Data
Schaller, Michael
The American occupation of Japan.

Bibliography: p.
Includes index.
1. United States—Foreign relations—Japan.   2. Japan—Foreign relations—United States.   3. United States—Foreign relations—Asia, Southeastern.   4. Asia, Southeastern—Foreign relations—United States.   5. Japan—History—Allied occupation, 1945–1952.   6. United States—Foreign
relations—1945–1953.   I. Title.
E183.8.J3S29   1985   327.73052   85-8818
ISBN 0-19-503626-3
ISBN 0-19-505190-4 (pbk.)

4   6   8   10   9   7   5   3

Printed in the United States of America

For Sue and Nicholas

PREFACE

On October 1, 1945, Foreign Service Officer John K. Emmerson began his formal duties in Tokyo by moving into the newly requisitioned offices of a major Japanese corporation. He arrived "just as a Mitsui junior executive was clearing the last items from his desk," the diplomat later recalled. Before leaving, the displaced manager "pointed to a map on the wall depicting Japan's Co-Prosperity Sphere. 'There it is,' he said smiling. 'We tried. See what you can do with it!' " For Emmerson, who had spent the previous year interrogating Japanese prisoners of war (POWs) in China, the words had a tremendous impact. At that moment, he noted, "the whole burden of American foreign policy in Asia hit me in the stomach. What were we going to do with it?"

By the spring of 1950, with the United States struggling to restrain the sweep of Communist revolution over Asia, the prophetic quality of these words seemed quite real. Diplomats such as George F. Kennan spoke openly of a need to create for Japan a new "empire to the South." That April, Japan's feisty, conservative prime minister, Yoshida Shigeru, discussed with one of Emmerson's successors the American pressure on Tokyo to accept a peace treaty that excluded China and the Soviet Union, yet granted the United States post-Occupation bases. Not only his left-wing critics but his right-wing colleagues as well, Yoshida complained, opposed what they saw as a willingness to subordinate Japanese interests to America's cold war policies. The prime minister's response sought to placate these criticisms by predicting that "just as the United States was once a colony of Great Britain but is now the stronger of the two, if Japan becomes a colony of the United States it will also eventually become the stronger."

Although the verdict on Yoshida's prophecy can be disputed, few question that U.S. policy toward Japan after the Second World War, like that toward its Axis partner Germany, stands out as one of the few triumphs in postwar diplomacy. Unlike the clouded, even tragic, American crusades in China, Korea, and Vietnam, the legacy of the Occupation seems one of progress, prosperity, peace, and democracy. Even more unusual, this achievement took place under the supervision of America's most controversial military hero, Gen. Douglas MacArthur.

Although most accounts of the Occupation portray it as a unique and distinct event in postwar diplomacy, the spectacle of Japan's recovery from disaster confirmed more trends in cold war history than it contradicted. America's handling of both Axis partners cannot be understood without examining the political, economic, and military crises that swept over the world after 1945. The break in Soviet–American relations, the economic collapse in Western Europe and Japan, the surge of Asian nationalism, and the Chinese Revolution all provided the context in which MacArthur, the Truman administration, and the Japanese themselves charted an uncertain course. Planning and implementing Occupation policies never occurred in a vacuum, before or after surrender. Conversely, concern for Japan's future shaped aspects of the most controversial American actions in postwar Asia, such as the interventions in China, Korea, and Vietnam.

Even before the atomic bombs fell in August 1945, policymakers in Washington pondered how to exercise control in Asia through the deft manipulation of Chinese, Southeast Asian, and Japanese aspirations. But the tide of revolutionary nationalism engulfing this vast region outraced all presurrender predictions, forcing the Truman administration toward new strategies. Once resolved to implement a containment program along China's periphery, the United States rebuilt Japan as the pivot of what American officials called the Great Crescent, a barrier of anti-Communist states stretching from Hokkaido to Pakistan. Usually described as a series of offshore island strongpoints, this defense perimeter actually encompassed a complex network of economic, geographic, political, and military relationships. Moreover, from the middle of 1947 through the outbreak of the Korean War, most of President Harry S. Truman's advisers considered MacArthur's handing of the Occupation more an impediment to recovery and security than an asset. Increasingly, his personal agenda and political ambitions deviated sharply from the ways both civilian and military leaders in Washington envisioned Japan's future.

The decision of the Truman administration in 1947–48 to initiate a Japanese recovery program modeled on the Marshall Plan brought about a direct clash between the flamboyant Supreme Commander and almost all agencies in Washington. In defiance of MacArthur, the State and Defense departments halted many basic Occupation reforms in pursuit of economic recovery and political stability. This recovery drive also spurred growing concerns about where Japan would find suitable markets and raw materials, especially in light of China's revolution, Southeast Asian rebellions, and Tokyo's chronic dollar shortage. Without fully anticipating the consequences, the American government implemented a program in Asia that reflected a desire for Japan to serve as the hub of a new regional alliance.

This study does not pretend to dwell on the remarkable internal transformation of Japan during the Occupation years. That is, in great measure, another and equally important story. I have tried to place the Occupation in the context of overall American East Asian diplomacy from 1945 to 1950, an approach that reveals a long-obscured relationship between the successful centerpiece of American policy and the dubious campaigns to "secure the great crescent." In short, it provides a novel perspective on the origins of the cold war in Asia.

Tucson, Arizona   M.S.
January 1985

ACKNOWLEDGMENTS

Many friends, institutions, and organizations have assisted in this project. Leonard Dinnerstein, Robert Schulzinger, Akira Iriye, Walter LaFeber, Robert M. Blum, Lloyd Gardner, William W. Stueck, and Bruce Cumings all read the manuscript in part or whole, making suggestions for improvement for which I am indebted. Howard Schonberger, William S. Borden, and especially John W. Dower deserve special thanks. They shared a wealth of knowledge on this subject, allowed me to read their own works in progress on related issues, and scrutinized early drafts with tremendous care. I first explored some of these themes in a paper jointly written with James Elston for the Amherst Conference on Occupied Japan.

Numerous archivists and librarians provided help along the way. At the National Archives, Gerald Haines and John Taylor tracked down wayward documents with consummate skill. Dennis Bilger of the Truman Library and the professional staffs of the Center for Military History, the Center for Naval History, the MacArthur Memorial, the Princeton University Library, the Columbia University Library, the Washington National Records Center, and the British Public Record Office were consistently helpful and encouraging during my research.

Much to my surprise, the departments of State and Treasury processed numerous Freedom of Information Act (FOIA) requests in a reasonable period of time. In many cases, these materials provided a vital supplement to archival holdings. Unfortunately, my experiences proved almost unique in this regard, with later researchers finding these agencies increasingly unresponsive to FOIA requests.

Generous financial support came from many sources. The National Endowment for the Humanities, the John Simon Guggenheim Memorial Foundation, the American Philosophical Society, the Harry S. Truman Library Foundation, the Northeast Asia Council of the Association for Asian Studies, and the University of Arizona Humanities Research Fund provided assistance. My editor at Oxford University Press, Nancy Lane, also encouraged this project in many ways over several years.

Nikki Matz and Marilyn Bradian cheerfully typed more drafts of the manuscript than they or I wish to recall.

CONTENTS

Day off ?

THE AMERICAN
OCCUPATION OF JAPAN

SOVIET UNION
(U.S.S.R.)

SEA OF
OKHOTSK

Sakhalin

MONGOLIA

Kurile Islands

Vladivostok

Peking

NORTH
KOREA

JAPAN

CHINA

Seoul

Tokyo

SOUTH
KOREA

TIBET

Chunking

Nanking

Shanghai

Delhi

NEPAL

Bhutan

Okinawa

Iwo Jima

INDIA

TAIWAN
(FORMOSA)

Pacific Ocean

Calcutta

E.
BURMA
PAKISTAN
(Bangla
Desh)

Hanoi

Hong
Kong

MARIANAS
IS.

Bombay

THAI-
LAND

SOUTH

Tinian

Saipan

BAY OF
BENGAL

Rangoon

FRENCH
INDOCHINA

Manila

PHILIPPINES

Guam

CHINA

PHILIPPINE

CAROLINE IS.

Gulf
of
Siam

SEA

ISLANDS

SRI LANKA
CEYLON

MALAYA

Brunei

N. BORNEO

Palau Is.

Truk I.

SARAWAK

Singapore

SUMATRA

BORNEO

Moluccas

Admiralty Is.

CELEBES

(West
Irian)

SOLOMON IS.

Djakarta

Dutch East Indies

Timor

NEW GUINEA

Guadalcanal

JAVA
(INDONESIA)

Indian Ocean

Darwin

CORAL SEA

AUSTRALIA

Brisbane

JAPAN
and the
"GREAT CRESCENT"
after World War II

Perth

Adelaide

Sidney

Melbourne

Tasmania

1

THE END
OF THE PACIFIC WAR

As the Pacific War approached its fiery climax over Japan, few observers could have accurately predicted the eventual course of the Occupation. Still recoiling from the Pearl Harbor attack and its aftermath and reflecting generations of anti-Asiatic prejudice, American public opinion seemed determined to crush Japan. In 1944, a Gallup Poll revealed that 13 percent of the public favored exterminating all Japanese. A third of those answering a June 1945 survey said they would summarily execute Emperor Hirohito; most others said they would condemn him as a war criminal. Sen. Lister Hill (D–Alabama) urged the armed forces to "gut the heart of Japan with fire"; Sen. Ernest McFarland (D–Arizona) insisted that "the Japs . . . pay dearly through their blood and the ashes of their cities" for attacking America; and Sen. Theodore G. Bilbo (D–Mississippi), a notorious racist, wrote Gen. Douglas MacArthur shortly after surrender to urge the sterilization of all Japanese.

An adviser to the influential State–War–Navy Coordinating Committee (SWNCC) proposed the "almost total elimination of the Japanese as a race"; Japan ought to be bombed so heavily that there would be "little left of its civilization." In 1945, Elliott Roosevelt, the president's son, told former Vice-President and then-current Secretary of Commerce Henry A.

Wallace that the United States should "keep on bombing until we have destroyed about half the Japanese civilian population." Even Franklin Delano Roosevelt, the champion of liberty, revealed interest in a scheme to crossbreed the Japanese with docile Pacific islanders. Compulsory eugenics, he told Smithsonian anthropologist Arles Hrdlicka, might eradicate the "primitive" brains and "barbarism" of the enemy race.[1]

Some top military leaders planned to flaunt this contempt as part of their strategy. In July 1945, for example, Army Air Force Commander, Gen. Henry H. (Hays) Arnold, drafted a letter to be dropped over Japan. Beginning with the salutation, "Dear Hirohito," it threatened "completely [to] annihilate the Japanese people" unles Tokyo surrendred at once. Only vigorous objections by Secretary of War Henry L. Stimson and Under Secretary of State Joseph C. Grew persuaded Arnold to moderate his threat.[2]

Even discounting for the hyperbole and passion of wartime rhetoric, the actual violence of battle made most verbal attacks appear understated. For months, massive firebomb raids had reduced 50 percent of urban Japan to cinders. Allied sinkings of merchant vessels had imposed a tight blockade on food and raw material imports from Asia and the Pacific. Several million soldiers and civilians were hopelessly isolated in China and Southeast Asia. As "invulnerable" outposts, like Iwo Jima and Okinawa, fell to the Americans, tens of thousands of dispirited Japanese soldiers died or committed suicide. By August, two million Japanese had perished, a fourth of them civilians.

When the twin blows of the atomic bomb and the Soviet declaration of war struck Japan, the emperor took the initiative of accepting defeat. Speaking to his subjects by radio on August 15, he said the enemy had employed a "new and most cruel bomb" that inflicted a terrible toll on "innocent lives." Prolonging the war would not only obliterate Japan but threatened to destroy all "human civilization." Quoting Buddhist texts, he declared Japan would pave the way for peace by "enduring the unendurable and suffering what is unsufferable."

But many Japanese had already prepared themselves for defeat. The real question in their minds related to the shape of the Occupation, not its inevitability. Fujiyama Aiichiro, a business leader who later served as foreign minister, recalled that "when it was learned that the occupying power would be the U.S. . . . many industrialists uncorked their champagne bottles and toasted the coming of a new industrialists era."[3]

Months before Japan surrendered, influential officials in both Tokyo and Washington had begun to consider the outlines of a postwar era. Despite the fanatic pronouncements emanating from both capitals, these planners labored to anticipate the shape of a new Asian–Pacific order that would accommodate the desires of the United States and Japan. In-depth studies by the historians Akira Iriye and John W. Dower reveal (from very different perspectives) that by 1943 many Japanese bureaucrats realized the futility of the war and hoped to negotiate a conditional surrender. These middle- and high-level officials believed that Japan ought to try again to cooperate with the United States in developing the Asian economy by returning to the pre-1931 Wilsonian principles of nonmilitary expansion.

Akira Iriye has identified a cadre of Japanese Wilsonians scattered throughout various ministries who were determined to rectify the tragic "stumble" into the path of war that had been brought on by the depression and the seizure of power by militant nationalists. This group believed that Japan itself must initiate peace talks and purge the government of radical elements. Such a step might elicit American goodwill and speed Japan's eventual readmission to the ranks of the world's advanced industrial community.[4]

John Dower's study of the Japanese diplomat and prime minister Yoshida Shigeru revealed the equally important role played by traditional conservatives (often called moderates or liberals by American policymakers) in setting a postwar agenda. For example, he elucidated the activities of the so-called YOHANSEN group (Yoshida was a member), which served as the conservatives' spearhead after 1941. Drawing members from the nobility, the armed forces, the business community, and the bureaucracy, it considered the war an unwinnable blunder likely to bring revolution in its wake.

These traditionalists resented wartime economic controls and the expanded power of the military because they represented a new form of state planning that undermined the old order. They also feared a popular revolt from below, aimed at the old elite, should the war continue. A negotiated peace seemed the only alternative to domestic revolution or foreign destruction.

The YOHANSEN faction proceeded cautiously to place supporters in key government and military posts. Only when air attacks intensified greatly early in 1945 did the group's titular head, Prince Konoe Fumimaro, submit a memorial (composed in part by Yoshida Shigeru) directly to the emperor. A member of the nobility and a former prime minister, Konoe described a grim future should the war continue. On February 14, he told the emperor that the war held only the prospect of defeat, upheaval, and the destruction of the *kokutai* (the traditional imperial political system). Konoe condemned Gen. Tojo Hideki and his supporters as radicals who precipitated war as a pretext for their plan to reshape the Japanese state and economy on the Soviet model. Even though defeat is terrible, the prince had written in 1944, "leftist revolution" is "as frightening, or more frightening, than defeat." Although defeat might eventually be redressed, "if we have a leftist revolution, *Kokutai* and everything will be gone to the winds. . . ." An Allied victory, he noted in his 1945 memorial, did not necessarily threaten *kokutai*. Rather, the "communist revolution which may accompany defeat" could totally undo the traditional order.[5]

Konoe and Yoshida also warned the emperor of the growing Soviet threat. Russia had already displaced Germany as the arbiter of Eastern Europe. Should the Soviets enter the Pacific War, they could annex Chinese territory and spread Communist influence. The prince also noted the potential threat of the Chinese Communists and the handful of Japanese Communists and prisoners of war active in Yenan (Yan'an).*

Konoe urged the emperor to sanction a move against the military clique, who were determined to continue the war. Only their displacement, he insisted, could prevent an internal revolution and induce the Americans to soften peace terms. "Wiping out this ring and carrying out the reconstruction of the military" were the "preconditions and prerequisites for saving Japan from a communist revolution. . . ." Despite this plea, neither the emperor nor the YOHANSEN group had much impact on the extreme militarists until the climactic events of early August. Only then did the emperor feel secure enough to propose, and the military despondent enough to accept, surrender.[6]

The initial failure of the peace faction and Yoshida's arrest by the political police on April 15 had an important if unanticipated result. Yoshida's two-month detention certified his credentials as an antimilitary peace advocate acceptable to Occupation officials. Moreover, the contents of the Konoe memorial revealed that influential Japanese shared many of the identical political concerns being voiced by those Americans charting a future course for Japan.

Even before the outbreak of war, an informal "special research division" within the State Department had discussed the shape of a postwar settlement. Area specialists, like Hugh Borton, Robert Feary, and George Blakeslee, met occasionally with their counterparts in the War Department's Civil Affairs Division, which was under Maj. Gen. John H. Hilldring. But the planners remained marginal to the policy process. For example, they only learned of Roosevelt's Cairo Declaration (promising to strip Japan of virtually all its overseas territory) "as it appeared on the ticker tape." In 1944, however, the State Department's new Postwar Programs Committee (PWC) and the army's Civil Affairs Division (CAD)

---

* Throughout the book, Chinese names and places are shown spelled in the Wade-Giles system with the pinyin spelling in parentheses. The two exceptions, in which Wade-Giles only is used after first use, are Manchuria (Northeast), to avoid confusion, and Peking (Beijing), to avoid unnecessary repetition.

were given greater authority. General Hilldring prodded the two units to recommend an occupation plan for Japan, stipulating the nations to be involved, the program to be followed, and a method for disposing Japan's colonies and conquests.[7]

In March 1944, members of the PWC reported that they favored a nearly exclusive American occupation. Although token Allied forces might participate, no zonal divisions should be tolerated. In short, nothing should "prejudice the dominantly American character" of the operation. The PWC report favored utilizing the Japanese government for administrative purposes and, at least temporarily, retaining the emperor. Once Japan had been disarmed, democratized, and economically reformed, the group wrote, it could be allowed to rejoin the Asian–Pacific community. This agenda bore much resemblance to that put forward by the moderates in Tokyo.[8]

Hoping to coordinate these and other diplomatic ventures, three of Roosevelt's cabinet seretaries—Edward R. Stettinius, Henry L. Stimson, and James V. Forrestal of the State, War, and Navy departments, respectively—organized SWNCC in December 1944. Worried about the drift in policy as the president's vigor declined, Stimson hoped the committee might remedy the "present chaotic situation" in Washington. A crude predecessor of the National Security Council (NSC), SWNCC provided a forum for assistant secretaries and technical specialists from these three often-competitive departments to develop and coordinate policies without first going through the president.

SWNCC's Sub-Committee on the Far East formulated a program for Japan. It reconciled plans devised in each department and forged general policy in accord with the president's outline. The latter proved most difficult because Roosevelt generally neglected to inform even close subordinates about deals made with Allied leaders.

At the February 1945 Yalta Conference, for example, FDR reached a series of accords with Joseph Stalin and Winston Churchill regarding the future of China, Korea, Southeast Asia, and Japan. Yet, the president declined to tell SWNCC or the State Department that Russia would soon enter the Pacific War, that the Soviets were promised special economic privileges in Manchuria, and that Sakhalin Island would pass back into Russian hands. Planners had to rely on rumor and on Roosevelt's translator at Yalta, Charles E. Bohlen, for snippets of information.[9]

During the last year he lived, Roosevelt actually increased his reliance on personal diplomacy to settle complicated problems. For example, in 1944, he encouraged his friend, Treasury Secretary Henry Morgenthau, Jr., to take charge of planning for postwar Germany. The latter's Informal Policy Committee on Germany (IPCOG) recommended elimination of central political authority, dismantling of heavy industry, and a division of the country into occupation zones. In April 1945, when rumors swept the State Department that Morgenthau hoped to apply these ideas to Japan, SWNCC's Far Eastern Sub-Committee rushed to complete its own "U.S. Initial Post-Surrender Policy." Expanding on earlier reports, it urged exclusive American rule with no zonal division and utilization of the Japanese government to speed thorough but nonvindictive demilitarization, democratization, and economic reform. Although determined to stop war production, SWNCC planning opposed widescale dismantling of heavy industry.

Before Morgenthau could object, his patron died. President Harry S Truman, who long disliked Morgenthau, quickly eliminated the treasury secretary's special influence in the Oval Office. As Morgenthau fell from grace, the State, War, and Navy departments reclaimed their lost prerogatives. Now, such advisers as Henry Stimson, Joseph Grew, W. Averell Harriman, and James Forrestal came to the fore. Although this group had also served FDR, their views on the Soviet Union and postwar planning had moved in a different direction from his since the Yalta Conference. Roosevelt had selectively utilized this group, often playing them off against each other. Desperate for information, advice, and emotional support, Truman leaned on their judgment almost exclusively.

All these officials recognized the dilemma faced by Washington in its effort to defeat Japan as soon as possible. After the demise of Roosevelt's initial strategy of utilizing Nationalist China's large but unreliable army as a proxy, the campaign against Japan relied on island hopping and the prospect of future Soviet assistance. The seizure of Pacific islands allowed the air force and navy to impose a tight blockade and launch an air offensive against the home islands. Eventually, Soviet forces would smash Japan's largely intact army in Northeast Asia at the same time that the United States invaded Japan proper.

Early on, however, American leaders realized that Soviet entry into the Pacific War would, inevitably, extend Moscow's influence in Northeast Asia. At Yalta, Roosevelt sought to place limits on this expansion by trading concessions to Moscow in Manchuria for a Soviet pledge to support exclusively the beleaguered Kuomintang (KMT) regime of Chiang Kai-shek (Jiang Jieshi). Not only diplomats but military officials as well agreed on the necessity of striking this bargain. In February 1945, for example, Gen. Douglas MacArthur told a member of the War Department's General Staff that the Soviets "want all of Manchuria, Korea and possibly part of north China. This seizure of territory [is] inevitable; but the United States must insist that Russia pay her way by invading Manchuria at the earliest possible moment." When Secretary of the Navy James Forrestal visited the general in Manila a few days later, MacArthur repeated this view even more emphatically. Because China could furnish no help against Japan, "he felt that we should secure the commitment of the Russians to active and vigorous prosecution of a campaign against the Japanese in Manchukuo of such proportions as to pin down a very large part of the Japanese army." If the Russians could be induced to throw some sixty divisions into Northeast Asia, MacArthur asserted, American forces could more easily invade the home islands. Ironically, he predicted that Stalin might try to avoid fighting in Northeast Asia in order to divert American forces away from the critical invasion of Japan. As late as mid-June, MacArthur urged the Joint Chiefs of Staff (JCS) to try to hasten a Soviet attack from Siberia.[10]*

One development alone—unknown to MacArthur until late July—might alter these assumptions about reliance on the Soviets. Since 1941, American scientists working on the Manhattan Project had been constructing an atomic bomb. If perfected and used, it might compel Japan's surrender without either the prohibitive casualties of an American invasion or the political liabilities of Soviet entry into the war. By speeding peace, the United States might contain the Soviet sphere of control without any direct Russian–American confrontation.

Besides the human and political costs certain to result from prolonging the war, American planners recognized other advantages presented by the atomic bomb. The entire political superstructure of Asia neared collapse during the summer of 1945. China stood on the brink of civil war. Nationalists in French Indochina, the Dutch East Indies, and in the British colonies were prepared to resist the reimposition of colonial rule. Although while no one in Washington favored the maintenance of Japanese control, there was fear that a protracted war might precipitate a Soviet surge into the growing political vacuum of East and Southeast Asia.

Secretary of War Henry Stimson and Under Secretary of State Joseph Grew raised these issues frequently between May and August 1945. Stimson's detailed knowledge of the atomic bomb and Grew's position as America's senior Japan expert gave their opinions added weight within the Truman administration. Although not identical, their attitudes had a similar objective. Not incidentally, both men soon planned to retire after decades of public service, which added to their willingness to press controversial ideas on the president.

Grew took the initiative of asking the War and Navy departments and President Truman to reexamine the strategy adopted against Japan. In May, he urged that the United States abrogate the Yalta accords and seek

---

* Tokyo shared this growing concern over the potential for Soviet influence in Northeast Asia. During the spring and summer, the Japanese tried, unsuccessfully, to induce Stalin to mediate on their behalf some form of negotiated settlement with the Western Allies. The Russian leader declined.

a delay in Russia's entry into the Pacific War. Grew, unaware of the atomic bomb, felt that conventional arms and skilful diplomacy alone could induce Japan's surrender without paying the price for Soviet assistance. Sticking to the policy of unconditional surrender, he charged, would prolong the war, undermine the Chinese Nationalists (as Moscow might aid their Communist rivals), and risk a Soviet entry into Japan that might "adversely afect our long-term policy for the future treatment" of that country.[11]

On May 19, Grew composed another memorandum for his own files that detailed what he had unofficially told many colleagues. The aging diplomat compared the Soviet Union to Nazi Germany, stating that by taking charge of Eastern Europe, Stalin had already cloaked himself in Adolf Hitler's mantle. Once Russia entered the Pacific War, he predicted, the Soviets would replace Imperial Japan as the overlord of East Asia and the Pacific. "Mongolia, Manchuria, and Korea will gradually slip into Russia's orbit," he warned, "to be followed in due course by China and eventually Japan."[12]

Japanese officials in Tokyo and Europe understood that Grew spoke for those who would utilize the emperor as a force for order and social cohesion after surrender. Moderate elements, the Office of Strategic Services (OSS) reported to the White House, believed Grew's statements comprised a possible bargaining agenda. Reportedly, the Japanese minister in Switzerland, Kase Shunichi, hoped to initiate peace talks with America and Great Britain before the Soviets struck. Stating that Grew ("the best U.S. authority on Japan") shared his opinion, Kase listed just one precondition for negotiations—that the Allies approve "retention of the emperor as the only safeguard against Japan's conversion to communism."[13]

Such peacefeelers encouraged Grew to take his ideas directly to President Truman. In a conversation on May 28, he told the president that the United States must offer some concessions to Tokyo, especially assurances that a postwar occupation would avoid any program of revolutionary change. Stressing the essential moderation of both the emperor and his political advisers, Grew described the traditional conservatives as the "cornerstone" for "building a peaceful future. . . ." By offering the so-called peace faction face-saving conditions, America could consolidate its position in postwar Japan.[14]

Considering the same situation, Secretary of War Henry Stimson agonized over the human and political costs of a prolonged war. He recognized, with particular foresight, the dual nature of the atomic bomb. It might end the war quickly, permitting an orderly transition of power, but would do so at the cost of killing tens of thousands of civilians and undermining Soviet–American relations. For months, Stimson pondered the question of how to use the bomb's awesome power constructively. More than anyone in the administration, he tried to inspire discussion over how the weapon might preserve rather than terminate the wartime alliance.

A week after Grew met with Truman, Stimson spoke with the president about the political aspects of atomic power. The secretary of war still supported the ongoing policy of not providing any information to Moscow until "the first bomb had been successfully laid on Japan." Truman agreed, noting that the upcoming Potsdam Conference had been postponed in part to allow more time to test fire the weapon. Although neither man wanted to use the bomb solely to discipline the Soviets, both agreed that its use and a continued American monopoly might assist "settlement of the Polish, Rumanian, Yugoslavian and Manchurian problems" with the Russians.[15]

The Manchurian problem, as with the problems in Europe, arose from the accords reached at Yalta. Roosevelt had sanctioned special Soviet privileges over Manchuria's ports and railroads in return for a Russian attack against Japan and a promise not to assist the Chinese Communists. Soviet and Chinese Nationalist negotiators, however, he failed to resolve the details of such an arrangement. Truman's advisers now feared Stalin might use this impasse to annex China's industrial heartland or to assist a takeover by Mao Tse-tung's (Mao Zedong's) forces. Obviously, the sooner Japan capitulated, the less pretext or opportunity would arise for Soviet interference. Either the atomic bomb or a new diplomatic strategy might induce this surrender.[16]

Although considering use of the bomb, Stimson held out hope for negotiations. On July 2, he handed Truman a carefully crafted proposal. Given the fanatic defense put up at Iwo Jima and Okinawa, the secretary of war expected some sixty thousand initial and up to one-half million eventual American casualties should an invasion take place. Such an assault would result in a "far more bitter finish fight than in Germany," leaving Japan "even more thoroughly destroyed. . . ." As this cataclysm served no purpose, Stimson sought some formula to "secure for us the equivalent of an unconditional surrender" without an invasion.

Japan, he continued, was not led solely by mad fanatics with an "entirely different mentality from ours." That nation had a remarkable history, leaping from "isolated feudalism" to "the position of one of the six or seven great powers" in only fifty years. Before the "seizure" of power by the "fanatical military group in 1931," Japan had been a responsible great power. Prominent "liberal leaders," although now submerged, surely understood the military implications of further resistance. By cultivating these elements, the United States could begin Japan's "reconstruction as a responsible member of the family of nations" and as a "useful member of the future Pacific community."[17]

Like Grew, Stimson urged Truman to inform Japan of the "overwhelming character of the force" about to be unleashed as well as the limited plan to purge war criminals. Such an ultimatum ought to clarify that no wholesale revenge would be taken and that, once demilitarized and democratized, the nation would be allowed access to peaceful foreign trade. The secretary of war even suggested telling the enemy that the United States might eventually accept "a constitutional monarchy under her present dynasty." If presented before an American invasion or Russian attack, these terms might bring forth a new leadership. Like his counterparts in Tokyo, then, Stimson looked back toward the decade of the 1920s as a model for Japan and its cooperation with America.[18]

While Truman pondered these suggestions, another major figure argued on behalf of a compromise peace. Former President Herbert Hoover, a nonperson during the Roosevelt years, reemerged as a man of some influence in 1945. He quickly established cordial relations with Harry Truman—who was eager to step out from under FDR's shadow—and became an influential, if informal, adviser on national policy.

Preaching a sermon whose roots stretched back to 1918, Hoover feared that the collapse of Germany and Japan invited a Communist takeover throughout Eurasia. In a pair of memoranda (one signed, the other anonymous) circulated in the War Department and White House, the former president predicted a Soviet assumption of Japan's sphere in Asia unless a quick peace agreement ended the Pacific War. Only an immediate surrender could block Russian encroachment in Asia and prevent a complete collapse of Japan. In the rush to avenge Pearl Harbor, Hoover wrote, the Americans and British ought not to feed the forces of revolution.

Incredibly, Hoover suggested that Jiang Jieshi be made an intermediary to conduct secret talks with Tokyo. In return for an orderly evacuation of China, Japan would be allowed to retain Korea and Formosa. Japan's negotiated withdrawal would bolster non-Communist forces in China and preclude a Soviet thrust into Manchuria. With relatively few sacrifices, Japan could "return to cooperation with Western civilization" and become an anti-Communist bulwark. Spared further destruction, the former enemy would "make an economic recovery . . . to the advantage of all free nations," Hoover concluded.[19]

Although sympathetic to the assumptions presented by Hoover and Grew, Army Chief of Staff George C. Marshall and Secretary of War Henry Stimson dismissed them as impractical. Moscow would surely enter the war against Japan because it served Soviet interests, not because of promises or concessions made at Yalta. Rather than unleashing the Soviets, the Yalta accords placed some tangible physical-political limits on Russian expansion. Stimson told Grew that he could accept only part of the diplomat's argument—that America should pursue a negotiated peace and that Japan ought to be controlled through "exclusive occupation by our own forces."[20]

Similarly, General Marshall and his aides objected to Hoover's proposals. They could not discount Soviet military assistance while the atomic bomb remained an untested weapon. Nor were they certain that Japanese liberals would leap at the opportunity to depose the militarists. Only a decisive military victory would buck up the civilians' courage and erode the military's confidence. Marshall and Stimson both dismissed the Hoover-Grew proposal to denounce the Yalta accords. Far from deterring Moscow, such an act would "give the Russians . . . an excellent excuse for immediate aggression in the Asiatic area." Consequently, before—and even after—the bomb was tested, American military planners felt that "the impact of the Russian entry on the already hopeless Japanese [might] well be the decisive action levering them into capitulation."[21]

The debate over how to handle the Soviets in East Asia paralleled the larger strategic confrontation emerging during the summer of 1945. Disputes over German boundaries and reparations, the postwar regime in Poland, the Soviet-controlled Balkans, and many related issues cast a pall over the last Allied wartime conference at Potsdam. Meeting in the once-opulent suburb of Berlin, Joseph Stalin, Winston Churchill (replaced by Laborite Clement Attlee after the general election), and Harry Truman tried to resolve, or at least patch up, the outstanding problems of Europe and Asia. The slender ground for compromise seemed confirmed on the first day when, after Stalin renewed his pledge to attack Japan early in August, Truman allegedly remarked that he "could go home now."[22]

The quip proved prophetic; the three leaders failed to resolve any substantive issues about Soviet demands for German reparations or Anglo–American insistence that Moscow establish more representative governments in Eastern Europe. Each side appeared convinced that the other sought to dominate all Europe. Unable to resolve most disputes, the three nations deferred action by creating a postwar Council of Foreign Ministers (CFM) to meet at future intervals.

American delegates were nearly as concerned by their lack of access to President Truman as by the emerging confrontation with Stalin. Democratic political broker James F. Byrnes, the recently confirmed secretary of state, monopolized Truman and limited contact with him. Despite, or owing to, his own lack of diplomatic experience, Byrnes shunted aside such seasoned delegates as Ambassador Averell Harriman and Secretary of War Henry Stimson. Much to their consternation, these veterans were excluded from planning sessions at Potsdam.

Harriman thought he had successfully accomplished the transition from

Roosevelt crony to Truman crony, yet he found himself ignored on Kremlin affairs. Brynes, Harriman complained, "played his cards very close to his vest" and relied on his own judgment. Harriman and Stimson "sat in the sun together outside his [Stimson's] villa talking about when and how the Japanese would surrender and how to deal with the Russians after that." Stimson dryly noted, "My assistance, while generally welcome, was strictly limited in the matters in which it should be given."[23]

Stimson retained one area of influence at Potsdam, however. He was designated to deliver word about the successful test of the atomic bomb. On July 16, he handed Truman news of the detonation at Alamogordo, information that "greatly cheered up" the president and Churchill. The immense expenditures and unprecedented secrecy finally yielded a weapon that might compel a Japanese surrender on American terms without the risk of a Soviet attack. By July 21, when a full report reached the president, all those in Truman's entourage realized the importance of the weapon. Stimson described Truman as "tremendously pepped up,"and Brynes could barely contain his excitement. Walter Brown, an aide to Brynes, reported the secretary of state as convinced that the Americans no longer need haggle with the Russians over the details of joining the war. Brynes suggested that the British and Americans issue a joint ultimatum "giving the Japs two weeks to surrender or face destruction. . . ." The "secret weapon" would be "ready at that time."[24]

As the conference entered a second week, Brynes tried to "outmaneuver Stalin on China" and Japan. The American delegation, which initially hoped to speed a Sino–Soviet treaty, now urged Chinese Foreign Minister T. V. Soong to stall on Stalin's demands for a Chinese agreement on acess to Manchuria. Byrnes hoped this would delay Russia's entry into the war until the Japanese had accepted an American ultimatum. If the Soviets attacked, Byrnes fretted, he could not "save China" and Stalin might "take over."[25]

Stimson voiced greater caution over bandying about atomic threats, lest such talk destroy all hope of postwar cooperation and arms control. At the same time, he accepted the responsibility of helping Truman select target sights in Japan. Certain sensitive areas, like the cultural treasures in Kyoto, must be spared, he told Truman on July 24:

> [The] bitterness which would be caused by such a wanton act [of destruction might make it] impossible during the long postwar period to reconcile the Japanese to us in that area rather than to the Russians. It might thus . . . be the means of preventing what our policy demanded, namely a sympathetic Japan to the United States in case there should be any aggression by Russia in Manchuria.

Truman agreed on the need to spare both Kyoto and Tokyo, even though the "Japs" were "savages, ruthless, merciless and fanatic. . . ."[26]

As viewed most broadly at Potsdam, the bomb promised to give the United States leverage vis-à-vis both Japan and the Soviet Union and at the same time bolster American allies in China. Even if the Soviets entered the war following the bomb's use, a quick surrender would minimize the scope of penetration and constrain Stalin's claims. Increasingly suspicious of Soviet designs and ever more confident of America's ability to defeat Japan alone, Truman maneuvered on two fronts to isolate Stalin.

The president obliquely informed the Soviet leader on July 24 that the United States possessed a new, unusually powerful weapon. Equally nonchalant, Stalin hoped it would be used against Japan. Ironically, each nation's espionage and counterespionage activities had revealed enough about their mutual knowledge so that each knew what the other was talking about although neither mentioned the atomic bomb. Truman, perhaps, thought this vagueness both fulfilled diplomatic obligations and scared the Russians. Stalin, genuinely concerned about the American breakthrough, determined to feign indifference. The charade merely confirmed the widening gap between the Russians and the Americans.*

The distance between Russia and the Western Allies increased on July 26 when the Americans and British issued the Potsdam Declaration (based on Stimson's draft) without informing the Soviets (or General MacArthur) beforehand. Truman's advisers justified this act by noting that Russia had not yet declared war on Japan. Although technically correct, the secretive release smacked of an Anglo–American effort to induce a separate peace.

The declaration's effect, however, was dissipated by two significant omissions. It made no direct reference to the atomic bomb, and it failed to guarantee the emperor's position, as both Stimson and Grew had urged. The latter point reflected an intense debate among American leaders. For months, Stimson and Grew had argued that some such promise might speed a surrender as well as preserve order within Japan. Ambassador Harriman agreed and elicited support from Ernest Bevin, the new British foreign minister. The emperor, Bevin urged, was the "instrument through which one might have to deal in order to effectively control Japan." Recalling the First World War, he stated that by driving out the Kaiser in 1918, the Allies had preempted a constitutional monarchy and unintentionally opened the "doors to a man like Hitler."[27]

In contrast, Secretary of State Byrnes and the American military chiefs took a different view. They felt any pledge to the emperor would preclude later options. The military staff also maintained that only a decisive bat-

---

* This charade was also evident in the American reaction to Stalin's disclosure of Japanese peacefeelers. Through intercepts, American intelligence knew of Tokyo's efforts and Moscow's indifference to them.

tlefield engagement would convince Tokyo both to surrender and to accept an occupation. Byrnes probably shared this belief and presumably had a special sensitivity to a (1945) Gallup Poll that reported two thirds of the public favored Hirohito's arrest or execution. Unpersuaded of the need to repudiate the unconditional surrender doctrine inherited from Roosevelt, Truman sided with Byrnes and eliminated all reference to the emperor from the ultimatum. The president's confidence showed through at a party aboard the cruiser USS *Augusta* while returning from Potsdam. Truman boasted that he no longer had to seek compromises or assistance to defeat Japan. America had "developed an entirely new weapon of such force and nature that we did not need the Russians or any other nation."[28]

Although top military planners were not quite so confident about the bomb's effectiveness, they still expected a speedy end to the war. The Soviet entry along with the bomb, they believed, should induce a Japanese surrender. On July 25, General Marshall ordered General MacArthur (already designated to lead an invasion) to devise plans for an immediate end of hostilities and the occupation of Japan and southern Korea. If necessary, this might include a lightening move to preclude Soviet penetration.[29]

The possibility of an imminent Japanese collapse affected directly the survival prospects for the pro-American KMT regime in China. Before Potsdam and the successful atomic test, the United States had urged the Chinese Nationalists to accept Soviet demands for special rail and port privileges in Manchuria and de facto control of Mongolia. Now Washington balked. Harriman and Byrnes both encouraged Chinese Foreign Minister T. V. Soong to resist Soviet claims. But, on August 8, two days after the dropping of the Hiroshima bomb, the Russians entered the war—about a week earlier than Washington had expected. On August 9, Stalin warned Soong that unless he agreed quickly to Moscow's terms, the Chinese Communists would "get into Manchuria."

This threat frightened Byrnes and Harriman as much as it did Soong because Manchuria and Korea were key economic zones for both China and Japan. Soviet domination would give Stalin a potential lever over the future of the entire region. Harriman grew so concerned that he urged Truman to order preemptive American landings in Northeast Asia. Although military planners considered landings in Manchuria impractical, they quickly accelerated plans (which the Russians accepted) for an American occupation of Korea below the thirty-eighth parallel.[30]

Somewhat to the Truman administration's surprise, the Soviets and Nationalist Chinese did reach a settlement on August 14. Although the Russians obtained considerable economic privileges in Manchuria, they promised to withdraw their troops three months after the war ended. China's partial loss of sovereignty in one region seemed offset by Stalin's explicit promise to support only the government of Jiang Jieshi, leaving the Communists, as odd man out in the deal. In balance, the settlement actually pleased American observers and angered the Chinese Communists.[31]

During the final weeks of war, advocates of a compromise peace with Japan grew more outspoken in Washington. Commerce Secretary Henry A. Wallace exploded when he heard Joseph Grew's wife talk about "strengthening Japan" so it would fight Russia. The State Department crowd, he fumed, had a "great deal spiritually in common with Nazis and fascists wherever they may be." But such objections did not deter Grew and Stimson from continuing to discuss how a peace formula and occupation agenda could be devised without reference to the "current war hysteria." The two officials again urged Truman to approve a plan directed toward the "regeneration of Japan in the minimum amount of time" by using much of the existing government. SWNCC, too, rushed position papers to the president, which Truman quickly approved, that called for exclusive American control over an undivided Japan.[32]

As hoped, the impact of the two atomic attacks combined with the Russian invasion of Manchuria moved the Japanese toward surrender. On August 10, Tokyo notified Swiss intermediaries of its provisional acceptance of the Potsdam Declaration, providing that the "prerogatives of the Emperor as a Sovereign ruler" remained intact. For months, Truman and Brynes had scoffed at accepting such a reservation. Now, they suddenly changed tack.

At a cabinet meeting on August 10, the president explained that his inclination to meet the Japanese partway was due to his dread at the prospect of Russian divisions pushing "too far into Manchuria." The Chinese and Soviets had not yet agreed on treaty terms (they did on August 14), convincing Truman and Byrnes that Stalin intended to grab Chinese territory or, at least, set up the Chinese Communist Party (CCP) as his puppet. A softening of the Potsdam terms seemed about the only leverage Washington possessed to restrain Russian movement southward. Within China, the American theater commander, Gen. Albert C. Wedemeyer, had already developed elaborate plans with the KMT to redeploy Chinese and American forces northward to "preclude the movement of Communist troops" into critical areas. These plans included joint efforts with Japanese units throughout China after the surrender.

Although the president "interjected most fiercely" that he no longer expected Russian cooperation, he expressed a determination to "go ahead without them anyway." Truman ordered Tokyo to be told that if the emperor signed and issued surrender orders and pledged obedience to the American occupation commander, he could remain on the throne pending the "freely expressed will of the Japanese people." The entire tone of the meeting, Henry A. Wallace recorded in his diary, seemed to subordinate all other concerns to the determination to block Soviet expansion.[33]

Initially, Soviet–American discussions on the amended surrender formula appeared to confirm Truman's prediction that Moscow would not cooperate. Meeting with Foreign Minister V. M. Molotov on August 10 in the Soviet capital, Ambassador Harriman could not get him to promise that the Red Army would halt its advance once Tokyo accepted American terms. Harriman believed that the Kremlin wanted "to have the war continue" as long as possible to gain territory. Nevertheless, at a midnight meeting, he insisted on a Soviet pledge to accept the new conditions regarding the emperor.[34]

At 2:00 A.M., after conferring with Stalin, Molotov told Harriman of the Kremlin's conditional approval of the amended terms. However, Molotov now insisted that the Russians be consulted on the selection of the Occupation Commander* and alluded to a separate Soviet occupation zone. Rejecting these demands at once, the ambassador and foreign minister began to trade insults over which nation had fought harder and who deserved a larger role in Japan.

A few hours later, just before Harriman complied with Molotov's demand that the Soviet terms be sent to Washington, Molotov's translator called on the ambassador. Stalin, he explained, had reviewed the dispute and wished to restate Moscow's position. The Soviet Union demanded neither a veto over the naming of a commander nor its own occupation zone. It only wished a promise of consultation. On this basis, Harriman and the Russian translator quickly prepared an agreement on American terms. Quite impressed with his own achievement, the ambassador concluded that the future Soviet role in Japan (or lack thereof) "was settled that night."[35]

The speed with which the Soviets raised and dropped the issue of an enhanced role in the Occupation as well as their facilitation of the American occupation of southern Korea and their willingness to sign a treaty with the Chinese Nationalists suggests that they had little expectation of achieving the goals raised by Molotov. More likely, Stalin hoped to highlight his "moderation" as a debating or bargaining point for use with the Americans regarding the predominant Soviet sphere in the Balkans. In fact, the Russians raised this issue over the next few months. Whatever their ultimate motives, Harriman and most high officials of the Truman administration were convinced that they had successfully blunted the first wave in a coordinated Soviet plan to dominate much of postwar Asia. Assistant Sec-

---

* About August 8, Truman had decided to appoint MacArthur as the Occupation Commander, a move accepted by the Allies on August 12 and announced three days later.

retary of War John Jay McCloy, for example, only lamented that not enough had been done to contain the Russians. War weariness had dulled the judgment of many in Washington he told Harriman. Most were "only thinking about the end of the war"; too few were "thinking about the future of Japan. . . ."[36]

2

REMAKING JAPAN, 1945 TO 1948

More than a decade after his abrupt recall from the Korean battlefields, Douglas MacArthur recounted his pride in presiding over the "world's great laboratory for an experiment in the liberation of a people from totalitarian military rule and for the liberalization of government from within." Writing as the American escalation was beginning in Vietnam (1964), his words seemed to confirm the public view of the only major success in postwar Asian policy. To most Americans, MacArthur personified a Japanese Occupation that had accomplished more than anyone could have reasonably hoped.

Among the many anomolies of MacArthur's position was the fact that his reputation had never been high among New Dealers. In fact FDR had called him one of the "two most dangerous men" in America. Tarnished by his crude overreaction and posturing during the army's eviction of the ill-fated Bonus Marchers in July 1932, the debacle in the fall of the Philippines after the Pearl Harbor attack further diminished his standing. Although the public grew accustomed to press releases depicting a "heroic" MacArthur during the subsequent Pacific campaign, President Roosevelt, Secretary of War Stimson, and Chief of Staff Marshall grew weary of his continual grandstanding, his disputes with the navy, his complaints over alleged shortchanging of his theater of operations, and his flirtation with the 1944 Republican presidential nomination. Still, MacArthur's popularity and battlefield victories during the war convinced FDR and (later) Truman, to appease his demands and ego whenever possible.

A longstanding enemy of the general, Harold L.C. Ickes—who had sparred with MacArthur over the Interior Department's authority in the Philippines—indicated that Harry Truman shared his dislike and suspicion of the Supreme Commander. "In expressing his opinion of MacArthur," Ickes noted in his diary, the president "indulged in some pretty vigorous Missouri expletives. . . ." In a memorandum of June 17, 1945, while weighing the options for the final assault on Japan, Truman wrote:

> Mr. Prima Donna, Brass Hat, Five Star MacArthur. He's worse than the Cabots and the Lodges—they at least talked with one another before they told God what to do. Mac tells God right off. It's a very great pity we have stuffed shirts like that in key positions. I don't see why in hell Roosevelt didn't order Wainwright home and let MacArthur be a martyr. Guess he was afraid of the Sabotage Press-McCormick-Patterson Axis. We'd have had a real General and a fighting man if we had Wainwright and not a play actor and a bunco man such as we have now.

Truman went on to contrast such generals as Robert E. Lee, Eisenhower, and Bradley to the "Custers, Pattons and MacArthurs."

On August 10, as the president pondered Japan's tentative acceptance of the Potsdam surrender terms, Sen. Tom Connally called Truman to warn him that he would make a "big mistake in appointing Dugout Doug as Allied Commander in Chief to accept the Jap surrender." Connally predicted the general would use the position to "run against" the president "in 1948 if [Truman] built him up." Shortly after the Japanese surrender, Truman and Harold Ickes discussed these issues again. The interior secretary had persuaded the president to appoint Paul V. McNutt, a civilian, as the High Commissioner in Manila. Now that the general had bigger fish to fry in Tokyo, Ickes hoped he would leave Philippine affairs alone. In any case, the interior official recorded how Truman "in entire good nature" interrupted him to say:

> I couldn't blame on him the appointment of MacArthur as the chief commander in the Far East Area. I replied that I agreed with him thoroughly. Politically, he couldn't do anything else. That blame is due to Roosevelt. I remarked that Roosevelt had made a mistake in taking MacArthur away from the Philippines; that he should have left MacArthur to clean up his own mess and taken Wainwright out. Truman agreed, saying that Wainwright was a better soldier. He knows, as do others, that the Philippine campaign under MacArthur was a fiasco.[1]

At the time and afterwards, few knew about the violent policy disagreements between MacArthur and the Truman administration so far as Japan was concerned. Because the press generally reported events in glowing terms, the public had only a dim awareness that the Supreme Commander for the Allied Powers (SCAP) censored reporting and barred any offending journalists from returning to his theater of operations. Nor did most Americans know that from 1947 on policymakers in Washington so feared and resented MacArthur's leadership that they restricted his authority and themselves guided much of what transpired during the final four years of Occupation.

These contradictions arose for several reasons, not the least of which stemmed from the imposing personality of the Supreme Commander. Because Japan comprised a distant alien culture and was relatively passive and outside the main theater of the cold war, few Americans paid it much attention. As always, Asia seemed an amorphous, confusing region to Eurocentric American foreign policy. Before 1950, the public, the press, and the Congress lavished far more attention on the dramatic Chinese civil war (where American involvement remained minimal) than on the unglorious routine of reconstructing a shattered Japan. For at least eighteen months after the war, even the top officials of the Truman administration were content to leave MacArthur pretty much on his own. The president rarely troubled himself even to ask about Japan. Second-level bureaucrats forged a reform agenda that they delivered to SCAP in 1945 and, then, mostly forgot about the problem.

Even one of the most knowledgeable junior diplomats sent to Japan in an advisory capacity admitted how little he or his colleagues thought about the future. On October 1, 1945, John K. Emmerson arrived in Tokyo after spending part of the war years interrogating Japanese prisoners in China. Assigned to an office in a former corporate headquarters, he arrived "just as a Mitsui junior executive was clearing the last items from his desk." Before leaving, the dispossessed executive hesitated and "pointed to a map on the wall depicting Japan's Co-Prosperity Sphere. 'There it is,' he said smiling. 'We tried. See what you can do with it!' " Like nothing yet had, this remark brought home to Emmerson the vast scope of the Occupation.[2]

At the other extreme, Gen. Douglas MacArthur radiated authority and self-assurance about Japan's future. He announced, periodically, new victories in taming and spiritually transforming a warrior race. His optimism and messianic certainty contrasted with the escalating reports of crisis coming from the Truman administration as it tried to deal with the Soviets, China, and postwar Europe. Even as Truman went before Congress in March 1947 to plead for more money and weapons to resist Communist pressure and restore European industry, MacArthur proudly announced a new political victory in Asia. With little assistance or encouragement from a fumbling administration, the general declared, he had remade Japan to the degree that it now deserved a peace settlement. A German solution, in contrast, seemed years away.

As SCAP—an acronym applied both to the Occupation headquarters and the general himself—MacArthur cut an Olympian image of a "lone figure" (in an aide's description) guiding through inspiration. Following an almost-invariable routine, he was driven from his residence at the American Embassy in Tokyo to SCAP headquarters in the Dai Ichi Insurance Building daily at 10:30 A.M. After lunch and a midday nap at home, he returned to the office for evening work. The general entertained only at luncheon and rarely socialized with Japanese officials. Aside from his regular commute, he saw nothing of Japan. In fact, he left Tokyo only twice before the Korean War—to visit Manila and to visit Seoul briefly. Few important emissaries came from Washington during the first two years, and the Supreme Commander made only minimal efforts to keep the U.S. government informed of his activities. MacArthur cultivated the idea that he alone determined the course of events within Japan. Initially, few questioned the validity of this assertion. The mile and a quarter between his residence and office comprised virtually his entire physical experience of the nation he "ruled." MacArthur, like God, commented one journalist, did "not choose often to expose himself."

Although not exactly heaven, Japan did provide a unique stage for the general's talents. Surely, military and civilian leaders were pleased to have the very senior and very opinionated MacArthur out of Washington and Europe. In either place, his impulsive and controversial style might cause problems. For his own purposes, the post in Tokyo met the general's need for a high profile job with maximum independence. Japan, like the Philippines from 1935 to 1941, provided a stage to demonstrate a degree of political and administrative talent that complemented his vaunted military reputation.

As with his wartime Pacific command, the SCAP assignment offered the desired distance from Washington along with the opportunity to blame others for slighting him because of their emphasis on Europe. He could attribute success to his own prowess and blame failure on Washington's penury. For a general whose only remaining promotion could be election to the presidency, these circumstances seemed ideal. Much of what MacArthur did and said over the next several years had as large an American as a Japanese audience.

After the terrible expenditure of blood during the Pacific War, the American landing in Japan seemed almost anticlimactic. Marines did not storm beaches nor fight fanatics to the death. Immediately after Japan accepted the surrender on August 14, 1945, the Imperial government obeyed

MacArthur's command to dispatch a small delegation to Manila to make preliminary arrangements for the surrender of their empire. On August 28, after delays caused by a typhoon and fears of possible attacks by rebellious kamikaze pilots, about two hundred army technical experts landed at Atsugi Naval Air Base to prepare for the arrival of MacArthur. Two days later, after more troops had landed, the Supreme Commander set foot on Japanese soil. The airfield, formerly headquarters for a suicide squadron, was decorated festively. Instead of storming Tokyo, one journalist remarked, the conquerors seemed to have arrived at a proper "lawn party." This symbolic taming of a "warrior race" suited the general's plan exactly. Then, on September 2, during solemn ceremonies aboard the USS *Missouri*, MacArthur accepted Japan's formal surrender, closing the most awful war in history.[3]

Both MacArthur and his closest aides cultivated a heroic myth regarding the Occupation. Brig. Gen. Courtney Whitney, who became the head of SCAP's Government Section, later recalled his commander's inspired, if offhand, remarks during the fateful flight to Tokyo. These, he claimed, set the "policy under which we would work and live for the next six years." Possessing an unsurpassed knowledge of the "Oriental mind, [MacArthur] paced the aisle of an unarmed plane" and casually outlined the transformation of a nation. He would "first destroy the military power," then build representative government, enfranchise women, free political prisoners, liberate farmers, establish free labor unions, destroy monopolies, abolish police repression, liberate the press, liberalize education and decentralize political power.[4]

Whitney's account neglected to mention that on August 29 while en route to his new command MacArthur had received an advance copy of the "Initial Post-surrender Policy for Japan" (SWNCC 150/4/A), which included virtually the entire reform agenda in the order of his recitation. Officially approved by President Truman on September 6, 1945, this document culminated several years of planning. On November 3, a related paper put out by the JCS augmented the program for Japan.[5]

Following the broad outlines of the Potsdam Declaration, the postsurrender policy ordered the Supreme Commander to disarm and demobilize enemy armed forces and establish a representative government. He was to promote individual liberties, free speech, and a free press. Among its goals, the Occupation was to encourage a peacetime economy sufficient to meet normal requirements. To assist his rule, MacArthur could utilize both the emperor and the existing government so long as they accepted his authority and did not impede progress toward democratic goals. SCAP had the power to remove the militarists and ultranationalists from office and from positions of influence. In addition, SCAP was not to oppose grass roots efforts to remove current leaders so long as these changes did not endanger American forces. The initial policy guideline proclaimed a variety of basic liberties, such as freedom of religion, the right to form political parties, the abrogation of discriminatory laws, and it also ordered the release of political prisoners. It mandated creation of a democratic judiciary and the reform and decentralization of police powers.

Planners in Washington acknowledged the important economic dimension of the Occupation, a concept integral to the orders given MacArthur. They insisted that strict limits and controls be placed on heavy industry. MacArthur was to encourage a free labor movement and a "wide distribution of income and of the ownership of the means of production." Reflecting the common assumption that giant monopolies, the *zaibatsu* (literally, money clique), had countenanced aggression, SCAP was to purge business leaders and initiate a "program for the dissolution of the large industrial and banking combinations [that had] exercised control of a great part of Japan's trade and industry." The document also proclaimed that the Japanese, not foreign benefactors, must "undertake the burden of repairing the damage" the war had brought about. Japan would have to rely on its own ability to resume peaceful trade and could not expect to enjoy a standard of living above that of its Asian neighbors.

Both idealistic and punitive, the agenda given MacArthur reflected extensive debate among and within the State, War, and Navy departments. Unaccountably, neither Roosevelt nor Truman had indicated any detailed concern about the Occupation. Initially, at least, deep concern with transforming Japan outweighed considerations about the potential Soviet threat, the impact of China's civil war, or the nationalist uprisings in Southeast Asia. The middle-level planners in Washington and in SCAP believed that America's victory entitled and required the United States to remake Japan along liberal, democratic lines. The Potsdam Declaration and the SWNCC and JCS directives all spoke of going beyond mere demilitarization and the elimination of military potential. The Occupation would also seek to eradicate the structures of Japanese society that had impelled that nation to expand since the late nineteenth century. Besides punishing war criminals and their business and political allies, the Occupation would establish an economic system tolerant of trade unions and unfettered competition. This, American planners insisted, would provide a real basis for democracy. Sensitive to Asia's historic agrarian exploitation, American reformers were determined to promote a peaceful revolution in tenant-landlord relations.

During the initial reformist stage of the Occupation, lasting through early 1947, Washington encouraged SCAP to pursue a program that reflected the most progressive tendencies of the New Deal. Even as American domestic and foreign policy lurched to the Right, MacArthur and his aides remained committed to a reform agenda abhorrent to most of the general's conservative constituency in the United States.

In addition to this idealistic facet, another impulse shaped the first years of the Occupation. For both Americans and Asians, the Pacific War had been incredibly brutal. Racial conflict, outrages against prisoners, and gross indifference toward civilian suffering had characterized Japan's behavior. Shortly after surrender, Truman had few qualms in describing the Japanese as "vicious and cruel savages" largely deserving of their fate at Hiroshima and Nagasaki. These sentiments lasted among Americans for several years and continued to affect many Asians for decades.

The dread of resurgent Japanese militarism impelled the United States to insist on sweeping demilitarization and the control of future military potential. In 1946, this sentiment undoubtedly shaped MacArthur's determination to impose a constitutional prohibition on Japan's right to wage war. Even those military planners in Washington who came to favor using Japan as a forward base for the navy and air force had mixed motives. Besides the nation's utility as a staging area in case of war with the Soviet Union, stationing American forces on the islands would insure control of an untrustworthy Japan during and after the Occupation.

· During 1947, as the cold war intensified both in Europe and Asia, the Truman administration and (more slowly) MacArthur discarded many of these assumptions. Whether they viewed Japan either as a major ally or as a prize in the contest with the Soviet Union, their concerns with liberal and punitive reform diminished. Nevertheless, for at least the first two years of this period, the administration and SCAP remained committed to the wartime legacies of liberal transformation.

Americans arriving in Japan encountered a bleak and shattered land. Although the killing had ended, living conditions were nearly as uncertain as during the war. Now severed completely from imports of food, fuel, and raw materials, the civilian economy approached collapse. American soldiers' letters described Japan's major cities as "completely flat with destruction." On approaching Tokyo from its outlying airfield in September 1945, one GI described the eerie sensation of thinking he was driving away from a great metropolis as "there was practically nothing left; the rubble did not even look like much." About the only major structure he observed, a gas storage tank, remained "completely untouched." Fire bombs, he lamented, "seemed to have destroyed everything but the obvious military targets."[6]

Actions by the Imperial government in August made the situation still worse. Immediately after surrender, government officials and their corporate allies looted the large stockpiles of supplies amassed since 1941. Brought to a halt only after the Americans arrived, this organized pillage contributed to commodity shortages for almost two years. Similarly, the Japanese government showed an eagerness to discharge financial obligations for war contracts through a huge currency issue. Along with chronic shortages, this set off a wave of inflation that continued for four years, eventually driving wholesale prices up thousands of times over pressurrender levels. Nearly 40 percent of Japanese cities lay in ashes, and poor harvests in 1945 added to food shortages. War damage, technical obsolescence, and the loss of raw materials from its empire further undermined the Japanese economy.

As if these factors were not enough, the loss of the empire stranded nearly seven million Japanese troops, officials, colonists, and merchants in the Pacific, on the Asian mainland, and in Southeast Asia. Protecting them from the wrath of the local population and returning them to a Japan many barely knew proved a formidable task. Under American naval supervision, the Japanese assembled a transport fleet of nearly four hundred ships that spent months repatriating these displaced persons. Ironically, the Americans postponed the removal of many Japanese army units from north China, Indochina, and the East Indies. To the shock of many Asians, these forces joined the KMT in its battle with the Communists and assisted the French and Dutch colonial administrations in efforts to prevent the emerging nationalist forces from consolidating their power in the wake of Japan's defeat. Although the bulk of these Japanese army units were evacuated during 1946, a few units fought with the KMT until the end of China's civil war in 1949.

The Supreme Commander in Japan, Gen. Douglas MacArthur, occupied a dual role. As SCAP, he nominally represented all the Allies and served as their delegate in carrying out the terms of the Potsdam Declaration. He also functioned as the American in charge of the Far Eastern Command. As such, he bore responsibility for all American forces in Japan, southern Korea, and the surrounding region. As during the war, China remained outside his jurisdiction. Under this arrangement, the Sixth and Eighth armies garrisoned Japan. Initial disarmament and demobilization of enemy forces went so smoothly, however, that the Sixth Army departed on January 1, 1946, leaving Lt. Gen. Robert L. Eichelberger's Eight Army as the garrison force.

SCAP's command post lay inside the Dai Ichi Insurance Building, one of the few major structures left in the heart of Tokyo. Before September 1945, American officials had not formally resolved whether to administer Japan directly (as in Germany) or to rule through the existing government. Once in Tokyo, MacArthur decided to utilize an indirect method. As a result, many of the hundreds of American army officers trained for military government served in Korea rather than Japan. In place of a military administration, MacArthur established some dozen special staff sections that paralleled the Japanese cabinet structure. But in many instances, he preferred the counsel of loyal subordinates over that of specialists.

The general turned toward old acquaintances from the Philippines or the recent Pacific campaigns for assistance. Members of the so-called Bataan Club, for whom he felt affection or responsibility, became high-level administrators in Tokyo. As one veteran and critic of the Occupation, Harry Emerson Wildes, put it, "neither ability nor special training was a necessary requisite for appointment to these positions of honor, privilege and power."[7]

MacArthur named former Manila lawyer, Brig. Gen. Courney Whitney, to head the all-important SCAP Government Section. This group supervised the emperor, cabinet, Diet, courts, and civil service. Former advertising manager, Brig. Gen. Ken R. Dyke, ruled the education system, the press, and cultural affairs although he lacked a college degree. Initially, MacArthur tapped a long-time aide and conservative businessman, Col. Raymond C. Kramer, to take charge of the Economic-Scientific Section. Maj. Gen. William F. Marquat, a former automotive journal editor, soon replaced him. The official SCAP historian boasted as his main qualification experience as an assembly line superintendent.

The lower staff positions, where most real supervision took place, were filled by more qualified candidates. These came largely from civilians and military officers serving in Washington who were lured to Japan by SCAP recruiters with promises of power and influence. Nevertheless, chronic personnel problems left many key technical posts vacant in Tokyo throughout the Occupation. The entire effect of SCAP's operation allowed the Japanese government a great deal of informal leeway in dealing with their American overseers.

The SCAP organization and the Japanese government communicated through the Central Liaison Office. Staffed mainly by former Japanese diplomats, this office transmitted American orders to the government bureaucracy and reported on the implementation of policy. In fact, each SCAP section cultivated its own Japanese clique and forged separate links with both it and MacArthur. Because only a few hundred technical experts worked in SCAP—assisted by the Eighth Army's military observer teams in the outlying areas—the Japanese interpreted, enacted, and reported on the progress of reforms without intensive scrutiny.

For example, months after the Occupation began, the economy seemed to spiral downward, completely out of control. As inflation raced ahead, production plummeted and raw materials disappeared. Yet, as late as January 1946, only one SCAP officer supervised the development of policy toward the *zaibatsu* monopolies that dominated heavy industry. Only two officers supervised the vital textile industry, one of whom returned to America in January 1946. This lack of oversight allowed the Japanese to ignore or defy many unpleasant demands or, more important, to distort the information on which SCAP relied.[8]

The most important SCAP subunits were the Government Section (under Courtney Whitney), the Economic-Scientific Section (under William Marquat), and the Counter-Intelligence corps (commanded by the extremely conservative Maj. Gen. Charles A. Willoughby—he later became an advisor to the Spanish dictator, Francisco Franco). These three generals formed a tight circle around MacArthur. Although sometimes bitter rivals for his patronage, they remained intensely loyal to the Supreme Commander personally. It is not surprising that the State Department worried about its bureaucratic isolation in this arrangement.

Pressure from Washington did cause MacArthur to accept a small Diplomatic Section in SCAP, referred to as the Office of the Political Adviser. Initially, the talented career diplomat, George Atcheson, Jr., headed this office. After having spent several years in Chungking (Chongqing), he developed a keen understanding of the forces at work in postwar Asia. Although he served in Tokyo for two years (until his death in a plane crash), Atcheson realized early on that he filled only a ceremonial role. In November 1945, he complained to Under Secretary of State Dean G. Acheson that on all matters of substance, "General MacArthur or his Chief of Staff and other members of the Bataan Club who act as his Privy Council or *genro* wish if possible to keep the State Department out. . . ." The diplomat grew increasingly disillusioned with MacArthur's machinations, especially the general's refusal to acknowledge that "policy is made at home and that, after all, the making of foreign policy is centered in the State Department." Not surprisingly, SCAP got on better with Atcheson's successor, William J. Sebald, usually served as an uncritical conduit for the general's views.[9]

The actual course of reform in Japan involved a convoluted interplay between MacArthur (who followed an agenda developed in Washington) and the Japanese elites who maintained control of political and economic life throughout the Occupation. Each sought to preserve and change selected aspects of the system to achieve specific goals. Sometimes, the Japanese and Americans agreed on ends but not on means to achieve them. Occasionally, disagreements had a more fundamental basis.

One example, which typified the jockeying of the next several years, surfaced on October 4, 1945, when SCAP issued a civil liberties directive that paved the way for a new political system. (These directives, or SCAPINs, were orders transmitted to the Japanese government for implementation.) This SCAPIN directed the release of political prisoners; abrogated limits on speech, assembly, and political parties—including the Communist party; and abolished the Home Ministry, which had supervised police repression. Startled by the order, the cabinet of Prime Minister Higashikuni Toshihiko resigned in favor of a new cabinet under the venerable diplomat Baron Shidehara Kijuro. The directive so frightened Prince Konoe that he visited MacArthur to warn of a revolutionary threat, just as he had done with Hirohito eight months before. Konoe and the new foreign minister, Yoshida Shigeru, feared that by design or error, the Americans had opened the door to chaos, communism, and disaster.[10]

Konoe and Yoshida, as they had held earlier, considered the war years an aberrant period in Japanese history. They believed that the depression and world crisis of the 1930s had led the military and ultranationalist fanatics to seize power. Because Japan had only "stumbled" or "strayed" from the path of acceptable behavior into armed aggression, a selective purge of the guilty should be sufficient to restore Japan's international legitimacy. Among Americans, Joseph Grew and Henry Stimson advanced similar arguments about the nature of the proposed Occupation.

MacArthur, like the SWNCC planners who devised the "U.S. Initial Post-Surrender Policy," saw a deeper problem rooted in the nation's historical development. Even worse, they believed that the legacy of political oppression and maldistribution of wealth endemic to Japan nurtured totalitarian movements of the Left and Right. Unless the United States effected fundamental social and economic change, Japan might once again threaten world peace.

Initially, at least, most Americans concerned with these matters (whether in Tokyo or Washington) supported a controlled revolution that would peacefully transform Japan from a state of feudal authoritarianism to a state of liberal, democratic capitalism. Gross disparities in class, wealth, and power, they believed, invited the seizure of power by extremists, be they Fascist or Communist. Despite his own critique of the New Deal and identification with Herbert Hoover's traditional conservatism, MacArthur endorsed his own subordinates' attack on the wealth concentrated among the *zaibatsu* business monopolies. Among other considerations, in his opinion, the elimination of extreme economic privilege was a prerequisite for protecting Japan from revolutionary upheaval.

OCCUPATION REFORMS

No single issue aroused more conflict during the Occupation than attempts to restructure Japan's economy. Official statements, such as the Potsdam Declaration and the basic JCS directive given MacArthur in November

1945, emphasized the fundamental importance of this. Besides such obvious targets as the cessation of war production, the JCS instructed SCAP to seek both economic disarmament and reparations as well as "reduction or elimination of certain branches of Japanese production," such as iron, steel, chemicals, nonferrous metals, aluminum, magnesium, synthetic rubber, machine tools, automotive vehicles, ships, heavy machines, and so on. Individuals of "important responsibility" in the economy who had been "active exponents of military nationalism and aggression" were subject to removal by purge. The JCS also empowered MacArthur to promote a wider "distribution of income and of ownership of the means of production and trade," to encourage labor unions, and to implement an antimonopoly program—all as part of the effort to reduce the power of the traditional economic elite.[11]

These directives resolved a debate over the political, economic, and philosophical dimensions of occupation policy that had raged near the end of the war. Generally, economists in the State and War departments argued that the immense power of the Japanese monopolies, the *zaibatsu*, depressed domestic consumption and promoted overseas aggression. The power of these cartels, sanctioned by law and tradition, led to political repression and imperialism.

Some of the more conservative area specialists in the State Department, led by Joseph Grew, contended that Japan's dependence on imported raw materials and the need to keep its export prices low justified a degree of monopoly anathema in the West. Whatever the merits of their argument, the Japan-hands lost much of their influence by the war's end. Neither Secretary of State James Byrnes nor his under secretary, Dean Acheson, had much use for Grew and his clique, who were pressured out of office shortly after Japan surrendered. Equally important, a number of popular and scholarly accounts appeared in 1945 attacking the *zaibatsu* as a particularly odious feature of Japanese society. William Johnston's *The Future of Japan*, Owen Lattimore's *Solution in Asia*, Andrew Roth's *Dilemma in Japan*, and Thomas A. Bisson's *Japan's War Economy* along with many articles in *Pacific Affairs*, the *Nation*, and *Amerasia* all warned that a real transformation of the enemy was impossible unless the business conglomerates were dissolved and replaced by a "democratic economy."[12]

Economist Bisson, who later worked for SCAP, exemplified these critics. His wartime writing described how the *zaibatsu* had abetted and benefited from aggression, especially as heavy industry depended on resources from the empire, China, and Southeast Asia. Cooperating with the militarists, the *zaibatsu* monopolized capital and used their "control associations" to allocate raw materials to enhance their domination of industry. Cleverly,

Bisson wrote, the *zaibatsu* had tried to obscure their support of the war, intending to blame the military establishment and protect themselves from retribution in case of defeat. But, he concluded:

> [The *zaibatsu*] working hand-in-hand with the Army molded Japan's economy for war during the pre-Pearl Harbor years. If the Zaibatsu are permitted to survive the conditions of defeat, they will continue to dominate Japan's postwar government. With the experience gained in this war, they will be able to prepare even more thoroughly for the next attempt to conquer East Asia by force of arms.[13]

Economist Jerome Cohen, who served in Japan briefly with the Strategic Bombing Survey, detailed many of the techniques used by the government and its business allies during the 1930s and 1940s to boost war production at the expense of consumer goods. The *zaibatsu* shaped the domestic market by exploiting new areas in conquered Asia. Both Bisson and Cohen showed how the share of heavy, war-related industry in the economy rose fivefold between 1931 and 1941—from a tiny base to a commanding 72 percent. As further evidence of this symbiotic relationship, they noted that during the two weeks between the informal surrender and the arrival of occupation forces (August 15 to 30), the government handed over vast sums of yen and stockpiled raw materials to the *zaibatsu*—insuring their postwar advantage.[14]

Although the size of the Japanese economy remained smaller than the American, the relative role of the *zaibatsu* surpassed many times that played by analogous American conglomerates. As economist Eleanor Hadley (another SCAP veteran) demonstrated, Mitsubishi's market position in 1944 resembled, in relative terms:

> U.S. Steel, General Motors, Standard Oil of New Jersey, Alcoa, Douglas Aircraft, Dupont [*sic*], Sun Shipbuilding, Allis-Chalmers, Westinghouse, A.T.&T., RCA, IBM, U.S. Rubber, Sea Island Sugar, Dole Pineapple, U.S. Lines, Grace Lines, National City Bank, Metropolitan Life Insurance, Woolworth Stores and the Statler Hotels.

All of this fell under the control of one extended family.[15]

Many *zaibatsu* combines originated in the nineteenth century and benefited from state-subsidized industrialization after the Meiji restoration. As closely held family enterprises, they operated on a scale not permitted American corporations. Law and tradition allowed the Mitsui *zaibatsu*, for example, to conduct a vast range of industrial, commercial, and financial business, employing about 1.8 million workers at home and abroad. The *zaibatsu* divided up markets with other cartels, fixed prices, allocated materials, operated joint subsidiaries, and often enforced business agreements on nonparticipating companies. Through their banking outlets, they even controlled credit to small businesses.

These combines operated according to a four-level pyramid, with the family on top. They comprised an informal business entity, ruled by a family council that enforced a strict business and social code. The council controlled the top holding company, or *honsha*, which served as the second level of the pyramid. The holding company, directly or indirectly, presided over the major operating subsidiaries (the third level), often giants in their own right. At the fourth level stood the underlying network of smaller enterprises owned in whole or part by the major subsidiaries. Through this mechanism, the Mitsui family owned at least 356 major companies.[16]

In the fervor of imminent victory over Germany in April 1945, President Truman created a special reparations committee to implement industrial reforms in Japan and Germany. He selected California oil entrepreneur and Democratic fund-raiser, Edwin Pauley, as its head. A self-made man, Pauley had few ties to corporate giants and much antipathy to monopolies. Excited by the opportunity to smash business combines in the two Axis nations, he and his staff anticipated extracting large-scale reparations from *zaibatsu* facilities.

Expecting an assault, the Japanese government and their business allies planned a counterstrategy. Relying both on private contacts with SCAP officials and public appeals for moderation, the Japanese elites hoped to stave off any radical change. During October 1945, *zaibatsu* representatives met with SCAP's economic chief, Col. Raymond C. Kramer, proposing a deal. The plan, advanced by the Yasuda family—and later endorsed by the Mitsui, Mitsubishi, and Sumitomo clans as well—proposed a voluntary dissolution of the holding companies and the resignation of family members and associates from major subsidiaries. Family shares in the holding companies would be sold to a liquidation commission, with the proceeds invested in ten-year government bonds. Although the plan made no provision for dissolving the major operating subsidiaries—the heart of the operation—or for distributing ownership and control more widely, MacArthur and Kramer indicated approval. Kramer even admitted that the plan would allow identical individuals to replace the former *zaibatsu* elite. He saw nothing wrong with this because it would speed Japan's reassertion of control as the "natural leader of Asia."[17]

Encouraged by informal approval, foreign minister Yoshida Shigeru revealed his government's views at an October 19 news conference. Hoping to sway foreign opinion in favor of the Yasuda plan, Yoshida denied that the *zaibatsu* had encouraged or benefited from the war. In most cases, he claimed, the combines were barred from the newly conquered lands because the military disliked the old *zaibatsu* and promoted the new monopolies in which they had special interests. During the war, the foreign minister insisted, the military forced big business to produce weapons for meager profits. Thus, for financial reasons alone, the old conglomerates "rejoiced at the war's end." Angered by what he saw as the hypocrisy of the West, Yoshida, citing du Pont as an example, condemned the huge profits reaped by American industry since 1941. If any one desired the war to continue, he suggested, it might have been these capitalists.[18]

American officers who had informal contacts with Japanese business leaders during the autumn of 1945 heard a similar story. Theodore De Barry, for example, became friendly with a member of the powerful Kawasaki clan who tried hard to convince the young soldier and linguist that most capitalists had opposed the war and chafed under the military's control. The military clique, according to this scion of a *zaibatsu* family, had forced peaceful industrialists into producing for war, had wrecked the economy, and had nearly destroyed Japan. The main ally of the militarists, he claimed, were big landlords who sought foreign conquest as a safety valve for peasant discontent. Similarly, an influential investment banker told another American that not only were the *zaibatsu* guiltless, but that SCAP would probably leave them untouched. "I doubt if they will do anything serious," he said. Although MacArthur and the reformers in Washington might first appear determined to restructure the economy, he expected that "the U.S. and England, being capitalistic countries, would sooner or later send over businessmen to handle this side of things."[19]

Traditional conservatives like Yoshida and Kawasaki were not wholly duplicitous or fawning in their claims. Certainly, some important business interests preferred peaceful penetration of Asian markets to outright conquest and war with the Western powers. Also, as the efforts of the YO-HANSEN group in 1944–45 testified, they saw many of the ultranationalists and militarists as radical upstarts who would wreck the carefully crafted *zaibatsu* control of the economy. Yoshida acknowledged a need (and, under the surrender terms, a responsibility) to tinker with the old system. Of course, war criminals should be punished and the militarists and their allies driven from positions of authority as much for the stupidity of their actions as for any moral lapses. But these attacks must be kept to a minimum while Japan worked to rejoin the community of advanced industrial nations. Because traditional conservatives shared the values and interests of the economic elite, they considered it vital to preserve as much of the status quo as possible.

Initially, MacArthur and Kramer took the hook that Yoshida had baited. Seemingly interested more in the appearance of effective action than in real reform, the Supreme Commander accepted the essence of the Yasuda plan. On November 6, 1945, his headquarters issued SCAPIN 244, an order to dissolve the family holding companies. Family shares would go to a Holding Company Liquidation Commission (HCLC), leaving the two bottom levels of the *zaibatsu* pyramid intact. The plan ignored the large operating subsidiaries and made no provisions for regulating the sale of holding company stock.[20]

This move stunned many in the State Department and SWNCC who had expected a more fundamental assault on the combines. The Yasuda plan left the *zaibatsu* free to operate through their subsidiaries and virtually encouraged a new elite to purchase control of holding company shares. William Clayton, Assistant Secretary of State for Economic Affairs, pressed the Justice Department to form a special mission on Japanese combines to redress the problem. Led by Northwestern University economist, Corwin D. Edwards, the mission visited Japan early in 1946. Its work overlapped that of the Pauley reparations mission, seeking "ways and means that would effectively destroy the powers of the Zaibatsu."[21]

The Pauley mission arrived first in Tokyo, bringing more than a dozen technical experts to survey the enemy's economic structure. Chief of Staff H. D. Maxwell supervised a group that had already thought deeply about how to use reparations, both to restructure Japanese industry and to speed economic development elsewhere in Asia. The mission was less concerned with pastoralizing Japan than with reversing the dependency relationship and the disparities in development between Japan and its neighbors. Industrial disarmament, in other words, would be futile so long as the defeated Axis power remained the industrial hub to a network of states producing raw materials. In a preliminary analysis sent to MacArthur as the group began its work, Pauley stated that reparations created a unique opportunity to propel all "Eastern Asia [toward] political stability and peaceful progress." Japan should neither be "pauperized" nor allowed to recover in a "form which will allow her to gain control, or to secure an advantage over, her neighbors."

Reparations could involve both transferring selected industrial plants to appropriate areas and helping poorer nations to "round out their own economies in accordance with a broad and consistent economic program. . . ." Japan would not be allowed "any plant which represents a key phase in the processing of raw materials of any of her neighbors," Pauley wrote. Eventually, Japan might again play a major part in the Asian economy, "though no longer a place of leadership and control."[22] The mission began work in Tokyo during November 1945, later traveling to the Philippines, Korea, and China. Several staff members toured the Communist-held portion of Korea and Manchuria, surveying Japanese-built facilities in those regions. SCAP officials never cooperated enthusiastically with other staffs, taking as their cue MacArthur's objection to any outside group poaching on his turf.

The participation of such knowledgeable, articulate, and well-known experts as Owen Lattimore in the Pauley mission raised further hackles among the Bataan Club. A popular political journalist, bold Asian explorer, and respected scholar, Lattimore brought a unique perspective to his assignment. The author of *Solution in Asia*, he had analyzed Japan's development in relation to China and Southeast Asia. Lattimore concluded that Japan consistently retarded regional development and must be prevented from doing so again. Reparations and other forms of aid to backward economies appeared the best way to speed progress and promote stability. Appropriately, Lattimore served as the mission's specialist on the structure and problems of the Japanese economy in relation to East Asia.

Within a week of his arrival, Lattimore forecast trouble ahead. Since surrender, he informed H. D. Maxwell, Japanese "moderates" had done everything possible to cooperate with SCAP. But when the Occupation began to implement economic reforms that would result in the "self-destruction of themselves," this same group would "force a crisis." Yoshida's attempt to distinguish between the old and new *zaibatsu*, for example, showed the elites' tactic of sacrificing their less important components in order to shortcircuit reforms. But if the Occupation attempted to go after Mitsui, Lattimore predicted, the moderates "with whom we are dealing will stage a ready-made panic."[23] The Japanese would probably use the spectre of revolution to "stampede" the Americans, he stated. The current regime might even provoke chaos or economic collapse—on a controlled scale—to make the threat credible. A growing leftist vote, "labor unions out of hand, peasants on the rampage, Russian Bolshevism ready to pop in at the back door" were conditions likely to widen the schisms already existing within the American camp. Afraid of the spectre of revolution, the United States, Lattimore wrote, would probably abandon radical programs and encourage a comeback for "the very Japanese whom up to now we [have been] forcing to back down. . . ." Not words, but deeds alone could break the power of the *zaibatsu* and create a real basis for democracy in Japan. The Occupation, he said, must attack monopoly and create new groups of independent businesses and peasants to break the political stranglehold of the combines.

Going beyond internal reform, Lattimore stressed the need to transfer basic industries to China and Southeast Asia. Their industrialization would coincide with a new economic structure within Japan. Transfers would also insure that as "Japan begins to recover, there will be more local strength" to prevent aggressive expansion. Thus far, SCAP seemed intent to dismantle only direct war-producing facilities, leaving Japan the "dominant . . . focus of American policy in Eastern Asia, with lines of economic and, hence, of political operations radiating outward . . . to other Asiatic countries. . . ."[24]

The entire reparations mission paid attention to how the *zaibatsu* relied on foreign supplies. They hoped to devise a transfer program that moved industries to those areas whose exports sustained production. Ideally, this would promise efficiency, speed growth, and eliminate Japan's ability to threaten or to dominate China and Southeast Asia. For example, if iron and steel mills were transferred from Japan to Manchuria, with its coking coal and iron ore, China would possess a marketable product with many outlets. Japan would have to buy industrial products from its neighbors, whereas China would be spared the "economic aggression" previously inflicted on it.[25]*

As the reparations group prepared their report, several prominent Japanese alumni of Johns Hopkins University hosted Owen Lattimore at dinner. After vainly trying to get the American to tell them what the Pauley report would recommend, they initiated what Lattimore described as a "new twist in the old Japanese propaganda line of being the bulwark against Bolshevism in Asia." These self-styled moderates warned of war between Russia and the West, saying the first battle had already been joined in China. America must "protect Japan against Russia" and should rebuild its former enemy for use "against Russia." These liberals, Lattimore noted with disgust in his diary, showed "delight, glee and gloating" over the fact that American marines were currently fighting Chinese communists.[26]

Spurred on by such behavior, Lattimore and the rest of the staff submitted a report that called for both a vigorous antimonopoly program and massive industrial transfers. Even before reporting this to the president, Pauley urged MacArthur to initiate a quick assault on the *zaibatsu* by beginning an "interim program" to seize their "excess capacity." On December 6, 1945, Pauley announced his intention of asking Truman to order drastic cuts in most industries, the elimination of all war-production capacity, and the confiscation of all overseas assets.[27]

On December 18, 1945, Pauley forwarded a hard-hitting report to the president, rebuking those who called for an accommodation with Japan. Directing this criticism partly at MacArthur, Pauley noted that compared to their victims, the Japanese still enjoyed a high standard of living. Reparations should not be considered solely a punishment for defeat. Rather,

---

* Ironically, after the Communist revolution in China, American planners stood this logic on its head. Chinese control of vital industrial raw materials, they feared, would allow the regime to blackmail Japan. This, then, justified the rebuilding of heavy industry in Japan.

the policy represented an effort to correct a history of physical and economic abuse inflicted by Japan on the rest of Asia. In any case, the report noted, Japan retained a large "excess capacity" of industry that depended on war-related orders and foreign raw materials. In addition, many secondary, war-related facilities could be transferred abroad without impairing Japan's domestic standard of living.

Pauley complained that MacArthur had done little to demilitarize basic industry and that some SCAP personnel even helped industrialists shield their factories from scrutiny. The situation, he said, demanded the immediate seizure of twenty-seven of the "most important machine-tool manufacturing plants, which produce almost exactly half of Japan's total." Pauley proposed to eliminate or restrict severely the airplane, ball bearing, and shipbuilding industries and to reduce steel-making capacity from 11 to 2.5 million tons annually. In addition, he recommended that all overseas facilities be confiscated by local authorities as ill-gotten gains. This interim program, Panley stated, would pave the way for an even more thorough housecleaning later on.

Through such action, the Occupation would restructure Japan's economy. Renewed stress would have to be laid on food production and the manufacture of light, consumer goods for export. Japan would have to deal with new industrial exporters in Asia as trading partners, forcing the country to compete as an equal. Using the stick of reparations, Pauley continued, the Occupation authorities could compel the breakup of *zaibatsu* enterprise, forcing industry to become more competitive. As long as the *zaibatsu* survived, the staff noted, "Japan will be their Japan."[28]

Truman reacted quickly to the document, telling Secretary of State Brynes that he "approved of Ambassador Pauley's report and it should be implemented as soon as the necessary details are worked out." The JCS, however, responded with greater restraint. Endorsing the principle of reparations, nonetheless, they granted SCAP permission to exempt specific industries from removal under the "interim program" if it threatened to undercut a "minimal" acceptable level. MacArthur's fierce opposition to any mandated program delayed implementation. Ultimately, the administration's change of heart unhinged the entire program.[29]

Although both the Pauley and Far Eastern Commission guidelines were designed to permit a standard of living equal to the 1930-to-1934 level, MacArthur criticized them as unrealistically severe. After long postponement, in April 1947, SWNCC resolved that SCAP should begin the distribution of some sixteen thousand machine tools to Japan's Asian claimants. These so-called advanced transfers were to be counted against the reparations quotas set for each nation. In effect, however, this allotment both began and completed the reparations program.

Attempts to smash the *zaibatsu* monopolies followed a similar pattern to the reparations fiasco—again an initial reform impulse fell victim to a conservative trend. The postsurrender instructions given MacArthur recommended dissolution of "large Japanese industrial and banking combines or other large concentrations of private business control." This concern reflected the fact that some ten *zaibatsu* families controlled nearly three fourths of Japan's industrial, commercial, and financial resources. Obviously, any program to curb this power and redistribute the "ownership and means of production and trade" required a tremendous effort and will.

Late in 1945, both the State and Justice departments agreed on the need to dispatch a mission on Japanese combines led by economist Corwin D. Edwards. Active in Tokyo during the first few months of 1946, the Edwards mission labeled the *zaibatsu* among the "groups principally responsible for the war and . . . a principal factor in the Japanese war potential." Edwards denied that his antagonism toward the industrial combines signified a radical or Marxist attack, rather, it represented a key element in the "broad program of democratization and demilitarization." The guilt of individual business leaders had little relevance, given the overwhelming power of the institutional structures. For decades, Edwards wrote, a few great combines had enforced "semi-feudal relations between employer and employee, held down wages, and blocked the development of labor unions." By stifling the growth of small, competitive business, they "retarded the rise of a Japanese middle class," which Americans considered the foundation of "humanitarian sentiments" and a "counterweight to military design." Low wages paid by the *zaibatsu* had stifled domestic consumption and intensified the drive for exports, thus giving "incentive to Japanese imperialism." The size, power, and influence of the combines made them primarily responsible for Japan's criminal behavior, Edwards concluded.[30]

The Edwards mission rejected the initial SCAP program because it failed to address the monopoly problem below the level of family holding companies, left large operating subsidiaries intact, ignored the pattern of intercorporate ownership and joint management, and failed to decree how *zaibatsu* assets should be sold off. The mission wanted the conglomerates broken into small competitive units that would lay the "foundation for a Japanese middle class and competitive capitalism." It opposed both nationalizing industry or permitting its control by organized labor. Advocating an American style antimonopoly program preceeding in two stages, Edwards called for the dissolution of the combines into constituent units by the forced sale of stock to smallholders—former owners would receive partial compensation. Rigorous antitrust legislation controlling the size, scope, and ownership of new business enterprises would prevent the growth of new monopolies.[31]

Initially, General MacArthur disliked these proposals as much as those regarding reparations and for many of the same reasons. SCAP's higher echelon objected to outsiders imposing any standards or taking any credit for the Occupation. Gen. William Marquat, head of the Economic-Scientific Section, told the JCS early in 1946 that, although the "objectives" of the Edwards report were "admirable," the "practical execution of such a program except in broad outline" was impossible. He questioned whether the United States intended to "establish an ideal economy" or whether it should be content with the "introduction of such democratic methods and the abolition of such menaces as to insure the disability of Japan to make future war." If planners in Washington expected to create an "ideal" society, then the JCS would have to order "complete reorganization" and a vast expanion of SCAP. Marquat characterized Edwards's recommendations as "too sweeping," "unworkable," "too liberal," and "unwise."[32]

Although the JCS sent General MacArthur the Edwards report as an "interim directive" in October 1946, SWNCC took no official action on it for a year. Finally, in May 1947, SWNCC forwarded the report (now called SWNCC 302/4) to the Far Eastern Commission for its approval. Bearing the new tag, FEC 230, the document asserted that the monopolistic powers of the *zaibatsu* had strangled political and economic freedom in Japan and encouraged aggression. The report declared that "the dissolution of excessive private concentration of economic power [constituted], in the United States view, one of the major objectives of the Occupation."

As presented to the Far Eastern Commission, the American proposal defined "excessive concentration" quite broadly. Almost any large-scale, diverse enterprise that tended to restrict competition might be in jeopardy. Although making some provision for limited compensation to *zaibatsu* shareholders, the report recommended selling assets to "such persons as small or medium entrepreneurs and investors . . . agricultural or consumer cooperatives and trade unions, whose ownership of these holdings would contribute to the democratization of the Japanese economy." Loans and technical advice should be furnished to these purchasers so that their acquisition of *zaibatsu* property would not be limited by "ability to pay."[33]

Ironically, by the time the Far Eastern Commission considered this proposal, most State Department and military planners had reversed their outlook. But, as with several other reform proposals, a kind of inertia carried the recommendations forward because no clear center of opposition had coalesced in Washington. Even more remarkable, the most vigorous, initial opponent of the proposed reform, Douglas MacArthur, now championed Edwards's call for *zaibatsu* dissolution. Influenced both by liberal members of SCAP's Anti-Trust and Cartels Division and by his own estimate that an antimonopoly program would be popular among most Americans, he pressed the Japanese government to enact vigorous antitrust legislation. Incredibly, officials in Washington now accused "radicals" in SCAP and MacArthur, himself, of undermining capitalism. The general, in turn, condemned the administration for defending anticompetitive economic oligarchs and for virtually insuring a popular uprising against the old order.

Besides MacArthur's discomfort with prodding in any direction from Washington, SCAP confronted Japanese government resistance to most aspects on the reform program. Economic deconcentration, land reform, political liberties, constitutional revision, labor rights, and political purges, all were pushed through an unenthusiastic bureaucracy charged with their administration. Not surprisingly, the Japanese fought hardest against plans for economic deconcentration. Their ultimate success in blocking substantial change reflected both native skills and the support they eventually derived from changes in American foreign policy.

The pattern of reform through mid-1947, the period before Washington took direct interest in MacArthur's activities, seemed one of frequent repetition. In anticipation of a SCAP command to, say, deconcentrate industry or revise the constitution, Japanese leaders would admit the need to make changes in the system. The government would appoint a committee to recommend some specific, often cosmetic, alterations in response to SCAP's orders. By offering minimal reform proposals, the Japanese hoped to deter more radical alternatives or, at least, achieve a compromise between extremes. Although sometimes falling flat, this tactic delayed the implementation of many orders until the Americans either had a change of heart or lost interest in rigorous enforcement.

As with their effort to preclude radical deconcentration of the *zaibatsu* by offering the Yasuda plan, the Japanese government attempted to finesse the sensitive problem of preparing a democratic constitution. After informal prodding by SCAP, Japanese officials began to revise the Meiji Constitution. On October 13, the government named lawyer Matsumoto Joji to head a formal revision committee. The draft he presented to the Americans in early 1946, however, included few substantive changes. On two crucial points, diminishing the emperor's political authority and confirming parliamentary control of government, the proposals seemed particularly inadequate.

During January and February 1946, about two dozen members of the Government Section worked furiously to prepare a draft constitution that fulfilled SCAP criteria. In a dramatic meeting on February 13, Gen. Courtney Whitney and his staff presented their handiwork to the Japanese. They applied tremendous pressure for quick acceptance of the document, hoping to put it in place before the newly formed Far Eastern Commission met in Washington to discuss this and related issues.

The Americans dismissed the Matsumoto version as totally inadequate. Whitney announced that unless the government accepted the SCAP version before the scheduled spring elections, "General MacArthur was prepared to lay this statement of principal directly before the people." Both sides understood the significance of this threat. Placing the basic national charter in the hands of the public for ratification might fatally fracture the elite, conservative hegemony over the political system.

Whitney relished the impact of these threats on the Japanese: He noted how "Mr. Shirasu straightened up as if he had sat on something. Dr. Matsumoto sucked in his breath. Mr. Yoshida's face was a black cloud." Leaving the group alone to discuss the ultimatum, Whitney and his aides informed the Japanese they would take a stroll in the garden to "enjo[y] your atomic sunshine." At that moment, by chance or arrangement, "a big B-29 came roaring over us," Whitney recalled, leaving an impression that was "indescribable but profound." By the time the Americans departed, they knew their draft "would be accepted as the basis for the revised constitution."[34]

The new constitution stripped the emperor of temporal political authority, strengthened the Diet, broadened voting rights, expanded the power of local government, provided for nominal sex equality and, in Article 9, forbade creation of armed forces or the conduct of war as a national right. This unique proposition testified to the intensity of American feeling about Japan's war guilt. Although the conservative cabinet initially balked at the provisions reducing the emperor to a mere symbol of the state, Hirohito intervened directly in the debate. On January 1, 1946, he issued a proclamation denying his divinity and, parenthetically, denouncing "radical tendencies" among the people. MacArthur lauded the emperor's initiative, describing his brave decision to take a "stand for the future along liberal lines."[35]

Not only did this imperial initiative reduce the likelihood of SCAP ever charging Hirohito with war crimes but it deflated conservative efforts to rouse public opposition to the constitutional reforms. Eventually, the cabinet, now headed by Prime Minister Yoshida, introduced the new constitution as a "government draft" in the spring of 1946. Arguing that it both reformed past abuses and preserved the essence of the traditional political structure, the government obtained Diet approval. The new constitution, technically a revision of the existing document, took effect in May 1947. For all their anguish, the conservative ruling group had avoided a popular referendum, managed to preserve and protect the emperor, and, over time, found it possible to thrive under the liberalized principles of the so-called MacArthur Constitution.

Land reform created another dilemma for SCAP and the Japanese. About half of the labor force worked in agriculture, and nearly half of this number farmed as tenants. Most small owner-cultivators fared little better than the landless. Chronic rural poverty limited domestic consumption and tended to push Japan toward expansion. Theorists often asserted that the oppression and poverty of rural Japan nurtured the displaced violence that Japanese soldiers exhibited to conquered people during the war.

Once again, in late 1946, SCAP planners sparred with local officials over plans to break this pattern. The Americans rejected a series of proposals to tinker with the rural structure and supported a more radical alternative. SCAP wanted to eliminate the economic and political power of landlords and to build up a viable smallholder rural base. This, they hoped, would transform the agricultural economy, expand production, enlarge the domestic market, and reduce potential revolutionary fervor in the countryside. In this regard, the contrasting model of China leaped forward.

More thoroughgoing than many other Occupation reforms, the Diet legislation (passed with SCAP sponsorship) forced the government to purchase most large landholdings. The system provided for subsequent credit sales to small farmers. Compensation paid to landlords profited them little because spiraling inflation reduced the yen's value to virtually nothing. Over several years, more than one third of farmland changed hands, which affected 30 percent of all Japanese. Not only did the program accomplish many of its economic goals, but it also created a class of small landowners loyal to the conservative parties who first opposed the reform. As MacArthur anticipated, Japan avoided the types of rural insurgencies that engulfed China and Southeast Asia during the following decade.[36]

In accord with the Potsdam provisions and postsurrender policy, MacArthur moved to purge undesirable elements from Japanese political, economic, and cultural life. Initially, many Japanese conservative politicians approved the principle of a limited banishment of those militarists and ultranationalists who had displaced them and warred against America. However, SCAPIN 550 (January 4, 1946) shocked the conservatives by its scope. The initial purge order required the removal from national government of politicians, bureaucrats, military officers, and police linked to aggression. A few months later, the purge expanded to include local governments, educators, and (in January 1947) corporate executives.[37]

Needless to say, the unexpected dragnet shocked its early supporters. Nevertheless, the fact that the purge relied almost exclusively on the Japanese government for administration (only about twenty Americans supervised its operation) mitigated its impact on the nearly 2.5 million citizens subjected to its provisions. Eventually, about two hundred thousand individuals were formally purged, the overwhelming majority of whom came from military ranks. Despite claims in both Tokyo and Washington, relatively few business leaders suffered its effects. In any case, purged business leaders often continued to exercise unofficial influence or moved into new jobs that paralleled their former positions.

As with antimonopoly reforms, the purge underwent fundamental changes over time. Reacting to criticism from Congress, the press, and American business, SCAP switched emphasis away from the elimination of right-wing influence in Japan. By 1949 and 1950, the purge functioned as an instrument to search out and eliminate left-wing and Communist influence in the public and private sectors. Communist leaders, radical intellectuals, and about twenty thousand workers eventually felt its effects.[38]

Between 1945 and 1950, many other Japanese institutions experienced equally dramatic transformations. SCAP took initiatives to restructure public education, the police system, and labor unions. In the first two instances, reformers stressed the advantages of decentraliziation and local control along the American model. The schools adopted more liberal curricula and substituted sports for military training. Former New York Police Commissioner Louis J. Valentine was brought to Tokyo as an adviser; he described his goal as the creation of police units that exhibited "kindness, gentleness, and symspathy . . . along the lines of the New York force."[39]

Besides farmers, few groups benefited from initial change more than industrial workers. Long victimized by tough antilabor laws and police-employer collusion, unions responded enthusiastically to SCAP decrees and new laws that allowed them to operate freely. Both the SCAP civil liberties directive of October 1945, SWNCC 92/1 of November 1945, and a trade union law passed by the Diet that December provided an expanded basis for collective activity. Within a few months, unions passed their prewar membership peak of four hundred thousand. After a year, more than four million workers belonged to some seventeen thousand "enterprise unions" organized on a plant-by-plant, rather than industry wide, basis. By March 1949, some seven million workers belonged to trade unions, nearly 50 percent of the urban work force. Because of their superior organization, the Communists proved among the most effective organizers during the first few years of the Occupation. As a result, most local unions were loosely federated with either the pro-Communist Sanbetsu Labor Federation or the smaller, anti-Communist, Sodomei.

Despite initial SCAP encouragement, MacArthur grew increasingly alarmed at the political activism of the labor movement by 1947; in February of that year, he banned a threatened general strike. At the same time, SCAP either sponsored or encouraged a series of new laws that limited labor rights. Legislation of July 1947 and December 1948 severely restricted the union activities of public employees, and laws passed in 1949 increased government control of trade unions in the private sector. SCAP eventually encouraged the AFL–CIO to organize a central labor federation in Japan to undermine the influence of the Communists and other groups on the Left.[40]

Not only a changing international environment but the presurrender decision to utilize the existing Japanese government shaped these developments. Even if the rationale for this choice made sense—SWNCC planners argued that only a handful of Americans possessed the language and political skill required for administrative supervision—some contemporary critics understood its likely result. The iconoclastic journalist, I. F. Stone, for example, claimed that the decision to work through the Imperial government prejudiced the entire Occupation. How could the United States really expect to democratize Japan, he asked, "if we confine ourselves to operating through a government which remains [the] instrument [of the old ruling class]"? He criticized the decision to "leave in power the very elements we are pledged to eradicate." When only a few weeks after the surrender MacArthur declared demilitarization a fait accompli and lavished praise on officials in Tokyo, Stone feared SCAP had shored up a foundering regime.

The journalist also recognized that more profound issues than Mac-Arthur's personal behavior underlay the policy line. He guessed that someone like Assistant Secretary of War John J. McCloy had persuaded the administration that in Japan, as in Germany, the United States required a "bulwark against the U.S.S.R. and communism." The old "pro-Axis" and "anti-Soviet" crowd, he warned, now favored "softer treatment for both Germany and Japan."[41]

Actually Stone's assessment of McCloy came close to the mark. In February 1946, following a brief visit to Tokyo, McCloy expressed fear that liberal reforms would drive Japan "further left." Tampering with the economy or the government structure would cause "emotional upset and political unrest." McCloy thought the United States had "little to gain and much to lose" by indicting Hirohito or abolishing the emperor system. He also denounced the trial of war criminals as a total "fiasco." It made little sense to assess guilt, McCloy argued because "most Japanese look alike, in more ways than one." He attributed the Occupation's initial success to the "incredible discipline of the Japanese people" rather than to social engineering. If the Americans lingered too long and concerned themselves with cultivating democracy, he predicted, the operation would soon appear "more untidy and less successful."[42]

Writing nearly eighteen months later, John Maki, a former Government

Section staff member, confirmed Stone's prediction. Despite the constitutional reform and legalization of political activities, Maki argued, the
Occupation only partly altered the nature of Japanese politics. The powerful bureaucracy remained intact, hardly touched by the purge or the
political process. Traditional conservatives still dominated the Diet. Maki
traced these failures to the "decision to act through a Japanese government,
[which had] the inevitable result of creating both the appearance and ac-
tuality [of suporting that government on issues of critical internal importance. . . ." Whether or not MacArthur and the United States had intended
it, their actions had "created an identity of interest between the Occupation
and the government."[43]

Not even MacArthur's most bitter critics would deny that real changes
occurred during the Occupation or that the Japanese cooperated with many
reforms. Rather, critics complained that SCAP's fixation with democratic
forms, such as holding rapid parliamentary elections and mandating speedy
constitutional revision, neglected more important structural changes. Merely
allowing the proliferation of political parties did not foster creation of mass-
based, issue-oriented movements. Nor did high levels of voter turnout
indicate popular understanding of the democratic process. Yet, MacArthur
and his staff pointed to such quantities as a measure of the quality of the
spiritual revolution they had brought about.

At least superficially, most Americans in SCAP wanted to transform
Japan. Still, few approved uncontrolled change that might take unpredictable directions and destabilize the Occupation. Although MacArthur's
orders from Washington made it clear he was not committed to defend the
current regime, inevitably, routine contact between Americans and those
already in power created shared interests. These sanctioned the status quo
and widened the distance between SCAP and opponents of the old regime.

Over time, many observers came to feel that MacArthur used the issue
of reform largely as a platform for his presidential aspirations. A short,
inexpensive occupation that utilized local talent would demonstrate his
own political and administrative qualifications. When caught between charges
of either pushing liberal reform too far or not far enough, the Supreme
Commander finessed the problem. His staff issued "radical" decrees that
would be greatly modified as they filtered through the Japanese bureaucracy. The general could (and did) point to a record of promoting reform
and preserving tradition.

MacArthur's critics in the State and Defense departments detected just
such evidence of the general's grandstanding during the tumultuous Diet
debate over the *zaibatsu* deconcentration law late in 1947. Ignoring pleas
from Washington that he withdraw the proposal from consideration,
MacArthur pressed the Japanese government to pass a comprehensive bill

attacking the basic structure and ownership of industry. Free enterprise and democracy hinged on its enactment, he proclaimed. Just how deeply the general believed in his antimonopoly program and how much favorable publicity he hoped to gain from a posture of defying Wall Street and Japanese big business came into question in a confidential report circulated in Washington in December.

An anonymous American in Tokyo ("Mr. Wm. W.") reported to Army Department officials in Washington that MacArthur had mostly cynical reasons for pushing the law. Just before a final vote, SCAP aides were telling Japanese officials that the controversial law "had to be passed so as not to embarrass the Supreme Commander who is expected to run for president." MacArthur, his spokesman revealed, did not care a great deal about the actual application of the radical program. He did, however, care very much about appearances. There must "be no sign to the world of dissension" in the ranks, no hint that the Japanese did not unanimously see him as an enlightened reformer fighting against entrenched, small-minded politicians in Tokyo and Washington. Should passage of the law be delayed (as virtually all high State and Defense officials demanded), this action would "prejudice the future of Japan when the Supreme Commander became President."[44]

The bitter debate over the fate of the *zaibatsu* caused the most direct clash between MacArthur's program and the interests of the Japanese ruling class. However, the conflict evolved partly from the general's need to create a vivid record of reform for use in an American political contest. In addition, his somewhat atavistic conservative philosophy rested uneasily with the structure of modern big business. Although MacArthur and Japanese conservatives often squabbled over tactics and sometimes over deeper issues, a complex symbiotic relationship evolved between them. More often than not, entrenched interest groups tolerated or even benefited from changes initiated by SCAP. By the time the Occupation ended, it seemed clear that the reform program, if taken as a whole, created the framework for an efficient, modern, and conservative Japan.[45]

Despite an eventual accommodation, the political process often seemed fractured, especially before mid-1948. Led by a series of weak cabinets, the Japanese government failed to confront the dilemmas of inflation, falling production, labor discontent, or food shortages. Neither conservative nor leftist parties mustered the determination or support to move the nation in a clear direction. In many ways, all Japanese political factions appeared determined to wait out the Occupation. The Left hoped SCAP would clear away the power of the old elites; the conservatives anticipated the moment when the Americans would lose interest in reform and set about rebuilding traditional power bases.

Although SCAP policy and the purge swept away the prewar political parties and disqualified many former members of the Diet from running again, it did not significantly alter the spectrum of politics. On the Right, two major parties, the Progressives and the Liberals, held sway. The Progressives were led by Baron Shidehara who served as Prime Minister from October 1945 to May 1946. Hatoyama Ichiro led the Liberal party until his purge in May 1946, which permitted Yoshida Shigeru (who had acted as foreign minister in the Shidehara cabinet) to assume control of the Liberals and serve as prime minister from May 1946 until May 1947. The exchange of power between the two conservative groups held few surprises because both had similar programs. Personality issues and ties to specific business interests rather than ideology distinguished them.

In contrast to the relatively strong conservative parties, groups on the Left emerged from the war fragmented, disorganized, and inexperienced. The Social Democrats were split between a mildly socialistic faction and a competing conservative element, socialistic in name only. The tiny Communist party, whose leadership had spent years in prison or exile, possessed a strong idology, dynamic leaders, and little popular following. The labor movement, a potentially powerful political base, began to grow only in late 1945 and had few initial ties to political parties.

The disorganization of all progressive groups in 1945–46 insured the short-term dominance of the entrenched conservative parties and the career bureaucracy. The SCAP-drafted constitution, which retained the emperor as symbol of the nation, strengthened the aura of a link between the American program and conservative hegemony. When MacArthur decided to hold early Diet elections (in April 1946, allegedly to speed the Diet's ratification of the constitution), the vastly superior resources of the Right ensured a conservative electoral victory.

In the first postwar election, out of 466 seats, the Liberals, Progressives (the conservatives), and their minor allies won in 325 instances. The Socialists captured 92 seats, the Communists only 5. The results allowed Yoshida Shigeru to form a conservative cabinet based on a shaky alliance of the Liberals and Progressives. Although he retained power for a year, Yoshida did little to alleviate the food shortages and economic problems besetting the population. Most of the year was taken up by the cabinet's bickering with SCAP over the implementation of various reforms.

Despite his own distaste for Yoshida, MacArthur expressed concern over the growth in union militance and left-wing organizations during 1946–47. In advance of the scheduled April 1947 Diet elections, SCAP permitted election law revisions designed to add a few seats to the conservative column. Nevertheless, the Socialists emerged as the largest party, although with only a plurality of Diet seats. From June 1947 until February 1948, Katayama Tetsu led a coalition Socialist cabinet rent by factionalism.

After the collapse of the Socialist coalition, the pendulum swung right again. Ashida Hitoshi, of the Democratic (formerly Progressive) party formed a new coalition cabinet. Riding the conservative drift in Japan and American policy, Yoshida organized a new Democratic-Liberal party in the spring of 1948 and this group took control after an electoral victory in October 1948. Its majority bolstered early in 1949, Yoshida's cabinet held power through the end of the Occupation.[46]

Union militancy probably presented the most dynamic political challenge during the Occupation. The SCAP decrees and Diet legislation of 1945–46 made it possible to organize millions of factory workers and government employees in a short period of time. Besides the enabling legislation, the virtual collapse of the economy following surrender spurred union activity. From 1945 through 1947, unemployment, inflation, and chronic food shortages devastated the urban work force. Neither the series of conservative nor the mildly socialistic cabinets seemed interested in, or capable of, organizing a rational recovery program. Many charged that the conservatives and their business allies actually stimulated inflation and black market activities to sabotage and frustrate SCAP reforms. In any case, within a year of surrender, the inflation rate approached 1000 percent and production diminished to a fraction of capacity.

In January 1946, SCAP calculated that an average worker with three dependents earned less than half the monthly 519 yen required to live. The desperate urban working class depended on barter with farmers: clothing and household possessions in return for rice. Even pay raises won by collective bargaining were quickly wiped out by inflation. In response, both unions and spontaneous groups of workers abandoned classical tactics and adopted direct action.

An early popular tactic, production control, involved seizure of factories and mines by workers who managed the enterprise themselves. In April and May 1946, unions led mass demonstrations in Tokyo and other large cities demanding larger food rations, wage increases, and the resignation of the Shidehara and, then, the Yoshida cabinets. Although unorthodox by American standards, these marches and sit-ins remained peaceful. Moreover, they spoke to the fact that the Japanese government had responsibility over prices, wages, and food rationing.[47]

On May 19, the so-called food May Day demonstrations at Yoshida's residence and in front of the Imperial palace elicited an angry statement from MacArthur. The next day he issued a "Warning against Mob Disorder or Violence" that decried a "growing tendency towards mass violence" and "intimidation under organized leadership." Violence by "undisciplined elements," he claimed, threatened "orderly government" and the basic purposes and security of the Occupation itself. Unless the Japanese government took steps to bring "disorderly minorities" and "minor elements" under control, SCAP would intervene to "control and remedy such a deplorable situation."[48]

Mark Gayn, an American jouralist sympathetic to the protestors, described the "startling effect" of MacArthur's warning. It stunned both leftist activists and union leaders to hear the Supreme Commander likening them to desposed "feudalistic and military" leaders. Conservatives, on the other hand, reacted with "undisguised jubilation." SCAP intervention drove a wedge between elements of the disparate leftist-labor alliance. Yoshida, previously hesitant to select a new cabinet, moved quickly to form a governing coalition. All along the political spectrum, Gayn wrote, the Japanese considered MacArthur's action as a "prop" for conservative rule.[49]

Over the next three years, SCAP and the conservatives chipped away gradually at labor militancy and independence. In the summer of 1946, MacArthur condemned "strikes, walkouts, or other work stoppages which are inimical to the objectives of the occupation. . . ." His aides issued verbal threats to union leaders that strikers might be arrested.

Then, the Supreme Commander issued a lengthy statement on the anniversary of surrender (September 2, 1946) that clearly articulated the political direction of the Occupation. In his typical grandiloquent prose, the general remarked:

> Over all things and all men in this sphere of the universe hangs the dread uncertainty arising from impinging ideologies which now stir mankind. . . . [W]hich concept will prevail over those lands now being redesigned in the aftermath of war: this is the great issue which confronts our task in the problem of Japan—a problem which profoundly affects the destiny of all men and the future course of all civilization.

The "democratic way of life," MacArthur asserted confidently, had already filled the "complete vacuum" of defeated and demilitarized Japan. America's soldiers, armed with a "spiritual quality" had demonstrated the false values and idols held up to the Japanese by their warrior caste. Almost "overnight," he wrote, [a] spiritual revolution ensued which . . . tore asunder a theory and practice of life built upon two thousand years of history and tradition and legend." This new Japan would thrive "unless uprooted and suppressed by the inroads of some conflicting ideology which might negate individual freedom, destroy individual initiative and mock individual dignity."

MacArthur called on the Japanese to reject the "slanted propaganda" of the "extreme radical left." To safeguard his charges, the general promised to take Japan along the "great middle course of moderate democracy," destroying "what should yet be destroyed, preserving here what should be preserved and erecting here what should be erected." He concluded this proclamation with an explicit reference to Japan's future role as an American ally. Under his guidance, the nation could become "a powerful bulwark for peace" rather than a "dangerous springboard for war."[50]

Despite these warnings, a deteriorating economy and disgust with the Yoshida government moved many unions to formulate plans for a general strike. Neither Prime Minister Yoshida's characterization of the plan as "subversive" nor informal warnings by SCAP officials slowed the mobilization for the strike. At the last moment, on January 31, 1947, MacArthur intervened personally to ban the scheduled February 1 strike. He accused the unions of wielding a "deadly social weapon" that risked chaos and starvation. According to the general, the union leaders represented a "small minority" eager to plunge Japan into a disaster, as had occurred during war.[51]

During 1948 and 1949, SCAP followed up this assault by promoting passage of revised labor legislation that eroded the political and economic power of organized labor. In a series of actions, the Diet banned strikes by public workers, abolished collective bargaining in the large public sector, and, finally, placed tight controls on labor activity in the private sector. A series of austerity plans, promoted by the Americans and the Yoshida government in 1949, led to purges of leftist activitists from industry, a policy expanded just before and during the Korean War.

Most of the initial American efforts to uproot entrenched elites and institutions gradually lost momentum or changed direction in 1948. As early as 1947, planners in Washington expressed greater concern over mounting Occupation costs than with the need for reform. Besides the widely held concern over trends within Japan, influential Americans saw the collapse of Nationalist China, anticolonial rebellions in Southeast Asia, and the rise of Soviet power as integrally related to Japan's future. Containing both Soviet power and a more amorphous Communist threat as well as building a pro-American alliance in Asia seemed to pivot on the theme of Japanese recovery. Recovery, in turn, appeared to rest on the reconstruction of a highly centralized, regionally predominant economy. Conservative political forces within Japan joined with their American sponsors to rebuild the nation in ways that bore an uncanny resemblance to the prewar order.

3
NORTHEAST ASIA AND THE PACIFIC, 1945 TO 1947

In a conversation with Adm. Forrest Sherman (a naval commander in the Pacific) on November 9, 1944, Douglas MacArthur revealed anxiety over postwar politics. Admittedly, the general was in a bad temper, having just learned of Roosevelt's reelection. "[The] American people," he complained, "[had chosen] further regimentation and had forsaken the things for which our forefathers had fought." MacArthur went on to predict a postwar world divided between the United States and the Soviet Union. The Russians, he felt, had begun to "unify Europe economically" and would next try to reap political benefits. Germany appeared "ripe for going to the left" and France, after a civil war, would probably go Communist as well. In the Far East, MacArthur warned, the Soviets would "eventually tak[e] over North China and compet[e] for the hegemony of the Pacific."[1]

Fears of Soviet or revolutionary advances in East Asia underlay most postwar plans and postsurrender policies. Intelligence studies prepared both by the British government and the American JCS during 1944–45 predicted an Asia wracked by nationalist rebellions and susceptible to Soviet influence. The British sent a report to American military planners anticipating an effort by the Kremlin to link Siberia "together with Manchuria, Korea, Sakhalin and the Kuriles into an economically and industrially self-sufficient block . . . capable of maintaining powerful military forces." Thus, a major thrust of Russian policy would be to "deny Japan the resources" of Northeast Asia. Intelligence studies by the JCS declined to predict the ultimate limits of Kremlin policy, but seemed certain of an eventual Soviet–American confrontation in Asia.[2]

State Department Asia specialists confirmed these gloomy assessments in a long report sent to the War Department two months before the Pacific War ended. Japan, the report predicted, would be reduced to a smoldering ruin, garrisoned by American troops. China, far from being Roosevelt's cherished "policeman of Asia" would fall victim to civil war and possible Soviet intervention. A wave of nationalism would sweep over the remainder of Southeast Asia, making it difficult or impossible for the European powers to reimpose colonial rule. Finally, "a rising force" of Soviet ideology "throughout the Far East" would threaten to close off the entire region to Western influence.[3]

A detailed study of early postwar global security policy by historian Melvyn P. Leffler revealed how American planners "considered the preservation of a favorable balance of power in Eurasia as fundamental to United States national security." At least until 1948, neither diplomats nor military officials anticipated a direct Soviet armed threat against either the United States or other areas outside Eastern Europe. In the initial postwar period, Soviet military strength was judged vastly inferior to America's and the Kremlin's policy aroused only moderate concern. However, planners reacted anxiously to the "growing apprehension about the vulnerability of American strategic and economic interests in a world of unprecedented turmoil and upheaval."[4]

These uncertainties applied particularly to East Asia and the Pacific. As American strategists anticipated Japan's defeat, the decline of the great European empires, China's civil war, and the possible extension of Soviet power into Northeast Asia, they resolved to enhance their nation's security through a defense in depth that was based on control of the Pacific Ocean. Although many tactical differences persisted among the armed services, virtually all civilian and military policymakers conceived of the problem in similar terms. The United States, they believed, must maintain exclusive control of the crucial Pacific islands and Japan while neutralizing or cutting its losses in China. As the Asian mainland became more unstable after 1945, the United States increased its determination to safeguard its interests in Japan, the Pacific, and Southeast Asia from Soviet influence.

THE OFFSHORE DEFENSE STRATEGY

Emotional memories of the Pearl Harbor attack, the fierce battles to dislodge Japanese forces from the Pacific islands, the advent of atomic weapons and long-range bombing, and technological and budget developments focused American attention on building a network of forward bases beyond Hawaii. As early as 1943, Army and Navy planners resolved to establish a defense in depth by taking permanent control of the mandated islands acquired by Japan after the First World War. These included such hard-fought-for prizes as the Marshalls, Marianas, Carolines, and Marcus islands. The Ryukyus (which included Okinawa) had been acquired by Japan during the nineteenth century. But, from the perspective of military planners, its location required that it become a major base. Despite alternative claims by New Zealand, Australia, and native inhabitants, the JCS insisted on absolute American control. They rejected suggestions by the State Department that Washington seek UN authorization to acquire the islands as trust territories. Roosevelt's influential military aide, Adm. William Leahy, fumed that not a single island could be surrendered to "even partial control of another nation" without jeopardizing national security. The JCS professed astonishment that civilian officials would even suggest that the future of the islands be made the "subject of discussion with any other nation." Roosevelt failed to resolve the debate before his death, leaving the ill-prepared Truman to mediate a solution.

During the autumn of 1945, civilian leaders of the War and Navy departments, the JCS, Admiral Leahy, and Secretary of State Byrnes reached a general consensus on the need to create a comprehensive base system in both the Atlantic and Pacific oceans. Although important differences persisted over such points as whether to annex outright the desired islands or seek a UN sanction, the fundamental policy had been set. Air and naval bases in the Philippines would be retained after the grant of independence because of their proximity to Southeast Asia. From Okinawa, American forces could control the Yellow Sea and the bulk of Northeast Asia. By retaining the former Japanese mandated islands astride the Pacific trade routes, the United States could interdict any aggressor far from the homeland. This new strategic frontier would assure American access to Asia, deny the region's resources to an enemy, safeguard lines of communication, and permit an air offensive against any Asian power, including the Soviet Union.

Angered by the State Department's continued effort to have the United Nations place a mantle of legitimacy over these annexations and by the department's claim that sovereignty over the Ryukyus should eventually revert to Japan, the JCS stepped up their campaign for outright annexation. In March 1946, the JCS expressed the view that "experience in the recent war demonstrated conclusively that the defense of a nation, if it is to be effective, must begin beyond its frontiers." The advent of atomic warfare only compounded this fact, they insisted. The "further [*sic*] away from our own vital areas we can hold our enemy, through the possession of advanced bases . . . the greater our chances of surviving successfully an attack with atomic weapons and of destroying the enemy which employs them against us."

Admiral Leahy, President Truman's Chief of Staff, maintained this drumbeat in the White House. In October 1946, he defended annexation as required not so much by immediate security considerations of a Soviet threat but because of a long-term strategy. Some day, the United States would need wartime access to the resources of Southeast Asia as well as a "firm line of communication from the West Coast to the Asiatic mainland, plus denial of this line in time of war to any potential enemy.[5]

Despite the military's clamor for control of the Pacific, historians Roger Dingman and Stephen Pelz have pointed out that strategic planning for this immense region remained chaotic in practice. During the five years leading up to the Korean War, the JCS and their subsidiary planning committees continually ranked East Asia and the Pacific as a third security priority, behind Western Europe and the Middle East. In case of Soviet aggression, the JCS assumed the United States would launch a counter-attack from the Pacific islands and (possibly) Japan, using conventional and atomic weapons. (Of course, before 1948 too few atomic bombs and suitable aircraft existed to play a real part in such a projected war.) But, military planners neglected to predict why or how the Russians would attack anywhere in the region. In fact, most war planning assumed a Russian–American conflict fought largely in Europe and resembling the Second World War.

China did appear to be a possible target of Soviet attack. But a Russian invasion seemed irrelevant, given the pace of the civil war after 1947. In any case, occupying that vast and poor country would be more of a liability than an asset. As for Japan, neither military nor civilian estimates predicted that the Soviets would attempt to seize more than Hokkaido during the initial phases of an all-out war. In fact, before mid-1950, the State and Defense departments could not agree internally or with each other over the questions of Japanese rearmament or the aquisition of post-Occupation offensive bases.

When military planners outlined scenarios for retaliatory air strikes against Soviet Far Eastern targets, they could not decide what military value these attacks would have. Army, navy, and airforce strategists also waffled on the question of committing ground forces to the Asian mainland. Most incredibly, the JCS never determined what kind of regional conflict (as distinct from a global war) might require American intervention. Accordingly, force structures and war plans were better prepared for direct confrontation with the Soviet Union than for a more likely limited conflict at such flashpoints as Korea and Southeast Asia.[6]

Uncertainties about Soviet intentions, China's civil war, and increasing Southeast Asian resistance to European colonialism combined to shift the focus of defense planning toward an insular strategy. The JCS sought to sway Truman to support their plans for the outright annexation of many Pacific islands by pointing out additional technological facts and budget constraints. Between mid-1945 and mid-1947, defense spending and force levels dropped precipitously. Troop strength fell from 12 to 3 to 1.6 million in twenty-four months. The arms budget, which reached $81.6 billion in fiscal 1945, fell to $44.7 billion the next year and only $13.1 billion in fiscal 1947. These figures virtually required that America rely on the use of naval and air power, not massed troops, to deter or attack an aggressor. Such forces could function best from forward bases like those in the Pacific. Positioning power on the mandated islands or Japan itself seemed vital to deter or counter any Soviet move into mainland Asia or against Japan.

The more apparent the deterioration of Chinese Nationalist strength became in 1946–47, the more military planners grew convinced they must pursue a pacific strategy. A relatively small strategic bomber force and navy, operating from the mandated islands, Okinawa, and (possibly) Japan, could deter, interdict, or retaliate against any enemy advance. Operating from bases distant from America, bombers with a three-thousand-mile range could hit deep inside the Soviet Union provided they made one-way runs and ditched in friendly territory. War plans evolved from 1945 to 1947 were predicated on unleashing atomic air raids against Soviet territory from bases in the Ryukyus, Japan, England, and, perhaps, Egypt and India.

Through 1946, the JCS did not consider it necessary or advisable to make Japan a major offensive military base. Instead, they emphasized the importance of insuring that Japan's large military potential and manpower be denied to the Soviet Union. However, the armed services insisted on outright annexation of the islands captured from Japan—this included Okinawa—and their conversion into major bases. Although the service branches argued incessantly over who would garrison these facilities, the islands figured prominently in all war plans. Gradually, war plans came to include staging air attacks from Japan, as well. However, Okinawa emerged as the critical focus of war plans by 1947, even though only limited development of its facilities took place before 1948.

Military planners envisaged the mandates, the Ryukyus, and Japan as inseparable elements to this defense in depth. Dismissing State Department calls for placing the mandates under some form of UN trusteeship (so as not to undermine the "moral prestige" of the United States), the JCS demanded total domination of the Pacific. As they summarized their case in 1947, the "ultimate security of the United States . . . rests on the ability . . . to control the Pacific Ocean and since no such control can be effective unless it is complete," any gaps in the system of bases "tend greatly to weaken if not vitiate the effectiveness of the system as a whole." The most distant and peripheral islands were actually the most important to counteroffensive operations because the goal of strategic attack was to begin operations "from points farther from our own vital areas and nearest those of the enemy." Both the JCS and General MacArthur warned it might prove "militarily disastrous" to compromise control over any Pacific territory."[7]

Torn between the military's demands for the outright annexation of the Pacific islands and the Ryukyus versus the State Department's insistence that the United States seek both a new UN sanction for its control of the mandated islands and consider the eventual return of Okinawa to Japan, Truman ordered a face-saving compromise. Later, in 1946, American officials prepared a special plan for a "strategic trusteeship" over the mandated islands—the plan left Okinawa's status undetermined for the time being. Presented to the Security Council on a take-it-or-leave-it basis, the formula discounted the Pacific islanders' claims for independent or self-governing status. It provided for virtually total American control for an indefinite period that was subject to almost no outside interference. Despite grumbling by Great Britain, Australia, New Zealand, and the Soviet Union, the United Nations approved the formula in April 1947, granting the United States military control over a vast part of the Pacific.[8]

ISOLATING JAPAN

Just as the United States maintained a tight grasp over the far-flung Pacific islands it had conquered, it also quickly resolved to seal off Japan from postwar Soviet influence. On August 16, 1945, when Stalin accepted the designation of Gen. Douglas MacArthur as Supreme Commander for the Allied Powers, the Russian leader stunned Truman by renewing a request for a Soviet occupation zone on Hokkaido, Japan's northern island. This, he claimed, would bolster the Russian people and repay the debt incurred by the Japanese during their occupation of Siberia from 1919 to 1922.[9]

Interpreting this as a power grab, Truman and his aides rushed to quash the initiative. The president reiterated that although Soviet forces could accept the Japanese surrender in Manchuria and the Kuriles, only token Russian forces, under MacArthur, might enter Japan. Washington would not budge from the principal of an American-controlled Occupation without zonal divisions. In a fast reversal of roles, Truman demanded that the Soviets permit American air force and weather units access to their occupation zones in the Kuriles. Now Stalin cried foul and each leader accused the other of trying to upset a delicate balance.[10]

In Moscow, Ambassador Averell Harriman, although suspicious of Stalin, believed that the Russians were only testing the waters. He guessed the Kremlin would back off quickly and was more interested in receiving nominal parity than real influence in Japan. Harriman suggested that Stalin could be mollified by membership on a prestigious but impotent supervisory commission for Japan modeled on the "pattern set in Hungary, Bulgaria and Rumania" by the Soviets. But secretary of State Byrnes, jealous of the ambassador's initiatives, rejected this advice and spurned Harriman's request for consultations in advance of the upcoming foreign ministers' conference in London. The secretary of state, Harriman complained, did not care to be "confused by other people's judgments."[11]

Despite his reluctance, Byrnes was forced to take some action because the British government raised similar demands for a voice in Japan. London had also called for creation of a two-tiered council (composed of greater and lesser powers) to advise MacArthur. Byrnes responded by unveiling a contingency plan devised by SWNCC months earlier should the Allies make such claims. He informed London and Moscow of Washington's willingness to convene a Far Eastern Advisory Commission (FEAC) composed of the major allies along with France, Canada, Australia, New Zealand, the Netherlands, and the Philippines. Based in Washington, it would remain strictly advisory and have no authority over MacArthur.[12]

From then until the London foreign ministers meeting convened on September 11, both powers attacked this offer. The British deprecated the idea as mere window dressing, whereas the Russians declared outright their refusal to participate in the powerless FEAC. Brushing aside all protests, Assistant Secretary of State James C. Dunn bluntly proclaimed that under no circumstances would the United States permit a "control Council in Japan" to diminish American influence.[13]

Throughout the tendentious London Conference, the Japan issue lurked beneath the surface of other debates. British, American, and Soviet delegates argued at length over procedural questions, on whether to admit France and China to their deliberations, over how to resolve territorial disputes, and, most intently, whether to honor the peace treaties Moscow had signed with the Soviet-created governments in Bulgaria and Rumania. Byrnes rejected the validity of the satellite states but suggested no grounds for a compromise. His refusal to bargain prompted Molotov to accuse the Americans of trying to play "dictator to the world."[14]

Byrnes disdained both colleagues and adversaries at London. A self-made politician who excelled at inner-party politics, Byrnes viewed the career foreign service with contempt. At one point during the conference, he allegedly said, "God Almighty! I might tell the President sometime what happened, but I'm never going to tell those little bastards at the State

Department anything about it!" Harriman, in contrast, although intensely anti-Communist, had some empathy with the Russians' fixation on security. Personally, he shared Molotov's frustrations with Byrnes and feared that a deadlocked meeting would only encourage greater Soviet hostility. The ambassador understood that Japan ranked high on the "hidden agenda" of Soviet concerns. Moscow worried that Washington intended to "use Japan against them" and for this reason refused to allow even a nominal control commission in Tokyo. Instead of trying to contain the Soviets by freezing them out, Harriman again suggested "following the pattern of the Balkan commissions," which would provide Stalin a face-saving role while preserving for MacArthur "the final voice." The dampening of Soviet–American tensions over Japan might also temper Russian behavior elsewhere in Asia, he believed.[15]

Harriman understood in part that this dispute comprised only one element in a broader deadlock over the atomic monopoly, the fate of Germany and of Eastern Europe, and the civil war in China. Although the president and the public were aroused by the Russians' brutal determination to hold an inviolable sphere, many American actions paralleled those of the Soviets, at least in their intentions. In the name of national security, Truman had just repeated Washington's resolve to prevent "interference by any non-American power in the affairs of . . . North, Central and South America." The American Navy proclaimed a moral right to annex hundreds of Pacific islands, and, during the London meetings, President Truman publicly reaffirmed that Washington would continue its unilateral control of Japan. Even Byrnes voiced misgivings at this last remark because it made Stalin think we were "going off in a unilateral way [in Japan] as the Russians were going off in the Balkans."[16]

But Byrnes's insight faded quickly. During the final week of the London conference, Harriman vainly sought to persuade the secretary of state to see contradictions in American policy. Washington could not expect the Soviets to broaden the Balkan regimes while proclaiming an exclusive American monopoly in Japan. Molotov seized on just such points to "divert attention" and pillory the United States. Byrnes agreed finally to suggestions from Harriman and Charles Bohlen that he keep negotiations going by expressing a willingness to reconsider (if not accept) Moscow's treaties with Rumania and Bulgaria. However, he still refused to ask the Russians to join an oversight commission in Japan.[17]

During the next three months, Byrnes stubbornly resisted striking a compromise over Japan and the Balkans. He found comfort in comments from Admiral Leahy and General MacArthur that opposed any sort of Allied control mechanism: Leahy feared a council was only a first step toward Communist "control of Japan"; MacArthur told a Truman emissary that Moscow would use local representatives to "demoralize" the Japanese and to "create an environment for a successful communist revolution." Byrnes continued to ignore Harriman's argument that Stalin placed first priority on winning for Russia acceptance as a "great power," which would be signified by Russia's playing some role in Japan. Secondarily, the Kremlin wanted to trade its subordinate position in Japan for a similar subordinate American position in the consignment of the Balkans to a Russian sphere. Of course, Russia was interested in Japan, but Harriman believed that the Kremlin's policy concerned itself more with establishing a relationship of equality with the United States than with expansionist plans.[18]

Harriman returned to Moscow from London in mid-October carrying a conciliatory personal message from Truman. The Russian capital was "rife with rumor" about Stalin's prolonged seclusion and an alleged power struggle. The ambassador forcefully demanded to see Stalin and, on October 24, flew to a Crimean resort for a special meeting. The letter from the president called for a resumption of Soviet–American negotiations along the lines of the Yalta accords. Although not ready to accept the Soviet-controlled Balkan regimes, Truman expressed a willingness to resume discussions over their legitimacy on terms more pleasing to Moscow.[19]

To the ambassador's surprise, Stalin immediately turned the conversation away from the Balkans and complained that Truman had "not touched upon" the "Japanese question." He wanted to know if the United States would create a "control commission" in Tokyo named and structured like the similar organs in Soviet-dominated Hungary and Rumania. To Harriman, Stalin's focus on this point and his insistence that such bodies be called "commissions" instead of the American preferred "council," confirmed his belief that the Russian saw Japan as the American political analogy to Eastern Europe.[20]

The next day, the Soviet leader lashed out strongly against American action in Japan. MacArthur had treated his representative in Tokyo, Gen. Kuzma N. Derevyanko, like a "piece of furniture." Instead of being relegated to a "satellite of the United States in the Far East," perhaps the Soviets should boycott cooperative efforts. Unless treated with equality and asked to join a substantive control commission in Japan, Stalin warned, he might pursue an isolated (meaning independent) policy in Asia.[21]

This discussion and subsequent Soviet behavior convinced Harriman that Stalin had no master plan to subvert Japan. Rather, the Russian leader worried over what the Americans intended to do and knew he had little ability to influence the course of events. The genuine anxiety in Moscow about the "constant menace to Russian security in the Far East" posed by Japan, Harriman explained to Byrnes, made Stalin even more argumentative and skittish than usual. This might explain why the Soviets requested and then rejected a new American offer to create an Allied military council based in Tokyo and a Far Eastern Commission headquartered in Washington. The Russians insisted that the "council" be called a "commission" and that the Far Eastern Commission possess a veto over SCAP policy. Washington, of course, would never allow the Soviets a controlling vote in Japan.[22]

Belatedly, the secretary of state accepted the ambassador's proposal to engage the Soviets constructively by tying a compromise over Japan to a deal on the Balkans. Byrnes proposed to reconvene the CFM in Moscow in mid-December, with attendance limited to the big three—the United States, the Soviet Union, and the United Kingdom. Despite an inauspicious beginning (typically, Byrnes neglected to consult with the British), some real progress took place on key issues.

The Americans hinted that they would accept a new Soviet formula (really only a token) for broadening non-Communist participation in the Bulgarian and Rumanian governments—Stalin and Byrnes did not finally agree on the terms until December 26, as the conference ended. This allowed the United States to abandon its stance of refusing to recognize the satellite regimes while they remained Russian pawns. The Soviets accepted Byrnes's offer to join a Far Eastern Commission in Washington and a smaller Allied Council for Japan (ACJ) in Tokyo. The Far Eastern Commission would act as an advisory board of eleven (later, thirteen) nations. Its decisions were not binding unless the United States and the other "great powers" were in agreement. In cases of dissent, Washington retained the right to issue binding "interim directives" on all matters. The smaller Allied council, composed of the Soviet Union, China, the United States, and the British Commonwealth, was empowered to consult with Gen. Douglas MacArthur, "the exigencies of the situation permitting." However, he need not heed any ACJ advice and, on all matters of substance, his decisions were "controlling." In essence, the Russian's accepted a nominal role in Japan with about as much influence as the Americans gained in the Balkans.[23]

Resolution of the Japan–Balkan dispute had a positive effect on a related international troublespot, China. Since mid-August, the United States had agonized as civil war spread in north China and as the Soviets occupied and looted Manchuria. The KMT and CCP armies faced off as some fifty-five thousand American marines, several million armed Japanese, and a large Russian occupation army looked on. American officials feared that the KMT could neither contain nor defeat the Communist forces and that a widening conflict might suck in both the marines and the Soviet troops.

To complicate matters still further, the mercurial ambassador to China, Patrick J. Hurley, had resigned late in November, charging that the Truman

administration coddled Communist sympathizers and weakened the Nationalists by pressing for a coalition government. The president sought
some way to tamp down the domestic reaction to these wild claims and to
defuse a dangerous crisis in China that might lead to an unwanted Soviet–
American collision. Once again, Washington tried to mediate among the
Chinese, this time by sending the highly respected Gen. George C. Marshall
as the president's special representative.

Initially, Truman and Byrnes feared a hostile Soviet reaction to the
Marshall mission. At Moscow, however, the Russians proved rather conciliatory. Foreign Minister Molotov did make some blunt remarks early in
the conference demanding the speedy withdrawal from China of the marines, who had sided with the Nationalists. But, to Byrnes's delight, Stalin
tempered his aide's statements. The Soviet leader professed strong support
for a negotiated settlement in China, although he doubted either party
really sought peace. He promised to remove quickly his own occupation
forces from Manchuria, and he applauded Marshall's appointment. The
two delegations also agreed to resume efforts toward establishing a viable
trusteeship in divided Korea, an issue discussed later in this chapter. Stalin,
it appeared, preferred to minimize China as a zone of international rivalry
and saw the Marshall mission as a good faith effort.

Despite the apparent goodwill and the accords achieved at Moscow,
Truman revealed a growing distaste for both his secretary of state and for
compromise with the Soviets. Byrnes's haughty behavior and minimal consultations with the President during and after the Moscow meeting convinced Truman that his aide sought to appease Stalin's appetite while
slighting his own chief. Moreover, the administration's foreign policy had
come under growing attack by influential Republicans and an increasing
number of in-house critics. Early in January 1946, on Byrnes's return to
Washington, Truman penned a letter to the secretary of state that he
declined to send but claimed to have read to Byrnes as part of an oral
dressing down.

The president launched into a wide-ranging denunciation of Soviet behavior in Eastern Europe, Iran, Turkey, and the Mediterranean. Even the
Russian entry into the Pacific War, which Truman admitted Americans
desired at the time, had proved unnecessary and a "headache to us ever
since." Truman declared, "Unless Russia is faced with an iron fist and
strong language, another war is in the making." Stalin understood only
one language: "How many divisions have you."

In light of this, the president expressed a determination to make the
Russians loosen their hold over Eastern Europe and back away from the
Near East. To keep the peace, America would "maintain complete control
of Japan and the Pacific." The United States would attempt to "rehabilitate

China and create a strong central government there" as well as in Korea, where Byrnes had agreed to resurrect a trusteeship with the Russians. After accomplishing this, Truman continued, he would demand the return of ships given the Soviets in wartime and "force a settlement of the Lend-Lease Debt of Russia." He was, in short, "tired of babying the Soviets." Although George Marshall's difficulties in China and the de facto division of Korea soon demonstrated the impossibility of imposing unilateral settlements in those nations, the president renewed a determination to brook no interference in Japan and the Pacific. His vivid outburst revealed the ugly tensions engulfing Soviet–American relations globally.[24]

The superficial agreements over China and Korea and the Allied representation in Japan soothed tempers without altering fundamentally the relationships among the powers. Neither the Far Eastern Commission nor the ACJ played much of any role during the Occupation. Not until 1947, for example, did the Far Eastern Commission even get around to sending an advisory "Post-Surrender Directive" to SCAP. Even then, the directive only repeated the basic American agenda of 1945. MacArthur met only once with the ACJ, at its first session in Tokyo during April 1946. The general appeared briefly to instruct the delegates on their duty to support SCAP loyally. He then turned the chair over to his deputy and never paid the group further attention. In his memoirs, MacArthur accused the council of "nuisance and defamation" that caused him endless bother.

Gen. Courtney Whitney and other SCAP representatives saw the ACJ as an enemy, searching for "sensationalism" and scandal. Whitney lambasted the Soviet delegate whenever he spoke and delayed answering inquiries, sometimes for months. By issuing informal "suggestions" to the Japanese government in place of formal orders, MacArthur claimed a right not to inform the council of his actions. Eventually, MacArthur's deputies chose to adjourn meetings only moments after they began. As the British Commonwealth delegate, Australian William MacMahon Ball, described this charade, the intense distrust and hostility between the Americans and Russians "cast its shadow" over all the council's work. Nothing could be examined on its merits because there "were no problems of Japan." Every issue was "considered for its effect on Russian–American relations."[25]

Nevertheless, the Soviets initially accepted this disposition as the best they could expect. Stalin made this evident in his final meeting with retiring Ambassador Harriman in January 1946. Although the Russian admitted he would prefer to abolish the emperor system, overall, he confided, the great powers had found "common ground and things were proceeding well in Japan." He also claimed to be as confused about China as the Americans were. He told Harriman that both the Nationalists and Communists rejected his advice and mediation offers. Just as Jiang Jieshi balked at following American orders, Mao Zedong did "not agree with the position of the Soviet government on China" and declined to follow Moscow's advice. The only Chinese Stalin had something positive to say for was the Generalissimo's son, Jiang Jingguo (Chiang Ching-kuo), who had lived in the Soviet Union during the 1920s, married a Russian woman, and paid a friendly visit to the Kremlin in December 1945.[26]

Years later, Harriman concluded that Stalin had meant what he said about China—that the Kremlin had no plan of conquest, did not control the CCP, and probably preferred a coalition government that would leave the country weak and outside any sphere of influence. At the time, however, the ambassador still feared Stalin planned to dominate mainland Asia, beginning with Manchuria and spreading south. Discussions he held in China and Tokyo en route to Washington confirmed this anxiety.

Late in January, T. V. Soong, Jiang's American-educated brother-in-law and sometimes foreign minister, passed "secret information" to Harriman. Soong alleged that in December (in Moscow) Stalin had told Jiang Jingguo of a "master plan":

> [The Soviets intended to] industrialize Siberia during the next fifty years. During that period there was no chance that the United States would want war and this would give him time to strengthen his weak position in the East. He said that China and the Soviet Union must work together and that the production of Manchurian industry was essential to the carrying out of the industrialization of Siberia, which could not be accomplished otherwise.

Harriman, in fact, harbored just such worries about Russian intentions, whatever the accuracy of Soong's source. Yet, he also viewed the KMT regime as too corrupt, unpopular, and faction ridden to survive even with American assistance. This made Japan all the more vulnerable to Soviet pressure and important to American security.[27]

Compared to the chaos and despair of postwar China, Tokyo seemed an oasis of stability and hope. Although he often cold-shouldered visiting civilians, especially diplomats, MacArthur lavished attention on Averell Harriman when he arrived early in February. Perhaps the conjunction of their strategic views promoted this accord. Both worried that the Russians intended to take all Korea in order to "expand their narrow strategic position in the Far East." Harriman predicted a Soviet campaign to integrate the economies of Siberia, Korea, and Manchuria, thereby threatening Japan's economic and physical security. MacArthur professed to be so taken by the ambassador's grasp of Asian events (or so intent on flattering someone about to report to Truman) that he offered him a top-level job with SCAP.

Seventeen years later, Harriman encountered the aging general at a dinner hosted by publisher Henry Luce to honor those who had graced the covers of *Time*. Even though Harriman had sided with President Truman in urging the general's recall in 1951, MacArthur spoke warmly of their 1946 meeting in Tokyo. Still the charmer, Douglas MacArthur told Harriman that he had been the first to sound the tocsin proclaiming the Communist threat in Asia. "You were the first one to warn me to be careful of the Russians. . . . It helped me a lot. I have always been grateful to you [for it]," he confided.[28]

MACARTHUR'S VISIONS

MacArthur's geopolitical vision was neither so naive nor so sophisticated as he would have his contemporaries believe. Although the predominant figure in the Japanese–American relationship (at least until 1947), he frequently altered his analysis, depending on the time and his audience. Often, he reversed the relative importance of China, Japan, Korea, Taiwan, and Southeast Asia to American security. He failed to specify if the "enemy" presented primarily a military, economic, or political challenge to Western interests in Asia. Until the North Korean attack of June 25, 1950, he had been among those most eager to write off the American commitment to the Syngman Rhee regime. Although while often implying that the United States must defend Nationalist China, he shrank from actually recommending such a course. Yet, the general continually offered bold, if Delphic, pronouncements on "oriental psychology" and world power, which were directed more toward shaping a political following at home than formulating a viable strategy in Asia.

Pushing aside the rhetoric, fluff, and frequent contradictions in his pronouncements, MacArthur held steady to a few basic strategic concepts through 1949. The Supreme Commander took seriously the "peace constitution" that he had largely inspired. For a variety of motives, he favored the real elimination of Japanese military power and even opposed the long-term maintenance of American bases on the islands. Until shortly before the outbreak of the Korean War, the general disputed efforts by the State and Defense departments to revive a small Japanese defense force, to resume some military production, or to require that the Japanese grant the United States extensive military-base rights as the price of a peace settlement.

However, none of these points suggests that MacArthur should be considered a closet pacifist. Both American security and that of Japan, he maintained, could best be protected by creating a strong island defense perimeter off the Asian mainland. Because he, like most military planners, doubted that the Soviets would directly assault Japan, its security did not hinge on rearmament. MacArthur felt that a local police force and, perhaps, a small symbolic American garrison would suffice to assure Japan's physical integrity. He vigorously supported the JCS's efforts to secure complete control of the mandated islands and Okinawa for use as air and naval bases. From these positions, MacArthur believed, any thrusts originating on the Asian mainland could be deterred or beaten back. Despite his frequent warnings about the global Soviet threat, the general predicted that the Russians would accept and honor Japanese neutrality if the United States did not remilitarize its former enemy. Ironically, he stood almost alone in this belief.

Except for China, MacArthur said very little about developments in the rest of Asia. Despite his long connection with the Philippines, he consented to only the briefest of visits to Manila, on the occasion of independence in 1946. Although he assisted in the return of Syngman Rhee to Korea, MacArthur joined the Joint Chiefs in urging the early withdrawal of American forces, even if this resulted in the collapse of the anti-Communist regime. His public and private references to China's civil war continually wavered, depending on the audience. Although sometimes appearing resigned to the Nationalists' defeat, he occasionally endorsed schemes to intervene covertly against the Communists. Certainly, the administration was at fault for whatever went wrong. In effect, the general strove to confirm his hardline anti-Communist credentials without appearing as a reckless adventurer willing to become trapped in a major war on the Asian mainland. Nevertheless, he proved a constant irritant to the president and his administration.

Only three weeks into the Occupation, for example, MacArthur released a statement in which he complemented himself for winning not only the greatest gamble of the war, but "in history." He applauded his decision to permit the Japanese government to take charge of disarmament and lavished effusive praise on the talents and cooperative spirit shown by the vanquished enemy. On his his own authority, he predicted that American occupation forces could soon be "drastically cut" to about two hundred thousand troops and that as "rapidly as ships can be made available," the "boys" would be sent home. Eighth Army Commander, General Eichelberger, went even further, hinting that the entire operation might be wrapped up in a year.[29]

Not surprisingly, these assertions infuriated President Truman, members of his cabinet, and the service chiefs. Millions of armed Japanese troops still occupied large parts of China and Southeast Asia, many of them sandwiched between contending local armies and European colonial forces. The British, Russians, and Chinese were complaining about their exclusion from any form of consultation or power sharing in Tokyo, where many members of the old regime remained in power. The elaborate American reform agenda had hardly begun to be implemented, yet the Supreme Commander and his aides spoke of winding down the Occupation. MacArathur's glib talk of "smooth progress" and "sending the boys home" played havoc with efforts by the armed forces to demobilize millions of restless troops in an orderly fashion. Finally, the general's assertion seemed directly at odds with the president's effort to have Congress approve peacetime extension of the draft—politically unpopular and certainly unnecessary if surplus forces already existed. (MacArthur, in private, supported the draft but refused to say so publicly.)

MacArthur's cavalier attitude toward Truman personally and toward administration policy also showed in his rejection of two requests that he return home for a visit. The Supreme Commander rejected an invitation from Truman, forwarded by Marshall on September 17, 1945, that he come to receive the kind of congressional and popular acclaim accorded other ranking generals. SCAP replied that conditions in Japan remained too sensitive. The next month, on October 19, Truman directed Marshall to send another more forceful message to urge MacArthur to "make a trip home at such time you feel that you can safely leave your duties." The general again declined, citing the "extraordinarily dangerous" situation in Japan. These rebuffs seemed rather at odds with the general's public pronouncements of mid-September. Truman, in turn, ordered MacArthur to adhere to policy directives and to desist from making unauthorized statements. Privately, Truman told one adviser that the press releases from Tokyo could only be viewed as a "political statement." Eben Ayers recorded his boss as saying that he "was going to do something with that fellow [MacArthur], who . . . had been balling things up. He said he was tired of fooling around."[30] (See the references appendix on p. 342.)

The following month, MacArthur offered additional insights into his attitude during a conversation with presidential envoy Edwin A. Locke. Declaring that he possessed a unique understanding of "oriental psychology," SCAP boasted that he would utilize Japan to serve American interests. MacArthur spoke to Locke in the company of Col. Raymond C. Kramer, then SCAP's chief economic expert and an extremely conservative businessman in civilian life. Both worried that occupied Japan might become an "albatross around our necks" should its economy falter. This seemed a real danger, given the loss of access to Korea and Manchuria, "without which existing industry in the home islands of Japan is badly unbalanced." The postsurrender reform plans given SCAP acknowledged the imbalance but sought to rectify it by extracting industrial reparations. The Occupation authorities had other ideas.

MacArthur and Kramer described a plan to promote stability and recovery by permitting the Japanese to enact cosmetic economic reforms. Some superficial changes would be made in the way the *zaibatsu* monopolies operated, but the new managers would, in substance, be "identical" to the current oligarchs. Kramer cautioned against transferring major Japanese-owned facilities in Korea, China, and Manchuria to the "incapable" hands of the local population. Instead, they might be "acquired . . . on a 99-year lease basis . . . by the fifty leading industrial concerns in America. . . ." American management would "safeguard the broader interests of the United States in the Far East" while maintaining the flow of vital raw materials to Japan.

MacArthur minimized the threat from recalcitrant militarists and fanatic nationalists. "Underground communist agitation" sponsored by the Soviet Union represented a greater threat. All SCAP policy, he claimed, "took into consideration the factor of Russian activity in the Far East." The United States and the Russians were locked in battle for control of the world and he assumed that Moscow's local agents, masquerading as "so-called liberals" had targeted the nation for a "successful communist revolution."

Although only a few weeks had passed since the formal surrender, MacArthur and Kramer described the two nations almost as nascent political allies. Once stripped of its military forces, Kramer told Locke (in MacArthur's presence), Japanese industry should be given the "green light" to expand. Given their superior "industry, discipline and honesty," the Japanese could soon become more than "ever before . . . [the] natural leaders of Asia."[31]

Although Locke wondered if MacArthur might have indulged in some poetic license in advocating policies that seemed to contradict the formal position of the United States, a variety of other Americans heard similar reports. Early in 1946, for example, a Treasury Department representative, D. R. Jenkins, traveled to Tokyo to investigate economic conditions. He reported to the department that the *zaibatsu* industrialists and their allies in the bureaucracy seemed firmly in control of the economy. Many officers on MacArthur's staff told him that "Japan should be considered as a base for possible future military operations against Russia." Because of this, they insisted that the "Japanese economy should be restored rather than weakened by reparations removals" and other reforms. Similarly, W. W. Butterworth (later head of the State Department's Office of Far Eastern Affairs [FE]) heard such statements when he served in the Embassy in China during 1946. American military officers throughout Asia, he reported, indulged in "open talk" about restoring Japan as "our future bulwark" and base for "strategic operations" against Russia.[32]

During 1946, MacArthur's articulation of a regional policy evolved in an ad hoc manner. In July, discussing policy with visiting Navy Secretary James Forrestal, the general complained that the Truman administration had failed either to restore Japan's strength or to halt the march of Chinese communism. Fears of reparation removals, he claimed, made it impossible to revive basic industry and prevented Japan from earning enough to pay for vital imports. He condemned critics who favored more extreme purges, arguing that only a small clique of militarists bore responsibility for aggression. In particular, MacArthur defended the emperor as a virtual captive of the military fanatics who, himself, was liberated by the American victory. In fact, discussions with Hirohito had led to the possibility of the emperor's religious conversion. MacArthur told Forrestal he now had before him the question of "permitting the Emperor to become converted to Christianity."

Christianity, as a political ideology, seemed to dominate MacArthur's outlook. It served as a barrier against both communism and left-wing journalists and diplomats who, he claimed, planned to subvert Japan. He told the navy secretary—a man predisposed to see communism as the work of the anti-Christ—that throughout Asia the Americans had joined a battle against communism and for Christianity. The general portrayed his own labors in Tokyo as a symbolic crucifixion. Japan formed the "western outpost of our defenses," he assured Forrestal, protected by the twin strengths of American military power and the Christian faith.[33] In fact, MacArthur's aides humored him by vastly inflating the numbers of Japanese converts.

Religious imagery permeated the general's public statements. His attacks on labor unions and leftists often contrasted the "extreme radical left" to the "true liberals" who participated in the "spiritual revolution" underway in Japan. By the first anniversary of surrender, he described the conquered nation as having become a "Powerful bulwark for peace" in the Pacific. Early in 1947, in a message to Congress, MacArthur boasted of his leading a "reformation of the Japanese people," taking them from adherence to mythical teaching of "legendary ritualism to the maturity of enlightened knowledge and truth. . . ." Economic recovery and political reform, he claimed, formed only a part of this renaisssance. He took equal pleasure in the fact that an "increasing number of the Japanese people—already estimated at over two million" had spontaneously "moved to embrace the Christian faith as a means to fill the spiritual vacuum left in Japanese life by the collapse of their past faith." This "spearhead of Christianity," he predicted, would sweep over Asia, transforming "hundreds of millions of backwards peoples. . . ."[34]

In commenting on the selection of moderate socialist Katayama Tetsu as prime minister in May 1947, MacArthur laid particular stress on the "spiritual implications" that outweighed the "political implications." For the "first time in history," the nation had a "Christian leader," a lifelong member of the Presbyterian Church. The Supreme Commander considered it a momentous event that Katayama's election coincided with the rule of fellow Christians Jiang Jieshi and Manuel Roxas, in China and the Philippines, respectively. "Three great Oriental countries now have men who embrace the Christian faith as heads of their governments," he beamed, predicting that the "steady advance of this sacred concept" would unify Asia and America by erecting an "invincible spiritual barrier" against evil ideologies such as communism. It must have jolted MacArthur's faith when, shortly thereafter, all three leaders were deposed.[35]

When confronted by serious challenges from officials in Washington, the general often turned the argument toward religion. Early in 1948, for example, he tried to parry the attacks of a particularly skilful adversary, George Kennan, by delivering a lecture on evangelism. Sent on a fact-finding mission to Japan, the diplomat tried unsuccessfully to engage MacArthur in a discussion of labor, economic, and security policy. Responding in a two-hour monologue, the Supreme Commander expatiated on the history of the world and his personal mission in Asia. He told the skeptical visitor that the Occupation's most spectacular achievement, perhaps,

> lay in the fact that it was now bringing to the Japanese two great appreciations which they had never before perceived and which were destined to revolutionize their thinking, namely, democracy and Christianity.

Petty bureaucrats in Washington (like Kennan?), he complained, failed to understand that the "great events of the next 1000 years would transpire" in the Far East. "Through the Japanese" he intended to "plant the seeds of . . . democracy and Christianity" among a "billion of these Oriental peoples on the shores of the Pacific." Japan, MacArthur claimed, would transplant American values on a mission that would "fundamentally alter the course of world history."[36]

Sir Alvary Gascoigne, head of the United Kingdom Liaison Mission, often discussed Asian strategy with MacArthur and, though friendly, had a fairly low regard for the general's intelligence. MacArthur, he commented, talked a good deal about the Russian threat but lacked any practical ideas about how to safeguard Japan once the Americans left. Nor did SCAP seem aware that the old ruling class had not collapsed but had only chosen to "sit out the round" and wait for the Occupation to end. Without exercising coercion, MacArthur wanted Japan to become an "American puppet" firmly "planted in the American sphere." Unfortunately, he did not have a clue how to accomplish this mission.[37]

Gen. Charles Gairdner, Gascoigne's military aide, had similar misgivings. MacArthur often spoke to him about the "Russian menace to the

Anglo–American democracies" and said that the Soviets were planning to take Japan as a "first step toward world domination." At the same time, Gairdner noted, the general wanted desperately to proclaim an end to the Occupation, regardless of the fact that the nation remained unstable and defenseless.[38]

During the first three years of the Occupation, MacArthur showed a similar ambivalence toward the Chinese Revolution. Despite intense opposition to communism, he befriended Gen. Joseph W. Stilwell in 1945 after the American had been recalled from China for proposing a partial shift in miliary support toward the CCP. In 1946, MacArthur told Forrestal that the Nationalist regime must be supported despite its failings, lest the Soviets gain control of all Northeast Asia. He even accused the State Department's China experts of "disloyalty" for criticizing KMT corruption. But, on balance, MacArthur's ideas were neither solicited nor heeded by the Truman administration.

The general's concern with China waxed and waned in response to the political tide in the United States. From late 1947 through mid-1948, he evinced much greater interest in some form of American intervention in the civil war, reacting to the fact that a China aid bill was being attached to the European Recovery Program (ERP). In December 1947, for example, he told Sir Alvary Gascoigne that he had been mentioned as a possible "military advisor to Chiang Kai-shek." "Without committing himself," MacArthur made clear that he "would not be adverse to adding this responsibility to his present one in Japan."[39]

When the China bloc in Congress stepped up pressure for a new aid package, MacArthur escalated his attacks on the Truman administration's China policy. He told British officials in Tokyo that he would gladly lead American troops into Manchuria to fight the Chinese Communists on the Nationalists' behalf. The general boasted that he "could accomplish this in six months by air action with a force of 1000 suitable aircraft of the close support variety." He might even be willing to occupy Manchuria for a time as a "trustee" of the Chinese government. A "non-communist Manchuria," he told Gen. Charles Gairdner, held the key to control of all North and Southeast Asia.[40]

A few days later, he responded to a request by Congressman Charles Eaton of the Committee on Foreign Affairs for information on China's importance. MacArthur gave a ringing endorsement to all proposals to aid China, saying that nation (not Japan) formed the "fundamental keystone to the Pacific Arch." The Truman administration ignored this "global context" and only sought to defend Western Europe. Instead, fighting communism in China (and, he implied, all Asia), would comprise the first step in an "integrated solution" to the cold war.[41]

In one sweep, MacArthur attacked not only the administration's China policy but also its entire emphasis on the European recovery plans that were then pending before Congress. He proposed an unlimited crusade, more in line with the rhetoric of the Truman Doctrine than Truman's actual aid requests. At the same time, MacArthur carefully avoided backing a specific commitment to save the KMT or to send American forces into hopeless situations. When asked to be specific, in fact, the general admitted the same basic reluctance to intervene in China. Nevertheless, by the year's end, he adopted an I-told-you-so attitude and criticized the Truman administration for failing to stem the Red tide in China. In a report to the Army Department, he warned of Soviet and Chinese legions sweeping out of China into Japan and Southeast Asia, all because of stinginess toward the KMT. Japan now formed the remaining "bulwark of the new strategic line" and could only be defended by giving him greater authority.[42]

THE CHINESE TRAP

MacArthur tried to hitch his wagon to the China bloc in Congress as the administration moved in the opposite direction. Despite an early trend toward intervention after the Japanese surrender, during 1946 the U.S. government began to limit and reduce its support for the Chinese Nationalists. In December 1945, George C. Marshall told Truman that abandoning the KMT would lead to the "tragic consequences of a divided China and probably a resumption of Russian power in Manchuria, the combined effect of this resulting in the defeat or loss of the major purpose of our war in the Pacific." Whatever its doubts about its wartime ally, Washington must "swallow its pride and try to hold China together."[43]

Despite this admonition, Marshall spent his year-long mission in a complicated effort to secure a coalition government while extricating American, Japanese, and Soviet forces from China. Although both Soviet and American troops began leaving in the spring of 1946, Marshall's elaborate truce procedures failed to resolve the underlying Communist–Nationalist dispute. The KMT believed that, ultimately, Washington would back it in the civil war and the Communists feared the same result. Frustrated with countless truce violations by both sides, appalled by the KMT's corruption and brutality, and relieved at the Russian withdrawal from Manchuria, Marshall determined that the civil war in China did not warrant a major American commitment. Even a Communist victory did not directly threaten vital American security interests in Asia, especially if control were maintained over Japan and the Pacific islands. Implicitly, Marshall's departure from China in January 1947 (to become secretary of state) began the reorientation of American policy in Asia toward Japan.[44]

While still in China and, especially, after his return to Washington, Marshall remained vehemently opposed to any large aid program for the Nationalists. Given the growing demands for American assistance throughout the world, Jiang's "feudal-fascist" regime hardly seemed a priority case. Although suspicious of the Communists, Marshall (and most China specialists in the State Department) considered them possible heretics from Moscow. More certain was Jiang's determination to play on America's fear of Russia to "drag" the United States "through the mud." Marshall told John Carter Vincent of the Office of Chinese Affairs that resuming military assistance (suspended during truce negotiations in 1946) would only promote civil war and assist the worst "reactionaries" in the KMT to "maintain themselves" in power. Of course, Marshall lamented, domestic as well as international pressures probably required that "sooner or later," when the situation deteriorated or the Communists approached victory, "we would have to act. . . ."[45]

What remained critical, of course, was the direction of that action. Would the United States rationalize its policy toward China, eventually accepting a Communist government there? And, equally important, how would revolutionary developments in China and Southeast Asia affect the course pursued toward the new Pacific bastion, Japan?

As Marshall had predicted gloomily, the deteriorating military situation within China and the ensuing political reaction within the United States would force him to appease the KMT and its supporters. Although steadfast in opposing direct American military intervention, as it would only "provoke the U.S.S.R. to similar intervention on the Communist side," he resumed America's halfhearted underwriting of the civil war. During 1947, Marshall lifted the arms embargo imposed a year before; early in 1948, he asked Congress to authorize about $550 million in new economic aid to China. In April, Congress passed the China Aid Act, alloting some $400 million for economic aid and about $125 million for military uses.

Even in proposing this assistance, the secretary of state dismissed its importance. He told members of Congress and the administration that no amount of outside money would save China "under present conditions of disorder, of corruption, inefficiency and impotence of the Central Government." At the same time, Marshall and Truman feared that ERP might be kept hostage by the so-called congressional China bloc unless they relented and permitted token assistance to the KMT. The loose coalition of senators and representatives who pleaded for aid on the Nationalists' behalf never threatened the administration's overall control of policy. But the fact that several of its members (Sens. Arthur H. Vandenberg [R–Michigan], Styles Bridges [R–New Hampshire], Kenneth Wherry [R–Nebraska], William F. Knowland [R–California], H. Alexander Smith [R–

New Jersey], Pat McCarran [D–Nevada], and Robert Taft [R–Ohio]; Congressmen Walter Judd [R–Minnesota] and John Vorys [R–Ohio]) occupied influential committee positions convinced the administration to appease their passion. For Marshall, the China Aid Act of 1948 represented a hoped-for last installment on a bad investment stretching back to 1938. The future, Marshall and Truman believed, depended on Western European and Japanese recovery.[46]

THE KOREAN SIDESHOW

Like China after Japan's surrender, Korea emerged as an unexpected focal point of Soviet–American rivalry. This small, poor nation, traditionally a tribute state of Imperial China, became an object of great power rivalry in the late nineteenth century and, finally, a Japanese colony. Before August 1945, those Americans charting a postwar course paid only slight attention to its future. At Yalta, Roosevelt and Stalin discussed creating some form of international trusteeship over the Hermit Kingdom but deferred details. In fact, both State Department and War Department officials initially expected to entrust Korea's liberation from Japan entirely to Soviet forces. American troops had a more important task—invading Japan proper. Even during the Potsdam Conference, Army Chief of Staff George C. Marshall assured his Soviet counterparts that the United States did not anticipate sending troops to invade the peninsula. Within a few days, however, this relative indifference disappeared. As American officials began to understand the potential of the atomic bomb and considered how the outbreak of civil war in China might encourage Soviet expansion, they reassessed the question of occupying Korea.[47]

By August 10, following the atomic raids, the Russian entry into the war, and Tokyo's tentative acceptance of the Potsdam surrender terms, these issues became major concerns. From Moscow, Ambassador Harriman urged Truman and Byrnes to order preemptive amphibious landings in Manchuria and Korea, hoping to beat the advancing Soviet armies. That day, SWNCC made the hasty decision formally to partition Korea into American and Soviet occupation zones, at least for purposes of accepting the Japanese surrender. During a midnight drafting session in Washington, Col. Charles H. Bonesteel and Maj. Dean Rusk used a crude map (the only one available) to draw a demarcation line along the thirth-eighth parallel—roughly the same point at which Czarist Russia and Imperial Japan had discussed an earlier partition. To the apparent surprise of all the Americans involved, Stalin promptly accepted the proposal. Even though his forces could easily have taken the whole peninsula (American troops did not arrive until early September), the Communist leader agreed to a split that placed the capital, Seoul, in the American zone. In attempting to explain Moscow's conciliatory behavior, several recent studies suggest that Stalin placed relatively little importance on Korea's fate and saw its partition as a painless way to alleviate Washington's suspicions about Russian intentions. He may also have thought the zonal division would strengthen Soviet claims to similar rights in Japan. In any case, it appears that neither of the two powers considered the issue worth arguing over in August, 1945.[48]

Early in September, MacArthur designated Gen. John R. Hodge, a combat officer with few political skills, to land his XXIV Army Corps in the American zone of Korea. Without firm guidelines or an understanding of Korean politics, Hodge quickly moved to depose a provisional government, the Korean People's Republic, he found already taking root. As with Soviet commanders in the northern zone, the Americans utilized ideologically compatible groups to begin establishing local administrations. The American counterparts to the leftist guerrillas in the north were a ménage of Korean collaborators, Japanese holdovers, and returned right-wing exiles, such as Syngman Rhee. Without much forethought, Army officers delegated important civil and police powers to an elite, ultraconservative faction. Local decisions became formal policy without much regard to State Department recommendations. Yet, the often-contradictory record of events both north and south of the thirty-eighth parallel suggests that as of early 1946 neither Moscow nor Washington anticipated a permanent division of the peninsula.

For example, at the December 1945 Moscow meeting of foreign ministers, Byrnes and Molotov had undertaken several measures designed to reduce Soviet–American tensions in the region. The Russians agreed to participate in both the Far Eastern Commission and the ACJ. Stalin endorsed Marshall's mediation efforts in China and promised to withdraw his own occupation forces from Manchuria. Finally, the two powers agreed to resume efforts to create a workable trusteeship over all of Korea. A few months later, in the spring of 1946, the joint commission designed to discuss the trusteeship reached an impasse. Uncertain about what to do, Hodge continued to allow conservative elements to move in the direction of creating a de facto regime in the south, even though Washington officially supported the principal of a broader based and unified regime. As right-wing elements solidified their grip in Seoul, the Soviets assisted the Left north of the thirty-eighth parallel.

By the summer of 1946, the temporary division of Korea had begun to appear as an indefinite separation. The State Department's deep misgivings about the reactionary bent of Rhee and his supporters gradually paled as the United States grew more fearful of Communist pressure in North and

Southeast Asia. After touring Korea in June, reparations adviser Edwin Pauley warned President Truman about the challenge he perceived. Communist agents in the south (the people's committees), Pauley declared, planned to seize the industrial infrastructure built by the Japanese as a prelude to unifying the peninsula under Russian control. This would endanger both China and Japan, he maintained, as both nations had geographic and economic connections to Korea.

Pauley, of course, had been criticized by others for alleged radicalism because he supported a vigorous reparations program in Japan. But he had consistently held that reparations were one method to *strengthen* the capitalist structure throughout Asia. His concern over possible Soviet expansion into vulnerable areas led him to desecribe Korea as an "ideological battle ground upon which our entire success in Asia may depend." Pauley told Truman that in this relatively peripheral area, the postwar programs of the United States and the Soviet Union had collided in a unique test of strength. If Americans expected to retain and expand influence over more important parts of Asia, then they must expand the commitment to build a strong capitalist state in, at least, the southern part of the country. Truman responded enthusiastically to his adviser's report. Although the president still proclaimed Washington's support for a unified government, he permitted movement toward formation of a separate provisional government.[49]

Even though many elements in the Truman administration recognized that American prestige was tied up with the evolving South Korean state, they acknowledged that, militarily, the presence of American troops was costly, dangerous, and, ultimately, irrelevant in a general war. By mid-1947, the JCS urged withdrawing these forces as quickly as possible. Far Eastern specialists in the State Department also favored a withdrawal but felt the United States must continue to provide military and economic assistance to the anti-Communist government in Seoul. The Joint Strategic Survey Committee of the JCS aptly summarized the gap between Korea's objective and subjective importance to U.S. policymakers. Although the position was of negligible value in strategic terms, its prestige and symbolism could not be discounted. Only in Korea, the planners noted, had the United States "for almost two years carried on ideological warfare in direct contact with our ideological opponents." To lose "this battle would be gravely detrimental to United States prestige, and therefore security, throughout the world."[50] As American diplomats and military planners would belatedly discover, the burden of sustaining this symbolic battle proved far more costly than anyone anticipated.

4

REINTERPRETING THE POSTWAR WORLD

Even as the Truman administration backed away from the China cauldron early in 1947, it confronted new dilemmas. If China represented an emotional holdover from the war years, the growing tensions with the Soviet Union and the economic crisis among America's trading partners presented an extraordinarily grim prospect for the future. Nearly two years of mounting frustrations were punctuated in February 1947 by the British decision to halt financial support for the Greek government's war against leftist guerrillas. Immediately, this raised fears of a possible Soviet breakthrough into the Mediterranean and the Near East. But, as Harry Truman told his cabinet on February 25, the Greek crisis represented "only a part of a much larger problem growing out of the change in Great Britian's strength and other circumstances not directly related to this development." Two weeks later, in an address to Congress, Truman announced his proposal to assist Greece and Turkey against alleged Soviet threats and also signaled America's intention to restore the faltering economies of the capitalist world. As the European "containment program" took form, the United States determined that Japan, like Germany, must serve as a bastion against Soviet expansion and, more positively, a catalyst sparking regional recovery.[1]

Early in March, Navy Secretary James Forrestal sought out other Cabinet members to discuss the general economic crisis highlighted by events in Greece. Forrestal believed that if "we are going to have a run for our side in the competition" with the Soviet Union, "we shall have to harness all the talent and brains in the country just as we had to do during the war." He looked for these skills among the business leaders of all capitalist nations, including those in the former enemy states. Real security against Soviet pressure and subversion depended on the "restoration of commerce, trade and business, and that would have to be done by businessmen." Specifically, this required reviving the economic strength of the former Axis powers. In simplest terms, containment meant putting "Japan, Germany, and other affiliates of the Axis . . . back to work."[2]

Forrestal joined Commerce Secretary Averell Harriman, Secretary of Agriculture Clinton Anderson, Secretary of War Robert Patterson, Under Secretary of State Dean Acheson, and former President Herbert Hoover in criticizing both the cost and direction of Occupation policies in Germany and Japan. Hoover took the lead, declaring that Europe would never recover from dependence on American aid until the "ceiling on German heavy industry was lifted." Germany, Harriman agreed, should again become the economic center of Europe, the core of an integrated regional economy. Forrestal concurred, adding that everything said about "Germany and the need for making some restoration of its industry possible applied with equal force to Japan." Without full recovery, the occupied nations would drain American resources, stifle prosperity among their neighbors, and devolve into economic chaos that would entice the Soviet Union.[3]

Several members of the group had already heard complaints about General MacArthur's "wrecking" of the Japanese economy. Then, late in March, the general suddenly issued his own calls for a peace treaty, claiming nothing could be done to improve the economy until after the Occupation ended. Forrestal complained that the army had lost control over MacArthur, that it could not "issue a single order" to the general. Nevertheless, the group agreed, something must quickly be done to silence the "defeatist" rhetoric from SCAP. America had only little time to restore "hope of recovery to the Japanese" before a "complete economic collapse."[4]

Anxiety over Japan's future paralleled the broader developments of postwar policy. By early 1947, Truman's advisers perceived two distinct but related threats. The Soviet Union, no longer constrained by German and Japanese strength, loomed as the most powerful nation in Eurasia. Soviet support for revolutionary movements—(whether rhetorical or material—could transform the political balance of Europe, the Middle East, and Asia. Whether or not Moscow intended to advance communism on the tips of bayonets, the chaotic conditions in most of the postwar world created an irresistible target for Kremlin leaders, American officials believed.

The scope of the Second World War had completely altered the world economy. Partly because of physical destruction, but even more owing to structural imbalances, the United States emerged far more prosperous and productive than all its traditional trading partners. Fifteen years of global depression and war had unraveled the patterns of world trade, and postwar tensions doomed any facile recreation of the old system. Although President Roosevelt hoped to encourage the vigorous revival of relatively free trade under multilateral principles, in 1945 half the world's economy lay outside the capitalist system or shattered by war.

The Soviet Union, its East European satellites, and part of Germany no longer engaged in normal trade with non-Communist countries. Economic dislocation in western Germany and in Japan stifled efforts at restoring their self-sufficiency and made them increasingly dependent on American aid. The economic vacuum pervading Central and Eastern Europe and East Asia as well as a variety of other impediments to trade blocked recovery in Western Europe.

Traditionally, Germany, Great Britain, France, and the Netherlands, had relied on Eastern European resources and (except for Germany) the profitable export of Southeast Asian colonial products, both for their own industries and as a source of dollar earnings to balance their normal trade deficit with the United States. The Western European powers had already liquidated many of their overseas investments to finance the war. Political upheavals throughout Asia in the wake of Japan's defeat confounded hopes of rebuilding propserity on a colonial base. Civil war engulfed China and political disorders in India, Malaya, the East Indies, and Indochina diminished contributions from these colonies. Instead of being engines for recovery then, Germany, Japan, and the Asian colonial states became an unprecedented drain on the world trading system.

Although not unprepared for all these events, American planners had failed to anticipate their depth or persistence. During 1945 and 1946, the United States extended generous food, commodity, and financial aid to many former allied nations as well as to occupied enemy states. The British, for example, received a multibillion dollar loan. American assistance to the United Nations Relief and Rehabilitation Agency (UNRRA) programs made vital supplies available to devastated parts of Europe and Asia. In Germany and Japan, the army's Government and Relief in Occupied Areas (GARIOA) program distributed food, fuel, and medicine to impoverished civilians. However, all of this humanitarian aid was envisoned as a short-term expedient, a bandage to heal the wounded system until the "normal" pattern of world trade reestablished itself. Initially, Germany, Japan, and the colonial areas were all expected to participate in this recovery as well as Eastern Europe and, perhaps, the Soviet Union.

The profound failure of world trade to stabilize after 1945 rendered American planning totally obsolete. A gap, or shortfall, between the value of American exports and the amount of dollars foreign customers had to pay for them grew quickly between the war's end and 1947. In 1945, the dollar gap stood at $7.1 billion; in 1947, it ballooned to almost $11 billion and threatened to grow larger. Whatever its size, the imbalance could only persist so long as either private American lenders or the government agreed to finance foreign purchases on credit. To refuse further loans risked losing America's best foreign customers and incurring severe domestic economic costs because about 10 percent of industry and an even larger percentage of agricultural production depended on foreign sales. Once cut off from dollar credits, other nations would have no choice but to turn toward restricted economies and closed trading blocs, as they had during the depression. Alternatively, desperate nations might be attracted by Soviet economic blandishments or fall victim to economic chaos and subversion. Either development would threaten American prosperity and augment Soviet strength.

Japan faced a particularly difficult situation immediately after surrender, with the underpinnings of its industrial society shattered. Actual physical destruction from bombing comprised the smallest part of the problem, reducing capacity by only 15 to 20 percent. During the war, escalating production demands resulted in the overuse and undermaintenance of machinery. Scarce parts and equipment were cannibalized, with much of the textile industry, for example, smelted for arms. Technological obsolescence also played havoc, for example, the loss of the Japanese silk industry. Before the war, silk comprised Japan's largest dollar-earning export to the United States. Following the trade cutoff in 1941, American government and industry promoted the development of synthetics like nylon. This versatile, inexpensive substitute displaced silk almost completely after 1945.

The loss of the silk market and its foreign exchange earnings typified the many problems besetting Occupied Japan. Jerome Cohen, a contemporary economist, described the postwar situation as a "hare-and-tortoise-race" between a "mounting inflation on the one hand and a slow revivial of industrial activity on the other."[5] Although neither the Japanese government nor the American authorities exercised effective control over the money supply, a shortage of raw materials and diminished purchasing power depressed production to less than half the 1930–34 level.

Unlike America, where only about 10 percent of industrial production went into exports, about 25 percent of Japanese industry depended on foreign sales. The resource-poor nation relied on cheap sources of imported raw materials (and a protected market) in Taiwan, Korea, Manchuria, and North China to keep export prices competitive. But defeat had stripped away the formal empire and wartime memories made Japan feared and resented as a trading nation throughout Asia.

Since the early twentieth century, substantial amounts of food, coal, and raw materials flowed from China to Japan. Following the invasions of Manchuria (1931), North China (1937), and the attack on Pearl Harbor (1941), China became the major supplier of Japanese industry and an important consumer of manufactured goods. Japan's surrender in August 1945 sparked the resumption of civil war in China, making it impossible for that nation to conduct substantial business with Tokyo. Anti-Japanese sentiment aside, the nearly total disruption of Chinese life until 1949 removed the largest nation in Asia as an economic factor to be reckoned with. This placed Japan in a relationship to China similar to that experienced by the Western Europeans who hoped to salvage their economies through boosting Southeast Asian and Eastern European trade.

These several factors conspired to drive foreign trade into a downward spiral during the first two years of the Occupation. A good deal of hardship, of course, had been predicted because Japan had developed a top-heavy industrial economy geared toward war production. But American planners had expected stability to follow a short period of readjustment. Japan, they assumed, would import raw materials and export light manufactured goods and textiles for Asian consumption. As it turned out, however, Japan faced a closing economic circle. Lagging raw material production in Asia forced Japan to import high-priced American cotton and other commodities. The profits reaped from restricted textile exports proved inadequate to pay for needed food, fuel, and industrial materials. This hindered production, drove up costs, and stimulated inflation—making Japan a high-priced, unattractive exporter. This, in turn, further restricted sales.

To cope with a hungry population, the American Army financed relief shipments valued from $350 to $400 million per year. These consisted largely of basic necessities, not raw materials needed for industry, which made little dent on the dollar gap. The acute dollar shortage arose from the fact that although Japan exported about 66 percent of its foreign sales to Asian nations and colonies, almost 90 percent of its imports came from the United States. Few Japanese products found a ready market in Western countries, with the result that Japan received soft nonconvertible currencies for its exports but needed to pay hard dollars for its vital imports.

Before the war, Japan had traded mostly within Asia, balancing its relatively small trade with the United States from currency earned on exports to the West and from "invisible exports," such as shipping fees and insurance premiums. Now, despite vastly increased dependence on American supplies, Japan sold only about 12 percent of its exports to the United States. Although, as Occupying power, the American government had a special responsibility for Japan, few other nations share its concern. Until 1949, the yen had no fixed exchange value, making it complicated and unattractive to enter trade agreements. Prices for exports were high, whereas their quality remained low. Security restrictions barred most Japanese travel abroad or visits by foreign business representatives at home. As a result of these many factors, 1947 gross exports reached only a tenth of the 1934 level, whereas imports declined to less than one third.[6]

This economic collapse had repercussions throughout the Far East and in Western Europe. Japan no longer provided a substantial export or import market for other Asian countries. Because Occupation authorities demanded that most purchases from Japan be paid in dollars, the normal dollar surplus in Southeast Asia (derived from sales of commodities like rubber to the United States) dried up. The European colonial powers also depended on dollar earnings from Southeast Asian raw materials to finance their own deficit in transatlantic trade. Declining exports to Japan as well as shrinking production owing to political upheavals in Southeast Asia deprived Great Britain, France, and the Netherlands of both dollars and low-cost commodities for their own hard-pressed industries.

Ultimately, the United States financed these interrelated trade imbalances through postwar assistance, culminating in the Marshall Plan. In Japan alone, during the period from September 1945 through June 1948, the nonmilitary expense of supplying food, fuel, medicine, and so on, reached nearly $1 billion and showed every indication of climbing higher. In 1949, overall Occupation costs amounted to some $900 million. This spectre—of endless costs and economic collapse—haunted policymakers in Washington who recoiled at General MacArthur's glib assurances that a solution could somehow be found after the Occupation terminated.

The parallel crises in Germany and Western Europe, which took an even greater toll, prompted the Truman administration to propose a broad recovery program going far beyond security assistance to Greece and Turkey. The administration requested that Congress finance the dollar gap for several years at great cost. Supplying industrial partners both dollars and raw materials would, they hoped, prevent dollar-scarce nations from severing trade with America, assist the restoration of faltering overseas production, and stem any drift toward an accommodation with Soviet power. Eventually, ERP, or the Marshall Plan, and the analogous Economic Recovery in Occupied Areas program for Japan emerged as the major initiatives in this direction. From 1948 until 1952, Congress appropriated billions of dollars, mostly to finance the purchase of raw materials and goods within the United States for delivery to Western Europe and Japan. The policy aimed at sustaining a high level of business activity at home while laying a foundation for economic and political cooperation abroad.

The Marshall Plan looked beyond merely extending new commercial credits or supplying raw materials from American stocks. It recognized many of the underlying structural imbalances that plagued the industrial nations of Europe and Japan. So long as they all remained dependent on importing relatively expensive dollar-priced raw materials, they would constantly experience a dollar drain. Because of high production costs, outdated technology, and restrictive tariffs, they would be unable to sell enough to the United States to balance their accounts. The solution, as initially conceived by such policymakers as Dean Acheson, James Forrestal, George Kennan, and Army Under Secretary William H. Draper, Jr., lay in promoting highly integrated regional economies that took advantage of efficiencies resulting from large-scale enterprises as well as from their concentrated power to develop new markets and cheap sources of raw materials.

Specifically, these planners envisioned three great interdependent zones of industrial power allied with the United States and against the Soviet Union. At the pinnacle stood the United States, predominant in the Western Hemisphere. A European zone centered around a restored Germany and an Asian component around Japan would complete the alliance. These two subordinate zones would become major regional centers of production and trade based on the exchange of their industrial products for raw materials with a network of less developed states. The creation of these integrated regional economies, with access to low-cost raw materials would alleviate demands for American aid and reduce the strain of dollar imports on Europe and Japan. It would also forge a matrix of anti-Communist states linked to America. The immediate challenge lay in securing enough time for a transition period during which America's allies could both restore productive capacity and reassert economic control of their own satellites.

The first obstacle blocking the path did not come from any imminent threat of Soviet invasion, although the Truman administration's public rhetoric obscured this point. Instead, the legacy of wartime rivalries, short-term dollar shortages, unequal development, and nationalist rebellions in colonial areas threatened to undermine the nascent alliance even before recovery began. The key to success, both in Europe and Asia, appeared as the restoration of German and Japanese productive capacity. With American assistance, they might serve as catalysts for the solution of regional economic, political, and military problems. Before mobilizing their idle capacities, however, the U.S. government had first to rationalize its own disorderly policymaking establishment.

Ever since the late 1930s, most observers agreed, chronic bureaucratic rivalries among civilian and military agencies in Washington had hobbled the formation and implementation of foreign policy goals. The armed services fought over budgets and missions. The State Department, laboring under an archaic geographic format, had played only a marginal role throughout the long dull tenure of Cordell Hull and the short stormy stewardship of James Byrnes. Without a central intelligence agency, little capacity existed either to gather secret information or implement policies covertly. Finally, the lack of coordination left each agency free to bombard the president with its own recommendations, regardless of redundancy or contradictions.

Although Truman expressed little personal interest in Japan (or most other foreign policy problems, for that matter), he acknowledged a need to reorganize the foreign policy bureaucracy. Frequently shortsighted and petty in his domestic political calculus, Truman, nevertheless, understood his own limitations in the foreign sphere and selected many advisers of real stature. Generally, they came from elite corporate business, the professional military, or, in a few cases, from the career foreign service. Most had little use for the New Deal's social reforms (Harriman was an ambiguous exception), and almost none thought it desirable or even possible to sustain cooperation with the Soviet Union.

The transformation began in January 1947 when Truman replaced James F. Byrnes with Gen. George C. Marshall as secretary of state. Marshall began reorganizing the State Department along more modern lines, creating, in May, the Policy Planning Staff (PPS). This special unit, he hoped, would devise "long-term programs for the achievement of . . . foreign policy objectives" by transcending narrow georgraphic and bureaucratic lines in the department. Marshall selected Soviet specialist George F. Kennan to head the PPS. He had come to Marshall's attention partly through the sponsorship of Navy Secretary James Forrestal, one of the earliest advocates of German–Japanese recovery. Forrestal, in turn, was also destined for promotion to a higher post.

In July, after prolonged and bitter debate, Congress passed the National Security Act of 1947. Among many provisions, it created a unified Defense Department, with Forrestal soon named as its secretary. He oversaw the national military establishment, which consisted of such semi-independent units as the JCS and the separate armed service branches, each with its own civilian secretary. Persistant rivalries among the services required a further centralization in 1949. Besides the new Defense Department, the 1947 act established a Central Intelligence Agency (CIA) and a National Security Council (NSC), both designed to coordinate policy and facilitate the president's access to vital information.

Although this reorganization left many bureaucratic problems unresolved, it augmented the power of the State and Defense departments enough for them to reclaim initiatives in the largely independent satrapy of Occupied Japan. Neither Marshall nor Forrestal stood in awe of MacArthur, an attitude they quickly transmitted to their subordinates. Just as Marshall relied on Dean Acheson and George Kennan for advice on Japan, Forrestal tapped a former colleague and vice president of Dillon, Read & Co., William H. Draper, Jr., as his under secretary of the army, a position that oversaw occupied areas. Leaving the army reserve for active service as a general in 1940, Draper stayed on in the War Department after 1945. During 1946, he played a major role in loosening economic controls and promoting business in Occupied Germany. Working individually and in tandem, Draper and Kennan sought to revise American policy in Western Europe and East Asia. Both men worked to modify socialeconomic reforms and to get Congress to fund substantial reconstruction programs. They considered it vital to delay peace settlements until after the German and Japanese business classes (and their political allies) were securely returned to power. These efforts brought both men into bitter disputes with some members of their own departments and, even more dramatically, with Douglas MacArthur.

In addition to the problem of reorganizing the ponderous foreign policy bureaucracy in Washington, the legacy of wartime and early postsurrender policies continued to plague the advocates of a new course for Japan. As of early 1947, several stringent Occupation policies affecting future economic activities remained in place. Although large-scale removals had not yet occurred, a major reparations program that called for the transfer of Japanese industry to China and Southeast Asia was still slated for implementation. Economic planners in SCAP and the Far Eastern Commission continued to discuss long-term arrangements for strictly limiting production levels in heavy industry. Under pressure from SCAP, the Diet had begun to consider a comprehensive plan to restructure the *zaibatsu* and to prevent the formation of future monopolies. This deconcentration law came into effect by the year's end. In January 1947, SCAP shocked many American conservatives by issuing an order to purge business executives linked to military aggression or ultranationalist groups. Thus, despite the intensification of the cold war and the reorganization of the executive Branch, Occupation policy in Japan continued to reflect a liberal reformist agenda.

What MacArthur thought about this is by no means clear. Although critical of large-scale reparations (which he feared would involve outside meddling by technical experts on SCAP's turf), he vigorously defended the bulk of his staff's activities, including the economic purge, deconcentration, land reform, and demilitarization. This, however, may not have reflected any ideological commitment. MacArthur, many observers noted throughout his career, simply could not stand being wrong or admitting error. Having become identified so personally with the early reform program, he may have feared embarrassment or ridicule or evidence of fallibility should he now take a new tack. Even worse, MacArthur recoiled at the notion of accepting criticism from the hated Truman administration and the president's policy advisers. His ambitious political agenda virtually demanded that he contrast his approach toward postwar problems with those evolved in Washington. Consequently, it did not matter exactly what advice for a revised economic program came from the State or Defense departments. MacArthur did not want either to admit error or accept recommendations from an administration he hoped eventually to displace. His disposition put him on a collision course with strategists like Dean Acheson, James Forrestal, William Draper, George Marshall, and George Kennan, who, whatever their vices or virtues, put their values and beliefs on foreign policy far ahead of partisan considerations.

Kennan's meteoric rise to a position of influence in Washington both affected and reflected the changing direction of policy during 1947. Although not the first or only official to question the basic nature of postwar international relations, Kennan epitomized (and gave a name to) the emerging containment policy. Even before he mobilized the PPS in the State Department, various area specialists in State and planners working for the JCS discussed a need to hasten the reconstruction and reintegration of the German the Japanese economies. However, no other individual or group articulated so fully the argument for adopting a novel economic and political strategy designed to enhance America's global interests.

Kennan first came to the attention of political officials during February 1946 while serving as the chargé d'affaires in Moscow. Worried by what he saw as America's indecisiveness in the face of Soviet belligerance, the diplomat dispatched a formidable report on Russian behavior to the State Department. At first of interest only to a small group, Navy Secretary James Forrestal circulated the report widely. Before long, it appeared that this dismal assessment of Moscow's policy became the new conventional wisdom. This influential report urged the Truman administration to abandon lingering illusions about cooperation with the Soviets. The United States, Kennan wrote, must rally its allies to resist implacable Soviet pressures to expand. Only by rejuvenating the sinews of democratic capitalism and restoring the European and Asian balance of power could America assure its security. Although hardly a novel idea, Kennan stressed the need to rationalize policy by selecting carefully among many possible commitments. As an added bonus, Kennan predicted that halting the growth of Russian influence would subject the Soviet empire to fatal internal pressures.[7]

Forrestal, Kennan's new sponsor, encouraged his return to Washington and appointment to lecture at the newly created National War College. His persuasive presentations and growing reputation brought him to the attention of George C. Marshall early in 1947. Kennan possessed exactly the kind of logic Marshall desired at the helm of the new PPS. Almost as soon as he assumed this PPS post in May 1947, Kennan achieved an unprecedented notoriety for a diplomat through the publication of his *X* article, which appeared anonymously in *Foreign Affairs*. An elaboration of the "long telegram," it introduced the word "containment" to the public and offered an intellectual framework for military, political, and economic resistance to the Soviet Union.

Two-and-a-half-years later, shortly before he left the PPS, Kennan doodled a drawing in the margin of a paper being drafted on policy objectives. It depicted a man struggling to pull a mule whose legs were firmly planted and who stubbornly resisted all efforts to move forward. In a sense, this caricature spoke to Kennan's struggle to advance his program along a path full of obstacles, not the least of which came from within the government's competing bureaucracies.

As an early advocate of what became the Marshall Plan, Kennan called for a recovery program that targeted vital centers of world power, especially Germany and Japan. Eventually, these restored nations would share the long-term burden of containment, reducing the stark, bipolar nature of the Soviet–American confrontation. Once the Western powers and Japan achieved stability, they could begin to exploit tensions inherent in the Soviet empire and between the Kremlin and the world Communist movement. However, before any of this came about, Kennan and his staff faced the grueling task of selling their program to the rest of the administration, Congress, and the American public.

As they began work in May 1947, Kennan had the PPS* rank-order "those areas of the world which . . . we cannot permit . . . to fall into hands hostile to us. . . ." Protecting these zones formed the "first specific objective" and the "irreducible minimum of national policy." Like Marshall and Acheson, Kennan did not consider the Red Army the initial or greatest challenge to global security. Instead, he identified the internal economic, psychological, and political weakness of Europe and Japan as the factors that most endangered the non-Communist world. In October 1947, he described the imbalance in Russian "political power" rather than "military power" as the immediate risk faced by the United States. The American counteroffensive, he argued a few months later, must be directed

---

* The Asia specialists on the PPS at first included John P. Davies, Carlton Savage, Barton Berry, George Butler, Jacques Reinstein, and Isaac Stokes.

against the "profound exhaustion of physical plant and spiritual vigor" in Western Europe. Communism would advance only in the wake of a Western collapse because the Soviets had neither the will nor ability to launch a war against America. They expected that political subversion and economic pressure would fatally undermine the exhausted nations of Europe, the Middle East, and Asia.[8]

Refining a line of argument developed over the previous eighteen months, Kennan told an audience at the National War College in September 1947 that "only five centers of industrial and military power in the world" mattered "to us from a standpoint of National Security." These included the United States, Great Britain, Germany and Central Europe, the Soviet Union, and Japan. These areas alone possessed the industrial strength needed for the "type of amphibious power which would have to be launched" to challenge America. As only the Soviet zone was now counted as unfriendly, the challenge ahead involved keeping the remainder of Europe and Japan in the American camp.*[9]

The rehabilitation of Germany and Japan as centers of regional power formed the core of Kennan's vision in the late 1940s. The restoration of their industries, he believed, would invigorate local forces determined to block Soviet expansion. Yet, these occupied nations remained isolated and condemned by the suspicions of their neighbors. Ironically, this policy impoverished the war's victims nearly as much as the Axis aggressors. The longer this situation continued, the more vulnerable the Japanese and Germans would become to Soviet threats or blandishments.

Yet, earlier suggestions about restoring the Japanese and German economies had outraged or terrified the Western Europeans and Asians. Kennan, along with Marshall and Acheson, envisioned only one path out of this dilemma. The United States must put forward a scheme for regional recovery centered on Germany and Japan. This, they hoped, would stimulate all parties, especially the Germans, to "see things in larger terms, to have interests elsewhere in Europe and elsewhere in the world, and to learn to think for themselves as world citizens and not just Germans." This idea formed the basis of the Marshall Plan as well as the parallel program of Japanese recovery.[10]

China fell conspicuously outside the strategy offered by Kennan. Besides the fact that it possessed no industrial base or offensive military strength, it failed to meet other criteria for aid developed by the PPS. In noncritical

---

* Although the ERP initially included an offer of aid to the Soviets and their satellites, neither Marshall nor Kennan desired or expected its acceptance. As historian John L. Gaddis notes, Kennan advanced the idea as a tactic to arouse tensions between the Russians and the people they dominated. Eventually, this might help nudge national Communist movements away from Soviet control (see Gaddis, *Strategies of Containment*, 38).

areas, Kennan argued, the United States should support anti-Communist regimes only if they were worth saving. Certain regimes might be adjudged simply too corrupt to loan any "moral prestige." If the Soviets threatened an area of marginal significance, it might be wiser to withhold aid rather than expend scarce resources on a hollow symbol. Kennan always maintained that the United States neither could nor should oppose all Communist movements to the same degree. Rather, it all "depended on the circumstances."[11]

Containment, for Kennan, despite the ambiguity of his *X* article, did not propose anticommunism as an "absolute factor." He refuted the logic of those in Congress who argued that the Truman Doctrine applied equally to all situations. "If I thought for a moment," he wrote in 1948, that the "precedent of Greece and Turkey obliged us to try to do the same thing in China, I would throw up my hands and say we had better have a whole new approach to the affairs of the world." In any case, he told an old friend, undue aid to China would starve the effort to keep "Russian hands" off Europe and Japan, the only centers of "military-industrial power on the surface of the earth" whose loss to the USSR could alter the strategic balance. Jiang Jieshi's regime, he added, had been "unsympathetic, unhelpful and irresponsibly shortsighted" in opposing American efforts in Japan. Thus, the KMT's demise would hardly worsen the Asian power balance.[12]

Kennan urged the Truman administration to "liquidate as rapidly as possible our unsound commitments in China. . . ." He acknowledged, unhappily, that some "minimum aid" might have to be continued to "satisfy American public opinion and, if possible, to prevent the sudden and total collapse of the Chinese government." But even if, as seemed likely, the Communists routed Jiang, their victory would not immediately enhance Soviet power. Whatever the Russians felt about their Chinese comrades, it was doubtful that, in power, the Chinese Communists "would retain the ideological fibre of their movement or the present degree of dependence on Moscow." Caught up in its own revolution, China would have little ability to export trouble. About the best the United States could do, Kennan said, was to keep a low profile and "sweat it out."

Given these factors, Kennan asked rhetorically, why involve America further in a struggle for which it had no solution? He contrasted the chaos of China with the potential stability and influence of Japan and the Philippines. There, he declared, Washington could lay the "cornerstones of . . . a Pacific security system. . . ." Effective control of these offshore bastions would preclude "any threat to our security from the East within our time."[13]

Calculated in this manner, American security did not require comprehensive accommodation with the Soviets or peace settlements with Germany and Japan. "First and foremost," Kennan argued, America needed to counterbalance the Soviet Union on the Eurasian landmass. "That balance is unthinkable as long as Germany and Japan remain power vacuums," he repeated frequently from 1947 through 1949. Instead of emphasizing punitive reforms or rushing toward peace settlements, American policy should attempt to restore the strength of the German and Japanese peoples "to a point where they could play their part in the Eurasian balance of power and yet to a point not so far advanced as to permit them again to threaten the interests of the maritime World of the West."

Kennan's synthesis, refined during the remainder of 1947 and early 1948, was partially anticipated by specific ideas and recommendations developed by the JCS, SWNCC, Japan specialists in the State Department, and influential persons outside the government. All placed a new primary emphasis on the economic and political dimensions of security. Downplaying the universalist rhetoric of the Truman Doctrine, all these groups joined Kennan in assigning priority to the preservation of economic and political links among Western Europe, Japan, and the Middle East to the United States. Revolutionary upheavals or Soviet threats elsewhere had only subsidiary importance.

In April 1947, for example, the JCS had issued a detailed study, "Assistance to Other Countries from the Standpoint of National Security." They identified the same vital economic zones as the PPS would over the next few months and argued for concentrating aid in these areas. The JCS stressed the need to restore economic interdependence among industrial nations and prevent Soviet control over additional industrial capacity and skilled populations. In Asia, they deprecated China's importance and favorably compared Japan's significance to that of Germany in Europe. Like its recent Axis partner, Japan was a defeated enemy, making the "idea of assistance to her . . . probably offensive to the majority of our people." Nevertheless, Japan had potentially great military importance as the "one nation which would contain large armed forces of our ideological opponents in the Far East while the United States and her allies in the West launched a major offensive in that area." For this "very simple reason," the JCS held, of "all the countries in the Pacific area Japan deserves primary consideration for current United States assistance designed to restore her economic and military potential."[14]

These ideas were incorporated into a massive reassessment of policy begun by SWNCC in March 1947 at the President's direction. Continually updated during the next two years, the SWNCC 360 report analyzed the role played by every country and region in the contest between the United States and the Soviet Union. It concentrated on the economic dimensions of security, especially the possible impact of a Western European or Japanese collapse followed by their entry into the Russian orbit. The persistent dollar gap in international trade, the report warned, represented the greatest short-term danger. The ballooning trade deficit endangered not only America's capacity to market exports but would soon cripple trade and recovery throughout the non-communist world. Only a dramatic increase in foreign assistance "to secure world economic stability and a desirable world trading system" while promoting American "political objectives in critical countries" could solve the underlying problem.

Although the SWNCC report placed greatest stress on Germany and Western Europe, its authors considered Japan the pivotal factor in Asia. As the region's sole industrial power, it desperately needed renewed access to the raw materials and markets formerly found in China, Southeast Asia, its own empire, or in the West. The Soviets, according to the SWNCC consultants, anticipated that an economic crisis in Japan would grow so severe after the Occupation that they could seize control through economic pressure alone, using access to Siberian and Manchurian resources as a lure to drag Japan behind the Iron Curtain.

Unlike MacArthur, they had little faith that the democratization and other reforms of the past few years would shield Japan from this blackmail or indirect aggression. An American failure to insure recovery would cause a "breakdown, gradual or precipitous," that would "represent a complete loss in the American investment in a stable, democratic and peaceful Japan and would seriously jeopardize the United States program for world wide economic recovery and political stabilization." SWNCC 360 proposed a half-billion-dollar aid program stretching over several years. Designed to finance raw material imports and rebuild industry, it would form part of a broader "program for expansion of Japanese import and export trade" with all Far Eastern countries that are "potential sources of raw materials for Japan and potential markets for Japanese products."[15]

These recommendations coincided with mounting public attacks on MacArthur's program and detailed government planning for economic recovery. Each reinforced the feeling that something was desperately wrong with the Occupation and that only outside initiatives could cure the problem. SCAP appeared less the solution to Japan's postwar dilemma than the source of it.

During the first few months of 1947, members of the State Department's Japan—Korea economic division undertook a reevaluation of the Occupation's economic premises. Under the direction of Edwin F. Martin, the staff concluded that, if properly managed, a Japanese revival might solve "a number of related problems" in East Asia. However, owing to changes in world trade patterns and a chronic shortage of dollars, Japan could neither reenter Western markets nor achieve a recovery on its own, as had been assumed earlier. As production stagnated for lack of raw materials, democratic reforms would falter and the nation would become either an American ward or a dangerous center of instability.

Such a failure would afflict all Asia, Martin believed, by depriving the region of "markets for their raw materials and sources of cheap manufactured goods." This left only one alternative. The United States could utilize Japan's idle industrial capacity by expanding its own raw material exports. Through priming the Japanese pump, eliminating most restrictions on production, and minimizing reparations, the United States could stimulate recovery based on a vigorous regional trade. Eventually, Japan would exchange its manufactured exports for inexpensive, Asian raw materials, alleviating a need for dollar aid. Japanese recovery formed a "circle" on which Asian prosperity depended. Following this line, Martin recommended funding an "economic crank-up," costing about $500 million over two years. As Japan became more fully integrated into the Asian economy, it would find a solution to its chronic dollar and raw material shortage while stimulating the development of neighboring states.[16]

The specialists in the Japan–Korea division stressed the importance of a regional economic plan rather than a compartmentalized program. For example, it would be impossible to boost production in Japan while planning to transfer the nation's heavy industry to Burma. Instead of attempting to relocate physically these facilities, the United States ought to limit reparations and emphasize the reduction of trade barriers throughout Asia. Martin reasoned that the greatest benefit to Japan's wartime victims would come from a growing exchange between their commodities and Japan's manufactures. America could stimulate this trade by promoting export production through raw material grants on a temporary basis.[17]

Nearly identical advice came from influential figures outside the bureaucracy, including former President Herbert Hoover. One of the earliest advocates of a "soft peace" with Japan, Hoover had urged Truman to envision Tokyo as an anti-Soviet ally even before surrender. In correspondence and verbal appeals to several cabinet members during the spring, Hoover expressed grave "anxiety over the situation in both Germany and Japan." Because these countries formed the "major fronts of Western Civilization" against Russia, a German collapse threatened to open "all Western Europe and the Near East" and, in Asia, Japan provided "the real ideological dam against the march of Communism."

The former president had visited Tokyo in May 1946 on a food relief mission. Then and afterwards, he voiced growing contempt for the "reparations and control policies" that caused an "industrial paralysis" and cost the American taxpayer hundreds of millions of dollars. Hoover cautiously skirted the issue of whether MacArthur himself should be blamed for the situation. This was not surprising because the Republican politician had a close personal and ideological affinity for the general, stretching back to the latter's service as army chief of staff in the early 1930s. Hoover played an important part in the "MacArthur for President" boomlet in 1944 and remained a strong political backer of the general in his 1948 quest for that office. However, the former president walked a narrow line by separating his criticism of "radical" reform from his continued support for MacArthur.

Writing to George Marshall and Robert Patterson, Hoover called for a "revolutionary review" of SCAP policies, especially the economic reforms that rested on an "illusion" about Japan. The "present economic paralysis" stemmed from limits on production, foreign trade, and the evils of attempting a "planned economy." Even if MacArthur were not personally at fault, Hoover considered it vital for the State and War departments to cancel existing plans to restructure or restrict industry. Other than prohibiting the production of weapons, he opposed any interference with market forces. Although Hoover claimed to approve "de-monopolized private enterprise," he balked at any rigorous attack on the *zaibatsu*. Social and economic experiments, he warned Secretary of War Patterson, would squander the "only possibility of holding her [Japan's] people as a bulwark against the Communist invasion of Asia." Constraints on Japanese industry, Hoover argued, formed a burdensome link of the economic "chains on the whole world." Americans ought to accept a "larger vision" that peace depended primarily on "productivity." Allowing the Japanese economy to drift or slip away would, ultimately, promote the "disintegration of Western Civilization everywhere."[18]

When *Newsweek* magazine printed a blistering attack on SCAP economic policy in January 1947, it revealed to the public that many powerful Americans and Japanese harbored grave misgivings about the Occupation. Although some liberal political journals, like the *Nation* and *New Republic*, had previously questioned SCAP's conservative bias, virtually no one had criticized MacArthur's program for being too radical or harsh. *Newsweek*'s foreign editor, Harry F. Kern, and Tokyo correspondent, Compton Packenham, saw things quite differently. Packenham had spent part of his youth in Japan and, as remembered by an associate, "looked upon most indicted war criminals in Tokyo as childhood playmates." Kern had similar feelings, having sympathized with Japan throughout the 1930s. He blamed Jiang Jieshi for "manipulating" Roosevelt into the confrontation at Pearl Harbor. This accounted, in part, for *Newsweek*'s rather tepid support for the Nationalists during the Chinese civil war. In fact, some of the magazine's Asia correspondents, like Harold Isaacs, were bitter critics of both the KMT and of the French in Indochina. Kern and Packenham detested MacArthur personally, believing that his reform agenda as well as that mandated by Washington left Japan destitute and vulnerable to communism.[19]

Newsweek appealed to more than an indignant readership. It counted among its founders, both W. Averell and his brother E. Roland Harriman. Kern remained close to Averell Harriman who, after his diplomatic service, served as Truman's secretary of commerce. Harriman had tried, unsuccessfully, to have General MacArthur voluntarily accept advice from business experts. After a rebuff in December 1946, Averell Harriman and other disgruntled officials used *Newsweek* as a forum to leak damaging information about SCAP.[20]

On January 27, 1947, *Newsweek* charged that the recently decreed economic purge in Tokyo would drive nearly thirty thousand talented, "active, efficient, cultured and cosmopolitan" managers from office. Destroying the "brains of the entire Japanese economic structure," Kern and Packenham wrote, would play into the hands of the "ever watchful Russians, the advocates of severe purges." The magazine sidestepped a direct attack on MacArthur, blaming, instead, his allegedly radical, antibusiness aides. It quoted a disillusioned Japanese businessman as asking why, "when America could have all Japan working in its own interest, it is now engaged in wrecking the country so as to leave it as an eventual prize for the Russians."[21]

In a rejoinder, carried by the magazine two weeks later, MacArthur refuted Kern's charges. Assuming personal responsibility for all SCAP actions, he denied that his subordinates had advocated radical reforms. He considered it utterly "fantastic" that anyone would question the purge of ultranationalist business leaders opposed to both peace and democratic capitalism. Unimpressed, Kern repeated his accusations and wrote additional articles about "trouble in Japan." Published over the next several months, they predicted that the economic and political radicalism encouraged by SCAP would open Japan to anarchy and communism. Kern even suggested that Japan be rearmed as a counter to Soviet and Chinese power.[22]

Despite these charges and specific allegations of gross mismanagement made by numerous cabinet colleagues, Secretary of War Robert Patterson seemed unwilling or unable to dispatch a new team of economic specialists to Tokyo. In a testy exchange, Patterson rejected Dean Acheson's request that the State Department be permitted to send its own experts to verify the rosy reports sent by SCAP. He insisted that no technical personnel could go to Japan without MacArthur's prior permission. This deference led Forrestal to complain that, in the past, the weak civilian leadership of the army "had not been able to issue a single order to MacArthur, and they couldn't now."[23]

The frustration voiced by cabinet members prompted the White House staff to begin investigating rumors of a civilian-military split over Japan. Robert N. Kerr, an assistant to Truman's aide Edwin A. Locke (who had visited Tokyo in 1945), met with State Department representatives on April 18, 1947. Ernest A. Gross, a deputy to Assistant Secretary John Hilldring, explained that disillusionment with MacArthur had little to do with conventional civilian-military conflict in Washington. He provided a detailed recounting of how the State, War, and Navy departments all proposed to reassess fundamental economic policy toward Japan. Gross persuaded Kerr to request a strong presidential initiative, including the dispatch of a "super diplomat," to break the grip of "General MacArthur, his Chief of Staff, and the 'Bataan Group' out there." Kerr passed on to Locke and Truman a warning he had been given. "The U.S. government" must soon choose between "saving the face of SCAP or wrecking its whole economic policy for the Far East."[24]

Despite this admonition, Truman seemed reluctant to move against MacArthur directly. The War Department, under Robert Patterson, and the armed services were in flux, about to be reorganized into a unified Defense Department. Until unification (in July 1947), MacArthur continued to run circles around his nominal superiors. However, the general realized that soon a powerful defense secretary might ally with Secretary of State Marshall and spur the president and his administration into action. Any degree of outside supervision or direction would diminish MacArthur's influence and subject his actions to scrutiny. His loss of exclusive control and the political spotlight that accompanied it threatened to destroy Japan's value as the general's presidential springboard. Rather than permit this, MacArthur launched a preemptive attack, proclaiming the success of the Occupation and calling for an international peace settlement to affirm his achievements. The longer a settlement was delayed, he knew, the less he could hope to dominate the tone and agenda of a peace conference.

During the first three months of 1947, as MacArthur witnessed the halo fading from around SCAP's brow, he began leaking reports that Japan deserved and required a restoration of sovereignty. Among other conduits, he turned toward British diplomat Sir Alvary Gascoigne on March 3 to deliver a lecture on the "three phases" of the Occupation. MacArthur boasted that he had "most miraculously" demilitarized Japan and nearly completed its "democratization." One final challenge remained—economic recovery. But, he claimed, a residue of international trade restrictions and discrimination by Allied governments threatened "completely and irretrievably [to] kill the Japanese economy." Nothing he could do nor any new foreign assistance would improve the situation, unless a peace settlement quickly restored self-rule. Unfortunately, MacArthur told Gasoigne,

Secretary of State George C. Marshall and his aides "paid heed" only to "Wall Street whose main holdings were in Europe." Consequently, Washington ignored Japan and directed all its attention toward Germany.

This updated Europe-first strategy, the general complained, ignored the fact that in Japan, in contrast to Germany, the United States had nearly a free hand. He dismissed the unresolved issues of reparations, levels of production, and trust busting as mere "technical problems." Security for the island nation, he insisted, could be assured through a "simple article . . . providing UN responsibility for future protection." In fact, MacArthur confided to the incredulous British diplomat, all of Japan's problems stemmed from the petty jealousies of Truman and his foreign policy advisers who hoped to inflate their own successes in Europe by making him appear a failure in Japan. But, he warned, unless Marshall made progress toward a treaty during the upcoming Moscow meeting of the CFM, he would shatter the "Pacific air" with his "cries" to "conclude an early peace treaty with Japan."[25]

MacArthur's worst fears were realized during the subsequent two weeks. The ill-fated Moscow meeting yielded no progress on the German or Japanese treaties. More significantly, the president's announcement of the Truman Doctrine on March 12 ended any likelihood of future Soviet–American cooperation. MacArthur then carried out his threat by making a rare visit to the Foreign Press Club in Tokyo where he encouraged reporters to take down an "on the record" interview. Without bothering to inform Washington, the Supreme Commander repeated most of what he had told Gascoigne privately. Recovery was impossible until a peace treaty stopped the "economic warfare" that inflicted even more damage than the atomic bomb. Under these circumstances, the general described himself as powerless to revive Japan's economy and dismissed any initiatives from Washington unless preceded by "peace talks."

Hoping to force the Truman administration's hand while he still controlled the Occupation, MacArthur praised the Japanese government as the fruit of his own "spiritual revolution." Blithely explaining away a half century of expansion and aggression, he told the American correspondents that Japan was merely a poor country that had taken a wrong turn in "reach[ing] out to get resources." It had been sufficiently punished by the loss of its overseas territories and owed nothing more to its wartime victims. Japan exhibited such "advanced spirituality," he claimed, that it should be considered immune from attack. MacArthur concluded by paraphrasing Winston Churchill's remark to the effect that the West's major European problem was "not to keep Germany down, but to keep it up." America's greatest "problem" in Asia, he explained, was to "keep Japan up."[26]

This blanket declaration absolving Japan of guilt and pronouncing it overdue for a peace treaty gravely embarrassed the Truman administration. Occurring at the very moment when the president sought to rally the American public, Congress, and European allies against the Soviet threat, MacArthur seemed to dismiss both the security and economic bases of the emerging containment policy. Japan, he claimed, required neither an American military umbrella nor an expensive recovery program. He implied that the adminstration had botched affairs in Europe and would now spend a fortune there, whereas SCAP had built a new Japan at bargain rates. Extending the Occupation and introducing costly new programs, he warned, would only wreck his achievements.

Virtually no officials in Washington shared this rosy assessment. Besides their political embarrassment at MacArthur's grandstanding, Marshall, Forrestal, Acheson, Kennan, the JCS, and the technical specialists in nearly every cabinet department feared that Japan would collapse economically and politically should the Occupation end soon. Unless fundamental policies were revised, the collapse might occur even while America remained in control. In fact, many suspected that this fear underlay MacArthur's haste. Probably, he wanted to "get out" of Tokyo while the Occupation still appeared successful and before a crisis tarnished his career or impeded his presidential aspirations. Few in the administration felt inclined to assist the general's obvious political ambition.

The host of studies and cabinet discussions carried on from January through April found public expression in a dramatic speech delivered by Undersecretary of State Dean Acheson. Speaking in Cleveland, Mississippi, on May 8, 1947, he refuted MacArthur's basic contentions and described the Truman adminstration's emerging strategy toward foreign economic policy. Acheson tied the burning issue of the growing "dollar gap" (the trade imbalance already exceeded $8 billion) to the "grim fact of life" that the "greatest workshops of Europe and Asia—Germany and Japan" remained idle. Because world economic stability and peace depended on their recovery, the United States could not await some distant political settlement with the Soviets nor subordinate economic recovery to peace treaties. Instead, Acheson pledged emergency financial aid to both the former Axis powers and their victims. America, Acheson announced, would reconstruct the two "great workshops" upon which the "ultimate recovery of the two continents so largely depends. . . ." In effect, the Truman administration had begun its counterassault on MacArthur's domain.[27]

5

AN ABORTED TREATY

Gen. Douglas MacArthur gambled that public pressure and his popular mystique would force the Truman administration to convene a peace conference. Ultimately, he had not only lost this wager but fatally undermined his elaborate political game plan involving both Japan and the presidency. The confusion and resentment he stirred up within the American government united a host of otherwise antagonistic elements against SCAP. The call for a treaty provoked precisely the sort of searching reexamination of the Occupation that MacArthur feared most. Ultimately, the State and Defense departments maneuvered a previously lethargic President Truman to strip the Supreme Commander of much of his power in Japan.

Ironically, the momentum for a treaty in 1947 came as much from within the State Department as from SCAP. A special working group, headed by Japan specialist Hugh Borton had been working on a draft since late 1946. Because no one had told them to stop, by March of 1947, they had produced a document calling for a long period of international oversight leading toward the restoration of sovereignty. The draft treaty relied on cooperation among members of the Far Eastern Commission to supervise closely military potential, heavy industry, and raw material stockpiles for up to twenty-five years. A council of ambassadors and a control commission would monitor Japanese behavior during the period. Stressing the international aspects of control, the draft made no provision for exclusive American military-base rights in Japan or Okinawa.[1]

Like many of the stringent economic measures that had been applied or remained under consideration, this document continued to reflect assumptions made before or shortly after surrender. The Borton group, although not at all vengeful, considered it necessary to supervise closely Japan's reentry into the Pacific and the world community. Both the wartime allies and Japan's wartime victims were accorded broad supervisory rights to ensure that Tokyo could neither restore its military power nor abandon basic Occupation reforms. The draft did not concern itself with utilizing Japan as an American military ally nor did it acknowledge any Soviet threat. Far from worrying about how to boost Japanese trade and production, the authors of the draft described a need for carefully monitoring and controlling industry so that Japan could not again dominate the regional economy.

Neither this draft nor MacArthur's independent call elicited much enthusiasm in Washington. The general objected to the Borton draft because it neither promised a quick restoration of full sovereignty nor provided for the kind of security provision the Supreme Commander favored. In fact, MacArthur's own formula for peace remained somewhat vague or, as critics contended, contradictory. He spoke against imposing any posttreaty controls or limits on sovereignty and opposed basing any foreign troops in Japan. He maintained that a guarantee from the United Nations would insure the nation's security without an American presence. However, his "neutrality" scheme presumed that Japan would be surrounded, or buffered, by a ring of American naval and air bases on the mandated islands and that Okinawa would be retained as a major base. Thus, Japan might remain demilitarized and ungarrisoned, but it would remain firmly under an American military umbrella.[2]

The secretaries of the armed services as well as the JCS condemned both the Borton draft treaty and MacArthur's scheme as naive, even dangerous. That MacArthur issued his proposals without bothering to consult military planners in Washington enraged them. Although not yet fully evolved, the strategic doctrines under discussion presumed that, in case of war, Japan would serve as a launching pad for conventional and atomic air raids against the Soviet Union. The JCS did not believe Japan was currently ready for a treaty or that an international guarantee could deny the islands to the Soviet Union. Even more troubling, MacArthur's neutrality proposal would deny American forces the right to utilize Japanese bases in peace or wartime. In fact, practically any treaty acceptable to the Soviets (or the Japanese) would diminish the degree of freedom now enjoyed by American forces. Until a decision had been reached on Japan's potential military role in U.S. strategy and on the sticky question of post-Occupation bases, the military establishment preferred to postpone all consideration of a settlement.

The Borton draft aroused related opposition among Pentagon planners. In fact, it made the situation worse by encouraging some form of multilateral military, economic, and political supervision of post-Occupation Japan. The State Department also made no provision for requiring the ceding of Okinawa as an American base. Together, these proposals seemed to undermine the whole concept of a Pacific defense perimeter.[3]

Despite the fact that a number of diplomatic and military planners objected to the timing and substance of these treaty provisions, a kind of bureaucratic inertia propelled them forward. Until August, PPS's reevaluation of policy continued to focus almost exclusively on European issues. Unsure of what to do with the draft treaty and increasingly embarrassed by MacArthur's pressure, the State Department issued an invitation on July 11, 1947, for all eleven Far Eastern Commission members to attend a mid-August preliminary peace conference.

This offer elicited hostile responses from the British Commonwealth nations, the Soviet Union, and the Nationalist Chinese. Because nothing could be accomplished in the Far Eastern Commission without their support, the initiative seemed doomed from the start. In a particularly inept move, the American invitation conflicted with a planned British Commonwealth meeting scheduled for August 26 in Canberra, Australia, where questions about Japan appeared high on the agenda. Because the British government could not negotiate with the United States before consulting the Pacific dominions, it politely declined the American invitation and suggested that the two nations begin private talks some time in the future.[4]

American handling of this episode confirmed London's misgivings about the entire Occupation. The British had been denied any substantial role in Japan. For a variety of reasons, they feared both an economic collapse of their former enemy as well as its complete recovery. An impoverished Japan would deflect American resources from Western Europe and inhibit the economic well-being of Southeast Asia. At the same time, a strongly resurgent Japan might gain a commanding position in Southeast Asia, driving Britain from this vital market. For example, Malaya's rubber and tin exports provided a major portion of the dollar earnings that Great Britain used to balance its transatlantic trade deficit. In addition, Australia, New Zealand, China, and the Philippines all worried about resurgent Japanese imperialism and opposed any treaty that lacked provisions for strict international controls on armaments and industry.[5]

Members of the British Cabinet and Foreign Office characterized American policy as a "strange neo-imperialism of a mystical irrational kind" combined with a "drive for exports which has acquired a certain force of desperation." The Americans appeared to want a Japan predominant in both North and Southeast Asia; the Soviets were equally determined to resist Japan's reemergence as a military power. The British worried most that in rebuilding their former enemy, the United States would enhance the Japanese position in Southeast Asia to compensate for lost access to Manchuria and Korea. Although Washington emphasized a Russian threat, MacArthur seemed prepared to entrust Japan's future security to a UN resolution and Soviet goodwill. Uncertain over the goals of American policy (and unsure who spoke for the administration—MacArthur or the State Department), the British preferred to postpone consideration of a treaty.[6]

Although the commonwealth declined to attend pending their Canberra meeting,* the Chinese and Soviets dealt additional blows to the American proposal. The Russians insisted that any settlement should be considered by the CFM, in which they had a veto, rather than by the Far Eastern Commission, where a two-thirds majority held sway. The Chinese, caught between their American benefactors and Soviet neighbors and harboring deep resentment toward Japan, proposed a compromise. They suggested that the Far Eastern Commission consider the treaty but that its rules be amended to grant the great powers a veto. This pleased no one; soon nearly every invited nation, not just the Soviet Union, raised some contradictory objection to matters of procedure or substance. Inconclusive debate raged for months, leading first to a postponement, then abandonment, of the proposed conference.[7]

Instead of upsetting civilian and military planners, this chaotic episode and international rebuff had an energizing effect on them. As a spokesman for the Army Department's Plans and Operations (P&O) Division put it, the United States ought to consider it extremely "fortunate" that foreign opposition blocked a peace conference. Otherwise, it might have gotten stuck with an unacceptable treaty. In effect, the Soviets, British, and Chinese had granted the United States time to reconsider whether "there should be an early peace treaty with Japan at all."[8]

In early August, George Kennan assigned John P. Davies to "look over informally" the Borton draft treaty, which the PPS had finally received. Kennan also requested that Far Eastern specialists evaluate its implications for Japan and for the "situation likely to arise in Indochina."[9] Since his wartime service as political adviser to Gen. Joseph Stilwell in China, Davies

---

*At the Canberra Conference, Australia and New Zealand insisted on consultations in advance of a treaty and wanted the treaty to include strict industrial-military controls as well as extensive reparations. The British Foreign Office had already drafted its own agenda, which was widely at variance with American concerns. See Foreign Office Files FO 371/63766–63784 and Dunn, *Peacemaking and the Settlement with Japan*, 68–69.

emerged as the State Department's deepest thinker on Asian nationalism, communism, and revolution. When transferred to the Moscow embassy after Stilwell's recall, he helped educate George Kennan about East Asian politics. Davies originally advocated cooperation with the Chinese Communists, both because he understood the KMT's weakness and thought the CCP could be utilized to limit Soviet influence in China. As American ties with both Chinese factions deteriorated, however, Davies lost faith in the Communists' ability to contain the Soviet Union and with China's geopolitical importance. In contrast, a revived, if tamed, Japanese nationalism might well serve American interests in Asia by making of Japan a strategic ally.

The draft treaty horrified Davies. He told Kennan that it not only ignored major problems but practically encouraged "Sovietized totalitarianism." Instead of integrating Japan into a "Pacific economy" as a "ready and dependable ally," it would subject the nation to international supervision and permit Russia a major "disruptive" role. Because, he reasoned, Japan could "only gravitate into the oribit of one or the other of the super-powers," the Soviet Union could easily instigate a coup and take over. Before further consideration of the document, Davies argued, the PPS must clarify these "basic issues."[10]

Kennan agreed that the treaty draft did "not seem to be related to any realistic pattern" of American objectives in Japan or elsewhere. How, he rhetorically asked under Secretary of State Robert Lovett, could the United States consult with foreign powers before any consensus formed within the government? the entire matter must first be "systematically thrashed out. . . ." Greatly impressed by this critique, Lovett dismissed the draft treaty as "wholly inadequate in present form." It would, he promised, be "sent back" and the views of the PPS "passed along."[11]

Members of the Army Department's P&O Division reacted just as Davies and Kennan had to the draft treaty and to MacArthur's proposals. P&O spokesman Col. S. F. Giffen shared a litany of complaints with Kennan, starting with the fact that neither Borton nor General MacArthur had solicited the military's views. Relieved that the treaty conference had been blocked, Giffen insisted that Japan be treated as a "potential" military base. Under no circumstances should it be declared "neutral" or under UN supervision, for this would eliminate its value as a bastion against Soviet expansion in Asia and free the Russian hand for mischief elsewhere. Even if America did not permanently garrison the island nation, it must at least hold Japan for another few years, by which time it would be clear "whether war is a genuine likelihood. . . ." Neither the State nor Army departments, Giffen emphasized, should "acquiesce" to MacArthur's blackmail. A premature departure would only "breed communism" and require spending "vast sums to bring order out of chaos." Despite General MacArthur's many talents, he had no right to control "overall U.S. foreign policy" and, Giffen added, his superiors ought to make him understand this.[12]

This support from the Army Department bolstered Kennan's effort to build a coalition against SCAP. He found additional encouragement from the newly appointed head of FE, W. W. Butterworth. A Europeanist by training, Butterworth served in China during the Marshall mission and became Secretary Marshall's choice to fill the sensitive position in the summer of 1947. Unlike his predecessor, John Carter Vincent, whose career centered on China, Butterworth had few emotional ties to America's wartime ally. He needed little encouragement to see the value of focusing attention on Japan.

Even while serving in China, Butterworth seemed impressed by Japan's importance as a containment barrier. In August 1946, for example, he cabled the State Department that Moscow might use its control of Manchuria and Korea to extend its "imperium" over Japan through economic pressure. Accordingly, the United States must "align Japanese interests with ours" to "offset Russian imperialism" and compensate for "Chinese ineptitude." Still opposed to rearmament, Butterworth also urged linking the "Japanese economy with our own . . . and in general to direct Japanese industry, trade, and shipping to the mutual interests of both countries." The Japanese, Butterworth felt, were better qualified to dominate Asian markets than "any other people in the East," and he considered it high time to "deal with the Japanese as an alternative" to the Chinese.[13]

If anything, Butterworth became more fixed in these beliefs after his promotion. An enthusiastic ally of Kennan, the new head of FE promoted cooperation with the policy planners and minimized bureaucratic haggling over turf. Disillusion, even hopelessness, over events in China made most Asia area specialists acknowledge the need to do something different in Japan. As a first step, few doubted, this meant asserting civilian control over SCAP.[14]

Encouraged by the consensus within the State Department and the army, Kennan assigned John P. Davies to oversee preparation of an alternative draft treaty. Within five days, Davies's working group sketched out what became the model for the rest of the Occupation. Davies had less interest in stipulating exact terms than in outlining what must be done to prepare Japan for its future role. The "radically changed world situation," he wrote, required that Japan be made "internally stable," "amenable to American leadership," and "industrially revived as a producer primarily of consumer goods and secondarily of capital goods" in order to prosper and raise the "standards of living in non-communist Asia." Although "cranking-up" the devastated economy would prevent internal subversion, America must also seek permanent base rights and organize a central police force "susceptible to expansion and use in accordance with American military decisions." Instead of seeking international approvals, Washington should "undertake unilaterally whatever control" might be needed to rebuild the economy. To prevent its ever becoming an "instrument of Soviet aggression," America could bind Japan through a bilateral defense pact included in a peace settlement of its own devising.[15]

During the following two months, the PPS coordinated their work with the Army and Navy departments, who rejected the concept of Japanese neutrality. They dismissed the premise that the former enemy might regain an "independent identity." Realistically, Japan could "function only as an American or Soviet satellite." To poison Soviet–Japanese relations, they urged subtly agitating for Russia's return of the disputed islands near Hokkaido that were seized in 1945. With luck, this dispute might embitter the two countries' relations for years.[16]

By mid-September, these ideas appeared in a thirty-seven-page draft. Bearing the title, "U.S. Policy Toward a Peace Settlement with Japan," and with a top secret classification, all who read the document had to sign a register. A summary statement on the cover sheet described the contents:

> A major shift in U.S. policy toward Japan is being talked about under cover. Idea of eliminating Japan as a military power for all time is changing. Now, because of Russia's conduct, tendency is to develop Hirohito's islands as a buffer state. The peace treaty now being drafted would have to allow for this changed attitude.[17]

This reference to a potential restoration of Japanese military power (or American use of Japan as a military base) marked a startling reversal of the principles proclaimed in the Potsdam Declaration and initial postsurrender policies. Although the State Department did not take the initiative in projecting a military role for the former enemy, Kennan's staff seemed to acknowledge that at least some provision would have to be made for enhancing Japanese security or allowing limited post-Occupation American-base facilities. Still, the PPS continued to define the threat to Japan and to Germany largely in economic and political terms. They saw little likelihood of a Soviet invasion or internal Communist coup. The greatest challenge came from Soviet control over Manchuria, North China, Korea, and Sakhalin—all traditional markets or sources of raw materials for Japan. These areas, PPS said, might be used as a "lever for Soviet political pressure, unless Japan is able . . . to obtain these raw materials and markets elsewhere—particularly in South Asia and the Western hemisphere." Long-term security depended largely on the "willingness of this [the American]

Government to prime the Japanese economic pump." America ought to rehabilitate Japan's economy by "furnishing sufficient funds over a period of four to five years" to put industry back on its feet.[18]

Within the Office of the Assistant Secretary for Occupied Areas, a few voices spoke out against the new approach. Encouraging the reemergence of old business leaders, one critic noted, resembled the "reinstatement of Schacht, the directors of Farben and the Ruhr on the grounds that compared with the SS [*Schutzstaffel*]" or the Communists, they were the "strongest force in Germany for stability and moderation" and had "natural ties with the United States." Emphasizing "stability over reform" paralleled the arguments of Japanese Fascists, who also raised the danger of Soviet influence. So far, the Occupation had sought to foster democracy and economic reform; it was also American policy to "contain Soviet expansion." However, to "seek the latter by abandoning the former" was "to argue that democracy must be abandoned in order to be defended."[19]

But remarkably little opposition emerged from anywhere inside the government to the PPS's work. Even some of Hugh Borton's early collaborators now rejected the preliminary draft treaty. Edwin F. Martin, head of the Japan–Korea Division, for example, stated that his initial support for an early peace arose from assumptions of "doubtful validity." "Economic conditions in Japan and the Far East" had so deteriorated that he now believed it would take "a number of years" and substantial American aid before the Occupation could end.[20]

Kennan's army allies, such as Gen. Cortland Van Rensselaer Schuyler, also commended the efforts of the PPS. Schuyler informed the new Army Under Secretary, William H. Draper, Jr., that both State Department and Army Department planners agreed on the need to make Japan "politically independent of the U.S.S.R." and would push a new program for Congress to "underwrite the initial economic rehabilitation of Japan." Even though the army still differed with MacArthur and the State Department on the question of post-Occupation bases in Japan, Schuyler anticipated a breakthrough on the thorny issue of fortifying Okinawa. Despite the fact that many diplomats insisted on its rapid reversion to Japan, the emperor, he revealed, had secretly suggested that Washington take a long-term military lease over the Ryukyus as part of a bilateral security pact and treaty. Apparently, the Japanese government felt that giving this prize to the American military would hasten a peace settlement, regardless of international opposition.[21]

In mid-October, Kennan distilled the essence of his staff's findings for Secretary of State Marshall and Under Secretary Lovett. Although a definitive judgment awaited the visit of some "high official" to Tokyo, Kennan alerted his superiors that MacArthur's behavior and the existing Occupation program encouraged "communist penetration of Japan." No more thought should be given to a peace treaty, he cautioned, before Washington had laid the groundwork for economic recovery and made arrangements for adequate military security. He reported that owing to wartime destruction and

> the loss of its markets and raw material resources in Soviet-dominated portions of the mainland, with highly unstable conditions prevailing in China, in Indonesia, in Indochina, and in India, and with no certainty as to the resumption of certain traditional exports to the dollar area, Japan faces, even in the best of circumstances, an economic problem of extremely serious dimensions.

The magnitude of these problems, he told Marshall and Lovett, dictated that Washington not disrupt Japan further before the State Department reassessed basic Occupation goals. Marshall not only agreed, but promptly ordered that all future planning for Japan be coordinated with the PPS. He also decided to send either Kennan, Butterworth, or Charles Bohlen to Tokyo.[22]

Kennan continued to lobby furiously during October and November, cultivating his patron, the new Defense Secretary, James Forrestal, as well as Army Secretary Kenneth Royall, and Adm. Sidney Souers, head of the recently created NSC. He told this group they must reverse policies toward both Japan and Fascist Spain. Just as Spain had a vital position in the Mediterranean, Japan represented the key to stability in Northeast Asia. Kennan alleged that his staff had actually uncovered a program for the "socialization" of Japan, including attacks on business and encouraging labor radicalism. He condemned MacArthur and the past two years of reforms for letting the country deteriorate so much that if he turned it "back to the Japanese," it would mean "economic disaster, inflation . . . near anarchy which would be precisely what the communists want."[23]

. Kennan's impact seemed confirmed during a cabinet meeting with President Truman on November 7. George Marshall praised the initiation of the containment program since the previous March. The United States, he believed, had found an antidote to Soviet expansion. America must now fund a multiyear recovery program and guard against a "panic" reaction by Moscow. Ultimate success depended on restoration of the "balance of power in Europe and Asia and . . . all action would be viewed in light of this objective." James Forrestal endorsed this conclusion, pressing Truman and the rest of the cabinet to proclaim publicly that the United States intended to restore the industrial strength of "both Germany and Japan." The survivial of the entire non-communist world, he intoned solemnly, now depended on rebuilding the "two nations we have just destroyed."[24]

6

THE CONSERVATIVE
RESPONSE TO
LIBERAL REFORM

Despite the convergence of ideas among officials like Marshall, Forrestal, Kennan, and Acheson in mid-1947, the administration made no immediate headway in altering the direction of the reform program in Japan. Even Kennan's success in halting consideration of an early treaty had depended, to a large extent, on the fortuitous opposition of the British, Soviets, and Chinese to the American proposal. Thus far, planners in Washington had only begun to define what they did not want to happen in Tokyo. They still had not mapped out an alternative agenda nor discovered how to constrain SCAP's independence. To make matters even worse, international pressure had grown to begin implementing the stringent reparations program recommended by the Pauley mission in 1945–46. Also, MacArthur and his top aides had come around to supporting a comprehensive anti-monopoly program designed to break up giant industrial combines into competitive units. Together, these economic reforms would transform Japan's internal economic structure while augmenting the economic independence of neighboring Asian states. Although these ideas reflected early postwar values, Kennan, Acheson, and Forrestal now spoke of restoring the central economic functions of Germany and Japan, making the former enemy states once again regional centers of capitalism.

Groping for a handle to halt these developments, civilian and military planners in Washington took aim first at the reparations program. Actually, Pauley's plan to hasten Asian development by breaking the hold of Japanese industry on the region's trade and technology had run into difficulty from its inception. MacArthur had always objected to poaching on SCAP's turf by Pauley's staff and considered some of its actions a criticism of his own industrial policy. Later, conflicting claims by potential recipients, civil was in China, and insurgencies in Southeast Asia had played havoc with Pauley's plan. In January 1947, Secretary of War Robert Patterson acknowledged these problems in dispatching a Special Committee on Reparations to Tokyo. Led by Clifford Strike, head of an engineering consortium, the mission received a charge to examine the technical condition of industry that might be removed in implementing the Pauley program. Strike, however, made no secret of his own view that it was "neither essential nor desirable" to adhere to the 1946 program. Even before traveling to Japan, he spoke of a need to leave "enough industry so that the Japanese economy will be self-sustaining" and capable of supporting its needs through industrial exports. Strike vigorously opposed "stripping . . . anything that Japan was likely to need in the future for building a normal economy. . . ."

State Department economic specialists like Edwin F. Martin admitted to curious members of the British Embassy staff that sentiment in Washington had turned strongly against any stringent reparations program. In place of Pauley's formula, Martin explained, the United States would probably impose a small, symbolic transfer of machinery from Japan to various claimants. But uncertainty over SCAP, with the tangled lines of authority within the administration and the Far Eastern Commission, led concerned British diplomats to conclude that no one in the American government "can authoritatively say what is the overall economic policy which the United States . . . pursues in Japan."[1]

Strike's conclusions, issued as a report to the War Department in February 1947, had relatively little to say about what machinery might fulfill the reparations quota. Instead, his report refuted the very premise of Pauley's assertions. Japan, Strike insisted, possessed little, if any, "excess industrial capacity." It must retain all available machine tools, any shortage of which would have to be replaced by American aid.[2]

Edwin Pauley continued to maintain that Japan could not only afford substantial industrial reparations but that stable, capitalist development elsewhere in Asia depended on such a program. Strike's assertions, he warned, represented a "complete repudiation of U.S. reparations policy" and would outrage Asian nations who expected the United States to fulfill pledges made in 1945–46. Confronted by such contrasting demands, SWNCC agreed to order the immediate distribution of some sixteen thousand machine tools to Japan's Asian claimants as part of an "advance transfer" program in April. But the tide was with Strike rather than Pauley. The "advance transfers" mobilized the advocates of a "reverse course" to push for termination of the entire program. Within a few months, the army would send Strike to Tokyo again with the understanding that he would advocate a drastic cut in reparations.[3]

The confusion surrounding reparations in the summer of 1947 also characterized the anti-*zaibatsu* program. As described earlier, the hard-hitting Edwards report of 1946 recommended a comprehensive program to deconcentrate the giant conglomerates and control the growth of future monopolies. Although MacArthur had received the report from the JCS as an "interim directive" in October 1946, neither SCAP nor SWNCC took official action on it for a year. Then, in May 1947, Washington forwarded the document, as SWNCC 302/4, to the Far Eastern Commission for its approval (there it assumed the tag FEC 230). Condemning the *zaibatsu* for having stifled both political and economic freedom in Japan and for promoting aggression, FEC 230 described the "dissolution of excessive private concentration of economic power" as one of the "major objectives of the Occupation."[4]

In Tokyo, Douglas MacArthur gradually embraced the ideal of (or, at least, the appearance of) the anti-*zaibatsu* program. He portrayed the reform as a litmus test of the Occupation's effort to stimulate a "controlled" revolution from above. The general also defended deconcentration as a strong vote of confidence in competitive private enterprise, not as an anticapitalist campaign, as critics later charged. When the Japanese government proved reluctant to move (both the Left and Right had qualms about breaking up the combines into small units), SCAP pressed the Socialist cabinet of Katayama Tetsu to introduce deconcentration legislation for Diet approval in July 1947.

By then, MacArthur's opponents in Washington perceived a triple threat. The spectre of a stringent reparations program, a radical assault on industrial combines, and the departure of American forces (should an early treaty come about) would, they feared, leave Japan in economic and political chaos. Responding to this challenge, leading officials in the State and Defense departments launched an offensive to reverse both fundamental occupation policies and MacArthur's unilateral power.

In July 1947, just as the administration drafted the ERP, the State Department submitted a Japanese recovery proposal to SWNCC that included features resembling those of the Marshall Plan. SWNCC 381, as the document became known, drew on studies of the department's Japan–Korea economic division in proposing a more than $500 million program to "render Japan self-sufficient by about 1950." It called for filling the raw material pipeline through some $400 million in new American aid combined with about $150 million raised from the sale of certain Japanese assets. The plan urged drastic reduction of reparations coupled with a higher ceiling on heavy-industry production levels. The temporary grant of American dollars and raw materials would establish preconditions for neighboring states to furnish "raw materials to Japan for processing into finished goods, some amount of these" to be "returned as payments to such countries." Citing Dean Acheson's appeal, the report held that only a cranking-up" of the economy would get Japan off the American dole. Although some at home and abroad might recoil at providing assistance to a former enemy, the State Department now concluded that American security required "substantial U.S. assistance to our ex-enemy, rather than to our ex-Allies in the Far East."[5]

Besides its call for economic assistance, SWNCC presented a startlingly revisionist view of recent Asian history. In complete contrast to the Pauley and Edwards reports, which chronicled Japan's record of economic, political, and military exploitation of its neighbors, the authors of SWNCC 381 likened Japan to nineteenth-century Britain, whose development stimulated the growth of Europe and North America. Martin and his staff predicted that Japan could duplicate Britain's progressive role on behalf of Asia, as they alleged it had begun to do through economic expansion after the First World War. Because it had been stripped of its military strength, they said, Japan ought now to be encouraged to reenter such natural economic frontier areas as Southeast Asia. Owing to its more advanced economy, it should soon enjoy a large trading surplus with its less developed neighbors, alleviating the need for further American aid. If Japan were permitted to repay its dollar debt in local soft currencies, Washington could use these funds to buy more raw materials for Japan or could return them to Southeast Asia with the proviso that they be tied to future purchases in Japan. SWNCC 381 predicted that Japanese recovery would thus stimulate regionwide development. And both Japanese and American influence in the area would be promoted without the outlay of additional dollars. As European influence waned, Japan would step into the breach, sealing off Southeast Asia from radical influences.[6]

By the summer of 1947, SWNCC planners concluded that the United States had little alternative but to promote Japan's recovery and its integration with the rest of Asia. And should the United States fail to fund such a program, they believed the outcome would be calamitous:

> [It would inevitably] result in a breakdown, gradual or precipitous, that would represent a complete loss in the American investment in a stable, democratic, and peaceful Japan and would seriously jeopardize the U.S. program for worldwide economic recovery and political stabilization.

But spending a huge sum on recovery could only be justified, SWNCC said, by including all Asian countries that "are potential sources of raw materials for Japan and potential markets for Japanese products."[7]

Both the civilian and military representatives to SWNCC endorsed the State Department's goals. However, settling on an actual plan to implement the crank-up proved more difficult. For nearly six months, the Army and State departments clashed over procedural issues. The army favored a unilateral recovery program that pointedly excluded consultations with other nations. Diplomatic officials considered it important to gain the political and economic cooperation of friendly Far Eastern Commission members. Military planners preferred to abandon all pretense of consultation, believing it would only impede recovery. As an army spokesman declared:

> I believe it appropriate for the United States to avail itself of its power to issue interim [i.e., unilateral] directives to the Supreme Commander for the Allied Powers. . . . I further believe it desirable for the United States to adopt the policy of exercising this power wherever possible in the solution of economic problems presented by the Occupation of Japan.

America, he felt, should act quickly and on its own to boost Japan's foreign trade, reduce reparations levels, and resolve the issue of the *zaibatsu*.[8]

The army's position hardened following the appointment of Gen. William H. Draper, Jr., as Under Secretary on August 30, 1947. A former vice president of Forrestal's investment firm, Dillon Read & Co., Draper had served the Army in several capacities since called from the reserves to active duty in 1940. Most recently, he had assisted Gen. Lucius Clay, Occupation Commander in Germany. There, many initial economic policies resembled those devised by SCAP and SWNCC for Japan. Draper revised basic labor regulations and industrial codes along more conservative, centralized lines. As Under Secretary for occupied areas until March 1, 1949, he coordinated the army's half of the "reverse course" in conjunction with the Department of State.

While preparing for a quick visit to Japan in mid-September 1947, Draper received two extremely critical evaluations of the Occupation there. One, assembled for his benefit by Assistant Sectetary of State Charles Saltzman, chronicled months of frustration in dealing with SCAP. It documented MacArthur's refusal to seek or accept assistance from civilian experts and his determination to enact "radical" reforms against the wishes of Washington, regardless of their economic impact.[9]

Harry Kern, the peripatetic editor of *Newsweek*, supplied more damning evidence. During the summer of 1947, Kern persuaded attorney James Lee Kauffman to take advantage of SCAP's relaxed rule on foreign visitors to travel to Japan. A prominent business lawyer who represented many corporate clients in prewar Tokyo (including Dillon, Read & Co.), Kauffman had been considered as a possible adviser to SCAP when the Commerce Department sought to send a delegation months earlier. While visiting Japan, he obtained a copy of the still classified FEC 230 report on *zaibatsu* dissolution. In essence, it contained the provisions of the deconcentration program MacArthur's staff placed before the Diet.

Although initally suspicious of the anti-*zaibatsu* campaign, the Supreme Commander had embraced it during 1947. Either because he was converted to its antimonopoly ideology or considered it a useful political ploy to enhance his standing as an enlightened man in America, MacArthur became the staunchest public advocate of the deconcentration program. In the report he prepared after this visit, Kauffman denounced FEC 230 and its pending legislative offspring as a "socialist idea" certain to destroy Japan. SCAP risked subjecting the nation to the "knife of the economic quack" wielded by "radical reformers" and "crackpots" enamored of Japan's "childlike" labor movement.[10]

Kauffman characterized the deconcentration proposals as a declaration of war against capitalism. The radical crackpots in SCAP maintained that peace and justice required the "dissolution of excessive private concentration of economic power," a term they defined loosely. If this standard became law, Kauffman warned, it would empower a future government to attack the wealth of virtually any domestic or foreign-owned company or individual. Even if *zaibatsu* owners received partial compensation, the deconcentration program would transfer ownership to unreliable consumer, labor, or cooperative groups—regardless of their ability to pay.

The bill before the Diet, Kauffman warned, went beyond attacking the *zaibatsu* families. It also targeted the large operating subsidiaries that dominated the structure of basic industry. The law would create a Holding Company Liquidation Commission (HCLC) empowered to designate companies for reorganization, purge officials, cancel debts, and force liquidations. This amounted to nothing but "good old socialism masquerading as democracy." Kauffman alerted *Newsweek* readers:

> [Japan] is still the leading oriental nation in ability, respect for law and order and desire to work. She is not communistic and while communism is growing, Japan will embrace it only as a last resort. Vis-à-vis our relations with Russia, Japan can be either for us or against us. We want her for us . . . the buffer against Soviet Russia on our Pacific side.

Not coincidentally, these words closely resembled the phrases chosen by George Kennan and John P. Davies in denouncing many Occupation reforms, the draft peace treaty, and MacArthur's behavior. Kauffman, in fact, had discussed his September 6 report with Kennan, Forrestal, Draper, and other influential officials.

Primed by Kauffman, Draper reached nearly identical conclusions during his own brief fact-finding tour of Japan late in September. On his return to Washington, he, Forrestal, and Army Secretary Kenneth Royall, agreed on the need to mobilize the administration against the deconcentration program and to place restraints on future action by MacArthur. Forrestal ordered his two aides to try to stop SCAP from pushing the controversial bill through the Diet; at the same time, Draper set about composing a brief declaration of principle which, he hoped, the Army and State departments could accept as a guide for action.[11]

When James Forrestal, George Kennan, Adm. Sidney Souers, and Kenneth Royall met on October 31, Kauffman's critique informed their discussions. Kennan's attack on SCAP's "socialization" program followed the Kauffman report on all particulars. He charged that radicals around MacArthur were determined to destroy Japan's natural resistance to communism and that the SCAP program of "economic disaster, inflation" and "near anarchy" was "precisely what the communists want." The group affirmed their determination to halt the deconcentration and reparations programs and to curb the power of organized labor in Japan.[12]

Kennan labeled the *zaibatsu* dissolution program as the central threat to Japan, a "vicious" scheme to destroy a modern industrial economy. It would strip power from those who had built a modern nation and put "labor unions" in control, making it "impossible" to run any business. Responding to this warning as well as the alarms raised by Kauffman, Forrestal complained to Kenneth Royall that SCAP's "socialization" program "would make it totally impossible for the country's economy to function."[13]

Early in October, Under Secretary of the Army Draper had introduced a new recovery proposal, called SWNCC 384, for interagency consideration. Although it proclaimed the same goals as the State Department's SWNCC 381, it called for unilateral action. Draper, Forrestal, and Royall proposed an immediate "shift in emphasis," as they called it, affording neither SCAP nor the Far Eastern Commission any opportunity to interfere. Unlike the Department of State, which still hoped for the cooperation of friendly Far Eastern Commission members, the army wanted to issue a proclamation that "indicated the economic recovery of Japan was a primary objective" of the United States and to use this as a justification for all subsequent action. The State Department representatives considered this a risky provocation because recovery plans dpended on expanded trade with Japan's neighbors.[14]

Besides his determination to pursue a unilateral program, Draper questioned other elements in the State Department's recovery proposal. He considered SWNCC 381 well intentioned but too limited in scope and time.

He preferred an approach recently drafted by SCAP's Economic-Scientific Section titled, "Economic Rehabilitation for Japan, South Korea and the Ryukyu Islands." Informally known as the Green Book (owing to its binding), the report expanded on the State Department scheme by positing a four-year recovery program during which Japan would receive about $1.2 billion worth of aid and industrial raw materials. This assistance, the Green Book held, would allow Japan to balance its foreign trade, pay for all its own imports by 1953, and sustain a standard of living at approximately the level of 1934. Although it avoided explaining precisely where Japan should expand exports and develop nondollar raw material imports, the report placed prime emphasis on ending the "log jam of raw material procurement" that blocked an industrial revival. Temporary American grants of cotton and other commodities, it claimed, would allow Japan to barter exports for future raw material supplies in Asian countries. Interestingly, this SCAP-generated proposal undercut MacArthur's claim that rehabilitation must await a peace treaty.[15]

Draper's staff soon reached a compromise with the State Department that involved asking Congress to fund an initial $180 million assistance package to run from April 1948 to June 1949. This Economic Recovery in Occupied Areas (EROA) program would supplement the existing $400 million already spent each year for food and vital supplies under the GARIOA program. Unlike the GARIOA program, EROA would provide industrial raw materials to insure export-oriented production. In many ways it resembled Marshall Plan assistance to Western Europe. Swallowing their doubts about abandoning the Far Eastern Commission completely, the State Department joined the army early in 1948 in submitting the proposal to the Bureau of the Budget and Congress.[16]

Now that the civilian and military planners adopted a united front, they feared that MacArthur's single-minded pursuit of the deconcentration program would frighten American legislators away from sinking new money into Japan. Already in a tight-fisted, budget-cutting mood, the Republican-dominated Congress appeared unlikely to appropriate new funds in the midst of an expanded purge, large-scale reparations, or an antimonopoly campaign. Fearing a delay, Forrestal, Draper, and Kennan maneuvered to isolate and neutralize the Supreme Commander.

Draper sent a pair of cables to MacArthur on October 20 and 21 instructing him to delay Diet consideration of the deconcentration bill. Much to the amazement of the army under secretary and Forrestal, the general reaffirmed his determination to pass the bill in the current session. Noting that SWNCC, the JCS, and the president originally supported the antimonopoly program, MacArthur claimed that the only people in Japan who opposed it were the *zaibatsu* themselves and the extreme Left, which favored state control. Debunking claims that he threatened Japan, the general insisted that the real conflict lay "between a system of free competitive enterprise . . . and a Socialism of one kind or another." The existing monopolies were actually a form of "socialism in private hands." By implication, then, MacArthur accused Draper and his group of supporting both Socialism and reaction.[17]

Responding to the Supreme Commander's visible pressure, the lower house of the Diet passed the deconcentration law late in November and sent it on to the upper chamber. Angrily, Army Secretary Royall accused MacArthur of promoting a redistribution scheme that went "beyond American philosophies" and threatened the basic "concept of private property." He demanded a delay in implementing the law (were it passed) so that a review board from Washington could oversee its application.[18]

William Draper responded to SCAP's audacity by orchestrating a public attack on MacArthur and deconcentration that began with *Newsweek*. He persuaded Harry F. Kern to devote part of the magazine's December 1, 1947, issue to a scathing critique of SCAP. The published account described Draper's struggle to prevent Japan from becoming a "permanent ward of the United States. . . ." Printing selections from both FEC 230 and Kauffman's report, *Newsweek* accused MacArthur of promoting programs "far to the left of anything now tolerated in America." The purge, reparations and deconcentration were all described at "lethal weapons" of socialism.*

A few days later, the president of Libby-Owens-Food Glass, John Biggers, discussed these issues with James Forrestal. Biggers, who knew Kauffman and had helped circulate his critique in Washington months earlier, expressed surprise that the administration had not squelched MacArthur's radical economic program. He also wanted help in having a Japanese employee of Libby-Owens "de-purged." Forrestal lamented that no one could make "MacArthur realize what [is] involved. . . ." SCAP seemed oblivious to both the dangers of the program and the need, should it pass, to "get some business people over there to administer the law. . . ." The whole situation, Forrestal complained, had been "scrambled" terribly by MacArthur.[19]

The administration's worst fears were realized on December 8, when the upper chamber of the Diet passed the deconcentration bill. Draper reacted by circulating a confidential memorandum he had just received purporting to describe SCAP's cynical political maneuvering. The information, passed to Draper by a "confidential" source in Tokyo, "Mr. Wm.

---

* MacArthur responded in kind a few months later when he labeled *Newsweek* correspondent Compton Packenham a "reactionary" element and barred him from reentering Japan. In March 1948, Army Secretary Royall reversed the order.

W.," portrayed MacArthur as vain, unscrupulous, and prepared to sacrifice Japan for his presidential ambitions.

"Mr. Wm. W" provided a firsthand account of how SCAP forced the Japanese government to approve the anti-*zaibatsu* program. He alleged that a radical antibusiness clique in SCAP (including Edward C. Welch, Theodore Cohen, Sherwood Fine, Irving Bush, Lester Salwin, and Col. William T. Ryder) presented a draft bill to Social Democratic Prime Minister Katayama Tetsu in July. Because the Social Democrats preferred to nationalize rather than dissolve the *zaibatsu*, Katayama opposed the bill. Speaking through intermediaries, MacArthur not only refused to meet with the prime minister but warned him to avoid future "insulting" behavior. Unless the government acted quickly, SCAP "would not be so kind in the future."

Just before the upper chamber considered the deconcentration law, General Marquat's aide, Colonel Ryder, passed another warning to the prime minister. The law, he declared, must "be passed so as not to embarrass" MacArthur who "expected to be nominated for President." The general did not care about enforcing the law, Ryder claimed, only that there "be no sign to the world of dissension" in Japan. That would tarnish his image and "prejudice the future of Japan when the Supreme Commander became President."

As if this were not damning enough, the informant also claimed MacArthur lied to influential American conservatives about his role. In late November or December, he met with a pair of prominent executives from Northwest Airlines ("Hunter and Stern"), one of whom sat on the Republican National Committee. MacArthur said he had "nothing to do with the reforms" mandated by FEC 230. All the radical proposals came from Washington. He was a "proponent of capitalism, but the men under him . . . well, he could not do anything about it, because Washington Democratic Reds sent them. . . ." These lies, Draper's informant wrote, were the "forerunner of the destruction of the capitalist system . . . and would ruin the very democracy that you and I fought for."[20]

British diplomat Sir Alvary Gascoigne also commented on MacArthur's manipulation of his position for domestic political gain. During December, he tried to use Gascoigne to leak information critical of both his Democratic and Republican opponents. The general claimed that he, unlike the cowardly Truman, would have taken military action to save China. As for Thomas E. Dewey and Robert A. Taft, the two leading Republican presidential contenders, MacArthur dismissed them as "very shopworn" and "provincial." When he suggested that a "dark horse," perhaps a military man might be nominated, Gascoigne asked if he meant Gen. Dwight D. Eisenhower. Obviously furious at the suggestion, MacArthur attacked his former aide's character, politics, and heritage. Eisenhower should not be considered either presidential or even a "good Republican" as he had the contamination of "Jewish blood in his veins." Although coy about his ambition, MacArthur told told Gascoigne that if, "by chance" his own name was put forward, "he as a good citizen would accept the nomination."[21] *

State Department officials appeared flabbergasted by these events. Unsure of how to handle MacArthur, they suggested that Draper issue a statement endorsing *zaibatsu* dissolution, praising SCAP, and announcing that the reform agenda had been completed. This, possibly, might assuage MacArthur and blunt his drive to enforce deconcentration. But Draper preferred a direct approach, such as issuing a statement stressing that serious, conflicting "opinions and judgements" existed among Americans about how to reform the Japanese economy. Instead of holding fast to an initial program, future actions must take careful account of Japan's new place within the "ever changing world situation."[22]

Draper also resolved to bring intense congressional pressure on MacArthur, who had been largely immune from political attack. He got Harry Kern to forward a copy of FEC 230 to Sen. William F. Knowland (R–California). For months, Draper had cultivated Knowland by drafting a program for credits to make California's large cotton surplus available to Japanese textile mills. After receiving the technically classified FEC 230 proposal, Knowland took the Senate floor to denounce it.

Without attacking MacArthur by name, the senator accused the "doctrine set forth in FEC 230" of resembling proposals by the "government of the U.S.S.R. or even by the labor government of Great Britain. . . ." Knowland charged an anonymous clique, either in Washington or Tokyo, with devising radical schemes that MacArthur had "no choice" but to carry out. Ironically, he pointed a ritual finger at the State Department as the primary culprit promoting the "most socialistic" ideas "ever attempted outside Russia." But Knowland also threatened to investigate other government agencies as well, an implied threat against SCAP.

Several members of the House of Representatives followed Knowland's lead by demanding an "investigation of the secret rule of Japan by confidential State Department directives to the Far Eastern Commission." This policy, they charged, was "bringing socialism to the former enemy nation." Simultaneosly, conservative newspapers like the *Chicago Tribune* and the

---

* Ironically, Eisenhower had returned from an October 1947 visit to Tokyo with a warning for President Truman. According to James Forrestal, MacArthur revealed to Ike his plan to leave Japan in 1948 to launch a presidential campaign. On the other hand, Truman remarked wryly, "another visitor to Tokyo had brought him a message warning . . . that Eisenhower would be a candidate. . . ." See Forrestal diary, October 6, 1947.

Washington Times-Herald attacked MacArthur indirectly through their criticism of administration policy. The economic reform program, the *Tribune* claimed, was solely an effort to "New Dealize Japan." The *Times-Hearld* protested that "if a bunch of New Deal socialists or semi-socialists have framed up a socialist future for Japan with everybody sharing the poverty and no big, efficient, privately owned industries permitted to exist—we should all know about it." The *San Francisco Chronicle* denounced FEC 230 and called for assurance that the reform policy would not get "anywhere." Numerous other newspapers voiced satisfaction that the American people had finally begun to receive valid information about Japan, "not merely the official account of what goes on" as decreed by "General MacArthur's command."[23]

Building on the momentum provided by Knowland's attack, Army Secretary Kenneth Royall delivered a major statement on Japan to the Commonwealth Club of San Francisco on January 6, 1948. Following a line of argument suggested by Draper, Royall explained that America had willingly assumed the burden of defeating Japan, punishing aggression, and promoting a host of needed, democratic reforms. Actions already taken had proved so successful, he boasted, that the power of the *zaibatsu* was "virtually abolished." Hereafter, the United States faced the challenge of creating a "self-supporting economy" no longer dependent on "hundreds of millions of dollars" to survive. Admittedly, this new "economic approach" led to "inevitable" conflict between the "original concept of broad demilitarization" and the new goal of "building a self-supporting nation."

Quickly, Royall debunked nearly every tenet of the original Occupation program. Destroying "synthetic rubber or shipbuilding or chemical or nonferrous metal plants" did more damage to "peace potential" than to war potential, he claimed. "Extreme deconcentration," must cease before it wrecked the entire economy. Japan could not "support itself as a nation of shopkeepers and craftsmen and small artisans" but had to increase "mass industrial production."

Royall called on Americans to face the facts:

> The men who were the most active in building up and running Japan's war machine—militarily and industrially—were often the ablest and the most successful business leaders of that country, and their services would in many instances contribute to the economic recovery of Japan.

The army secretary then confirmed that deconcentration and reparations were being "re-examined," even though this aroused strong "differences of opinion" among American officials. Henceforth, the United States would build a Japan "strong and stable enough to support itself and at the same time . . . serve as a deterrent against any other totalitarian war threat which might hereafter arise in the Far East." With a rhetorical flourish, Royall transformed Japan from a defeated enemy into the guardian of American interests in East Asia.

Ten days later, Royall sent Congress a draft bill requesting funds for "economic rehabilitation of occupied areas [EROA]." The new program would go well beyond humanitarian relief, granting the army authority to finance industrial recovery and raw material imports. All the relevant government agencies, the army secretary emphasized, supported this departure.[24]

When asked for his endorsement, however, MacArthur stunned both the army and members of Congress by lecturing them on economic history. He recounted how Japan's industrialization depended on control of resources in Formosa, Manchuria, and Korea. All this had been lost since 1945. Nevertheless, he stated, under SCAP's guidance "amazing strides" had been made toward industrial "rehabilitation and recovery. . . ." MacArthur attributed much of the success to mandated structural reforms. He continued:

> "Traditionally [a people] exploited into virtual slavery by an oligarchic system of economic feudalism under which a few Japanese families directly or indirectly, have controlled all of the commerce and industry and raw materials of Japan, the Japanese are rapidly freeing themselves of these structures to clear the road for the establishment here of a more competitive enterprise—to release the long suppressed energies of the people toward the building of that higher productivity of a society which is free.[25]

The renewed stress on the anti-*zaibatsu* program, provoked William Knowland and other senators to raise new questions about the goals of economic policy in Japan. In fact, Draper, Royall, and Forrestal probably encouraged Knowland to resume his attack in the hope of embarrasing a politically vulnerable MacArthur. In his remarks of January 19, Knowland again denounced deconcentration as a "socializing trend." Although still offering some ritual praise of MacArthur's military prowess, the senator remarked that the military phase of the Occupation had ended "months ago." Recovery demanded that new talent replace the "doctrinaire New Dealers" in SCAP who "found their activities limited in Washington and signed up for overseas occupation service. . . ."[26]

The erosion of MacArthur's position convinced the State Department to cast its lot with Draper. Early in January 1948, W. W. Butterworth decided to support the army's version of the recovery program, even though this meant a break with the Far Eastern Commission. Butterworth thought much of the civilian-military impasse reflected a fixation on semantics rather than a "serious matter of substance." In any case, he informed his aides, Japan would have to recover through the "normal operation of merchant greed," not the idealistic reforms favored by some Americans. If necessary, the United States would "ride roughshod over the other FEC [Far Eastern Commission] countries."[27]

Following Butterworth's lead, state and army representatives arranged a compromise over the wording of SWNCC 384. Assistant Army Secretary Gordon Gray told the conferees that however they worded it, Congress needed evidence of a "shift in emphasis" before it would appropriate new funds. On January 21, 1948, after softening provocative phrasing, the committee approved the unilateral recovery program. The next day, both MacArthur and the Far Eastern Commission were notified that the United States intended to make Japan self-sufficient through the "early revival of the Japanese economy." Industrial growth and foreign trade would be encouraged so that Japan could make its "proper contribution to the economic rehabilitation of the world economy. . . ."[28]

A few weeks later, Draper dropped the other shoe by releasing a report on Japanese industry prepared by Clifford Strike's engineering firm, Overseas Consultants Incorporated (OCI). In his second study for the army, Strike expanded on an earlier warning that reparations would cripple Japan. Although still agreeing that "primary war industries" should be destroyed, OCI decided that most heavy industry previously defined as "war supporting," should be exempt from reparations. These included twelve basic categories, such as pig iron, steel, machine tools, ball bearing, and chemicals. In essence, the OCI report rejected the spirit and letter of the Pauley reparations program by concluding that little, if any, "excess capacity" existed. At most, Strike's group recommended that reparations totaling 172 million (prewar) yen be taken from "war supporting" facilities. This comprised less than a fifth of levels considered feasible by SWNCC a few months earlier and was only a tiny fraction of what Pauley envisioned. The OCI group defended these changes as required to achieve two essential ends: the reduction of "costs to the American taxpayer" and the "reconstruction and use as quickly as possible [of] the bulk of [Japan's] industrial capacity."[29]

The approval of SWNCC 384 and the release of the OCI report revealed the determination in Washington to "shift emphasis" as rapidly as possible. But instead of acquiescing, MacArthur redoubled his public opposition to the altered national policy. On February 1, 1948, the general responded by letter to questions raised by senators William Knowland, Brien McMahon, and Bourke Hickenlooper. He refuted their attacks on his economic policy (and sought to shift any blame) by charging that whatever SCAP did was "limited to the execution and implementation" of Washington's directives. "I am hardly in a position," he wrote, "ten thousand miles away to participate in the debate" over Japan's future.

But, of course, the general intended precisely that. He first tried to shift responsibility onto the shoulders of the administration for the genesis of the deconcentration program. Then, he launched into a spirited attack on the "traditional economic pyramid" that gave a "few Japanese families direct or indirect control over all commerce and industry, all raw materials. . . ." SCAP had done nothing more radical than to attempt the demolition of that pyramid in order to build a democratic society and free enterprise system. If the United States abandoned this program, he warned, "there is no slightest doubt that its cleansing will eventually occur through a bloodbath of revolutionary violence."[30]

By justifying his policy as the main barrier to revolution, MacArthur tried, in effect, to turn the tables on his enemies. The same day, he issued a public letter to a group of American citizens, recounting (in words similar to those of early statements by the State and War departments) how the *zaibatsu* were responsible for "economic exploitation at home and aggression and spoilation abroad." So long as these giants existed, he wrote, they comprised a "standing bid for state ownership and a fruitful target for Communist propaganda and collectivist purposes." Unless SCAP acted on their behalf, the Japanese themselves would act "through the violence of revolutionary means" after the Americans left.[31]

But the final provocation, so far as the administration saw it, came later in February when the deconcentration law took effect. The HCLC mandated by it possessed authority to order the dissolution or reorganization of both the *zaibatsu* and their major subsidiaries. The HCLC promptly designated over three hundred companies, comprising over half of Japan's commerce and industry, for possible dissolution as "excessive concentrations of economic power." Financial institutions were anticipated as the next targets. Appalled by this action, the State and Defense departments' leadership resolved to throttle MacArthur. From this point on, they viewed the Supreme Commander as the greatest single danger to Japan's security.

7

SETTING
A NEW COURSE

Reflecting on the event years later, George Kennan wrote that besides the Marshall Plan, setting the "reverse course" in Japan was "the most significant contribution I was ever able to make in government." Except for the one other case, he never made "recommendations of such scope and impact" and on "no other occasion" did his proposals "meet with such wide, indeed almost complete, acceptance." Working together with Army Under Secretary William H. Draper, Jr., Kennan disposed of the anti-monopoly and reparations programs, prodded the president to limit SCAP's independence, helped steer a recovery package through Congress, and assured a conservative political hegemony within Japan.[1]

Because Japan, like Germany, formed a pivot of his ideas about recovery and containment, Kennan took an intense, personal interest in the decision to "shift emphasis." Having convinced leading figures in the administration that MacArthur had done "precisely what the Communists want," George C. Marshall selected Kennan to visit Tokyo to ascertain the "steps which can be taken now to speed Japanese recovery." His mission coincided with another led by William Draper. Together, their critique of SCAP policies effectively ended MacArthur's near unilateral control of Japan.

The secretary of state had jousted with MacArthur ever since their encounters during the First World War. A veteran, he tutored Kennan on how to assuage MacArthur's ego and suspicions. Marshall suggested that he ask the Supreme Commander first to expatiate on "our world strategy" and how Japan fit into it. After MacArthur completed his disquisition (which might take some time), Kennan could bring up the "considerations which we here had in mind." Marshall warned Kennan that MacArthur's aides were sycophants and vipers, ready to distort any offhand comment into a personal attack. Above all, Kennan ought to maintain a public facade of total approval, voicing criticisms only to the general in private.[2]

Before his departure, Kennan revealed how Japan fit into his security and economic schemes. In a PPS review of foreign policy, he called on the administration to accept the limits of American influence among the "Asiatic peoples." As they evolved politically they would reject liberalism and "fall for varying periods, under the influence of Moscow" whose ideology had a great appeal in poor areas. Consequently, Americans should abandon the "aspiration to be liked," should dispense with concerns about "human rights" or "living standards," and should "deal in straight power concepts." American security in Asia only required liquidating "unsound commitments in China," maintaining control of the offshore Pacific islands and harnessing the "economic potential" of a "truly friendly Japan."[3]

The deconcentration program, Kennan maintained, posed a greater threat to Japan than Soviet military power. Before departing, he insisted that the State Department notify other agencies and the Far Eastern Commission that the deconcentration policy did not reflect the "current views of the American government." As a result, the department ordered Far Eastern Commission delegate, Gen. Frank McCoy, to begin a "calculated policy of delay," preventing further consideration of the FEC 230 program and other issues still before the commission.[4]

Although Kennan and the State Department leadership tried to maintain a low, nonprovocative profile, the Defense Department and army civilians took steps certain to antagonize SCAP and, presumably, put MacArthur in his place. Army Under Secretary Draper's office leaked information to the United Press and the International News Service, which put out reports under leads such as "Drastic Change in Policy of U.S. Envisaged—Kennan Visits seen as Move to Build Up Japan as Anti-Red Bulwark." Other headlines described Japan's vital role in countering Red infiltration of Asia. The stories claimed Kennan would order MacArthur to hasten economic recovery and, perhaps, rebuild Japan's military power to create a new "bulwark against Soviet expansion in the Far East." The Truman administration, according to these reports, had abandoned all hope of stabilizing China and believed Japan must become the new center of economic and political resistance to communism in Asia. Although a bit exaggerated, it

was true that on February 24, Defense Secretary Forrestal ordered the
Army Department to prepare a study of the feasibility of "limited military
armaments for Germany and Japan." Forrestal wanted to know whether
the time had come to begin raising a small Japanese army for post-Occupation duties.[5]

Kennan's trip began inauspiciously with a grueling transpacific flight. On
landing in Tokyo, the diplomat and his Army Department companion,
Gen. C. V. R. Schuyler, were summoned to MacArthur's residence, where-
upon the general "turned his back" on Kennan and delivered a two-hour
monologue. "Thumping the table for emphasis with a single vertically held
finger," the Supreme Commander lectured Schuyler on the history of oc-
cupations since Caesar and his own crusade to bring democracy and Christianity to Japan. After satisfying himself and exhausting his audience, he
dismissed the two visitors.

Although infuriated by his treatment, Kennan recalled Marshall's advice.
Instead of complaining about his being foisted off the next day on a series
of minor SCAP officials, Kennan sent MacArthur a polite note requesting
a personal audience. He professed a desire to learn firsthand how the
general would protect Japan "from aggression" and sought MacArthur's
views on devising "an intensive program of economic recovery."[6]

The Supreme Commander responded immediately to this flattery by
setting up a private meeting. Knowing the general's views on Pacific strategy, Kennan announced his own belief that Japan's physical security could
be assured by American control of the Pacific island chain. MacArthur, of
course, agreed, adding that this offshore defense perimeter ought to stretch
in a U shape, embracing the "Aleutians, Midway, the former Japanese
mandated islands, Clark Field in the Philippines, and, above all, Okinawa."
From these bases, MacArthur said, he could use air and sea power to
control "every one of the ports of northern Asia from which an amphibious
operation could conceivably be launched." American control of this line
made it unnecessary to establish bases on the Asian mainland or Japan.[7]

A gap opened between the two men when Kennan referred to the economy. MacArthur denied any responsibility for economic problems in Japan.
The fault, instead, lay with all the other nations of Asia that discriminated
against Japanese exports. The only business leaders purged, he claimed,
were "elderly incompetents," the "counterparts of the most effete New
York club men." Nor, MacArthur insisted, was the deconcentration program as "extreme" as some argued. He blamed its questionable elements
on a few "academic theorizers of a left-wing variety at home and in Tokyo"
whom he intended to eliminate from SCAP. The general could not resist
telling Kennan that such unsavory types also stalked the corridors of the
State Department. In any case, MacArthur suggested that he would not
push the deconcentration program much further.

Kennan worked to win over the Supreme Commander by attacking his favorite villain, the Far Eastern Commission. The envoy suggested that both SCAP and the American government could justifiably ignore the commission on the grounds that it possessed authority to supervise only the initial surrender, not the subsequent administration of Japan. Now that the Occupation had entered a later stage, the Far Eastern Commission should be permitted to wither away. This pleased the general so much that he "slapped his thigh in approval" and told Kennan they had achieved a "meeting of the minds." To show his sincerity, MacArthur thereafter spared no effort in hosting Kennan, even supplying him with a private railway car.[8]

Probably, neither man fooled the other. Kennan felt nothing but contempt and loathing for nearly everything he saw in Tokyo. He wrote to W. W. Butterworth how he recoiled at the "stuffiness" and "degree of internal intrigue" around MacArthur, which reminded him of "nothing more than the latter days of the court of the Empress Catherine II, or possibly the final stages of the regime of Belisarius in Italy." SCAP functioned as a parasite, demonstrating a startling "American brand of Philistinism" and a "monumental imperviousness to the suffering and difficulties of the [Japanese]. The Americans in Tokyo "monopolized . . . everything that smacks of comfort or elegance or luxury." The "idleness and boredom" of the Occupation force contrasted with the "struggles and problems of a defeated and ruined country" filled Kennan with "despair." The "monotony of contemporary American social life, its unbending drinking rituals, the obvious paucity of its purposes, and its unimaginative devotion to outward convention in the absence of inner content or even enjoyment" seemed "pathetic" and destructive.

MacArthur's underlings and their "shrill cackling" wives behaved as if the war had been fought so that they might have "six Japanese butlers with the divisional insignia on their jackets" or so that "Miss Z might learn her skiing in the mountains of Hokkaido" at Japanese expense. "I know," Kennan lamented to Butterworth, that the army had fought hard and that "many of the Japs deserve a worse fate than to have the tastes and habits of American suburbia imposed upon them." But victory had no meaning without a proper peace and so far, to most Japanese, the American Occupation was not "intelligible."[9]

Although Kennan's complaints revealed the depth of his own alienation from American society and culture, he insisted that the idealistic reforms of 1945–47 had no basis in Japanese life. The nation would reject them like an infection once the Americans departed. Only the resilience of traditional conservative groups could protect Japan from an even more radical infection—communism—after the Occupation.

MacArthur's court, Kennan remarked, reminded him of nothing so much as the Kremlin under Stalin (both had a "fragile psychic quality"). He wanted badly to return to Washington with his report. However, he resolved to wait until March 22 in order to confer with Army Under Secretary William Draper, who was scheduled to arrive with a business delegation.

While cooling his heels over the next week, Kennan began to compose a report for the department. Here and in letters to Marshall and Butterworth, he complained that MacArthur and his entourage thought little about the future security of the Pacific and lacked any "over-all strategic concept." Little had been done to fortify Okinawa or other strong points on the island defense perimeter, he lamented. Although economic recovery would insure Japan's internal stability, it would have to rely on this island defense shield for external security. After taking a side trip to the Philippines, Kennan concluded that, aside from Japan, the United States had little in common with, and no obligations to, most Asians. The "vast Oriental world," he wrote to Butterworth, stood "far from any hope of adjustment to the requirements of an orderly and humane civilization." America, unfortunately, had nothing much to offer the "billions [of] pathetically expectant . . . oriental eyes."[10]

In Tokyo, Kennan began drafting what became PPS 28, a policy analysis completed three weeks later in Washington. In a densely packed forty-two page commentary, he condemned SCAP as a parasite gorging on Japan. It squandered nearly a third of the nation's budget while mandating destructive radical reform. With industry crippled by purges and threats of dissolution, Japan teetered on the brink of collapse. Considering these problems, Kennan declared, no responsible official could support a peace settlement. The problem required more aid and fewer experiments. Instead of imposing new rules, SCAP ought "steadily but unobtrusively [to] relax pressure" to enforce existing policies. The purge, reparations, deconcentration, war crimes trials—all the elements of the reform agenda—ought to be reviewed. Nothing should continue that "operated against the stability of Japanese society" or stood in the path of the "prime objective," economic recovery. Kennan favored turning as much authority as possible over to the Japanese government and establishing a central police force or small army to resist subversion. When the Soviets observed Japan's internal stability and the security provided by the Pacific base network, Kennan guessed Moscow would accept an accommodation with Tokyo.[11]

Kennan's efforts in Tokyo received powerful support from William Draper. The army under secretary had had been lobbying Congress on behalf of the recovery program and, especially, for a special revolving credit to supply raw American cotton to the textile industry. Testifying before the House Foreign Affairs Committee on March 5, he described the EROA program as "analogous to the so-called Marshall Plan for Western Europe." By encouraging production, it sought to reduce the long-term cost to the American taxpayer and enable Japan to stimulate the "economic revival of the Far East," just as Germany would do in Europe.*

As in Germany, Draper explained, defeat cut Japan off from its traditional foreign sources of supply and markets—Korea, China, Formosa, Southeast Asia, and so on. He considered it doubtful that Japan would ever sell enough to the United States to earn the dollars needed to pay for American raw materials. Thus, long-term recovery required Japanese access to nondollar sources of supply. "By starting the flow of essential raw materials and filling the pipeline" and by providing working capital and other assistance, Draper testified, EROA would lay the basis for a self-supporting Japan "no longer dependent on the United States. . . ." Rebuilding Japan, he told the committee, had priority over aiding the beleaguered Chinese Nationalists because its recovery, not China's, would stabilize the region and provide the "focal point in the whole recovery of the East from the effects of war."[12]

During early March, Draper completed arrangements to lead a business delegation to Tokyo. He expected its influential membership to spearhead an attack on "radical policies." The delegtion included Percy H. Johnston, chairman of the Chemical Bank and Trust Company, serving as nominal head; Paul G. Hoffman of Studebaker, who was soon to be appointed by Truman to administer the ERP; Robert F. Loree, chairman of the National Foreign Trade Council, and Sidney H. Scheuer, owner of a large textile firm. Draper made certain the group would issue a report that buttressed his "own recommendations to the President, and [that] the Secretary of State and the Congress . . . [would] change the instructions to MacArthur. . . ." They and he both agreed that Japan's economy, save for American charity, was a "morgue."[13]

Dreading Draper's visit, MacArthur "spoke most bitterly" to his friend Sir Alvary Gascoigne about "American tycoons," such as Forrestal, Royall, Draper, and Harriman, who opposed the purge and deconcentration "because they thought they would conflict with their own business interests." MacArthur claimed Draper had no authority to visit Japan and insisted he would not "accept orders" from a mere under secretary. The general again portrayed himself as an "international official" who could not be ordered about by a "purely American official."[14]

Draper quickly confirmed MacArthur's worst fears when the army official along with Kennan and General Schuyler met the Supreme Commander

---

* Originally, the ERP, China Aid Act, and EROA for Japan were lumped in one package. To expedite passage of the Marshall Plan, the administration prevailed on Congress to separate the Japan proposal.

on March 21, 1948. MacArthur exploded when Draper asked him to comment on Forrestal's proposal to establish a "small defense force for Japan" to be ready for the eventual departure of Occupation troops. He first tried to dismiss the notion as too hypothetical becuase no early treaty now seemed likely. The Soviet Union and Nationalist China, he complained, both wanted to weaken Japan to boost their own control in Northeast Asia. Still, MacArthur declared, the United States should try to line up other nations, "even if it should be necessary to exclude Russia," in preparation for a treaty. He hoped this strategy would convince the Soviets to participate. In any case, he cautioned, the Occupation could not really end until Washington and Moscow reached some sort of bilateral agreement.

As to the question of defense forces, MacArthur emphasized his belief that American troops were not actually vital for the physical defense of Japan. Rather, they sent a signal, to the Japanese and the rest of the world of "our refusal to permit forces of communism to make further advances in this country." Then, the Supreme Commander unleashed his feelings against Draper. He absolutely opposed replacing the current SCAP structure with a civilian American administration because, he claimed, the Japanese would only obey him. He attacked the idea of raising a Japanese army now or even after the Occupation, saying it would violate international agreements, undermine three years of reform, defy the Japanese constitution and public opinion, impose impossible costs on a shaky economy, and needlessly provoke the Soviet Union. Finally, a Japanese army served no possible military purpose because the stationing of American forces on the Pacific islands and Okinawa provided every conceivable level of security for both the United States and Japan.

MacArthur's intense feelings on this subject must have made an impression on both Draper and other army planners for they agreed, reluctantly, to confine a Japanese army to the planning stages for the time being but to augment police and coast guard forces. However, as their discussion progressed, the general and the army under secretary did establish one important point of agreement. Both (along with Kennan) had no use for the Pauley reparations program. They felt that Japan required "every tool, every factory and practically every industrial installation" it had at that time. Ridiculing the original reparations program as wasted charity for underserving Asians, the groups pledged to terminate the transfer scheme before it went any further.[15]

Except for this shared determination to jettison the reparations program, which MacArthur always considered outside meddling, Draper and his delegation devoted most of their efforts to undermining SCAP programs the general cherished. They conferred with numerous Japanese officials and many *zaibatsu* representatives whose operations were targeted for reorganization. Although their formal report did not appear until late April, they revealed most of their conclusions while still in Japan.

Newspaper accounts about the Draper-Johnston mission described their "businessman's solution to Japan's economic ills." The group "expressed themselves freely" to the effect that Japan must must be made economicaly self-sufficient as soon as possible. They accepted the testimony of corporate leaders that radical labor unions, reparations, the deconcentration law, and the purge must all be swept away. By scrapping controls and providing a half-billion dollars in new aid, they would assist the former enemy to reemerge as the "workshop of the Far East." Reportedly assuring business leaders that the bad times were over, Draper promised the Occupation would never again "go to extremes."[16]

The British government, always worried that the sudden reversals in American policy might endanger its own Asian interests, sought all the information it could gather about Draper mission. Eventually, embassy officials in Washington convinced one of Draper's aides (possibly Col. T. N. Depuy) to speak off the record. The informant explained that because military security depended as much on economic stability as armies, the United States wanted to prevent Japan from becoming so desperate that it "might throw her lot in with Russia." America would see to it that Japan had a "sound economy" to "enable her to look after herself and to take the present burden off the American taxpayer." Although never particularly enamored of MacArthur, the British expressed concern about his possible replacement, especially when *Newsweek*'s Harry F. Kern told an embassy staffer that he and other "influential persons would press for the appointment of Draper as Supreme Commander." Hubert Graves, who heard this, speculated how British interests would fare in Southeast Asia if the "former Vice-President of Dillon, Read & Co." took charge of Japan.[17]

When the formal report of the Johnston committee appeared on April 26, it confirmed many of these fears. It endorsed the goal of self-sufficiency by promoting Japan's access to Asian raw materials and export markets. It urged the elimination of most restrictions on production and the cancelation of reparations. To help achieve the needed ninefold increase in exports, the report called for an "eventual shift in Japanese food and other imports from the dollar area to the sterling and Far Eastern Areas," with payment made in Japanese industrial exports. Production was to be accelerated by the drastic relaxation of antimonopoly measures, placing severe curbs on organized labor, controlling inflation, fixing the yen's foreign exchange value, and discouraging domestic consumption in favor of exports.

Reparations were to be virtually eliminated. In 1946, Pauley called for removing industrial facilities valued in prewar yen at 990 million. The OCI group, in 1947, recommended transfers worth some 172 million prewar yen. But now, the Johnston committee proposed taking no more than 102 million prewar yen. Even more dramatically, the committee advocated retention of selected "primary war industries," formerly a taboo subject. Overall, the report would eliminate some 90 percent of proposed reparations in the heavy-industry category and 60 percent in the war-industry category.[18]

Almost simultaneously with the release of the Johnston report, Draper appointed and dispatched to Tokyo a Deconcentration Review Board (DRB). The army under secretary insisted that the panel possess the "broadest possible authority" to review the antimonopoly program and make the "final recommendations direct to General MacArthur on the specific application of the law to individual concerns." Army Secretary Royall told James Forrestal that the DRB would demonstrate that the deconcentration law would not be permitted to "interfere with the economic recovery of Japan."[19]

During May, the DRB quickly began to eliminate businesses from jeopardy under the new laws. It overturned or amended almost all the original 325 reorganization decrees issued by the liquidation commission. Plans to move against financial institutions were shelved. Although its members claimed that their actions signaled no "basic change" in policy, the actual standards imposed by the DRB made it nearly impossible to prove a monopoly existed. Edward C. Welsch, head of SCAP's Anti-Trust and Cartels Division, described the situation in these terms:

> What was initially considered . . . a major objective of the Occupation [had] become . . . a major embarrassment. . . . Without formally questioning the desirability or broad pruposes of the policy, it was decided to take measures which would minimize the actions prepared for carrying out the policy. Facts of the last war faded . . . and conjectures on the next war took their place.[20]

Despite his harsh, personal, attacks on Draper, MacArthur appeared to have lost either the will or the ability to fight for his program. For one thing, the general's political star fell swiftly during the spring. On March 9, 1948, he had finally declared his willingness to accept the presidential nomination. With "due humility," he described his willingness to save the country in its "hour of momentous import, national and international, spiritual and temporal. . . ." His subsequent press releases emphasized the title, Supreme Commander, perhaps to suggest that he already outranked Truman, the Commander-in-Chief.

The drama aside, MacArthur's campaign floundered quickly. With no coherent program and little organization (outside of a few wealthy, ultraconservative patrons), his campaign generated little enthusiasm. On the eve of the vital Wisconsin primary, that state's junior senator, Republican Joe McCarthy, attacked him as a tired old man, tainted by personal misconduct (a divorce), and long out of touch with the nation. Defeat in Wisconsin led to further losses that spring. At the Republican convention in June, MacArthur received only seven first-ballot votes, all of which soon deserted him in favor of Thomas Dewey.[21]

Both MacArthur's supporters and opponents within SCAP observed the erosion of the general's influence in Washington. Guy Swope, for example, left SCAP's Government Section in the spring of 1948 expecting to be snapped up by the Economic Cooperation Administration (ECA) or some other foreign aid agency. Instead, he reported to his former colleagues, service in Japan "aroused very little interest" and much hostility among the ECA, State Department, and other groups. Once he revealed his SCAP background, the "high command" in Washington labeled him one of the "small group of long haired boys . . . who have helped General MacArthur put over his socialistic schemes and was blackballed for that reason." Not only the Democrats but the Republicans, too, Swope wrote, were planning to "force MacArthur out." To an equal degree, both Dewey, Truman, and the "powerful American interests" were "plenty sore at the Big Chief" for what they considered his "drastic" economic directives.[22]

With MacArthur's power down, if not out, William Draper pushed the EROA aid program and other matters through Congress. In complicated maneuvering that involved partisan debate over foreign aid funding levels, the House Appropriations Committee moved to shorten the program from fifteen to twelve months, reducing spending from about $180 million to $144 million. Fearful that Congress might actually adjourn without approving anything, Draper had the administration reintroduce the EROA package as part of the broader GARIOA program. Things became more confused when the Bureau of the Budget sought to impose a $150 million cap on EROA, and opponents of the ERP insisted that any funds for Japan be subtracted from European aid appropriations.[23]

Draper worked to break this logjam in two ways. First he released the Johnston report to Congress and the public, providing assurances thereby that new aid would not be squandered on "radical reforms." Then, he began speaking of a Communist threat to America's "key" Far Eastern bastion. In a widely publicized address delivered in San Francisco, the army under secretary compared Japan to Germany and emphasized that its security depended on economic recovery and foreign trade. EROA would both reduce huge Occupation costs and assure that "democracy will find good soil in which to grow and in which those philosophies and ideologies which thrive upon hunger and confusion will lose their appeal."[24]

Following extended debate, Congress funded both the ERP and, on June 20, a slightly trimmed EROA aid package. EROA for Japan, Korea, and the Ryukyus totaled $125 million. But because it formed one part of the much larger GARIOA program (PL 793), the army had some discretion in shifting funds between the $422 million Japan-GARIOA budget and the smaller Japan-EROA budget. Draper augmented this still further by capping months of intensive lobbying for a cotton credits bill. Congress passed PL 820, establishing a revolving fund for the purchase of American cotton by Japanese mills. With exports of finished textiles slated to repay the fund, the program constituted a new source of foreign exchange earnings.[25]

During the following six months, prodded relentlessly by William Draper and George Kennan, the administration extended control over Occupation policy. As Kennan steered a new strategic agenda through the national security bureaucracy, Draper expanded his campaign to unleash Japanese industry by promoting an export-oriented economy. By the end of 1948, President Truman approved these programs, which formed the outline of a new Japan.

Kennan pressed his staff to rework his impressions of Japan into a formal document for governmentwide adoption. Submitted to the NSC on June 2, as NSC 13, it codified the ideas put forward by both State Department and Defense Department planners. Proclaiming economic recovery the "prime objective," it touted economic growth and political stability over a quick peace settlement or social reform. NSC 13 proposed to halt further destabilizing reforms, to curb the power of organized labor, and called for greater efforts by SCAP and the Japanese government to promote both industrial discipline and production for export.

Pointing out that few Americans yet agreed on how to insure future Japanese security, Kennan's staff urged postponing any decision to either rearm the old enemy or to insist on post-Occupation bases. When treaty negotiations actually began, a solution appropriate to current political conditions could be devised. Rather than trying to bully the Russians with the spectre of Japanese power, Kennan preferred to use the base issue as a bargaining chip. Because he doubted the Soviets planned to attack a reasonably stable Japan, the nation's security could be assured through domestic recovery and maintenance of an American defense network along the Pacific island perimeter. If these two factors were present, neither large Japanese nor American forces would be needed to defend the home islands. In fact, Kennan often warned, a preemptive move to rearm Japan or develop its offensive capacity in alliance with the United States would scuttle the chances for an eventual deal with Moscow.

On the questions of rearmament and bases, major differences developed with military planners. Accepting some of MacArthur's points about the costs and dubious value of rebuilding a Japanese army, the Army Department agreed to defer any immediate decision. Planning should proceed, however, and internal security forces, such as the police, should be recentralized. (Kennan concurred on this.) But, in any case, top army planners were not primarily concerned with the assistance Japanese forces could render in time of war. What mattered most was simply denying Japan to the Soviet Union and utilizing Japanese territory for offensive air attacks against the enemy. Thus, preserving control of post-Occupation base facilities loomed as a major issue dividing State Department and Defense Department planners.[26]

Eager to obtain Commonwealth support for this approach, Kennan and Butterworth conferred several times with British Under Secretary for Foreign Affairs, M. E. Dening. Although generally sympathetic, Dening worried that an unduly resurgent Japan might displace British interests in Southeast Asia. Dismissing this concern, the Americans argued that because current policy practically invited a Soviet breakthrough in Asia, the United States had no choice but to restore Japan's economy as fully as possible. Overlooking British fears (and that of most Asians) about resurgent militarism, Kennan compared the Occupation's reforms to the "softening up" pushed in "Soviet Occupied countries in Europe." Regardless of international concern, the United States would emphasize "stability as opposed to uncertainty."[27]

W. W. Butterworth explained to Dening and his aides that Washington would not rush into a peace treaty while Moscow held "the key to raw materials and fishing areas in Northeast Asia" which were critically needed for Japan's recovery. Dening lamented that American officials considered the United States the "sole power which can insure security in the Far East" and that all its allies should be "satisfied with any measures they think appropriate." Sometime later, Butterworth responded to British misgivings by saying that although London might not be thrilled with the State Department's recovery program, alternative proposals by the "Army extremists" would disregard completely Commonwealth interests and boost Japan even more.[28]

During the autumn, William Draper spread the same message among influential business and trade groups. In a speech to the Council on Foreign Relations, for example, he reported that, in light of the Communist sweep through China, Japan was the "logical stopping place for Russian aggression." Apart from other considerations, it was "definitely in America's interest to rebuild the Japanese economy." Two weeks later, on November 9, Draper again compared Japan to Germany and thanked his audience (the National Foreign Trade Council) for helping to bring about a change in Occupation policy. American forces would stay in Japan, he reported, until the world had "stabilized" and "economic health and well-being" had been regained.[29] On July 26, a National Foreign Trade Council delegation, including representatives of General Electric, ITT, and other large corporations, called on Army Department and State Department officials. They denounced SCAP, the economic reform programs, and the purge, complaining that MacArthur had sacrificed the "best managerial brains" in Japan. The group's head, Robert Loree, who had accompanied Draper to Japan, urged the president to take charge and to "reassure the Japanese industrialists and give them the confidence . . . to go ahead." Loree demanded that SCAP's power be turned over to the Japanese.[30]

Although General MacArthur still insisted that the State and Army departments lacked authority to alter such things as the purge and deconcentration program, many of his actions belied his tone. Over the next eighteen months, he frequently delayed or amended initiatives from Washington but ultimately gave in. Moreover, despite his rhetoric about holding true to the original Occupation program, during the summer of 1948 he, too, moved forcefully to the Right. SCAP began to act against left-wing political and labor groups, promoted industrial "discipline," and initiated a new purge against "radicals" within its own organization.[31]

A member of the British liaison mission in Tokyo, with the unlikely name of Ivan Pink, provided some of the most graphic accounts of the "almost hysterical" anti-Communist "witch hunt" begun in Japan. During the summer, he reported, both the English-language and Japanese press carried a "steadily increasing volume" of anti-Communist material, reflecting the "obsession" in SCAP's general headquarters. The "communist menace" had replaced "facism and militarism" as "enemies of the Occupation." Pink reported to London that Gen. Charles A. Willoughby's Counter-Intelligence Corps (CIC) propagated the panic. With "teutonic rigidity" (Willoughby spent his early childhood in Germany), American officers "look left . . . and fail to look right because no one has told them to." The Japanese played up to this fixation and the more enthusiastically the CIC responded to their reports, the more right-wing informants scrambled to "collect every scrap of information they could find [or invent] on this subject." Eventually, Japanese officials realized they could use the Red menace as an excuse to stall SCAP or wring from it desired decisions.[32]

Pink and one of his colleagues, L. Col. John Figgess, described the situation on Hokkaido, cited by Americans as a "hotbed of communist activity." British diplomats had traveled extensively on the island and found much labor activity but none of the violence and anarchy described by SCAP officials. Even though the railway unions were among the nation's most radical, the trains, Pink noted tartly, "were running on time." The real trouble, according to Figgess, came from the fact that the CIC considered any assertive union activity a Communist threat. The idea that "strikers" might have legitimate grievances was deemed "not worthy of consideration." Thus, they reported all political and labor protests as "communist agitation." MacArthur and his conservative Japanese allies, Figgess concluded, played up the Communist threat as an excuse for all unsolved problems and a justification for upgrading Japan's "future role."[33]*

Even as Draper and Kennan called for greater labor discipline, SCAP began its own assault on organized labor. For several months, rising prices and food shortages had led to a growing tide of demonstrations, strikes, and other job actions. The well-organized and highly politicized government workers' unions played a central role in the movement. In addition to white-collar employees, their membership included the blue-collar workers of such public enterprises as the railroads, communications, tobacco monopoly, and so on. General MacArthur followed the advice of Gen. Courtney Whitney and his aide, Blaine Hoover, of SCAP's Government Section, in stripping all these workers of their right to strike or bargain collectively. Despite objections from James Killen, his Labor Division chief, MacArthur passed this order to Prime Minister Ashida on July 22, 1948.

In a long, rambling letter, the general ordered revision of the national public service law. Quoting FDR, but evoking Calvin Coolidge, MacArthur condemned public employees for impeding the "efficiency of governmental operations" and blamed strikers for trying to "subvert the public interest" on behalf of a minority interested in "anarchy, insurrection, and destruction." The Ashida cabinet responded by issuing a special ordinance on July 30 forbidding strikes and labor agitation by government employees, pending formal Diet amendment of the public service law. When the Communist party and many unions protested this action by staging walkouts and rallies, SCAP encouraged the Japanese government to arrest strikers, labor organizers, and Communist activists.[34]

Virtually all Far Eastern Commission members, including the British, condemned his action. When Sir Alvary Gascoigne brought an official protest to General MacArthur, the Supreme Commander, he reported to London, "shout[ed] at me without stopping for one and three-quarter hours." In a meeting that Gascoigne characterized as his most "painful . . . duty in Japan," MacArthur accused the British Commonwealth nations

---

* The U.S. Army's 1948 estimate of Communist strength presented a much less threatening picture. Hard core party membership stood at around fifteen thousand, with some seventy thousand close supporters—out of an eighty million population. The Communist newspaper *Akahata* boasted of one hundred thousand party members. Many more Japanese voted Communist, of course, but were not organized along violent lines.

of siding "with the Kremlin" and "betraying" the United States. Henceforth, the general declared, the Commonwealth delegate to the ACJ ought to quit assisting the Soviet plot to "corrupt labor . . . and cause disruption and chaos." In the future, MacArthur shouted, the man ought to "keep his mouth shut."[35]

In October, in the wake of a huge bribery scandal, Japanese politics lurched further to the Right following the collapse of the centrist Ashida cabinet. The leader of the conservative Democratic Liberal party, Yoshida Shigeru, formed a new government and by November 30 pushed the revised public service legislation through the Diet. MacArthur applauded the new law as a way to break the "spell" exercised over workers by a "licentious minority" and Communist influence. The limitations on union power, he insisted, preserved the "integrity of representative governments over those who would leave government easy prey to minority subjugation."

In the wake of these upheavals, the Social Democratic party fractured into rightist and leftist factions and Yoshida's conservative forces emasculated the most active and articulate element of the labor movement. Encouraged by SCAP's endorsement of police and legal assaults on public service unions, private sector employers began to crack down on their own labor adversaries. During the next eighteen months, "radical" labor federations were confronted by a host of legal, political, and organizational challenges, including moves by the AFL–CIO to sponsor anti-Communist Japanese offshoots. In private, MacArthur boasted, the revised public service law deserved credit for breaking the power of radical labor, for splitting the Socialist party, and for giving business a tool to control workers.[36]

As the year wore on, the State and Defense departments also moved to bury the remnants of the reparations program. Although virtually no one still believed in the principal of industrial transfers, some State Department officials feared an abrupt cancelation of the program would provoke Asian nations to retaliate against Japanese trade. Charles Saltzman and Willard Thorp, assistant secretaries of state, as well as W. W. Butterworth sought some compromise falling midway between the Pauley and Johnston recommendations. Saltzman suggested to the army that a nominal program be continued, allowing SCAP "strictly [to] limit the amount" that could be taken. After a time, the United States could simply declare the program terminated, leaving the bulk of industry intact. Even MacArthur, Kenneth Royall informed George Marshall in July, had endorsed the Johnston committee's proposed slash of reparations levels. With SCAP on board, Royall declared, he and Marshall should meet and consummate an agreement.[37]

In October, after the NSC finally approved NSC 13 (amended as NSC 13/2 on October 7 and signed by the president two days later), Secretary of State Marshall asked George Kennan to work out a final compromise with William Draper. In a quick agreement reached October 28, the two men settled on a reparations level approximating the army's position. Relying on the findings of the Johnston report, they resolved to permit only a trickle of reparations to continue, and that for only a few months longer. Substantial transfers were all but prohibited by empowering SCAP to impose a strict policy of setting tight delivery schedules and assessing high transportation costs for claimants. In addition, MacArthur could order blanket exemptions for many heavy-industrial and primary-war facilities. As expected, few Asian states could meet the announced timetables, provide transportation, or absorb service charges assessed by SCAP. China, wracked by civil war, could take almost nothing. By May 1949, the United States announced that the time during which removals could be taken had lapsed and declared the program "successfully terminated."[38]

Truman's endorsement of NSC 13/2, the winding down of the Occupation's initial economic reforms, and the implicit curb on MacArthur's powers, put Draper in a position to implement his larger goals for Japan. For several months, the ideas of an army economic adviser, Ralph (Rex) W. E. Reid, had caught Draper's attention. Before becoming the army under secretary's chief economic aide, Reid had worked for SCAP and developed a deep suspicion of MacArthur's program. He worried that revolutionary movements in Asia made Japan dangerously dependent on American raw materials and that recovery could be achieved only by integrating Japan into a regional program. For EROA to work, he informed Draper, general assistance to the Pacific and Southeast Asia had to be extended "in an integrated fashion" that shifted the "sources of Japanese imports from dollar to non-dollar areas." Reid called for authorities in Japan to allocate raw materials in ways that promoted export production over domestic consumption, limited social welfare spending, and compelled workers to accept a reduction in living standards and wages. These actions, he believed, would permit Japan to reestablish itself as the industrial hub of the Asian economy. Not only would this insure economic recovery, it would also promote political and military stability over a wide region.[39]

Draper parlayed Reid's recommendations into a formal directive for the president's consideration. Working in conjunction with the State Department, he composed a decree ordering MacArthur and the Japanese government to take "whatever measures may be required . . . to achieve fiscal, monetary, price and wage stability in Japan and to maximize production for export." It mandated a balanced internal budget, speedier tax collection, limits on government credit, wage and price controls, and the allocation of scarce raw materials on a priority basis to maximize export production. It also authorized SCAP to establish a single foreign exchange rate for the yen, replacing the multitiered system used in foreign trade.

Acting Secretary of State Robert Lovett gave the directive his "full sup-port" and signed a "memorandum of understanding" that pledged both departments to share information on orders sent to MacArthur and to monitor his compliance with them.[40]

For practically the first time since the surrender, Harry Truman used his authority directly to mandate a policy for Japan. Following up on his October 9 approval of NSC 13/2, the President issued a nine point stabi-lization directive. Using the draft supplied by Draper, Truman's December 10, 1948, order announced appointment of a special emissary to oversee the Japanese economy. Joseph Dodge, a Detroit banker who had worked with Draper on German monetary reform before becoming head of the American Bankers Association, would now assist MacArthur. Although Dodge initially declined the appointment, he accepted after Truman called him to the White House and emphasized his full support for the program.[41]

Typically, MacArthur revealed several reactions to the initiative from Washington. In a series of angry cables during December, the general denounced the form and substance of both NSC 13/2 and the stabilization directive. MacArthur professed outrage that Draper had "informally" ap-prised him of these policy shifts. Such orders, he insisted, must come to him formally, as "interim directives," issued by the JCS. MacArthur com-plained that *Newsweek* had received more authoritative word of the policy shifts than had SCAP. Even when the JCS dispatched the required "interim directive," MacArthur was not appeased. The stabilization program, he warned, would wreck the economy, reward the *zaibatsu*, and undermine "many of the fundamental rights and liberties heretofore extended to labor and other segments of Japanese society" under the Occupation. Faced by an assault on their living standards and rights, workers would become susceptible to Communist influence and "explosive consequences may well result."[42]

MacArthur launched a similar tirade against NSC 13/2, telling Draper the new policy, although authorized by the President, did not apply to him. As "Supreme Allied Commander," he declared, international agree-ments made in 1945 dictated that on issues not primarily related to the status of American forces, he was bound by decisions of the Far Eastern Commission. In a remarkable about face toward two powerless organs he had long despised, MacArthur claimed that the Far Eastern Commission and the ACJ were "constantly alert to any action even remotely violative of FEC policy decisions or which might lay the basis for impeachment before the several governments concerned of SCAP's stewardship of his international authority." Being "subject solely" to these commissions, MacArthur informed Draper, he had no responsibility "in any way for its

[NSC 13/2] implementation or for any form of report which might imply SCAP responsibility for its implementation."[43]

State and Army officials recognized this defiance as a profound challenge to both the reverse course and, more importantly, to presidential authority. MacArthur's move to cloak himself in the mantle of "international" authority also raised troubling complications for Washington. However, the representatives of the two departments guessed, correctly, that a united front within the administration and Truman's personal endorsement of the Dodge stabilization mission, would, eventually, force MacArthur to back off.[44]

Despite his fury over lost prerogatives, General MacArthur actually accepted many elements of the reverse course. For example, even while denouncing the stabilization decree and NSC 13/2, he informed Prime Minister Yoshida that he would enforce their provisions. Neither left-wing labor or political agitation would be permitted to block the new program. To boost exports and balance the costs of imported raw materials, he told Yoshida, all labor and political activity would be "subordinated to a primary purpose common to all of the people." Japan had no choice but to accept "increased austerity in every phase of . . . life" and to "surrender" some of the privileges and immunities inherent in a free society." MacArthur promised to "curb" any attempt to interfere with the "acceleration of production." He also warned: unless the stabilization program is successful, "Japan may perish."[45]

Joseph Dodge established warm ties to several of MacArthur's most severe critics before his February 1949 arrival in Tokyo. In addition to his record of close cooperation with Draper in Germany, Dodge knew journalist Harry Kern and other members of the anti-SCAP network. Six months earlier, Kern, James Lee Kauffman, Compton Packenham, and Eugene Dooman organized a lobbying organization called the American Council for Japan. Composed of some two dozen journalists, business leaders, reitred diplomats and military officers, this "Japan lobby" worked hard to alter Occupation policies.[46]

Just before his departure for Tokyo, Kern gave Dodge a report on "Japanese policy" prepared by the Council members. It denounced SCAP as inefficient, corrupt, and radical. MacArthur, allegedly, had destroyed the "very individuals and classes" who supported America and permitted the Communists free reign. Instead of relying on conservative business, political, and military groups, SCAP cultivated a "bureaucratic, inefficient, dictatorial, vindictive and at times corrupt" administration. The Japanese had grown so disillusioned, Kern's report warned, they might "turn to the only alternative to Western democracy in the World today—Communism."

Dodge thought well enough of this critique to make the report required reading for his assistants.[47]

Kern had another ally in high circles by late 1948. He recommended Gen. Robert L. Eichelberger (who had recently retired from commanding the Eighth Army in Japan) for a position in Draper's office. Unlike most of MacArthur's "inner circle," Eichelberger maintained his psychological independence and objectivity throughout the war years and his service in Japan. The army under secretary hired Eichelberger to work with Tracy Voorhees, the new assistant secretary of the army. The retired general, an in-house critic of SCAP policy, served as liaison between the American Council for Japan and the Army Department.[48]

The American Council for Japan demonstrated its informal influence on policy when Kern arranged a reception for high-ranking Army Department and State Department officials. On February 5, Harry Kern informed William Draper that he, James Lee Kauffman, and other council members would host a dinner in Washington to promote cooperation with "executive agencies" in "every reasonable way." Draper forwarded both the invitation and the council's Japan report to Army Secretary Royall, then in Tokyo with Joseph Dodge. He suggested Royall study it during the long return flight. Noting Kern's history of bitter disputes with MacArthur, Draper commended his use of *Newsweek* as a forum to support "our recovery program." Kern could be relied on in the future to back the "State and Army general policy toward Japan."[49]

The dinner sponsored by the council on February 16 brought together an impressive official guest list. Besides Army Secretary Kenneth Royall, it included William Draper, Assistant Secretary of State Charles Saltzman, Robert Eichelberger, W. W. Butterworth, Assistant Army Secretary Tracy Voorhees, and half a dozen other foreign service officers who specialized in Asian affairs. Discussions centered around the council's critical report, with most speakers endorsing its recommendations. The general conclusion was that Japan's productivity and trade must be expanded, as an increasing degree of political-economic autonomy returned to the Japanese government.[50]

This social gathering cemented the Japan bloc within the administration and between it and influential private citizens. Although MacArthur continued during 1949 to delay, impede, and criticize many aspects of the reverse course, he no longer commanded the power or authority to set the Occupation's agenda. Besides their disdain for the Supreme Commander, this group offered an alternative vision of Japan's future, one in which the former enemy would cooperate with the United States in dominating the future of Asia.

8

REGIONAL ECONOMIC INTEGRATION AND THE RISE OF SOUTHEAST ASIA

The stabilization decree of December 1948, when combined with EROA, the cotton credits, and NSC 13/2, provided a mechanism for an economic crank-up geared toward export production. But how, ultimately, could Japan be freed from dependence on expensive dollar-based commodities that forced up the price of its manufactured goods and limited market outlets? How could the United States use the recovery program to stimulate trade between Japan and nondollar Asian producers and consumers? Some form of regional economic integration, many believed, held the best hope for achieving self-sufficiency and security by the early 1950s. As one State Department economic analyst noted in 1948, EROA would create a "purely nominal trade balance" in Japan. Real self-sufficiency required the revival of Far Eastern productivity to a point where Japan could "buy her imports from those non-dollar areas which constitute her export markets." "Genuine and lasting" recovery would remain a phantom until the United States undertook a regional approach to improve "economic conditions in the Far East as a whole. . . ."[1]

Once begun, talk of cranking-up Japan's economy inevitably led to the question of where in Asia the required raw materials and markets could be found. Some analysts proposed that because the "raw material interrelationships with Korea, Formosa, Manchuria and North China" formed the "essential core" of Japan's industrial economy, the United States ought to encourage a restoration of these ties. Robert W. Barnett, an aide to Edwin F. Martin, argued that there was much merit in Japan's "plan for a Great East Asia," which only its reliance on military force had corrupted. Barnett suggested that Sino–Japanese trade not only made economic sense but might even soften or co-opt the radical doctrines of the Chinese Communists. Even as China succumbed to communism, it might simultaneously forge ties to a strongly capitalist Japan. Serving as something of an American proxy, Japan might even develop trade links to the Vietminh in Indochina and the insurgents in the Indonesian Republic. Barnett hoped this approach might ensure the "success of the crank-up for Japan" while reducing the pro-Soviet orientation of Asian revolutionaries.[2]

Other economic specialists in the administration feared the political consequences of encouraging Japan to reenter a Communist "China market." Joseph Jones, a top administrator of the ECA, for example, proposed that the United States take the lead in clearing China of communism on Japan's behalf. In a proposal written to coincide with the expected election of Thomas Dewey, Jones urged ECA head, Paul Hoffman, to bring together all the disparate aid programs in Asia, including those in China, Korea, Japan, the Philippines, and colonial Southeast Asia. To stem the revolutionary tide in China, Jones argued, ECA should insist on "drastic change in the size and character of U.S. aid."

Hoffman should impress on the new president and Congress the "importance to China of trade with Japan, the importance to Japan of trade with China, Southeast Asia, [and] the Philippines. . . ." Since 1945, Jones recalled, "civil war in China, anarchy in Southeast Asia," an inefficient Occupation in Japan, and the "hatreds and resentments aroused throughout the Far East by Japanese invasion" had prevented the revival of integrated trade. Congress, he said, must "adopt an integrated program that has a chance of knitting that shattered area back into an economic whole" and thereby create "conditions resistant to Communism and anarchy." Unless the United States committed itself to driving the Communists from China, he held, little hope existed of putting "Japan, or Korea or China on a stable and self-sustaining basis."[3]

Jones, like many others in and out of government, guessed wrong about the 1948 election. Truman's victory over Dewey confounded advocates of military intervention in China. Neither Truman nor his new secretary of state, Dean Acheson, nor the Asia experts of the State Department entertained visions of American forces sweeping back Chinese communism. Nevertheless, the idea of regional economic integration impressed many officials as the key to Japanese recovery. In contrast to Jones, however, they looked south, as well as north, for a solution. If properly developed, Southeast Asia might serve as a substitute for the China-Manchuria-Korea market. Not incidentally, the disputed colonial states of Southeast Asia also appeared as practicable spots to "draw the line" against Communist expansion beyond China.

Late in 1948, Army Under Secretary William Draper had this idea in mind when he pressed his staff to consider an "economic aid program, similar to the Marshall Plan, for the Far East." Working together, economic adviser Ralph Reid and the army's Civil Affairs Division prepared a plan to hasten Japanese recovery while fostering in Asia "strong, independent Governments, friendly towards the United States and opposed to Communism in order to provide a bulwark against Soviet encroachment, to assure the U.S. sources of strategic raw materials, and to deny to the Soviet Union the manpower potential of the Far East."

Recovery and containment, Reid informed Draper and Joseph Dodge, formed two halves of the same walnut. The United States must insure stability by shifting Japan's trade "to a non-dollar basis as rapidly as possible." Unless Congress funded a "regional recovery program . . . comparable in nature to the ERP and tightly meshed with the latter through the medium of the European colonies in the Far East," Japan would remain an American dependent. This program would constitute the "American reply to the twenty nation Asian Cominform," Reid proclaimed. Although Army Department and State Department planners acknowledged a necessity to permit some Japanese trade with China, they emphasized the long-term goal of forging trade links with non-Communist Asia.[4]

Traveling to Japan several times during 1948–49 as Draper's representative, Reid worked closely with Joseph Dodge. These visits confirmed his belief that economic-political stability required that Japan establish close trade links with Southeast Asia. To his relief, Reid discovered that the staff of SCAP's Economic-Scientific Section (ESS) endorsed a similar concept. Although MacArthur still fumed about NSC 13/2 and the stabilization directive, the ESS staff set to work on a recovery proposal that resembled the one from Washington. Their "Program for a Self-supporting Japanese Economy," issued in November 1948, and known colloquially as the Blue Book (owing to its binding), postulated achieving a trade balance in 1953 through the "most rapid possible re-entrance of Japan into world markets, particularly in the Far East. . . ." The ESS estimated that $1.3 billion in American aid over the next four years would permit Japan to export enough to balance the cost of imported raw materials.[5]

The Blue Book linked recovery to finding "key markets and indispensable sources of raw materials . . . in the natural market areas in Asia. . . ." Japan would exchange capital equipment and consumer goods for the "industrial raw materials and foodstuffs which they can offer." By encouraging the Japanese to cultivate markets not directly important to the American economy, the United States would reduce the need to assist Japan without sacrificing profit. A temporary infusion of new dollars and raw materials coupled with strict reductions in domestic consumption should allow Japan to balance its trade and capture new markets within four years.[6]

The tenets of the Blue Book so impressed William Draper that he urged the State Department to join the army in using it as a guide for future economic planning throughout Asia. As Draper put the idea to then Acting Secretary of State Lovett, the Blue Book, stabilization decree, and Dodge mission heralded an "integrated and expanding program of American aid for Asia." Henceforth, he hoped, the department would join the army in proposing a means to ensure the "necessary expansion of trade" between Japan and its neighbors.[7]

An outline proposal of a "Marshall Plan for the Far East," composed by Ralph Reid and Assistant Army Secretary Tracy Voorhees, whetted Draper's enthusiasm. Prepared in February 1949, it postulated an ERP-type program for Asia that linked Japan to a ring of Asian states capable of resisting communism. Accepting the Communist conquest of China, Reid and Voorhees recommended a Western commitment to suppress the nationalist rebellions in Southeast Asia as a prelude to linking the region to Tokyo. Centering on Japan and spreading outward (vivid color charts portrayed Japan as the hub of the prewar Asian economy), beginning with economic aid, and moving toward military assistance, the new plan would "create democratic governments, restore viable economies, and check Soviet expansion." In one master stroke, the two men asserted, the United States could both "advance the dignity of man" and keep "vital raw materials" out of Communist control.[8]

State Department officials voiced misgivings about making any glib analogies between the ERP and the rest of the world. Except for Japan, East and Southeast Asia needed not a reconstruction program but primary political and economic development. The Marshall Plan helped rebuild, not create, advanced industrial economies. Moreover, most Asian states would resent bitterly any American-sponsored plan to subordinate them to a Japanese "workshop." Economic experts in the State Department supported bilateral rather than comprehensive recovery programs. The United States could sponsor currency convertibility agreements between Japan and Southeast Asia, subsidize short-term payments deficits, and, perhaps, fund a small development bank to boost the production of raw materials needed by both Japan and Western Europe. But any attempt to sponsor a "significant increase in the standard of living of the billion inhabitants of Asia," W. W. Butterworth warned Robert Lovett, would only bankrupt

America. Butterworth complained that the fixation on integration voiced by Draper and Voorhees sounded to him as if the Army wanted to "recreate the Greater East Asia Co-Prosperity Sphere." The West Europeans had the industry, management, and "complementary economies" to pull off recovery. In Asia, he warned, "except for Japan . . . you [don't] have any of this."[9]

Persuaded by Butterworth to resist endorsing any comprehensive army scheme, Acting Secretary of State Lovett declined Draper's proposal that they jointly ask Congress to link all future assistance to Japan to an "integrated and expanding program of American aid for Asia. . . ." Although admitting the importance of boosting the "export productivity of other Asiatic countries" as a step toward helping Japan, he stressed the disagreements between the two agencies on how to bring this about. Until this was resolved, the State Department would not recommend to Congress a major change in the patterns of assistance.[10]

Although Draper had failed to win over the State Department to his Asian Marshall Plan scheme, he pursued other avenues toward the same end. Throughout 1949 and the first half of 1950, Joseph Dodge's program in Tokyo (the so-called Dodge Line), applied stringent doses of neoclassical economics and government control to transform Japan into a low-cost, high-volume industrial exporter linked to its Asian neighbors. By curtailing public spending, discharging many employees, and reducing lending by its own Reconstruction Finance Bank, Dodge forced the Japanese government to slash the huge internal budget deficit.

In a move designed to restructure the industrial economy in an opposite way from what the Pauley and Edwards missions envisioned, credit to many smaller enterprises ceased. Not only would this limit inflation, Dodge held, but tighter credit along with the preferential allocation of raw materials would assist large-scale enterprises producing for export. At the same time, American and Japanese authorities promoted new labor laws, initiated a "Red purge," and promoted the formation of conservative unions. As with the recipients of Marshall Plan aid, the Japanese government also had to create a special yen counterpart fund that matched at least part of the assistance granted by Washington.

Many aspects of the Dodge Line resembled Japan's prewar economic program. Like the planners of the 1930s, he sought to bolster large business to take advantage of economies of scale. By assisting production for export, he hoped to make prices more competitive and, thus, attractive to the large but relatively poor Southeast Asia market. The creation of the powerful Ministry of International Trade and Industry (MITI) in 1949 bolstered the government-business partnership.

Both at the time and afterwards, this austerity program aroused intense controversy. Although Dodge took the credit for halting inflation, prices had already begun to moderate when he began to slash spending. Unquestionably, forced reductions in government expenditures nearly doubled unemployment during the eighteen months preceeding the Korean War. Nevertheless, the American envoy remained certain that Japan required this tonic. As prices dropped and the value of the yen stabilized, he predicted, exports would become competitive, find new markets, and spur a strong recovery. Yet, until the Korean War created an entirely new political and economic situation, the economy showed little evidence of the heralded rebound.

Like his close associate, William Draper, Dodge perceived an intimate connection among industrial recovery, increased exports, and containment of revolution. Once restored as a stable industrial power, he believed, Japan would serve as a key "border area in the world-wide clash between communism and democracy." Linked by ideology to the West and by commerce to Asia, Japan could deflect "totalitarian pressures" by counterbalancing the Communist "Pan-Asiatic movement." Through this new ally's economic power, America could exercise "tremendous influence over our relations with all of the Orient." Shortly before the Korean War, Dodge told a congressional committee that, in the future, Japan would be "used as a springboard for America, and a country supplying the material goods required for American aid to the Far East."[11]

Although both Dodge and Draper had been disappointed by State Department reluctance to cosponsor an Asian Marshall Plan, they hoped to take advantage of the next best thing—the ERP operations in colonial Southeast Asia. These small projects in French Indochina, the Dutch East Indies, and several British colonies were designed to spur production of food and industrial commodities, thus reducing European dependence on dollar-priced American raw materials. Indirectly, this American aid also subsidized the mounting costs of the colonial wars borne by the Europeans. Nevertheless, Dodge believed that the ERP might provide a mechanism for Japan to extend its ties to Southeast Asia.

Soon after reaching Tokyo, the new "economic czar" notified ECA head Paul Hoffman of his interest in coordinating Japanese recovery with Southeast Asian development projects. Dodge proposed the "greatest possible integration of U.S. aid programs" so that each dollar "may be used several times over in the achievement . . . of recovery and reconstruction throughout the Far East." Both Dodge and Draper praised a then-recent decision by the ECA to grant several million dollars to the Dutch East Indies to finance the purchase of Japanese textiles. This, they hoped, would serve as a model for future sales. Such cooperation among SCAP, the Army Department, and ECA, Dodge told Hoffman, would facilitate even larger "reconstruction projects whose completion . . . served two or more of those countries whose recovery the U.S. seeks to assist." In anticipation of future cooperation, Draper appointed his imminent successor in the Army Department, Tracy Voorhees, and Deputy Assistant Secretary Robert West as liaisons to the ECA.[12]

During the next several months, Hoffman's deputy, Harlan Cleveland, met frequently with the army delegates. They agreed, in principle, that Japan should be used as a "source of supply" for American aid programs in East Asia. In other words, dollars for the purchase of supplies bound for the region could be spent acquiring these products in Japan, even though Japanese prices might be somewhat higher than for similar procurements in America. The benefit would come from the multiplier effect, in that the dollars would benefit both Japan and surrounding countries. Development projects in "colonial and other under-developed areas," they hoped, could be quickly and cheaply begun by utilizing both Japanese materials and technical assistance. Although many Asians might object to Japan's role, given their wartime experiences, the Americans believed the ECA could serve as a buffer inhibiting this reaction. Cleveland even thought the ECA might be willing to finance some trade with Manchuria to provide Japan access to coking coal and food from this Communist-controlled area at a price well below the cost of transporting it from the West. He hoped the whole topic might be examined by a "special consultant" selected by the army and ECA.[13]

Cooperation between the ECA and Draper and Dodge soon collapsed, however. A series of political, economic, and bureaucratic disputes revealed each camp had quite different ideas about regional integration. To begin with, early in 1949, despite conflicting advice, President Truman ordered the termination of all ECA programs in Communist-held parts of China. This eliminated any prospect of directly subsidizing Sino–Japanese trade. But this presented only one of several barriers. Draper, Dodge, Reid, and Voorhees thought that ECA expenditures for colonial Asia should primarily benefit the Japanese economy. Examples might be funding East Indian textile purchases in Japan, giving Japanese factories contracts to build transportation equipment for use in Southeast Asia, or development aid to boost commodity production in Asia for purchase by Japan.

ECA administrators, in contrast, justified expenditures in Asia as a method to hasten European recovery. They considered Asian development projects as useful sources of nondollar raw materials that would reduce the dollar drain on the British, French, German, and Dutch economies. A certain degree of coordination with Japan might facilitate these ends and reduce program expenses. Japan, for example, might serve as a convenient source of selected consumer goods and technical services for use in Southeast

Asia. But, as a rule, the ECA bitterly opposed any effort to grant Japan exclusive, or even privileged, access to Southeast Asia. If the European dependencies became a Japanese economic preserve, absorbing Tokyo's exports as payment for their food, minerals, and fibers, it would undermine the fundamental ECA interest in Southeast Asia—that of restoring the export of cheap raw materials from Southeast Asia to Western Europe and European sales in the other direction.

As this divergence of goals became increasingly apparent, army planners considered alternative ways to forge Japanese links with other Asian states. But political and military problems in East Asia proved even greater barriers to their ideas than ECA resistance or State Department skepticism. The collapse of the Nationalist regime on the Chinese mainland as well as the growing intensity of nationalist revolts in French Indochina, the East Indies, and Malaya threatened to seal off much of Asia from future cooperation with Japan. More than an economic problem, the Communist victory in China and pressure on Southeast Asia impressed many Americans as evidence of a strategic Soviet breakthrough in the East. Although the United States had successfully blocked the Soviets in the West, the Russians appeared to have turned their forces in an attempt to enter Europe through its back door. Once in control of continental Asia, they might quickly overwhelm Japan, dominate the Middle East, and sweep into Europe.

Japan held an ambivalent place in this scenario. On the one hand, its industrial potential seemed significant enough to affect the world power balance, should it come under Soviet domination. At the same time, Japan appeared a fragile giant, easily subdued through manipulation of its raw materials. Partly as a result of these fears, the contests for power in China and Southeast Asia were reinterpreted as proxy battles in a much larger contest.

THE RISE OF SOUTHEAST ASIA

The circumstances of the Pacific War, especially Japan's occupation of colonial Southeast Asia, virtually insured the demise of the prewar order. Not only had native populations witnessed the humiliation and defeat of their European masters by fellow Asians but the Japanese vigorously and often successfully cultivated anticolonial sentiments. Subject peoples reacted to these pressures in various ways, some actively collaborating with their new overlords, others leading resistance against them. Important groups in China, the Philippines, Indochina, the East Indies, Burma, and Malaya exhibited both responses, securing a novel political role for themselves. The mobilization of elites and the new avenues of expression for the masses fatally undermined the aura of colonial authority.

Japan's vigorous effort at driving Western imperialism from Asia had dire implications for both itself and Europe. With its historic economic ties to both Europe and Japan, Southeast Asia (more than China) formed a critical link between containment in the Pacific and Western Europe. The region's raw material exports provided its European masters great benefits, as a cheap source of supply for home industries and, since the First World War, as a means to finance the chronic dollar gap in transatlantic trade. To significant degrees, British, Dutch, and French industry relied on profits from investment and trade with their Southeast Asian colonies. For example, an estimated one Dutch citizen in five derived a living from commerce generated by the East Indies, and Malayan tin and rubber comprised one of Britain's few dollar-earning exports. Japan, too, had grown closer to Southeast Asia during the 1930s. During the war, it had tried, with limited success, to link its economy fully with its Greater East Asia Co-Prosperity Sphere. But since 1945, the region's political and military upheavals restricted its value to both Western Europe and Japan, leaving them increasingly dependent on costly American production and uncertain American aid.[14]

During the Second World War many American officials revealed a keen interest in how this new nationalism might affect Southeast Asia. Typically, President Franklin Roosevelt showed tremendous foresight but little follow through in seeking a diplomatic solution. Frequently, he called on the West Europeans and British to promise their dependencies postwar self-determination. FDR suggested several courses, ranging from the outright return of Hong Kong to China to placing Indochina under trusteeship and to granting the East Indies partial home rule. Although the small band of Southeast Asia specialists in the State Department applauded these ideas, most higher ranking diplomats and military officers had little sympathy for undermining further the status quo. When faced by mounting problems over coalition warfare, complaints by the Allies, Soviet expansionist tendencies, and the disintegration of the Chinese Nationalist regime, even Roosevelt drew back from his anticolonial position. By the time of the Yalta Conference, he largely abandoned efforts to compel decolonization and did little more than admonish the Europeans to liberalize their rule.[15]

Harry Truman, lacking the fervor and vision of Roosevelt, relegated colonial questions even further on the back burner. The new president seemed most comfortable with views expressed by the OSS and a spring 1945 Department of State study. The loss of Asian colonies, the OSS warned, would weaken and alienate "European states whose help we need to balance Soviet power in Europe." The State Department recommended support for gradual self-rule by colonial peoples, but cautioned against any moves to eliminate the "influence of the West" or cut off the "equality of commercial opportunity and . . . access to raw materials." By August, SWNCC had endorsed the principle of gradualism designed to insure that "self-governing states" in Asia would "cooperate with each other and with the Western powers on a basis of mutual self-respect and friendship."[16]

Although Truman and his advisers still considered themselves bound to the principle of self-determination, their actions during the closing months of 1945 indicated otherwise. Although calling for negotiated solutions with the anticolonial resistance movements in Southeast Asia, the administration approved Lend-Lease aid and other loans and provided logistic support for Dutch, British, and French efforts to retake their colonies in the wake of Japan's surrender.

Until the close of 1948, the overwhelming American concern with Southeast Asia related to its ties with the European political economy. As a State Department policy release admitted in September 1948, however, much as Washington supported the goal of self-determination, it accepted the French military campaign in Indochina because America's "immediate and vital interest" centered on "maintaining in power a friendly French government to assist in the furtherance of our aims in Europe." Similarly, the department feared the consequences should the Netherlands lose all control over the East Indies. It hoped for a compromise settlement between the nationalists struggling for independence and their foreign masters. Unless the Dutch held onto a major economic stake in the colony, the present government might be fatally undermined, a result considered extremely "prejudicial to the U.S. position in Western Europe."[17]

Administration spokesmen made similar arguments when testifying before Congress on behalf of the proposed ERP early in 1948. Under Secretary of State Acheson claimed that the success of the Marshall Plan depended on Europe's ability to maintain exports once American aid helped restore production. Acheson hoped that "most" or a "very large part" of these exports would "go to Southeast Asia." Before the war, he recalled, nearly a billion dollars of exports went to that region. But since 1945, "practically none." Economist Richard Bissell, speaking for the ECA, told senators that the European colonies in Southeast Asia were "extremely important" to the success of the Marshall Plan, not only as export markets but also as "earners of dollars for the home countries." Mineral exports, for example, were vital for generating British and Dutch revenues. Thus, estimates for the future duration and funding of the ERP reflected "in very substantial part," a judgment as to "when or if those territories will be politically pacified" and "how soon thereafter" they could begin making "substantial exports of petroleum products, rubber, tin and other minerals, which could make a decisive difference in the dollar interests of the controlling European countries."[18]

From 1945 to 1950, American policymakers worried most about the rebellions in French Indochina and the Dutch East Indies, where the Japanese occupation had fatally undermined colonial authority. Within two weeks of the Japanese surrender, Mohammed Hatta and Sukarno proclaimed the birth of an Indonesian Republic and Ho Chi Minh announced formation of a unified Democratic Republic of Vietnam (DRV). Although Indochina was one of the less prosperous colonies of Southeast Asia, its large population, pivotal location, and, above all, well-organized, Communist-led insurgency made it a particularly vexing problem for the West. In contrast, the East Indies' vast mostly untapped wealth made it a gem that the Dutch and their allies were reluctant to surrender. In contrast to the Viet Minh movement, however, Indonesian nationalism had only a small Communist element, a fact of great significance as time passed.

Immediately after the war, the United States, like the Europeans, vacillated over the claims of the Vietnamese and Indonesian nationalists. Some Officials in Washington and Paris, for example, favored negotiating a compromise settlement with Ho Chi Minh, assuming he would settle for less than full independence. The Vietnamese leader seemed interested enough to journey to France late in 1946 for what turned out to be futile talks. The French government considered only superficial concessions and refused to recognize the sovereignty of Ho's DRV over the entire colony. At most, Paris considered a partial grant of independence to the northern provinces, where the insurgents had greatest strength. The central and southern parts of the colony—Annam and Cochin China—were to remain French dependencies.

Before and after this episode, Ho contacted a variety of Americans to enlist their support. Some represented the OSS, which had coordinated anti-Japanese operations with the Vietminh guerrillas; others were attached to the State Department. Ho continually maintained his commitment to nationalism and expressed hope that America would furnish encouragement and support to his nation. Even those critical of his open Communist affiliations praised the charismatic revolutionary as a "symbol of nationalism and the struggle for freedom to the overwhelming majority of the population."[19]

By November 1946, the French resolved to force Ho's followers from their northern strongholds and bombarded the port of Haiphong, killing several thousand civilians. This incident initiated a full-scale guerrilla war that lasted until 1954. Gradually, through its support for France and general opposition to communism, the United States became a third party to the struggle.

Almost from the onset of the conflict till its denouement nearly thirty years later, American officials of six presidential administrations viewed events in a remarkably consistent way. They supported the principle of gradual decolonization and the transfer of power to non-Communist Vietnamese. But whatever else happened, the "least desirable eventuality," as the State Department put it in 1946, would be the "establishment of a communist-dominated, Moscow-oriented state in Indochina. . . ." Truman administration officials shoped that France would cultivate moderate nationalists and avoid a brutal military campaign that might turn the Vietnamese "irrevocably against the West and toward ideologies and affiliations hostile to democracies which could result in the perpetual foment of Indochina with consequences for all Southeast Asia."[20]

The State Department early on and consistently condemned Ho's "Vietnam Government" as a "small Communist group possibly in direct touch with Moscow and direct touch with Yenan." Allegedly, they used nationalism merely as a cover to advance Soviet interests in Asia. Yet, only if France accommodated moderate nationalists, Washington held, could some degree of Western orientation and an "antidote to Soviet influence" be assured.[21]

By the spring of 1947, in light of the emerging containment policy, recently appointed Secretary of State George C. Marshall evinced great concern with events in Southeast Asia. He informed Paris that the colonial war could "no longer be considered, if it ever was considered, to be of a local character." Even though the United States had "no solution of the problem to suggest," it had a "vital interest in the political and economic well-being of this area." By May, Marshall was worried that France's failure either to defeat the insurgents or to cultivate an alternative nationalist force threatened to permit this critical region to slip in the direction of "anti-Western Pan-Asiatic tendencies" where the "Communists could capture control." By failing to win the "voluntary cooperation" of the natives, Paris actually abetted the Kremlin's drive to capture "600 million dependent people."[22]

Yet, despite American pressure to deal with the Vietnamese honorably, the French resurrected a questionable politican from central Vietnam, Bao Dai, to serve as their hand picked "emperor." Although descended from a precolonial royal line, Bao Dai had abdicated his claim to power at the end of the war and had alternated his residence between Hong Kong and the Riviera. Initially, Marshall and his advisers were outraged by the "creation of an impotent puppet government," which implied that Western democracies were "reduced" to supporting "monarchy as a weapon against communism." American officials in Southeast Asia dismissed Bao Dai as a "dissolute playboy in the pay of the French whose total loyal following probably comprised some half dozen Hong Kong concubines."[23]

During 1947 and early 1948, the colonial war expanded while American policy continued to drift. Most foreign service personnel in Southeast Asia approved the concept of decolonization, but they feared that any rapid change would lead to chaos and communism. The more senior and influential Western European desk officers stationed in the State Department identified closely with the colonial powers and warned against doing anything to undermine the vitality of the empires. The handful of junior diplomats who questioned the implicit proimperialist policy were regarded, in the words of James O'Sullivan (former vice-consul in Hanoi), as among those who "heard for too long the patter of little brown feet and are therefore unreliable." On reassignment in Washington, O'Sullivan told his mostly unsympathetic colleagues that "alongside of Ho Chi Minh," the "rest of the Indochinese politicians are strictly bush leaguers."[24]

As 1948 wore on, American officials appeared increasingly confused and frustrated both by French intransigence and Communist strength in Indochina. M. E. Dening, the leading Asia specialist in the British Foreign Office, came away from a June conference with W. W. Butterworth and his staff perplexed by the drift in Washington's policies. The Americans opposed both French and Dutch efforts to destroy the insurgencies in their colonies, but they feared a victory by Communist guerrillas. They wanted to see power given to moderate Asians, but they feared such groups would lose out to hardened revolutionaries. When Dening asked Butterworth to cite an example of a currently acceptable Southeast Asian leader, the American began to praise the dead Filipino, Roxas. Dening quipped that although American diplomats formerly "seemed to think that every Nationalist must be good," they "now seem to see a communist behind every nationalist bush." Although agreeing with Butterworth that the Communists often did cloak themselves as nationalists, he thought it foolish for the Americans to forget that care "must be taken not to kill one with the other."[25]

During mid-1948, an upsurge of violence against colonial control in Southeast Asia frightened the United States more than ever. In addition to the Indochina war, long simmering anti-British sentiment in Burma and Malaya broke into open revolt. The on-again, off-again negotiations between the Indonesian Republicans and the Dutch threatened to explode into open warfare once more, wrecking the chances of a settlement. Then, in September, the Republican movement split when a Communist faction revolted against both the Dutch and the leadership of Hatta and Sukarno. American officials tended to view these events as interrelated, reflecting some new Soviet battle order that was supposedly laid down during a Communist conference held at Calcutta in February 1948.

The State Department moved quickly to convene a Southeast Asia Regional Conference in Bangkok that brought together an array of area specialists and military attachés. The conference ballooned into a major affair, one of its planners reported, with the "army, navy and, finally, SCAP, horning in." Although the agenda was kept "broad enough so that anything under the perpetual sun of SEA could be discussed," talk centered on the need to arrange a transition from colonial to home rule before Communist insurgents overran the region.[26]

Worried about a new Soviet challenge, the American delegates suspected Moscow ordered its local agents to intensify their anticolonial struggles to sever the economic links between Western Europe and Southeast Asia. Through this indirect attack, the Kremlin expected to nullify the Marshall Plan and cripple European recovery. Having failed to subdue Europe directly, Ambassador Edwin F. Stanton informed the State Department, the Soviets were "definitely concentrating on this area."[27]

American diplomatic personnel stationed throughout Southeast Asia reported on the links between the various colonial economies and the industry of Europe. Although each raw material or product exported might appear marginal to the world economy, together they played a fundamental part in the structure of trade. Malayan tin and rubber, for example, were significant not only as industrial commodities. If required, substitutes could be found. However, Malayan exports provided Great Britain with most of its hard-currency earnings, the essential "dollar arsenal" that defrayed part of the Anglo–American trade deficit. To greater or lesser degrees, the foreign exchange earned by other exports from the region helped offset the chronic trade deficits of the ERP nations, with the remainder made up by Marshall Plan aid. Any hope of achieving long-term liquidity seemed dependent on expanded trade with Southeast Asia.

American delegates accused both the French and Dutch of "playing the Communist game" by wasting on jungle warfare lives and money needed desperately for reconstruction throughout the world. The use of American supplies, provided indirectly to the colonial armies, turned the "thinking population" of all Southeast Asia against the United States and allowed Communist insurgents to pose as "Bolivars" freeing their people from outside oppression. Discussion at the conference revealed a near consensus that Western influence could only be assured if France and the Netherlands transferred power to non-Communist nationalists who could then lead their people toward an accommodation with the industrial powers.[28]

THE INDONESIAN MODEL

Indonesia provided an immediate challenge for those in Washington who thought it possible to steer a course between the twin evils of colonialism and communism. For over a year after the Japanese surrender, the Dutch had tried to destroy through force the Republican movement that had taken over parts of the archipelago. A truce reached in November 1946 (the Linggadjati Agreement) showed some promise for a negotiated settlement. But the Netherlands tried to confine the republic's sovereignty to part of Java and to create numerous other federated, or puppet, states linked to the mother country. When talks collapsed, the Dutch undertook a "police action" on July 20, 1947, that continued for six months. American officials worked hard to persuade both sides to resume negotiations, something achieved in the Renville Agreement of January 17, 1948.

The essentially moderate ideology of Indonesian nationalism impressed American diplomats both in Washington and in the East Indies. Although Hatta and Sukarno struggled for full political independence, they propounded only modest revolutionary, social, and economic doctrines. However, if frustrated, they and their followers might move toward the position of the tiny Indonesian Communist party (with some three thousand members) and create a movement one diplomat feared might soon be "comparable to that of Indochina." If that occurred, the United States might be forced to oppose independence as a "pawn in the hands of militant and organized communists."[29]

The Truman administration spoke with uncharacteristic unanimity on the Indonesian question during 1948–49. Both Secretary of State Marshall and Under Secretary Lovett made it plain to the Hague that Washington considered the Republicans a buffer against Indonesian communism. The colonial military campaign, they complained, threatened to drive "nationalism and communism into a united front against Netherlands aggression." Lovett urged the Dutch to accommodate "Indonesian nationalism . . . in a just and practical way as a condition precedent for dealing with Communism in that area. . . ." American mediation efforts in the East Indies, under the guidance of H. Merle Cochran, specifically sought to strengthen Hatta and Sukarno to enable them "successfully [to] liquidate Communists within the Republic."[30]

These concerns peaked in September 1948 when a small Communist faction revolted in eastern Java. American representatives on the island viewed it as a wonderful "opportunity" for the moderate Republicans to demonstrate their "determination [to] suppress Communism." Consul General Charles Livengood admitted to a "sensation of relief" now that the crisis had finally come and the Republicans could prove their mettle by destroying their former Communist allies. The suppression of the revolt, he and Cochran believed, would cleanse the republic of radicals, erode Dutch claims to be resisting communism, and commit the Republicans to a pro-Western orientation.[31]

Although the Republicans crushed the Communists quickly, Washington grew alarmed by the Dutch refusal to make political concessions. They shocked both Indonesians and Americans by launching a second "police action" against Republican-controlled territory on December 19, 1948. As Under Secretary of State Dean Rusk lamented, this action actually encouraged communism in Southeast Asia by sweeping aside the "moderate national elements" willing to work with Western powers. Although Washington would not risk a formal break with its European ally, word went out to diplomats they must increase pressure on the Hague.[32]

Almost immediately after these events, the State Department issued statements through American embassies condemning the Netherlands. The Dutch were charged with undermining the best opportunity to "hold a firm anti-communist front" in Indonesia and, like the French, were forcing the colonial population to choose between toleration of the "status quo or revolt under the Red Flag." Sukarno and Hatta, far from being threats to Western security, had "met and disposed of an all-out Communist offensive under a Moscow agent not only without help from the West, but under serious handicaps imposed" by America's ally, the Netherlands. The moderate nationalists in Indonesia held the key to control of 75 million people and vast mineral wealth. In the "long run," Robert Lovett declared, these moderates represented the "only alternative to the surrender of the whole region to Communist dictation."[33]

During the next six months, the American government escalated pressure on the Hague for a settlement. Washington supported a UN resolution demanding a resumption of negotiations and hinted it might cease Marshall Plan aid if the police action continued. Members of Congress, prodded by the administration, questioned why the American taxpayer had to subsidize a colonial war against anti-Communist Asians.[34]

Meanwhile, the State Department grew even more convinced about Indonesia's importance to the West. A major review by department specialists described it as the "southern anchor" to the American defense chain composed of Japan, the Ryukyus, Formosa, and the Philippines. Besides its strategic location, large population, and potential as a barrier to communism, its exports were "almost essential to the success of the European Recovery Program." An independent, pro-Western Indonesia might provide both a symbolic counterweight to revolutionary nationalism and a "base from which a beginning could be made in rolling back the Communist tide in Asia."[35]

Ultimately, the threats to suspend ERP aid and growing international isolation compelled the Dutch to resume negotiations with the Republicans. Between August and November 1949, the two parties conducted the Round Table Conference at the Hague, where they finally resolved the colony's future. Pressed by the United States, the Dutch agreed, reluctantly, to transfer sovereignty to an Indonesian Republic with broad powers over the many scattered islands of the archipelago. The formal grant of freedom on December 27, 1949, marked a singular triumph for American diplomacy in Southeast Asia.[36]

The elements on which the Indonesian success rested (a fairly maleable Dutch government and an anti-Communist nationalist movement) had few counterparts elsewhere in colonial Asia, India being the major exception. In many parts of Asia, moderate forces had practically ceased to exist. The KMT had already split in the face of Communist military advances, with its squabbling factions fleeing the mainland. A small, but violent, revolt continued in Malaya, complicated by Chinese–Malay ethnic rivalry. Indochina entered its third year of war with no settlement in sight. Although France reached an agreement on March 8, 1949, to install Bao Dai as "emperor" of an independent Vietnam, few Americans expressed optimism about his future or considered him a viable alternative to Ho Chi Minh. In contrast to the success in stabilizing Western Europe and Japan during 1948, most observers agreed that the non-Communist position in Southeast Asia had eroded significantly.

Troubled by the possibility of a Communist breakthrough in this region, the PPS initiated a reevaluation of American policy. John P. Davies, the group's foremost Asia expert, took the lead in December 1948, circulating a memorandum on the connection between Southeast Asian security and overall containment of Soviet influence. Davies acknowledged that most of the Asian mainland, from Manchuria to Indochina, would remain "hostile to us" for the "foreseeable future." By holding offshore island strong points in the Pacific, "from Hokkaido to Sumatra," the United States could easily resist Communist physical threats. But looking beyond a mere holding action, Davies urged that America consider "vigorous measures of political warfare to reduce Kremlin-directed influence in Korea, China, Indochina and Burma." More than anything, long-term success in the contest for Asia required:

Creating an apparatus which will enable us to employ our and Japan's economy as an instrument of political warfare with respect to Communist Asia; acquiring necessary raw materials for U.S. strategic and economic requirements; developing economic stability and interdependence among the Western Pacific islands (including Japan), Malaya, and Siam; encouraging a flow of raw materials from Southeast Asia to the ERP countries.[37]

Southeast Asia's importance to Western security, Davies emphasized, differed fundamentally from China's. Despite its size, China had only marginal ties to the Western powers, if somewhat greater significance to Japan. In contrast, the Southeast Asian economy had both immediate and future relevance to European and Japanese industry. Secretary of State Acheson made exactly this point in February 1949 when testifying before Congress on the extension of the Marshall Plan. European industry imported raw materials from Southeast Asia and the Middle East, produced manufactured goods, and reexported them, "which kept the economies going in South America, Southeast Asia, in India, in the Middle East and everywhere." The recovery of Western European productivity as a result of the ERP, Acheson explained, could be sustained only if prewar trade patterns with Southeast Asia were restored. But because of nationalism, colonialism, and Communist agitation, Acheson warned, the West faced a "race with time" to convince the Southeast Asians they needed Europe as much as Europe needed them.[38]

This focus on Southeast Asia's role in the world economy followed the consequences of the continuing China policy debate. In his testimony before Congress, Acheson bid good riddance to the KMT, declaring that any more assistance to it "would be silly beyond human description." The United States must wait until the "brick, dust and smoke clears away" so that it could "know what to do." For both foreign and domestic political reasons, Acheson sought to turn American attention away from China and toward reconcentrating Far Eastern strategy on Southeast Asia. Its vast economic wealth might be tapped for European and Japanese recovery, and, unlike China, its nationalist drive had not yet been monopolized by Communists. In line with Kennan's criteria for where to "draw the line," the region "mattered" to the non-Communist world but was not so far gone (like China) to make assistance futile.*

Consequently, early in 1949 Acheson asked Kennan to assign the PPS the task of developing a comprehensive Southeast Asia policy that transcended the narrow political and geographic prejudices of the department's West European officers. Kennan assigned his staff to devise a general guide

---

* Early in March, President Truman approved a series of NSC papers (originating in the State Department) that further disengaged America from China's civil war. The president opted against military aid or intervention, declined to protect Taiwan, and permitted some trade with the emerging Communist regime. See discussion below of NSC 34/2, 37/5, and 41.

for action, avoiding detailed prescriptions for every colony. In particular, he wanted them to elucidate the region's importance to Western Europe and Japan, whose stability counted most for America. The fruit of this investigation, a study entitled "U.S. Policy towards Southeast Asia" (PPS 51), formed the basis of Asian containment doctrine for the next two decades.

The PPS described Southeast Asia as a vital economic crossroads that had "become the target of a coordinated offensive plainly directed by the Kremlin." As in so many other areas, the war and postwar dislocations had smashed the old political order and disrupted the normal economy. Meanwhile, the atavistic colonial system only made matters worse by ruthlessly suppressing demands among Asians for economic progress and political liberation. As the leader of the non-Communist world, the United States bore responsibility for managing creatively the "extreme nationalist passions which now inflame the region." Prolonged warfare would only radicalize the region's politics and prevent it from making necessary "contributions to the ERP countries . . . to India's food problem, or to the orientation of Japan's trade southward in search of survival."

The predominant Soviet interest in the region, the PPS asserted, stemmed from a desire to deny Southeast Asia's mineral wealth to the capitalist world. Kremlin domination would create the "dramatic spectacle of the world divided in half by communism on a north-south axis." Coming so soon after the Communist's triumph in China, loss of Southeast Asia would appear "a major political rout the repercussions of which will be felt throughout the rest of the world, especially in the Middle East and in a then critically exposed Australia." Physically, Southeast Asia comprised a "vital segment on the line of containment, stretching from Japan southward around to the Indian Peninsula." Hence, the security of the "three major non-communist base areas" in Asia, Japan, India, and Australia, depended "in a large measure on the denial of SEA to the Kremlin." Economically, the colonial wars caused an immense drain on Europe and identified the United States (through the ERP) as an indirect oppressor. More serious than the indirect costs, the struggles poisoned the chances of a close post-colonial relationship between Southeast Asia, Europe, and Japan. In short, the loss of the region's commodities would jeopardize recovery among the capitalist democracies.

The PPS believed the crisis required indirect American intervention to "rationalize" the policies of the European allies. Currently, the French and Dutch were providing the "ideal culture for breeding of the communist virus." The "first essential requirement for resistance to Stalinism" in Southeast Asia, PPS stressed, was the "satisfaction of militant nationalism." Once, say in Indochina, real power had been transferred to Vietnamese, the United States would then have the opportunity to work "through a screen of anti-communist Asiatics, to ensure, however long it takes, the triumph of Indochinese nationalism over Red Imperialism."

The PPS urged cooperation with the British to impress other West Europeans that the future of Southeast Asia had to be viewed "in the context of a larger area embracing non-communist centers of power on either side and below." It comprised an "integral part of that great crescent formed by the Indian Peninsula, Australia and Japan." American political support for self-determination would enhance the region's ability to resist subversion. Once stabilized, the United States could begin

> vigorously [to] develop the economic interdependence between SEA as a supplier of raw materials, and Japan, Western Europe and India, as suppliers of finished goods, with due recognition, however, of the legitimate aspirations of SEA countries for some diversification of their economies.[39]

The PPS made a strong case for American involvement in Southeast Asia. As a geographic crossroads, an economic treasure trove, and a political cauldron, its ultimate orientation could influence the global balance of power. By supporting moderate nationalism, Kennan's staff emphasized, the United States had the best chance of containing China while safeguarding Japanese and European economic interests. A summary note of a discussion of PPS 51 by the under secretaries of state in April revealed this concern. "Not until the political problems of SEA are well on their way to solution can the region begin to fulfill its major function as a source of raw materials and a market for Japan and Western Europe."[40]

Given the poaching on bureaucratic turf inherent in PPS 51, the policy paper aroused strident controversy within the State Department. Most Europeanists (and a few Asianists) objected both to Kennan's conclusions and his presumption in discussing questions over which they had a say. Desk officers dealing with France and the Netherlands especially disliked the recommendations to compel acceptance of independence movements by the colonial powers whom they considered far more important than Asians. Although he tried to forge a consensus for PPS 51, Acheson delayed formal submission of the paper to the NSC.

The British government, for its part, seemed eager to assist American efforts in Southeast Asia, just as Kennan hoped it would. In a briefing for foreign secretary Ernest Bevin (scheduled to meet Acheson in April), Asia specialist M. E. Dening echoed closely the view of the PPS. Dening urged that Bevin consider the possibility of building a "common front" from "Afghanistan to Indochina, inclusive. . . ." This would make it possible to "contain the Russian advance southwards, to rehabilitate and stabilize the area, and to preserve our communications across the middle of the world." A stable, pro Western Southeast Asia might even make it "possible to redress the position" of the Communists in China. Although Dening (like Kennan) still felt the "strategic necessities of Europe and the Middle East" came first, the "requirements of Southeast Asia" were also of "vital" importance.[41]

When Bevin met face to face with Acheson in April, the Briton stressed the analogy between the Middle East and Southeast Asia. The Russians had targeted the "primary producing countries," he warned, as an indirect way of paralyzing their adversaries. The foreign secretary suggested that his country along with the United States, Australia, and New Zealand form a special economic mission to develop Southeast Asia.*

Although Acheson doubted the utility of a formal Pacific security pact, he shared Bevin's anxiety about a redirected Soviet threat. President Truman, in fact, had recently declared that the development and protection of the Middle East and Southeast Asia must be "regarded as the other side of the medal of Western European Recovery." If, when ERP aid ceased in 1952, the recipients had not developed new markets and sources of supply, Truman feared that the Soviet bloc would "exploit" the West's needs through economic blackmail.[42]

Although both Acheson and Bevin found themselves in general agreement that the Western powers ought to pursue a "realistic policy" respecting the Communist victory in China, the United States showed much less flexibility elsewhere in Asia. It had, of course, pressured the Dutch toward a compromise settlement with the Indonesians, once the Republicans had committed themselves to anti-Communism. But, Washington would not push the French nearly as hard. France, of course, was of far greater importance in Europe, and the Vietminh rebels were far more radical than their Indonesian counterparts. Together, these two features locked American policy in step behind French colonialism.

Thus, although almost all American diplomats expressed private misgivings over the phony grant of autonomy to Bao Dai and admitted there seemed "little chance the agreement would appeal to Vietnamese nationalists," they despaired over the lack of acceptable alternatives. A pair of cables drafted by State Department Asia specialist Charlton Ogburn and sent over Acheson's signature to foreign posts, lamented that while the "Bao Dai solution" appeared inadequate, Washington hoped that respon-

---

* London had already appointed a special commissioner general for the United Kingdom in Southeast Asia, Malcolm MacDonald. Based in Singapore, he advocated adopting a regional economic and military policy, an Asian equivalent of the Marshall Plan and the Atlantic Pact. He, too, believed the Russians had targeted Southeast Asia as a region of "vast importance in the world-wide struggle between Democratic and Communist causes, quite out of proportion to its industrial and political development."

sible Vietnamese would "appreciate the true character of the menace approaching from China" and "prefer to cooperate" with Bao Dai "rather than accept the alternative of continued resistance and risk the loss of real autonomy to the Chinese Communists." A second Ogburn-Acheson cable put the issue even more starkly. Ho Chi Minh, they asserted, was an "outright Commie" under Kremlin control. The depth or sincerity of his nationalism was "irrelevant" because, in colonial areas, "all Stalinists . . . are nationalists" who would take power to open the way to either "Kremlin control" or "Chi Commie hatchet men and armed forces."[43]

Lingering doubts about Bao Dai or French sincerity were subordinated to the fears of Soviet and Chinese Communist expansion. Moreover, the American Ambassador in Paris, Acheson's friend, David Bruce, fully supported the French and worked closely with them to bolster their case in Washington. Bruce privately assured Acheson that Bao Dai enjoyed great popularity and had been granted real authority. Against all evidence, he insisted, the March 8 agreements represented a triumph for Asian nationalism and a "milestone" of reform. America could not afford to let down its French and Vietnamese allies, Bruce argued. There was no point in criticizing either Paris or Bao Dai, the Ambassador held, "since no alternative" existed.[44]

On June 14, 1949, Bao Dai finally formed a government and proclaimed the existence of a Vietnamese state within the French Union and under French military protection. He made these pronouncements in a bizarre ceremony, surrounded by a host of security guards representing numerous secret criminal societies and religious sects (Caodaists, Hoa Hao, Ben Nguyen, and a Catholic local defense corps), which formed the basis of his local support. Although the American government waited some eight months to extend formal recognition, Washington praised the establishment of the "state of Vietnam" as a move toward the "reestablishment of peace in that country." All "truly nationalist elements," the State Department asserted, would cooperate with Bao Dai.[45]

These steps toward American involvement in the Indochina struggle marked many cruel ironies, not the least of which was the distortion of the PPS 51 study of Southeast Asia. Although providing a basic rationale for commitment to this region, the PPS had also called for a tough approach to the French and for extending American support for genuine nationalism. Kennan and his staff certainly carried no brief for Ho Chi Minh, nonetheless, they considered Bao Dai-like solutions a dangerous fraud. Yet, as with the implementation of his original containment doctrine, the administration had heard only part of Kennan's message. It accepted the argument that Southeast Asia formed a critical link in the Great Crescent, but it ignored the plea that the United States move with, as far as possible, a real nationalist tide.

The fate of the PPS 51 report mirrored this confusion. Because many Europeanists in the State Department opposed its harsh judgments of colonialism, Acheson waited for several months before submitting the paper to the NSC. When he did so, on July 1, the secretary of state did not press for its formal adoption as national policy. Instead, he asked that it serve as a reference point for other ongoing NSC studies of Asia. Two weeks later, Acheson dispatched the report to diplomatic posts as a "source of information" rather than as a formal policy statement.[46]

By the middle of 1949, the Truman administration seemed mired in a bureaucratic debate over where and how to implement an Asian containment doctrine. Kennan urged linking Japan to Southeast Asia and Europe while sitting out the last rounds of the Chinese civil war. Others, especially those in the Defense Department, worried that the imminent Communist victory in China would endanger Japan and accelerate the insurgencies in colonial Southeast Asia. All agreed that an indefinite Japanese Occupation would soon pay diminishing returns, requiring the United States to move toward some form of peace settlement. But none agreed on just how the overlapping interests of Japan, China, and Southeast Asia could be satisfied. For the subsequent eighteen months, the factions within the Truman administration structured their debate over containment in Southeast Asia or China largely in terms of how it would affect Japan's future.

9

THE PEACE TREATY: TRYING AGAIN

At an off-the-record press briefing on February 6, 1949, Army Secretary Kenneth Royall stunned reporters by expressing "grave doubts as to the strategic importance of Japan." In Tokyo to accompany newly appointed economic czar, Joseph Dodge, Royall described Japan as a backwater, distant from the Russian heartland, difficult to defend, expensive to support, and of little relevance in a new war. America could mount offensive operations against Asian targets more easily from "Okinawa, Alaska or possibly Formosa," the army secretary explained, and "with a great deal less expense." He even went on to minimize the threat posed to the region by the Chinese Communists. Under Prime Minister Yoshida, Royall complained, the Japanese had tried to inflate their importance to the United States as part of a scheme to squeeze more aid. The visiting American made it clear he expected the journalists to leak his remarks so that all concerned would "begin considering" arrangements for the "withdrawal" of Occupation forces. As we "picked up our hat and coat to go," he predicted, the Japanese would prove quite conciliatory. In the meantime, he hoped SCAP would turn over more authority to both American and Japanese civilians.[1]

Royall's blunt comments, so critical of both the Japanese and SCAP, shocked Yoshida, infuriated MacArthur, and confused almost everyone. The British foreign secretary complained that the "sensational nature" of the remarks would have the "most serious repercussions in Southeast Asia and indeed on the interests of the Western powers in Asia as a whole." The secretary of state had to provide assurances that the army secretary had spoken his own mind, without official authorization. Even if this were technically correct, Royall clearly floated his ideas as a trial balloon, hoping to move the discussion of Japan's future off dead center. It was time, apparently, to begin thinking about post-Occupation military, political, and economic arrangements and time, it seemed, to begin planning for SCAP's dissolution.[2]

Of course, Royall knew that the United States would not write-off Japan, nor did it really harbor grave doubts about its strategic importance. But he did hope to prod MacArthur and the Japanese into considering a settlement that satisfied the extensive appetite of the military establishment. Taking shape early in 1949, the renewed discussion of a peace treaty pitted the State Department (and some civilian military officials) against the JCS, the secretary of defense, and Under Secretary of the Army, Tracy Voorhees. The leadership of the state department, generally speaking, felt the implementation of new Occupation policies justified rapid movement toward a peace treaty with Japan. In anticipation of a settlement, it urged the reduction of SCAP's authority, the transfer of responsibility to both American civilian administrators and the Japanese, and the making of efforts to minimize the presence of post-Occupation American forces and base facilities. Unwilling to encourage rearmament, they opposed creating a new army. A recentralized police force seemed sufficient to maintain internal security. Given the new direction of policies, Acheson and his advisers considered the Occupation nearly past its prime. Henceforth, they feared, it might pay diminishing rewards and elicit greater Japanese resentment. In contrast, a rapid return of sovereignty accompanied by continued economic assistance would ensure a stable Japanese–American relationship.

None of this seemed obvious to the JCS, Defense Secretary Louis Johnson, or Tracy Voorhees, all of whom opposed an early American withdrawal. Military planners doubted that a delayed peace would sacrifice Japan's friendship or that a quick settlement would ensure Tokyo's future loyalty. But, most of all, they wanted to continue an arrangement that provided the United States optimum influence and control. Besides worrying about the possible loss to an enemy of Japan's military potential, the JCS stressed the nation's importance as a forward military base in American strategy. Aware that neither the Soviet Union nor China (not to mention Japan) were eager to grant the United States unlimited military-base rights in the post-Occupation period, the defense establishment was anxious to postpone a treaty. Furthermore, it had already urged (in May 1948) that plans go forward to lay the groundwork for a small Japanese army able to take over the duties of American ground forces. Because no progress had been made in this direction, largely owing to MacArthur's objections, the JCS and the defense secretary vigorously defended the status quo.[3]

Although unhappy with these views, neither General MacArthur nor the Japanese government had much impact on the treaty debate in Washington until the spring of 1950. Both advocated positions much closer to that of the State Department than to the military, however. Understandably, the Japanese wanted to regain sovereignty as quickly as possible and without having to accept permanent American bases or other restrictive provisions. They especially hoped to avoid a treaty that would antagonize their Communist neighbors, China and the Soviet Union. Only as a last resort, in 1950, did the Japanese government bend to American pressure to rearm and to sign a treaty wholly unacceptable to the Communist powers.

Although he still pined for a treaty to cap his achievements, MacArthur voiced similar misgivings about rearmament or extracting permanent bases. In his view, American forces based on Okinawa, the Philippines, and the mandated islands would provide ample protection against any threat to Japan. So long as Japan were not rearmed or turned into an offensive base, the general thought that the Soviets would agree to honor Japanese neutrality. The nation could be, he hoped, the "Switzerland of the Pacific." Only when he began to realize that virtually no one in Washington desired Soviet cooperation, did MacArthur come to support a blend of State Department and Defense Department positions.

In May 1949, President Truman approved a broadly worked NSC recommendation that plans be accelerated to remove "the regime of control" in Tokyo. But, as usual, he took almost no personal interest in pursuing this policy. Truman stood aside while his civilian and military advisers continued to work at cross purposes. The State Department position, as articulated by Dean Acheson, held that a treaty was needed to ease the "growing uneasiness and restiveness among Japs," especially in light of the Communist advance in China. (The military took the opposite view, that the Chinese Revolution made a pull out from Japan too risky.) Post-Occupation security would be assured by maintaining economic recovery, creating a central police force, and, possibly, retaining a leased naval base at Yokusuka. Unless given its sovereignty and encouraged to trade with its neighbors, Acheson warned, Japan might prefer an accommodation with the "Commie system in Asia." The longer the Occupation dragged on, the greater the drain on American resources would grow and the more "easy prey to Commie ideologies" Japan would become. The fact that the Soviet Union had issued a standing offer to discuss a treaty in the CFM created a constant temptation for the Japanese, which America had to counteract by an initiative of its own.[4]

The JCS ignored or disputed most of Acheson's appeal. Early in June, they notified the defense secretary of their views in a report, NSC 49, later circulated by the National Security Council. Although the secretary of state had pointed to the imminent establishment of a Communist government in China as a compelling reason to bind Japan to America by restoring its sovereignty, the JCS turned this argument on its head. In light of the "debacle" in China and the "developing chaos on the Asiatic mainland, together with its communistic trend," they wrote, America must not allow Japan to slip away. Continuing the Occupation, besides assuring the denial of industrial and military potential to Moscow, provided "us with staging areas from which to project our military power to the Asiatic mainland and to USSR islands adjacent thereto." In this light, the JCS insisted on prolonging the Occupation and pressing for the development of major bases for use by American forces in the posttreaty period. In addition, they urged serious efforts to prepare a Japanese army to take over from American troops.[5]

MacArthur, typically, took issue with both these positions, objecting to the JCS's demands for rearmament and bases as well as the State Department's insistence that SCAP surrender power to civilians in advance of a treaty. "By no stretch of the imagination," he informed Acheson, could the State Department compel him to transfer authority to American and Japanese civilians as had recently taken place in the Western zones of Germany. Once again, the Supreme Commander asserted that his special "international status" exempted him from normal control by Washington. Any premature reduction in SCAP's power, he warned, would give "greater impetus to the Communist drive to bring all Asia under control." In a jab directed at the State Department's China policy, MacArthur boasted of erecting a "strong spiritual front" against the "Communist advance." Unless Acheson was prepared to accept "catastrophic consequences," he ought to drop loose talk of dismantling the bulwark. Claiming that the Japanese viewed him with a "respect bordering on reverance and veneration," the general urged that he alone be entrusted with arranging a treaty, possibly through a "pledge on the part of the Soviet Union" to respect Japan's neutrality.[6]

Over the next several months, MacArthur continued to offend both State and Defense officials by asserting his right to define the pace and terms of a peace settlement. He hampered implementation of NSC directives, blamed Joseph Dodge for causing an economic crisis and "leaving SCAP to hold the bag," and complained that all demands from Washington undermined his authority. Gradually, however, the general resigned himself to the fact that virtually no one in a position of authority shared his interest in eliciting a Soviet pledge guaranteeing Japanese neutrality. Acheson and his diplomats simply distrusted Moscow. The JCS, in contrast, worried that Moscow really would adhere to a neutrality agreement, thereby blocking Japanese rearmament and offensive bases.

Late in July 1949, MacArthur began proposing a compromise between the State and Defense departments. Although refusing to appoint a civilian deputy, he privately stated that some American troops should remain in Japan "until such time when their withdrawal becomes feasible." He also withdrew his endorsement for negotiating a treaty directly with the Soviets in the CFM. Instead, he urged that all members of the Far Eastern Commission be invited to a peace conference, a forum more easily dominated by the United States. Even if the Soviets participated and issued a pledge to respect Japan, he explained, American troops should continue to garrison Japan for "a minimum of two years" and possibly longer.[7]

By September 1949, MacArthur essentially endorsed the State Department's initiative. Paraphrasing portions of NSC documents he had once objected to, the general informed William Sebald he had "completely changed his views regarding post-treaty controls for Japan." He now supported the State Department's idea of a simple treaty imposing few economic, political, diplomatic, or military restrictions. The United States, he agreed, should encourage the strengthening of Japanese "police forces and perhaps allow them some light arms." Given the instability throughout Asia, he also favored maintaining a protective American "military force in Japan for the indefinite future." This should be negotiated on a bilateral basis with Tokyo, outside the provisions of the formal peace treaty. MacArthur asked only one concession for his conversion to the State Department's position. He wanted the peace conference held in Tokyo with himself named as a "neutral chairman of the Conference."[8*]

Besides the signs of flexibility from Tokyo, other international developments appeared to favor the treaty initiative. Northeast Asia specialist, Marshall Green, noted the different circumstances in 1949 as compared to 1947. The "Communist successes in China and Communist threats to other parts of the Far East" he believed, caused a decisive shift in how the British Commonwealth and other Asian states viewed a treaty. Australia and New Zealand, for example, now paid only lip service to the "Japanese threat." Whatever fury they harbored about the past war, they had begun to rec-

---

* As part of the bait to convince Acheson to name him as the chair of a peace conference, MacArthur offered to approve a long-standing request to expand the diplomatic mission in Tokyo. He also invited the secretary of state to come for a visit. Reluctant to give the general this spectacular forum, however, Acheson declined all three suggestions.

ognize that Japan was no longer the "principal threat to their security." Instead, they hoped a Japanese settlement might pave the way for a Pacific equivalent of the North Atlantic Treaty Organization (NATO) alliance, which would protect them both against their former enemy, Japan, and their future Communist opponents.[9]

Great Britain, America's key ally, also proved extremely accommodating on the treaty issue. During September, Foreign Secretary Ernest Bevin and his top aide for Asia, M. E. Dening, met in Washington with their State Department counterparts. Discussion centered on the Western response to the formation of the Chinese Communist government and the Japanese treaty. Only in partial agreement on the first question, the two governments found much common ground on the second.

Dening chided W. W. Butterworth for Washington's delay in ending the Occupation. In 1947, London and the Commonwealth had urged caution, but they now believed that a prolonged Occupation would only alienate Japan from the West. Dening suggested that the United States not worry about whether China or the Soviet Union would support a treaty. Washington should devise a settlement of its choosing and protect its interests through a "U.S.–Japanese bilateral pact providing for post-treaty U.S. base facilities." Dening also suggested an American trusteeship over Okinawa and was "fairly certain the Commonwealth countries would have no objection" to the course of action he recommended. In any case, the continued drift of policy and the piecemeal diffusion of power to the Japanese represented the worst course. This made America's potential Asian allies angry and left everyone confused about Washington's commitment to the region.[10]

Bevin proved even more eager to assist a settlement. Acheson wanted assurances of Commonwealth support for a prearranged treaty that might be submitted to a peace conference. The British foreign secretary pledged that if Acheson told him "in advance" what Washington required, he "thought he could get the Commonwealth together to write the basic provisions of the treat which would be satisfactory to us." Dean Acheson, in turn, promised Bevin he would "line up" the JCS and the Defense Department by January 1950 so that Bevin could present the case to a scheduled Commonwealth gathering.[11]

Buoyed by the support he found in Tokyo and London, Acheson pressed Truman to put his weight behind the treaty effort. The president seldom expressed an opinion on Japanese matters, preferring to have his subordinates reach a consensus he could rubber-stamp. But the secretary of state feared that unless Truman put pressure on the Defense Department, the military establishment would block his effort to present the British with a

treaty outline. On September 16, Acheson convinced the president to order
the JCS to report formally their views on the "essential security requirements" of a treaty.[12]

Hoping to persuade the JCS and Defense Department officials to support
the State Department's initiative, Acheson and several of his aides (including W. W. Butterworth, John Allison, John B. Howard, and Robert
Feary) met frequently during the autumn months with military representatives. The secretary of state also laid the groundwork for a treaty in
testimony before the Senate Foreign Relations Committee. Relying on
arguments drafted by John Davies, Acheson told both the JCS and the
senators that Japanese security depended far more on its "political, economic and social health" than armed might. Only the "early conclusion of
a peace settlement" would counteract the impact of the Chinese Revolution
among Asians, he cautioned.[13]

In November, Acheson conferred with William Draper's successor as
under secretary of the army, Tracy Voorhees. The secretary of state made
a renewed appeal for army endorsement of a peace settlement. Pursuing
a line of argument developed by Butterworth and Davies, he sought to
refute the common assertion that Japan would be defenseless once the
bulk of American troops departed. Acheson insisted that only a treaty
could mobilize the Japanese behind American leadership. Without it, they
would have no positive incentives to cooperate with the United States.
Besides, he told Voorhees, the Soviets had made a standing offer to consider a treaty in the CFM. By delaying a settlement, Washington threatened
to alienate Japan and leave it susceptible to all manner of Communist
blandishments.[14]

The confidence exuded by the secretary of state reflected, to a large
degree, the strides already made within the department toward writing a
treaty. Since January 1948, a working group had prepared a series of drafts
for periodic review by Kennan, Butterworth, and Davies. On October 13,
1949, they submitted a comprehensive draft treaty that Acheson circulated
widely in the administration. This new approach bore little resemblance
to the 1947 document but a close similarity to the final treaty of 1951.

Besides some extensive clauses on property claims, trademarks, and the
like, the political and security sections of the proposed treaty were short.
It confined Japan to the four major and specified minor islands. The United
States would gain a trusteeship over the former mandated islands and
portions of the Ryukyus. Tokyo must pledge to maintain representative
government, although it might amend Occupation reforms. By prior arrangement, the United States and Japan would devise a security treaty
providing for American forces to be stationed in Japan after the Occupation
ended. The bilateral security pact would permit the United States to station

heavy weapons in Japan and put down threats to internal security. Although the draft retained a prohibition against rebuilding a formal Japanese army, it suggested that the ban be reassessed after five years.

Aware that both the Soviets and Chinese Communists would bristle at these provisions, Butterworth, Davies, and John Allison especially liked the idea of trading Chinese and Russian claims to Taiwan and Sakhalin for those nations' acceptance of the treaty. For example, Taiwan would revert to China only if Peking (Beijing) signed the American draft, and Washington would not formally cede Sakhalin (which the Russian's held since 1945) until Moscow signed. The document included no suggestion that Washington or Tokyo sound out the two Communist states about the possibility of genuinely neutralizing Japan.[15]

Much to Acheson's surprise and disappointment, George Kennan, the "father" of containment, evinced little enthusiasm for this approach. In fact, Kennan's objections marked a step in the alienation that soon led him to leave the department. His critique of Japan policy in 1949 resembled many of the objections he raised to the creation of the NATO alliance. As Kennan saw it, once Japan had been economically and politically stabilized, it faced little danger of subversion or invasion. As the Soviets realized this and so long as the United States did not appear to be turning Japan into an armed camp, the Kremlin might show serious interest in accepting a genuinely neutral solution. Acheson's effort to bring the military establishment and Congress on board, Kennan feared, would over-militarize Japan and turn containment in Asia (as in Europe) into more of a provocation than a defense. The new approach of the State Department, he lamented in his diary, reflected more an attempt to solve "internal administrative difficulties with our own government" than to put Japan on a stable course.[16]

SCAP's representative in Washington, Col. C. Stanton Babcock, expressed great enthusiasm for the draft treaty. Speaking on MacArthur's behalf, the colonel not only endorsed its provisions but approved the idea of cooperating with the Commonwealth nations to assure a friendly two-thirds voting bloc in the Far Eastern Commission. SCAP remained opposed to substantial Japanese rearmament, Babcock emphasized, but supported the retention of a moderate sized post-Occupation American force in Japan. An expanded Japanese constabulary would "deal with Communist or other internal attacks" and the American troops would serve as a trip wire to deter foreign aggression. MacArthur also endorsed the idea of placing all security provisions in a special bilateral pact, separate from the main treaty.

Although in substantial agreement with the State Department's position, MacArthur broke ranks on a related issue. Babcock told both State Department and JCS representatives that the Supreme Commander considered it "of the greatest importance that Formosa not fall under Communist control" (Americans often used the name Formosa in place of the Chinese name for the island, Taiwan). Although American control of the island was not required, "by hook or by crook we must keep it out of Communist hands." Speaking for MacArthur, Babcock proposed that Washington either declare a "trusteeship" and put the island under control of a "safe nation" or even return it to Japan for safekeeping.[17]

MacArthur, in fact, had recently grown more outspoken about the overall Communist threat in Asia. SCAP had invited British High Commissioner for Southeast Asia, Sir Malcolm MacDonald, to visit Tokyo for consultations. There, intelligence chief, Gen. Charles Willoughby, outlined a proposal for a new "line of resistance against communism" that included Japan, the Ryukyus, the Philippines, and Formosa. Criticizing the weakness he saw in the Truman administration's approach, Willoughby said SCAP placed "top priority on preventing Formosa from falling into communist hands." He asked that MacDonald try to reverse London's policy of seeking an accommodation with the Chinese Communists while MacArthur pursued the same goal with Washington. The two men agreed to coordinate future efforts and met several times over the following months.[18]

Douglas MacArthur, of course, was not unique in raising questions during this period about the future of Taiwan. At various times in 1949 and 1950, Dean Acheson, George Kennan, John Davies, W. W. Butterworth, and others in the State Department hatched ideas to foment coups or uprisings against Jiang Jieshi in order to install an "independent," non-Communist regime on the island. Circulated with varying degrees of seriousness, none of these schemes seemed practicable. Should they succeed, they would undoubtedly drive Peking toward even closer ties with Moscow, the opposite of what American policy intended. In this context, MacArthur's attempt to link the Formosa question to the Japanese treaty represented a twist on administration policy but not a fundamental contradiction.[19]

Far more serious than qualifications from SCAP were those emerging from the Pentagon. Early on in their deliberations, JCS representatives and Tracy Voorhees explicitly rejected the idea of a permanently demilitarized Japan. Speaking for Voorhees, Gen. Carter B. Magruder explained that he and "certain others in the Pentagon" felt a large Japanese army would be extremely useful as a supplement to American forces during a war. Japan, Magruder emphasized, must become more than a passive ally denied to an enemy. This theme underlay a critical report prepared for Voorhees and the JCS by the Joint Strategic Survey Committee (JSSC) on November 30. After weeks of deliberation, the committee dismissed the

State Department's draft treaty as premature and ill advised. Before any settlement came into effect, they insisted, the United States must possess permanent bases both in Japan and the Ryukyus and insure that Formosa remained out of Communist hands. Moreover, they considered it necessary that the Soviet Union agree formally to all these provisions. The survey committee realized, of course, that these provisions made a treaty nearly impossible. But, they held, the threat of communism in Southeast Asia, Korea, and Taiwan made the "continuation of our dominant position in Japan of paramount importance to U.S. Security" and made it "dangerous to take any action with respect to Japan now which might lead to an irrevocable loss of influence there."[20]

Not only did the JSSC oppose the neutralization of Japan on its own merits, but noted a clear connection between German and Japanese rearmament. Although the situation in both occupied nations was not "identical," the "underlying objectives of the United States and the U.S.S.R. toward both" appeared to be nearly the same, they said. Even if Japan could be safeguarded by a bona fide pledge of Russian respect for its neutrality, the military planners observed, this would have an undesirable impact "upon our future position in Germany" and the extremely controversial possibilities of rearming that country within NATO. After all, if Washington could accept a neutralized, unarmed Japan, many Western Europeans would question why a similar arrangement could not apply toward the still-feared Germans.[21]

As the Joint Chiefs worked the survey committee's report into a formal position paper, Tracy Voorhees also labored to undermine the treaty initiative. Meeting with British Embassy counselor, Hubert Graves, the army under secretary cited international law as a reason to stall a settlement. Any treaty that unilaterally abolished SCAP, he warned, would violate the Potsdam agreement and Moscow accords of 1945. Voorhees claimed "greatly [to] fear what Russia might do should a treaty be concluded without her." The Soviets might "seize Japanese ships and even bomb Japanese cities inasmuch as they would still be at war." Rather than risk such a confrontation, Voorhees suggested that Washington and London agree to create a "stand-by SCAP" that would oversee limited home rule in Japan. Instead of a formal settlement, the United States would simply allow the Japanese to manage their own affairs under the ultimate supervision of a skeletal SCAP and the protection of American forces. Technically, this would leave international arrangements in tact, offering the Soviets no excuse for interference. Meanwhile, Voorhees's aide, Goldthwaite Dorr, discussed this proposal with Acheson's assistants and suggested that a partial Occupation continue for as much as five more years.[22]

Voorhees even hoped he might persuade Douglas MacArthur to abandon support for a settlement at this time. In mid-December, the army under secretary traveled to Tokyo and laid out the Defense Department's position. But MacArthur hotly disputed Voorhees's contention that Japan must be retained for use as an offensive military position. All Japanese, the general insisted, wanted a genuine treaty now and resented bitterly the stalling in Washington or the talk of a partial settlement. The Soviets, he contended, would both honor Japanese neutrality and accept a treaty permitting a small American force of some thirty-five thousand men to remain afterwards. Instead of trying to "exploit its position in Japan for military purposes," MacArthur told Voorhees, the United States ought to develop bases in Okinawa and the Philippines and take the "necessary steps to deny Formosa to the Communists."[23]

Even though, by early December, the JCS, Voorhees, and Defense Secretary Louis Johnson had resolved to recommend that Truman not authorize further steps toward a treaty, they delayed informing the president of their opinion. First, the military leadership wanted to drag their heels until after the informal deadline for informing the British of the American position had passed. That way, Bevin would be unable to consult with the Commonwealth members at their upcoming January conference. Without assurances of Commonwealth support, Acheson could not place a treaty before the Far Eastern Commission. The longer they delayed consideration of a treaty, the military establishment believed, the greater the likelihood they could extract concessions on rearmament and the protection of Formosa from Acheson and Truman.

In fact, Deputy Under Secretary of the Army Robert West made these objections to a treaty quite explicit in discussions with British representatives. On December 2, Hubert Graves informed Dening that three major issues blocked progress toward a treaty by the State and Defense departments. The Defense Department, he reported West as saying, had determined to preserve the status quo until they received promises to speed Japanese rearmament, to protect Formosa, and *not* to recognize the Chinese Communist regime. Moreover, West complained, Dening had W. W. Butterworth "wrapped around [his] little finger."[24]

Still, Truman had instructed the JCS to make a formal report on their views, and they eventually did so in a way that cut the ground from under the State Department. Late in December, the JCS notified the State and Defense departments and the NSC that

> unsettled political and military conditions and uncertain military action on the Asian continental areas near Japan . . . the highly unstable political and military situation in Taiwan and in Southeast Asia . . . and the fact that a treaty consistent with the terms of the armistice by which Japan surrendered could not at this

time assure the denial of Japan's ultimate exploitation by the USSR or assure
her orientation toward the western powers made it important to postpone a
peace settlement.

If, despite this warning, the president wanted to pursue a treaty, the military
chiefs urged moves to bar the Soviets from stationing any forces south of
Sakhalin. The United States would require all its current Pacific bases as
well as permanent military facilities throughout the "four main islands of
Japan." Moreover, the JCS opposed concluding any treaty unless both the
Soviet and Chinese Communist governments accepted these provisions, an
event even the JCS described as "mutually exclusive." In something of a
tautology, they argued that the fact the Communist states would not approve a treaty partly directed against them confirmed that a settlement
with Japan remained "premature." Defense Secretary Louis Johnson added
insult to injury in forwarding his endorsement of these conclusions to
Acheson. Johnson suggested that the only major problem in Japanese–
American relations stemmed from too much loose "public discussion during
recent months about an early treaty," a debate, he said, incited solely by
the State Department.[25]

Nearly beside himself with frustration, Acheson hastily arranged a meeting where he, Dean Rusk, and W. W. Butterworth could confront JCS
chairman, Gen. Omar Bradley and Maj. Gen. J. H. Burns, reprsenting
Louis Johnson. Acheson ridiculed the military's contention that Washington should solicit Soviet and Chinese support for a treaty confirming Japan
as a forward American base. This fixation on a short-term military advantage, he charged, ignored Japan's greater political and economic importance to the United States. If also nullifed attempts to generate British
Commonwealth support for a unified Far Eastern policy.

Acheson hammered away at his most immediate problem, as well. Months
before he had promised British Foreign Secretary Bevin that the United
States would submit treaty terms that could be discussed at the upcoming
Commonwealth conference at Colombo, Ceylon (Sri Lanka). Because of
the Defense Department's calculated delays, he had to break this pledge.
If he offered no explanation or indication of where matters stood, he might
be accused of misleading vital allies whose cooperation was essential in an
eventual treaty. Consequently, Acheson proposed that Bradley and Burns
approve his sending Bevin a brief message about why the American government had been unable to resolve basic policy questions. He proposed
to say that different agencies in Washington favored alternative means of
resisting growing Soviet pressures on Japan and the rest of Asia. They also
were uncertain of how to assure non-Communist states in the region that

Japan posed no future threat. Although the United States did not consider the "rearming of Japan" an "acceptable" policy at present, the administration was agreed that extensive military-base rights must be retained in and around Japan after the Occupation ceased. Acheson admitted that a treaty that contained provisions unacceptable to China and the Soviet Union provided a "less secure basis" for peace than would otherwise be true. Still, the United States did not believe that excluding them from a settlement would impede an eventual treaty.[26]

Not surprisingly, Bradley and Burns appreciated Acheson's proposed message to Bevin. It indicated the beginning of an important switch in the State Department's position. Although still uncomfortable with the concept of immediate rearmament, Acheson appeared to accept the inevitable creation of a new Japanese army. Also, he agreed that some troops and bases should remain in Japan even after a peace settlement. Even though the scope of these concessions remained unclear and the subject for many later arguments, Acheson had framed his message to focus on the question of military (rather than political or economic) security in light of a Soviet threat. Bradley took this as the germ of a future agreement. He told the secretary of state that, although the situation in China, Southeast Asia and Taiwan remained too unstable to chance a treaty with Japan, in "six months or a year" things might evolve "in such a way that we would know better where we stood." Accordingly, the general suggested, why not lay preliminary plans for rearmament because it would "probably be necessary at some time to let Japan have armed forces."[27]

In effect, the JCS and the Defense Department had made Japan hostage to a successful resolution of other crises in Asia. For months, the military establishment had pressed Acheson and Truman to toughen opposition to the Chinese Communists and consider means of defending Taiwan. They wanted Japan as a strong link, an "active" not a passive ally in a military alliance. If the administration wanted the military to endorse a treaty, Bradley and Louis Johnson served notice, it had better swallow the Defense Department's prescription for the remilitarization of Japan and for more active opposition to Asian communism.

Nor was President Truman much help to Acheson. Although he resisted many of the pressures to move against China and supported the principle of a speedy settlement with Japan, Truman hesitated to overrule the JCS and the Defense Department on the details of a treaty. For example, on December 29, at the conclusion of a NSC meeting at which his civilian and military advisers clashed over China policy, the president expressed concern over the delayed Japanese settlement. The Soviets, he insisted, had not played a great role in bringing about Japan's surrender. Washington might permit the Russians to take part in a treaty, however, Truman had no doubt that the United States and the United Kingdom could negotiate a peace treaty with Japan whether the USSR participated or not." Despite this assertion, the president made little effort to press the Defense Department to fall in behind Acheson's initiative. Serious consideration of a settlement lapsed for several months, resuming only when the State Department adopted many of the hard-line policies of the military planners.[28]

The British government and its Asia specialists expressed great disappointment over the failure of the United States to put forward any terms. Dening felt nothing whatever would be accomplished so "long as Mr. Tracy Voorhees remained in office." It might be necessary, he advised his colleagues, for the foreign office to draft a "defense treaty between Japan and the United States" and submit it to Washington because the Americans seemed not to know how to secure their own "strategic interests." The Ambassador to the United States, Sir Oliver Franks, felt the problem went far beyond Voorhees. Actually, he complained, the Americans appeared to lack "any real . . . policy for the whole Pacific area." As Chinese–American relations deteriorated after January 1950, Franks noted, Japan remained the "one area" in Asia where the position of the United States "was for the time being secure." Any administration effort to improve Sino–American relations or defy the Pentagon's position on Japan would provide the Republican opposition new ammunition to attack an already battered Far Eastern policy.

About the best Dening and Franks hoped for was that the United States would salvage something in the region by increasing its involvement in Southeast Asia. They guessed that Acheson would try to divert the administration's critics from their China campaign by doing something "sensational" in "regard to U.S. aid for Indochina." The British agreed this was necessary both to change the terms of the debate in Washington and to protect vital interests that affected Europe and Japan. Diplomats in London and Washington believed that if the Truman administration hoped to implement a rational Japan policy, it would have to adopt new approaches toward events in China and Southeast Asia.[29]

10

JAPANESE RECOVERY PROSPECTS IN THE WAKE OF CHINA'S REVOLUTION

In October 1949, a few days after Mao Zedong (Mao Tse-tung) proclaimed the establishment of the People's Republic of China (PRC), the State Department convened a special meeting of diplomats and influential private sector outsiders. This group of entrepreneurs, educators, journalists, and China specialists discussed the implications of the regime for future policy. The so-called Round Table Conference coincided with another reevaluation of policy under the aegis of a blue-ribbon panel, the Far Eastern Consultants, led by Ambassador-at-Large Philip C. Jessup. Common themes emerged from the three-day conference as well as the several-month survey of the Far Eastern Consultants. The Chinese Communists, both groups agreed, took power through their own strength and the collapse of the KMT. American opposition would do little to shake their rule. However, if the United States maintained a low-keyed, noninterventionist approach to China, the Communist regime would inevitably grow disillusioned with its new Soviet ally. Those most familiar with China agreed that the United States should avoid any further military actions on the mainland or Taiwan. Instead, Washington ought to preserve informal links with Peking and await opportunities provided by a Sino–Soviet split.[1]

Repeating a theme he and the State Departments' specialists had elab-

orated since 1947, George Kennan told the Round Table that even a pro-
Soviet China posed little threat. As a desperately poor nation, it would
drain scarce Soviet resources, not enhance the Kremlin's power. Yet, he
continued, the Communist conquest of China might affect the United States
indirectly, especially through its impact on Japan. Kennan acknowledged
that Japan's recovery needs dictated some trade contacts with the new
regime but that long-term prosperity and security required a broader base.
"You have" the "terrific problem," Kennan explained, of how the "Japanese are going to get along unless they again reopen some sort of empire
to the South. Clearly we have got, if we are going to retain any hope of
healthy civilization in Japan in the coming period, to achieve opening up
of trade possibilities, commercial possibilities for Japan on a scale very far
greater than anything Japan knew before." Another conference participant
(a veteran of the Occupation), Phillip Taylor, agreed, observing that because Communists controlled Northeast Asia, "we have got to get Japan
back into, I am afraid, the old Co-Prosperity Sphere. . . ."

In addition, Kennan noted, the United States had to devise a recovery
formula for Japan that both stimulated its economy and kept the former
enemy to safe paths once the Occupation ended. Japan, in other words,
must be made both commercially prosperous and politically dependent.
The key, he argued, lay in devising "controls, . . . foolproof enough and
cleverly enough exercised really to have power over what Japan imports
in the way of oil and other things. . . ." By means of this strategic economic
leash, "we could have veto power over what she does."[2]

At about the same time, a group of Army Department officials and
SCAP representatives (including Robert West, Gen. Robert Eichelberger,
and Col. Stanton Babcock) met with British Embassy counselor, Hubert
Graves. The group hoped to convince the Commonwealth countries to
permit Japan greater access to Southeast Asia in place of China and Korea.
"Commercial expansion," argued Deputy Assistant Secretary of the Army
West, was vital "in keeping Japan to safe paths . . . since only a decently
prosperous Japan could be trusted to accommodate itself to Western strategic and political requirements." Now that China ("the continental market") lay within the Communist zone, Americans must insure that its allies
agreed to bring Southeast Asia "into relation with [Japan's] economy.
. . ." Graves reported to London that he had "been struck by the repetition
of this theme in various sectors of the Administration."[3]

Some prominent journalists also picked up the theme of how China's
revolution might affect Japan. Among the most prolific were Stewart and
Joseph Alsop. During the Second World War Joseph served as an employee
of the Chinese Nationalist regime and as an aide to Gen. Claire Chennault.
Stewart shared his concern with Chinese affairs and took an extensive tour

of Asia during the summer of 1949. He returned in August to prepare a
series of reports for his nationally syndicated column about a Communist
strategy to conquer the West by means of economic strangulation. Communism would expand from its relatively unimportant Chinese base, he
predicted, to overrun resource-rich Southeast Asia. From this position, the
Soviets planned to starve Japanese and European industry.

Stewart Alsop's first report, of August 22, accused the Truman administration of a do-nothing policy in Asia. The State Department's Far Eastern experts, he charged, ignored the fact that the Communist virus would
spread from China into Burma, Indochina, Siam, and Malaya, "not in the
distant future but in a matter of months, before the year is out." When
Japan's "vital industrial potential" had been added to the "Kremlin's vast
Asiatic empire," the global power balance would tilt fatally. Diplomats
who claimed that Japan was anchored securely to the United States failed
to realize that it was "nonsense to imagine that a non-communist Japan
could hold out against Communist pressure when her whole natural trading
area had been organized under Communist control."[4]

In subsequent installments, Stewart Alsop blended his own views with
information leaked by someone close to Defense Secretary Louis Johnson.
Reflecting a debate between Johnson and Acheson, he criticized the State
Department's policy as "feeble and diffuse." He advocated appointment
of a "supreme commander" to fight the cold war in Asia and an effort to
hold "the many independent remaining centers of resistance to the
Communists in South China." Slowing the Red tide for even a "few weeks"
might spell the difference between "holding Southeast Asia and
losing it."[5]

On August 29, Stewart Alsop charged the Soviets with planning to con-
struct a new Communist "Co-Prosperity Sphere." Besides directly helping
Russia, this bloc of Asian satellites would strangle Western Europe and
Japan. He warned:

> If Southeast Asia goes, Japan should not prove a difficult target, unless American
> troops are to hold Japan indefinitely by brute force. China and Southeast Asia
> comprise Japan's whole natural trading area, and economic pressure alone could
> be enough ultimately to bring Japan into the Soviet sphere. With Japan's in-
> dustrial potential added to the great riches and huge population of Southeast
> Asia and China, and the whole area under Soviet control, a vast upset in the
> world power balance will have occurred. It is worth recalling that we fought a
> long, cruel war with Japan to prevent such an upset in the balance of power.
> It is also worth recalling that Japan was not a European power, and the Soviet
> Union is.[6]

In mid-September, Joseph Alsop coauthored a more optimistic column
with his brother. Although both thought it doubtful that Truman or Acheson would reverse their China policy, they saw a hopeful sign in the ap-

pointment of Philip Jessup to conduct a general review of programs in Asia. Even though he had little use for the KMT, Jessup seemed to share the Alsops' concern with Southeast Asia, viewing it as an appropriate and practical place to draw the line against communism. They predicted Jessup would recommend that a special $75 million appropriation (Title 303: Mutual Defense Assistance Program [MDAP]), recently approved by Congress, be spent as "seed money" in the region to finance a covert offensive in the "battle for Asia."[7]

The debate within and outside the American government over East Asia policy revealed deep tensions over how to contain the Communist threat while building a core of stable, pro-American states in the region. Although some in the administration, Congress, and the press argued for a military solution (such as blockading or attacking China), others preferred to rely on economic and political means to enhance security among the region's vulnerable nations. Many expected that the Chinese Communists might eventually be turned against the Kremlin and toward a partial accommodation with the West. But would moderation or threats achieve this end more quickly? Given Japan's desperate need for trade outlets, could a limited relationship with China speed Tokyo's recovery and help to modify China's radicalism? Or would such an arrangement only bolster the Communist regime, providing it with an enhanced potential for blackmail? Yet, if Japan was kept isolated from China, where could alternative markets be found?

Before June 1950, the Truman administration never fully resolved these questions. Most actions taken during this period reflected shifting sets of alliances among competing elements in the policymaking community, as they all jockeyed for presidential support. Truman confounded both hard- and soft-liners by endorsing contradictory policies that reflected his own divided instincts as well as those of his advisers. At the same time as he approved Acheson's idea of maintaining private trade links with China, for example, he followed the advice of Louis Johnson that America honor the Nationalists' trade blockade of Chinese ports. Although halting military aid to Taiwan, Truman refused to sever diplomatic ties with the KMT. Although several American diplomats remained in China, he hesitated to permit any serious discussions between them and Communist authorities.

Besides insisting on these conflicting approaches toward China, the State and Defense departments disagreed bitterly over the terms of a Japanese peace settlement. The military establishment envisioned Japan as a semi-permanent military enclave. Diplomats, in contrast, stressed its value as an economic and political ally helping to integrate Asian nations into a pro-Western bloc. Its ultimate importance, they insisted could not be weighed by conventional military standards. As George Kennan put the argument to Dean Rusk, Japanese political and economic power in Northeast Asia held the only "realistic prospect for countering and moderating Soviet influence" there. Dismissing calls for further aid to the KMT or other Chinese anti-Communist factions, Kennan called for action to restore the "natural balance of power." Quoting historian Tyler Dennet's account of Thoeodore Roosevelt's policy during the Russo–Japanese War, he remarked that Washington should raise "no objection" to Japanese ascendency in Korea and its surrounding territory. Control by Tokyo "was to be preferred to Korean mismanagement, Chinese interference, or Russian bureaucracy." Kennan particularly liked a phrase uttered by TR to Sen. Henry Cabot Lodge in 1905. "It is best," he stated, that Russia "should be left face to face with Japan so that each may have a moderative action on the other."[8]

Dismissing China as a factor, Kennan proposed encouraging Japan to resume its traditional role as "power broker" in Northeast Asia. But even he realized that Japanese power depended on a sustained recovery. Conditions in East and Southeast Asia must not be allowed to deteriorate in a way that threatened Japan. How the Truman administration handled the demise of the KMT and the policy it adopted toward Southeast Asian nationalism would, as much as anything else, lay the foundation for Tokyo's future role, he concluded.

Broadly speaking, key decision makers in Washington fell into two antagonistic camps, with President Truman straddling the gap. The JCS and Defense Secretary Louis Johnson along with a small bloc of Congressmen advocated a high-profile anti-Communist policy toward China. They opposed recognition of the Peking regime, supported military aid both to forces on the mainland and to defend Taiwan, and favored imposing strict trade sanctions against the Communist regime. Both Secretary of Defense Forrestal (1947–49) and his successor, Louis Johnson (1949–50), typified this attitude. This group favored holding bases in Japan indefinitely as part of an overall aggressive strategy. They conceived of containment and security interests largely as military problems. In their view, active hostility toward the Chinese Communists would prevent the Soviets and their proxies from consolidating a victory or winning new victories beyond China.

No less anti-Communist, but far more sensitive to the complexities of Asian politics, the PPS and the Far Eastern Division of the State Department fought a spirited campaign to minimize further involvement in China's civil war. George C. Marshall and his successor, Dean Acheson, paid close attention to the advice of W.W. Butterworth, Philip Jessup, George Kennan, John Davies, and China specialist Philip Sprouse, who insisted that futile acts against the Communists would only drive the CCP closer to the Kremlin. Arming KMT remnants in China or Taiwan, this group argued, would encourage a shotgun wedding between Moscow and Peking, with the United States providing the shotgun. Not just the Communists, but most Chinese, they insisted, preferred the civil war to end quickly so they might resume normal living. Acheson and his advisers believed that allowing limited Sino–American trade and holding the door open to possible diplomatic recognition might induce Peking to behave moderately. Moreover, these diplomats knew, any strict trade embargo would sabotage Japanese recovery, boost Occupation costs, and cause bitter resentment in Tokyo and Western Europe. Besides the State Department's Asia area experts, certain civilian army administrators and most SCAP officials shared this concern about the value of trade with China.

Debate over China policy in 1949 often assumed grotesque proportions. Vociferous pro-Nationalist support ranged from the "comic" antics of Sen. Pat McCarran (D–Nevada) to the vitriolic attacks of Sen. William Knowland (R–California) and Gen. Claire Chennault. In February 1949, for example, McCarran sponsored a bill that called for $1.5 billion in new loans to China. Some fifty senators (nearly half of them Democrats) endorsed this proposal along with a call to send American combat advisers into Chinese battlefields. It soon became clear, however, that neither McCarran nor most of his nominal cosponsors really cared about the Nationalist cause. At its core, the aid bill actually represented the latest McCarran scheme for dumping surplus Nevada silver on world markets. The proposal, which its sponsor neglected to clear with other pro-Nationalist senators, soon collapsed.[9]

The tireless adventurer and flying ace, Claire Chennault, advocated other rescue schemes between May and August 1949. Encouraged by Sens. William Knowland and Sen. H. Alexander Smith [R–New Jersey], Chennault returned from China in April 1949 to lobby for covert military assistance to anti-Communist forces still active in western China. In congressional testimony and in several popular magazine articles (which bore titles like "Hold 'Em, Harass 'Em, Hamstring 'Em," and "Last Call for China") this Jiang family confidante and business associate claimed that a "modest" airlift costing several hundred million dollars per year could indefinitely sustain anti-Communist forces.[10]

Besides the logistical and political problems in the Chennault plan, several critics observed that the proposal hinged on giving a lucrative transport contract to Chennault's personal airline in China, Civil Air Transport. As with his misguided air-war strategy during the Second World War, the flying ace completely intertwined national policy with his own commercial and career success. Whatever enthusiasm existed for the idea of covert aid to Moslem anti-Communist forces in western China disappeared during the summer of 1949 when the leading candidates for aid, two generals surnamed Ma, suddenly opted to leave on a pilgrimage to Mecca.[11]

While the congressional China bloc and the private China lobby harassed the administration, more serious debate occurred internally. As had been true since the end of the war, the military establishment pressed Truman to expand economic and military aid to China. Army officials insisted that China was no worse adsministered than, for example, Greece. Like that nation, they claimed, it occupied a strategic location. In an attack on the State Department, Gen. Albert C. Wedemeyer told Defense Secretary Forrestal that, following the loss of China, Soviet forces would be "free to devote [their] entire energies and efforts to over-running Western Europe and the Near East." Russia could also proceed to dominate all continental and Southeast Asia, jeopardizing access to vital raw materials. Perhaps the greatest danger, he argued, would be:

> [the] interposition of an "iron curtain" between the Asiatic continent and Japan, foredooming to failure present U.S. efforts to make the Japanese economy self-sufficient. Japan would be deprived of the opportunity of establishing necessary markets in Asia, thus either imposing Japanese economic survival as a permanent burden on the U.S. taxpayer, or, failing that, forcing the Japanese to join the Soviet orbit as the only remaining means of survival.[12]

By late 1948, however, the JCS acknowledged the bleak prospects facing Jiang's regime. In February 1949, even so ardent a China supporter as James Forrestal admitted that the pace of the Red advance dictated a reduction or suspension of further military assistance. Belatedly, he recognized that much of the military equipment delivered to China soon found its way into the enemy camp. After discussions with members of Congress and the NSC, President Truman decided against formally terminating aid to China, lest it totally discourage "resistance to communist aggression." However, he ordered that "no effort would be made to expedite deliveries" to the mainland, in effect insuring that few military supplies would reach their destination before the KMT collapse.[13]

The pace of the Communist advance as 1949 began posed an additional problem for American policy. Should economic assistance, administered by the ECA under the terms of the China Aid Act, be continued in areas under de facto Communist control? Officials of the ECA serving in China, especially Roger Lapham, favored maintaining a low-key program that might help the civilian population and, perhaps, separate the CCP from the Soviets. However, when ECA officials suggested this tactic to the State Department in December 1948, both Acting Secretary Robert Lovett and the FE head, W. W. Butterworth, opposed the idea. In part, they feared a congressional retaliation against providing aid to the Communist areas. Discussions with Truman on December 20 revealed the president's opposition as well. The idea of such "positive" action to wean the Communists away from Moscow had, apparently, found little favor outside the State Department's PPS.[14]

However, a reluctance to permit aid to Communist areas did not mean the State Department desired to expand assistance to the Nationalist remnants on the mainland. In March 1949, as the China Aid Act neared expiration, the State Department sought to reword the law, permitting a more flexible interpretation. In early April, after much haggling with Senator Knowland, among others, the department got its way. An extended and amended China Aid Act, utilizing $100 million in unexpended funds from 1948, now permitted support to groups other than the "Government of China," including a possible successor regime on the mainland or on Taiwan. The new law did accede to the demands of the China bloc in Congress that aid only be given to the "non-communist areas of China." Nevertheless, as Dean Acheson explained, the State Department supported the revised act "in large measure" because it permitted extension of economic aid to Taiwan.[15] in fact, the overall policy of the State Department reflected this new preference for assisting a non-Communist island bastion, detached from the mainland and, hopefully, ruled by someone other than Jiang Jieshi.

In contrast the JCS and the secretary of defense continued to urge a last-ditch effort at military assistance to the mainland and an explicit American commitment to defend Taiwan. Not only might selective arms shipments to anti-Communist forces delay a complete Communist victory, they argued, but enemy control of Taiwan threatened the entire offshore defense line. If "Kremlin-directed Communists" held Taiwan, the JCS maintained, it would allow them to dominate the sea-lanes on which Japan, Malaya, and the Philippines depended.[16]

General MacArthur added to the din, claiming that if Taiwan passed under Communist control, "our whole defensive position in the Far East was definitely lost." America would be forced to move its "defensive line back to the west coast of the continental United States." MacArthur gave verbal support to a plan to provide Claire Chennault a five-hundred-plane airforce flown by American "volunteers" and even suggested transferring warships to the KMT navy to "blockade and destroy China's coastal cities." Late in 1949, the Central Intelligence Agency (CIA) uncovered evidence that SCAP permitted some Japanese aviators to assist Jiang on Taiwan. Yet, despite this rhetoric and encouragment, neither MacArthur nor the JCS favored committing American forces to the defense of Taiwan. They mitigated their tough talk by adovcating only indirect assistance and increased military aid.[17]

President Truman vacillated between support of the State Department and the arguments presented by hard-liners that China must be isolated by military pressure and Japan protected by rearmament. As a politician, he responded to pressures applied by members of Congress and some pro-KMT lobbying groups. Although not enamored of the Nationalists, he shared many of the gut-level, anti-Communist impulses so common among the military establishment. Despite his temperament, however, he usually allowed himself to be swayed by the more measured advice of Dean Acheson. The influence of the secretary of state remained especially strong from the spring of 1949 until January 1950. Thereafter, domestic pressures, a series of confrontations with the Chinese Communists, and personnel shifts within the state department undermined moderate elements and led Truman to support a tougher approach throughout Asia.[18]

During the spring of 1949, Acheson's advisers succeeded in pushing a relatively moderate program through the NSC, an approach geared toward buying time in East Asia. The diplomats predicted Communist forces would quickly consolidate control of the Chinese mainland and, probably, Taiwan. But on achieving victory, Mao's forces would face an immense task of national development. By avoiding provocations, Washington could encourage the "full force of nationalism" to turn against the Kremlin, which represented a new imperialism. Dismissing the anti-Communist remnants in China as only "slightly less impotent than Yugoslav royalists," the State Department's China specialists advocated a wait-and-see stance, guessing that internal cleavages would eventually moderate the Chinese Revolution. Internal pressures might then impel the Communists to seek "amicable relations with the world community." This evolution might take as long as twenty-five years, and thoughtless hostility would only delay its occurrence.

These arguments persuaded the NSC and Truman to heed Acheson's plea to avoid "military and political support of any non-communist regimes in China" unless they showed a real capacity to mount, on their own, "successful resistance to the Communists." Meanwhile, the administration ought to permit private business and philanthropic contacts with the "Chinese people" as one method of exploiting "any rifts between the Chinese Communists and the USSR and between the Stalinists and other elements in China both within and outside of the communist structure."[19]

Acheson also presented arguments against extending military protection to the Nationalists on Taiwan. He and his aides would have preferred to remove Jiang Jieshi as a prelude to assisting an independent Taiwanese regime. But they discovered such plans were complicated and dangerous. Almost any ruse, if successful, would still foster intense anti-American sentiment within China, just when Washington hoped to stimulate anti-Soviet feelings there in response to Russian meddling in Manchuria and Sinkiang (Xinjiang). If American tinkering with the island's future was to "have any hope of success," Acheson told an aide, "we must carefully conceal our wish to separate the island from mainland control." Early in March, the NSC and the president approved this formula. Although willing to provide some economic assistance to the island while sounding out options for local autonomy, Acheson convinced the administration not to commit American forces in the defense of Taiwan.[20]

Truman's agreement not to challenge the Communist regime directly preserved some latitude for informal Sino–American contacts. Acheson, Butterworth, and Kennan all guessed that China's need for trade and technology unavailable from the Soviet Union would, eventually, moderate Peking's behavior at home and abroad. Within the administration, the hard-liners and moderates continued to argue the significance of this fact. Some believed an economic sword would compel the Chinese to act acceptably or else perish. Others insisted that China could not only survive a long period of economic isolation, but that any trade blockade would have a dire impact on Japanese recovery plans. The United States and its allies, in other words, would pay the high costs for any economic warfare waged against the Communists.

Despite termination of ECA activities in China at the close of 1948, Truman's diplomatic advisers urged him to permit continuation of private trade. W. W. Butterworth stressed the advantages of procuring from China "exports vital to the Japanese economy" that would cost more elsewhere. The more foreign economic outlets it possessed, Butterworth argued, the less likely would be the "early application . . . of doctrinaire totalitarian controls by the Chinese Communists." Carefully regulated trade (which excluded strategic items), he insisted, would mostly benefit China's non-Communist partners, thus easing the Japanese and European economic drain on the United States. Attempts to use trade as a political bludgeon against Peking, he warned, would probably elicit "retaliatory measures" of greater cost to non-Communist economies.[21]

The question of Japanese recovery and trade had vexed Chinese of all political factions since 1947. Opposition to the "reverse course," the end of reparations, and American subsidies for industrial reconstruction had mobilized both Nationalists and Communists in China to denounce favoritism toward a hated enemy. Besides real fears of resurgent Japanese militarism, most Chinese expressed outrage at Washington's willingness to expend dollars on a former enemy while abandoning a former ally. As the Nationalists fled the mainland in 1949, Chinese Communist spokesmen took up the campaign against the threat of United States–Japanese imperialism.[22]

China's new rulers, however, retained a realistic understanding of their need for foreign trade, especially with Japan. Much of China's industrial infrastructure had Japanese components, and Japanese industry eagerly consumed exports of food, coal, and iron ore. Trade between the two countries grew to nearly $250 million during the 1930s and to over $600 million during the war years. As America's naval blockade tightened, China became the predominant source of Japan's imported raw materials. However, with surrender and China's civil war, Sino–Japanese trade shrunk to a tiny fraction of its earlier levels, fluctuating between $7 and $20 million per year.

For Communist leaders, like Mao, renewed trade promised to provide needed foreign exchange, access to technology, and a safety valve from complete dependence on the Soviet Union. In Peking, Communist officials approached Consul General O. Edmund Clubb in the spring of 1949 to inquire about reopening trade with Japan, especially exchanging coal, soybeans, and fibers for machinery. Clubb believed they were so eager for this commerce that Washington might use it to extract at least some political concessions. Meanwhile, economic specialists in the State Department agreed with the principle of replacing high-priced American raw materials imported by Japan with far less costly Chinese commodities. Some economists estimated that if political barriers came down, Sino–Japanese trade could rise quickly to $50 million in 1950 and five times that amount by 1953.[23]

Faced with a stagnant economy, limited outlets, and uncertain American-aid prospects, most Japanese were eager to conduct "business as usual," with the new Communist regime. Both leftists and conservative elements in Japanese political and business circles appeared reconciled to the Chinese Revolution. The predominant Right expected that any semblance of order in China would create major commercial opportunities. At the same time, they guessed, the Communists' victory in China would stimulate further the latent anticommunism among Japan's masses, thus augmenting the conservatives' domination in Tokyo.

In November 1948, Prime Minister Yoshida allegedly stated that he envisaged "without any anxiety the possibility of a total [seizure] of China by the Communists. . . ." the feisty conservative leader believed that the CCP would soon turn as nationalistic and antiforeign as previous Chinese regimes. Insisting that the CCP actually helped mitigate Soviet power in Asia, the prime minister believed Sino–Japanese contacts could be rebuilt to mutual advantage.

Yoshida's remarks typified the conservatives' hope that the Communist victory in China would both restrain the Soviets and give Tokyo new leverage over Washington. Peace on the Asian mainland promised to restore favorable trade conditions absent for years. In the spring of 1949, Yoshida told an American journalist, "I hate communism so much I avoid even reading about it." Still, he continued, he did not "care whether China is red or green. China is a natural market, and it has become necessary for Japan to think about markets."[24]

These jaunty remarks echoed other sentiments voiced in business circles. American economic analysts noted how distinctly assertive, unified, and confident the Japanese appeared on this issue, as compared to the almost cowering remarks on foreign policy that usually emanated from Tokyo. Perhaps, China's expulsion of American influence stimulated the Japanese desire for self-determination. The lure of trade with Peking as well as the symbolic impact of the CCP victory certainly stimulated desires for a restoration of sovereignty. As some Americans noted, this pattern held true especially for conservative politicians and industrialists. It would be "naive" to assume that the Japanese oligarchy would "remain a passive instrument for achieving American objectives in the Far East." Following a peace settlement, it was reported, Yoshida's political and business allies would "be ready to gamble on their own skill in pursuing an independent foreign policy, which will not necessarily be in accord with either the American or Soviet objectives." Late in 1949, Inagaki Heitaro, Japan's trade minister, confirmed this point, explaining that Tokyo hoped to conduct between one fourth and one third of its total foreign trade with China.[25]

The army's Civil Affairs and P&O divisions, both concerned with balancing Japan's foreign trade accounts through expanded access to nondollar markets, also considered trade with China as a vital element in any recovery. At a conference—including Butterworth, Niles Bond (of the State Department), Gen. Edward M. Almond (of SCAP), and officers representing the Civil Affairs Division and the under secretary of the army—it was agreed that Sino–Japanese trade ought to be permitted. The military officials who actually oversaw Japan's economy shared little of the enthusiasm of the JCS to pump aid to the KMT or blockade the mainland. It was not so much a matter of principle as one of "hard headed business," they reasoned. The Civil Affairs Division, under Gen. G. L. Eberlie, prepared a general guide for SCAP use, stating that trade with "Korea, Formosa, North China and Manchuria" remained "vital to the economic recovery of Japan." The guide also proposed that SCAP should permit China trade consistent with restrictions on trade with Russia and its European satellites. In many categories, Japan was to enjoy the same privileges as the ERP countries. Encouraged by their ideas, the Civil Affairs Division and Army Under Secretary Draper prodded MacArthur to expand Sino–Japanese commerce "to a maximum consistent with the economic requirements of the respective [Communist] areas and Japan."[26]

Eager to reduce its own costs and responsibility under GARIOA, the army's civilian command—Secretary Kenneth Royall and Under Secretary William Draper—broke ranks with the JCS and the secretary of defense.

Early in February 1949, while accompanying Joseph Dodge to Japan, Royall raised the sensitive issue of trade with China. During the same news
conference at which he called for an early treaty and blasted SCAP, he
also discussed the importance of restoring Japan's commerce in Asia.

The army secretary bid good riddance to the KMT and suggested that
the Communist Chinese posed little threat. In fact, the restoration of peace
on the mainland was probably "the best thing for China." It would permit
both Washington and Tokyo to resume normal trade and provide them
with "bargaining points" and "greater advantages for exploitation of China."
So long as Peking did not face an implacably hostile America, Royall
believed, the Chinese Communists would prove "tough babies" for Moscow to control.[27]

However, State Department and Army Department officials excited by
the prospect of Sino–Japanese trade still voiced concern over its implications. Some worried that a Japan not at all dependent on non-Communist
trading partners might loosen its political ties to the United States. Eventually, overdependence on China might even force a change in "Japan's
political and strategic orientation." Promises of preferred access to markets
and raw materials or threats of a "possible economic boycott by China"
might pull Japan "into the Communist bloc."[28]

For example, if Japan's steel industry recovered through utilizing Chinese
ore and coking coal, what would prevent Peking from someday abruptly
halting these supplies to "create a serious economic crisis" or to blackmail
Japan? For political security, both State Department and Army Department planners believed that Tokyo must have diversified outlets if it expected to rely on China while avoiding Communist pressure. The solution
might be to pursue a dual policy, promoting immediate trade with China
and laying the groundwork for a commercial development program in
Southeast Asia at the same time. Chinese exports could "reduce significantly" Japan's current dependence on American raw materials and food.
They would also provide a vital "breathing space before the development
of better trade conditions for Japan in Southeast Asia." As one State
Department survey concluded early in 1949, American development aid
to Southeast Asia should serve the "dual purpose" of consolidating American influence in that region while "providing insurance not only for Japan's
future economic independence" but also for the degree of economic stability required for "political independence throughout the Far East."[29]

On March 3, 1949, at a meeting of the NSC, the secretary of state pushed
through a policy directive reflecting these views. NSC 41, "U.S. Policy
Regarding Trade with China," called for tolerance of private trade between
China and the non-Communist world. The report asserted that any embargo or attempt at economic warfare would not only be ineffective but,

most likely, would backfire. Not only could China probably withstand any trade restrictions but the United States would find its own allies bitterly opposed to a quarantine. In contrast, a "positive" trade policy might serve as a carrot encouraging acceptable political behavior by China. In the absence of any effective "instrument," to cause the "defeat or containment of Chinese Communism," the State Department considered it preferable to "augment, through permitting restoration of ordinary economic relations with China, such forces as might operate to bring about serious rifts between Moscow and a Chinese Communist regime." An embargo, on the other hand, would only drive China closer to the Soviet Union, the opposite of what Washington desired.

But the core of the economic argument in the case Acheson presented to the NSC related to Japan. Chinese exports would be of "significant importance" to the goal of Japan's recovery and self-sufficiency. "Severe restriction on trade" would make it difficult or impossible to purchase raw materials from North China and Manchuria. This raised the awful prospect of "indefinite support of the Japanese economy by the United States." Acheson acknowledged that commercial relations between Japan and China constituted a risky proposition. Although China desired Japanese capital goods in exchange for raw materials, Japanese dependence on China "would provide the Communists with a potentially powerful leverage over Japan after the United States Occupation and financial support had been withdrawn." However, because America could not "underwrite the Japanese economy indefinitely," this had to be accepted as a "calculated risk." In the short run, SCAP would have to regulate trade carefully, halting any trend toward overdependence on China. This policy also sought to encourage the Japanese government to maintain controls on trade with China once it regained sovereignty.

NSC 41 proposed implementing the "R-procedure," originally developed for regulating commerce with the Soviet bloc. Certain strategic and high technology items in a "1–A" category were barred as well as certain less sensitive "1–B" goods. But most raw materials, food, and consumer products could be bought from or sold to China in accordance with normal commercial considerations. Meanwhile, the NSC and President Truman agreed that SCAP

[should] encourage trade with China on a quid-pro-quo basis but should avoid preponderant dependence on Chinese sources for Japan's critical food and raw material requirements. Every effort should be made to develop alternative resources on an economic basis, particularly in such areas as southern Asia where a need exists for Japanese exports.

From March 3, 1949 until the outbreak of the Korean War, this relatively flexible trade policy remained in effect. Some officials in the Office of the

Secretary of Defense and the JCS (although not the Army Department) tried to restrict Sino–Japanese commerce, but the exchange of products totaled some "40 million during the twelve months ending June 1950, nearly double the previous year's value.[30]

Even before approval of NSC 41, the Army Department had notified MacArthur that it, too, supported increased trade with China. In May, Deputy Assistant Secretary of the Army Robert West told SCAP in detail about Communist approaches to Consul General O. Edmund Clubb in Peking, noting that the State Department wanted the Chinese to make commercial deals through American consular officials. (The Communists refused to work through the consuls because Washington refused to recognize the PRC and maintained diplomatic relations with the Nationalist's on Taiwan.) Although eager to encourage trade, West also urged SCAP to avoid giving any impression that Japan desperately needed Chinese exports, nor should it permit any official trade missions to travel between Peking and Tokyo. But except for restrictions on 1–A and certain 1–B items, he explained, Japan was free to conduct business on a cash or barter basis.[31]

MacArthur, as ever, showed several faces on this issue. Despite his oft-stated sympathy for the KMT, he acknowledged the importance to Japan of expanded trade with China. Although barring official dealing or visits by Communist trade delegations to Tokyo (which might imply a shift in diplomatic recognition), SCAP encouraged commerce in even wider categories and with less regulation than the State Department preferred. In defiance of the State Department's preferences, he urged proceeding with trade even when Communist authorities insisted on bypassing American consular officials, who normally certified invoices. He took this position both to avoid delays and to make certain that diplomatic officers gained no added leverage over SCAP. In effect, State Department officials complained, MacArthur wanted "no procedural limitation on the development of Sino–Japanese trade that are beyond SCAP's control."

Yet, the general could make statements that seemed to defy all of his actions to stimulate commerce. In October and November of 1949, he informed British diplomats in Tokyo that, despite the importance of Sino–Japanese trade, he supported a blockade of China that would force the Communist regime from power. At the same time, his staff sought even greater latitude from the State and Army departments to expand Japanese access to Chinese markets.[32]

Ultimately, prospects for Sino–Japanese trade excited MacArthur because he, like Acheson, knew it benefited Japan directly. Thus, the general continually resisted pressure from the JCS and Defense Secretary Louis

Johnson to alter his position. In September 1949, he declined to endorse Johnson's proposal to amend the flexible trade policy. By then, President Truman had actually come around to Johnson's side, telling Acheson he considered NSC 41 "out of date." Yet, on November 4, with implicit support from SCAP, Acheson convinced Truman to maintain the status quo. Implementing a trade embargo, the secretary cautioned, would enrage the Europeans and Japanese and only marginally affect China. Over the long run, he warned, severe restrictions on Japanese trade with China would "pose a serious obstacle to achievement of Japanese self-support and would require a major" increase in the "future magnitude and duration of United States financial support for the Japanese economy."[33]

Acheson stuck to this argument into January 1950, when he explicated his policy before a closed session of the Senate Foreign Relations Committee. Describing his approach to Asia, the secretary urged patience. At present Washington must do nothing to drive Peking closer to Moscow. While awaiting a Sino–Soviet rift, the United States could shift its "real center of interest" to the countries bordering China. Rather than playing with counterrevolution in China, Acheson called for making containment work in the "crescent or semicircle which goes around . . . Japan at one end and India at the other." This required implementing a policy of regional integration for Japan, resembling that in Western Europe. Concentrating American efforts on an economic or military crusade against China, he warned, would actually devastate Japan, which "lived on foreign trade." Ironically, success in isolating China would make Tokyo a semipermanent "pensioner of the United States. . . ."[34]

In his testimony, Acheson countered almost all questions about aiding anti-Communist Chinese by stressing the need to assure Japan of trade opportunities. For the present, at least, China seemed Japan's only ready source of raw materials and its most appropriate market. In the long run, he hoped, defending and developing the Southeast Asia portion of the Great Crescent might provide an alternative economic zone. "At the present time," Acheson asserted, Japan could resist blackmail because it had "more to offer North China than North China had to offer Japan." In the "pull between them," the Japanese held the "superior" position. However, he doubted his leverage could be maintained "over a long period of time" if nothing changed. To build a more secure system, Acheson explained, all future assistance to the Far East should be extended "in such a way that we can get double benefits for them." By this he meant that development projects in East and Southeast Asia would be designed to help both the direct recipients as well as Japan.[35]

The idea of programming assistance in ways that would eventually benefit Japan gained additional adherents during early 1950. The JCS, Defense

Secretary Louis Johnson, Army Under Secretary Tracy Voorhees, and others championed a "southern strategy" to isolate China while making Japan the anchor of Asian containment. However, unlike Acheson or Kennan, they had little interest or faith in the prospect of separating China from the Soviet Union. Uneasy with permitting any non-Communist trade with China, they hoped to minimize Sino–Japanese links by developing alternative Asian outlets. For these varied reasons, a cadre of enthusiasts emerged who took the remarks made by George Kennan and Philip Taylor at the October Round Table Conference rather literally. Japan had to regain "some sort of empire to the South," something like "the old Co-Prosperity sphere. . . ."

11

NSC 48 AND THE RENEWED DEBATE OVER ASIAN COMMUNISM

The impasse over the Japanese treaty and still-contested policy toward China revealed a widening rift within the Truman administration. Rival civilian and military agencies disputed not only the details of a treaty or trade regulations but also what kind of threat Asian communism presented to American security. Acheson and his advisers considered it plausible to downplay China's significance while building alternative centers of strength in Japan and Southeast Asia. In contrast, Defense Secretary Johnson and the JCS wanted to utilize Japan, Taiwan, and Southeast Asia as advanced military outposts in an active campaign against Chinese communism. MacArthur, again, remained somewhere in between. Although opposed to moves aimed at remilitarizing Japan, he supported proposals to augment anti-Communist movements in Southeast Asia and argued for a commitment to Taiwan. Given these diverse concepts of containment and a defense perimeter, all three factions operated at cross purposes.[1]

The ambitious and acerbic Secretary of Defense, Louis Johnson, began to challenge Acheson's influence over Truman shortly after he replaced the ailing James Forrestal early in 1949. An influential Washington attorney and major Democratic fund raiser, Johnson had little respect for bureaucratic turf or professional diplomats. Unlike Forrestal or Acheson, the new defense chief surrounded himself with political cronies positioned to advance his own career. David Lilienthal, Chairman of the Atomic Energy Commission (AEC), described his discomfort at the sight of those who flanked Johnson: the "overfed, cigar-chewing, red faced . . . characters," the kind of "vultures" one saw "hanging around the courthouse" looking for public contracts. Lilienthal prediced the defense secretary's tenure would prove a "terrible strain for democracy."[2] Subsequent developments confirmed Lilienthal's predictions. The defense chiefs' petulant and unpredictable behavior compelled Truman to fire him in the autumn of 1950.

Unhappy with the recent NSC and presidential approval of the State Department's "moderate" program toward China, Johnson demanded a wide-ranging reexamination of policy. Through the NSC, he circulated a complaint that the "course of events in Asia," particularly the "successes of communism in China," threatened the "future security of the United States." Johnson stated that the relatively passive reaction to events in China overlooked "our best long-range interests." Because, he argued, containing communism required a "carefully considered and comprehensive plan," the defense secretary wanted the NSC to reexamine basic policies and devise "new courses of action—political, economic and military—which might be undertaken" in Asia.[3]

Johnson did not say so, but his interest in a new "plan of action" was stimulated by the administration's introduction of a large aid package to Congress. In July, Truman asked Congress to approve the Mutual Defense Assistance Act, which included the MDAP, a program that would provide funds for arms, defense production, and other activities in Europe and Asia. A billion-dollar plum that both State Department and Defense Department officials wanted to control, MDAP opened a new round of bureaucratic infighting in Washington.*

The idea of a large fund for supplying aid to allies originated as part of the SWNCC 360 study in April 1947. Superceded by the Truman Doctrine and Marshall Plan, the proposal languished for two years. Many members of Congress objected to the concept of giving the president nearly complete discretion over foreign aid and others felt the giveaway would only make the Europeans less willing to improve their own defense capacity. However, right after he signed the NATO treaty on July 23, 1949, Truman formally proposed creation of a $1.5 billiion MDAP. The administration claimed the program would put teeth in NATO by buttressing the European allies against either internal uprisings or the initial phase of a Soviet attack. In addition to granting weapons from American stockpiles, money might be used to stimulate European defense production. Implicitly, MDAP dove-

---

* The MDAP, in turn, funded Military Assistance Programs, or MAPs, in recipient countries. The acronyms were often used interchangeably.

tailed with Marshall Plan funding and represented a sort of "military" Keynesian foreign aid program. Later, after the ERP ended, many of its functions were continued under this military-aid program.

The bill encountered fierce opposition when first introduced to the Congress, however. Several senators cited criticism from journalist Walter Lippmann who condemned the proposed law as a "general license to intervene and to commit the U.S. all over the globe, as, when and how the President and his appointees decide secretly that they deem it desirable to intervene." Charging that Truman wanted a "diplomatic slush fund and military pork barrel," Lippmann predicted the law would lead to secret military commitments and interventions around the world. An irate coalition of liberals and conservatives dismissed Dean Acheson's explanations and compelled him to withdraw the bill. On August 5, the Senate received a hastily revised draft with some of the discretionary provisions deleted.[4]

The most strident members of the congressional China block (Sens. H. Alexander Smith, Owen Brewster, Styles Bridges, and William Knowland; Representatives Walter Judd and John Vorys) sized on the MDAP as a vehicle to reinvolve the United States in China's civil war. Although most of its provisions applied to NATO and, possibly Austria, MDAP might be utilized to extend aid to the Nationalist forces in Taiwan and the mainland. By making this demand their price for cooperation, the China bloc hoped to force the Truman administration to accede to its views.

Sen. H. Alexander Smith described how the China bloc hoped to extract concessions. The "strange combination of supporters" as he described them, included representatives who acted from a variety of motivations. Congressman Walter Judd was "completely emotional on the subject" of China. Sen. Pat McCarran made outlandish aid proposals "in part at least to create a market for the silver-producing states of the West." Sens. Owen Brewster and Styles Bridges, Smith admitted, "were motivated . . . by the desire to make the China crisis a partisan issue of the campaigns of 1950 and 1952." However, Smith felt that he himself and Sen. William Knowland were motivated by purer instincts. Also, they held seats on the key committees conducting the MDAP hearings.[5]

Knowland took the lead in proposing that MDAP be amended to include about $200 million for use "in the Far East to stop the spread of communism in that area." The wording was designed to permit activities outside of China because, Smith admitted, even KMT loyalists were "virtually agreed that further aid to the Nationalist Government would be money poured down the rat hole. . . ." Instead of locking funds into one project, it might be valuable to place a special economic weapon in the hands of the president, "to use at his discretion," to block Communist expansion in other parts of Asia.

Working with Senators Knowland, Vandenberg, and John Foster Dulles, (R–New York—filling out the term of the deceased Robert F. Wagner), Smith drafted the desired amendment. They hoped to make the MDAP hearings a forum to dramatize the "importance of the whole Far Eastern picture, . . . includ[ing] Japan and the islands of the Pacific, as well as Burma, Indonesia, Malaya and even India, as well as the specific crisis in China." Smith even invited MacArthur to testify, although the general declined in a flip manner, which angered his supporters in Congress. Ultimately, Smith believed the proposal to fund an Asian MDAP might even convince the "State Department leadership to work with us rather than against us."[6]

From August through September, the Senate Foreign Relations and Armed Services committees held joint hearings on the MDAP bill. Most Senators were far more concerned with technical features of how the bill would fund European defense industry than with its application to East Asia. Nevertheless, Knowland and Smith kept the China issue before their committees by continually charging that it made no sense to spend billions of dollars in Europe while denying a few million to halt the Red advance in Asia. Even some fellow Republicans, like Henry Cabot Lodge (R–Massachusetts), grew frustrated with Knowland's behavior. Lodge reported that he heard from reputable sources that the Nationalists were openly selling American weapons to the Communists. "If the Senators who want to send arms to China could see the procession of American weapons going down the streets of Shanghai carried by Communists, they would damned soon stop it." But Knowland persisted in his demands and on August 26 offered an amendment to allocate $175 million for China.[7]

Hearings in the House of Representatives followed a similar pattern. There, Congressmen John Vorys and Walter Judd berated the administration's desertion of China. Profound ignorance, if not treason, caused this failure to stand with a noble ally, they charged. The House Committee on Foreign Affairs, although quite willing to include some vague symbolic wording about stopping communism in Asia, refused to recommend that any China aid be included in the MDAP bill.

Both Gen. Omar Bradley and Secretary of State Acheson testified against funding a new China aid package. Bradley explained that as a "practical point," the Nationalists were finished on the mainland. Acheson offered a detailed analysis of Asian politics, citing the historical reasons for the Communist victory. He went on to caution members of Congress against concentrating "every thought we have on China." Now the time had come to refocus policy on how to "prevent the spread of this communist menace throughout Southeast Asia," Acheson explained. He promised that his aides would soon recommend new policies in this regard.

Even Acheson saw some benefits in making life "difficult" for the Chinese Communists through conducting limited guerrilla operations, but he preferred to expend major resources elsewhere. The secretary again stressed the importance of the "vast area which extends from Pakistan to Japan," convulsed by nationalism and hungering for change. America should direct its efforts toward winning the loyalty of these other Asians. This was especially important to America's most important regional ally, Japan, he noted, because it required strong economic ties with the nations of the Great Crescent.[8]

To speed passage of the MDAP legislation, Acheson proposed a compromise being discussed by several senators. Congress ought to "give the administration some money—not very much—which could be used in Asia on a confidential basis" at the president's discretion. The administration would pledge to use the money to fight communism "in China and elsewhere." But his suggestion at first fell flat. The House committee preferred to spend nothing on covert aid and Senators Smith and Knowland wanted a large sum committed to China.

Acheson pressed forward with a compromise. Covert funding, he suggested, should be pegged at no more than $75 million (instead of $175 million), and the president should be given the right to expend the money secretly, in any way he saw fit. Although most senators had opposed this principle in the original MDAP bill, the idea of a small, clandestine, unvouchered fund for Asia worried them less. Eager to pass the bill and appease their contentious China bloc colleagues, a majority of both committees expressed support for Acheson's proposal.[9]

Some additional problems arose as the Senate committee tried to write the text of an amendment. Knowland insisted that any money spent must actually benefit anti-Communist Chinese. At one point, he and Smith even demanded that Truman be compelled to confer with General MacArthur before spending any covert funds. But, eventually, most senators approved wording for Section 303 of the MDAP bill that appropriated an unvouchered fund for the containment of communism "in the general area of China."[10]

The formal committee report sent to the full Senate in September detailed the exceptional nature of the secret provisions. In effect, Section 303 provided money not for China, but for the nations on its periphery. Because the political situation in Asia was far less stable than in Europe, the report asserted, the president must be granted wider leverage. Therefore, Section 303 allowed the chief executive to transfer money, weapons, or services—with no accounting—to any part of Asia "threatened by communism."[11]

By early September, a few problems remained in reconciling the House and Senate versions of the bill. Following negotiations, the House dropped its provocative but empty call for the United States to sponsor an anti-Communist Pacific pact, a sort of toothless Asian NATO. Instead, it accepted the Senate amendment to create a special fund for containment in the "general area of China." The two chambers approved identical versions of the bill on September 28, which Truman signed as PL 329 on October 6, 1949.*

Louis Johnson already had this money and something like Section 303 in mind when he pressed the NSC to come up with an "action plan." Although the initial funds were comparatively tiny, any program begun under MDAP was almost certain to grow. If the Defense Department seized the initiative in proposing novel ways to use the money, it would stand a good chance of dominating both the president's attention and an overall Asian containment program. At a tactical level, Johnson also took advantage of the fact that the small, permanent NSC staff he asked to prepare the Asian policy paper tended to reflect the military's influence. Before this, most foreign policy studies were actually drafted by the State Department and merely circulated by the NSC for consideration.

Dean Acheson understood at once what Johnson had attempted. He, too, formed a special working group to devise a "new" Asia program for Congress and the president. On July 18, 1949, Acheson appointed Ambassador-at-Large Philip C. Jessup (a close friend) and two prominent "outsiders," Everett Case, Colgate University president, and Raymond Fosdick, former Rockefeller Foundation president, as special Far Eastern Consultants. Jessup assumed this task in addition to the related job Acheson had already given him, that of assembling the China White Paper. This exposé of KMT misuse of American aid since 1941 was designed to deflate those critics who charged the Nationalists had lost to the Communists because of inadequate foreign support. When released, Acheson guessed, the White Paper would contain any domestic political damage caused by the Communist victory in China. Meanwhile, his blue-ribbon panel would survey Asian policy and recommend forward-looking actions that might be taken outside of China. Together, the secretary of state hoped, these moves should dampen attacks by the congressional China bloc, partisan critics, and hard-liners within the administration—making it much simpler for Truman to support a moderate line.

Acheson phrased Jessup's appointment partly to undercut criticism from Louis Johnson and the congressional China bloc. "Take as your assump-

---

* Key supporters of this grant of power to the president included J. W. Fulbright (D–Arkansas), Jacob Javits (R–New York), and Wayne Morse (Ind.–Oregon). Ironically, all became leading critics of executive misuse of covert power in Asia during the 1960s.

tion," he instructed Jessup, that it is a "fundamental decision of American policy that the United States does not intend to permit further extension of Communist domination on the continent of Asia or in the Southeast Asia area." He ordered the consultants to devise "programs of action" for repelling any Communist thrust beyond China. The department, he said, would "make absolutely certain" it neglected "no opportunity that would be within our capabilities to achieve the purpose of halting the spread of totalitarian communism in Asia."[12]

Besides dispelling criticism that his department was doing nothing to resist Communist threats, Acheson thought the Far Eastern Consultants might offer suggestions on how to use MDAP funds or other aid money in Asia. The secretary considered it vital that civilians control any future aid program in East and Southeast Asia. Thus, during the remainder of 1949, the Far Eastern Consultants and the drafters of Johnson's alternative proposals, now labeled NSC 48, really fought to dominate the direction of Asian policy.

Early in August, Acheson tried to control terms of the debate by releasing the thousand-page China White Paper. This remarkably detailed chronicle recorded Washington's ten years of frustration with an inept and corrupt KMT regime. The message seemed clear, at least to those in the State Department: the Nationalists were doomed and not worth saving. However, to appease conservatives, Acheson added to the report a brief cover letter composed by a committee. It managed to offend nearly everyone through its hostile description of the Chinese Communists as Russian stooges and the KMT as inept, corrupt bunglers. Mao, Jiang, the China bloc, and many others dismissed the whole exercise as an American alibi, largely on the basis of this ill-tempered preface. The public and most members of Congress heard far more about the cover letter than the contents of the full report and remained as confused as ever about the administration's policy.[13]

Meanwhile, the NSC staff set to work on the task assigned them by Louis Johnson. From August through October, this group reduced hundreds of pages of data into a forty-page study that called on the United States to resist a Soviet breakthrough in Asia. In a neat twist, the NSC 48 draft depicted an effort by the Kremlin to build its own "Co-Prosperity Sphere" as a mirror image of the earlier Japanese version. Soviet proxies would use control of China and Taiwan to isolate and seize Southeast Asia. Once they dominated the region's transportation routes, markets, and raw materials, the Russians would have placed a noose around the neck of Japan.

The economic dimensions of the threat to Japan and the West loomed larger in these background studies than in most earlier assessments of East Asia. Previously, planners had focused on the internal recovery crisis resulting from Japan's economic isolation and the shift in world trading patterns. This, of course, remained a major consideration, but the NSC 48 drafts also indicated a growing concern about the consequences of Soviet control over Japan and Southeast Asia for American economic security. The NSC staff carefully weighed the effects of what would result from the Kremlin's harnessing of Japan's industrial base to its own base. They estimated that this would boost by some 25 percent Russia's military-industrial complex. If Northeast Asia as an economic unit (including Siberia, Manchuria, North China, and Korea) were rationally integrated, the Soviets could quickly alter the balance of world economic power.

In weighing the consequences of a Soviet breakthrough in Southeast Asia, the NSC staff perceived a grave danger to the interdependence of world trade. Although the direct American economic stake in the region might not be vital, that of Western Europe and Japan was, or might become so. As nationalist political agitation and rebellion drove out the colonial powers, these planners predicted, Communist elements would begin to close off the region's resources, with disastrous results. Hoping to prevent this shock and still avoid direct American intervention, the planners suggested that the United States encourage, or even underwrite, a new Japanese presence. Ignoring the fact that most Southeast Asians remained terrified of renewed Japanese influence, the NSC staff argued that an influx of Japanese technical personnel could replace departing Europeans and provide a vital cushion of "social and political stability" as the area traversed from colonialism to self-rule. Simultaneously, this strategy would provide a substitute for the promises, influence, and technical expertise of Communist agents and secure Japan a future role in Southeast Asia.[14]

Proposing a European analogy, the draft report described Manchuria as similar to central Europe and Japan as another England:

> The powder keg—Southeast Asia (Balkans, Middle East) occupies a similar position with the more or less secondary, but not to be overlooked India (Iberian Peninsula) in the offing. Therefore, to carry the analogy further, it must be concluded (tempered only by the broad concept of defense in the East and offense in the West) that a strong Western-oriented Japan, with access to the raw materials of as much of the rest of Asia as possible, is essential to the U.S.

Expanding on this domino theory, the NSC staff dismissed the likelihood or value of Chinese "Titoism" mitigating Peking's threat. Whatever face Mao showed, the United States must oppose "communism because of its basic evil." In this hierarchy, Japanese security rested on defense of, and access to, Southeast Asia. This, in turn, required a renewed campaign against Chinese communism and the defense of Taiwan. Despite initial losses, by "aggressively and effectively" backing "indigenous forces," the

United States could "commence the rollback of Soviet control" everywhere in Asia. Success depended on quick action and the appointment of a "high-ranking individual—military or civilian—to direct all United States efforts against Communism in China."[15]

The NSC 48 drafts produced by mid-October met all of Louis Johnson's criteria for undermining the State Department's policy. In contrast to the "moderate" view of the Chinese Revolution, the NSC portrayed the revolution as a first act in the conquest of Southeast Asia and Japan, with drastic repercussions inevitable in the West. To stifle Chinese communism in its cradle, the report called for a halt in all trade, a ban on all private contacts, and active support for anti-Communist guerrilla activities. Acting under the fig leaf of an American-organized, anti-Communist "Pacific Association," the NSC staff urged U.S. control of Taiwan. Even more pleasing to the defense secretary, the draft recommended that a wholly new, military-oriented agency be created to wage a "cold war in Asia."[16]

As word of the NSC deliberations filtered back to the State Department, Acheson redoubled his efforts to contain the offensive by the hard-liners in Congress and the Defense Department. The wording of Section 303 to the MDAP bill had prevented the China bloc from transforming that program into a vehicle solely for fighting the Chinese. In his testimony, the secretary of state redirected the anti-Communist impulse away from military actions in China and toward support for economic and military assistance in Southeast Asia and Japan. But when the issue resurfaced once more with the appearance of NSC 48, Acheson and his Far Eastern Consultants worked even harder to keep Congress and President Truman on track.

At the same time as the NSC staff developed their agenda for Johnson, Acheson's Far Eastern Consultants lobbied with members of Congress, journalists, business leaders, and the president on behalf of a "regional" strategy. Dismissing China's importance, even should it become a Soviet satellite, the Far Eastern Consultants urged policymakers to concentrate attention on the more important sectors of the Great Crescent. As early as August 29, they presented a package of recommendations to the secretary of state. To capture the psychological initiative at home and abroad, Jessup, Fosdick, and Case urged a bold statement endorsing non-Communist nationalism in Southeast Asia, renewed efforts to have Congress fund the Point 4 economic-aid program, appointment of a special high commissioner to Asia, rapid conclusion of a Japanese peace treaty, and special assistance to the Philippines and India so that they might serve as models of "the good life in a non-communist society."[17]

Early in October 1949, the Far Eastern Consultants helped conduct the department's Round Table Conference on China, where they presented their concepts to influential members of the business, press, and academic communities. At the end of that month, Jessup's group made a formal presentation to the secretary and the department's Asian specialists. To insure that Moscow did not "capture" Asian nationalism, they explained, the United States must encourage Chinese "deviation" from the Kremlin while turning Japan, Korea, Okinawa, and the Philippines into "demonstration projects." Achieving these goals, Jessup and the others stressed, required that Washington coexist with the new regime in Peking, do nothing to detach Formosa from the mainland, and remove "barriers to trade in non-military goods between Japan and China." However, the Far Eastern Consultants opposed any accommodation with Ho Chi Minh's guerrillas and endorsed the French scheme to transfer power to the Bao Dai regime in Indochina.[18]

Although Acheson's strategy appeared to gain adherents in Congress and in the private sector during the closing months of 1949, he found it difficult to hold Truman in check. The president had remarkably little feel or understanding of Asian politics and expressed contempt for both warring factions in China. Although disgusted by KMT corruption, he had a gut-level fear of the Communists that often set him thinking in a bellicose direction. In June 1949, for example, Truman vetoed an invitation (which Acheson, in any case was not keen to accept) for Ambassador John Leighton Stuart (then in Nanking [Nanjing]) to visit several of his former pupils, now important Communist officials in Peking.

During the summer and fall, Truman grew furious at the Chinese for holding Consul General Angus Ward under house arrest in Mukden (Shenyang) on charges of espionage.* He spoke of cutting off all trade with China and even blockading ports in retaliation. In October, the president told Acting Secretary of State James Webb of an idea to use the $75 million of covert funds in the MDAP bill to incite an uprising by anti-Communist Chinese Muslims. In mid-November he mentioned a plan to have the American Navy blockade North China and also to use Section 303 funds to sponsor guerrilla actions. Although all these references were vague and emotional, they revealed the president's inclination to listen with partial attention, at least, to ideas whispered by Louis Johnson.[19]

Given the president's skittishness, Acheson hoped the respected team of Jessup, Case, and Fosdick—none of whom were "tainted" as "China experts soft on communism—would soothe Truman's temper. After all, they, too, had an action plan, but one devoted to the positive goal of

---

* Some evidence indicates Ward's subordinates may have been spying. He was held partly as a scapegoat and partly as a bargaining chip by the Communists. Ironically, the CCP may have wanted to trade his release for recognition by the United States.

building positions of strength rather than the negative impulse to fight the Chinese. Early in November, the secretary met with the Far Eastern Consultants to prepare them for a meeeting, two weeks later, with the president.

Jessup ran through what he intended to tell Truman. An area approach that would knit together Japan and Southeast Asia would limit the advance of communism more effectively than any half-baked scheme to refight the Chinese civil war. Supporting nationalism and developing regional ties among the Japanese, Indians, and Southeast Asians, Jessup emphasized, would create a viable network of pro-Western, anti-Communist states. In this regard, the ambassador continued, the United States could utilize Japan to "influence . . . the countries of SEA" as they achieved independence. He even advocated formation of a new "Co-Prosperity sphere" with the "same phychology" minus the militarism of the 1930s. This time around, the United States could provide the temporary financing for "Japanese personnel to fill in shortages" as the Europeans left Southeast Asia. Eventually, he believed, just as the United States used the cover of "Pan-Americanism" to become the "indispensable" leader "economically and politically" of the Western Hemisphere, Japan and India might "become similarly indispensable in the Asian area."[20]

In view of Jessup's emphatic support for encouraging Japan's reentry into Southeast Asia, questions arise about the degree of differences between the State Department's agenda and that proposed by the Defense Department and the NSC staff. Both glibly spoke of sponsoring a new "Co-Prosperity Sphere," were committed to containment on China's periphery, and accepted the need to assist Japanese recovery. But they broke ranks sharply when it came to defending Taiwan, sponsoring military actions against China, and permitting Sino–Japanese trade. Defense Department enthusiasm for Japanese rearmament and opposition to an early peace treaty also divided the departments. MacArthur kept a foot in both camps, endorsing Acheson's views of the treaty, disarmament, and trade but also Johnson's attitude toward China and Taiwan. Given these divergent opinions, Acheson placed great stock in the impact of Jessup on Harry S Truman.

Jessup's group met with the president on November 17, making these points in some detail. Truman told Acheson that the presentation had been "tremendously helpful," providing him with a "new insight into the reasons for the Communist success in China" and a "better understanding of the whole situation" in Asia. Buoyed by this response, the secretary reiterated his own and the Far Eastern Consultants' main point: the best way to contain communism and modify Chinese behavior was to avoid provocations and encourage those "vigorous influences" that would drive Moscow and Peking apart. The entire situation, in fact, resembled closely "the case of Tito." Truman, however, would not so easily abandon his own visceral reaction to communism. He told Acheson that although he agreed, in a "broad sense," that a moderate, constructive policy might provide a long-term solution, he still lacked a "thorough understanding" of all the facts needed in "deciding the question."[21]

The president's wavering response—and well-known tendency to agree with whomever he last spoke—worried Acheson. The secretary of state knew that Louis Johnson was ready and eager to supply additional "facts" in the form of NSC 48. When Acheson and the Far Eastern Consultants finally saw the draft report in the latter part of October, they feared its "unrealistic, impractical and even starry-eyed" anticommunism might be exactly the kind of solution that appealed to Truman. If nothing else, its conclusions would be much easier to sell to a mass audience than the more subtle and sophisticated recommendations of the Far Eastern Consultants.[22]

The reaction of Everett Case typified that of most State Department officials. The concepts advanced by NSC 48, he exclaimed, varied from the "merely wishful and unrealistic . . . to the dubious and even disastrous." Talk about a Pacific pact or a UN-sanctioned American takeover of Taiwan was fanciful and baseless. How would Washington reconcile "refusal to recognize or do business on any terms" with Peking vis-à-vis "trade requirements basic to reconstruction of a sound Japanese economy? If America isolated China, how could it hope to "enlighten" the Chinese with respect to the Soviet Union? Negotiations and trade with the Communists must serve as carrots, not bludgeons. All references to seizing Taiwan, blockading trade, or backing guerrillas, Case insisted, must be stripped from NSC 48. As area specialists in the Office of Chinese Affairs pointed out, American attacks on China would do little to dislodge the Communists but would provide the new regime with a perfect alibi for its own failures and give them "no incentive to change their attitudes and policies toward us."[23]

Alerted by his staff, Acheson quickly appointed a special working committee headed by John Allison to emasculate NSC 48 before it caught the president's fancy. The trick, they believed, was to preserve the flamboyant anti-Communist rhetoric of the original draft and at the same time gut its conclusions and recommendations for action. Besides their determination to cut the plan's call for intervention in China and Taiwan, Acheson and Allison hoped to recast NSC 48 in a manner that boosted their program for Japan. As it stood now, Allison noted, a "policy paper purporting to deal with all Asia" but that made no provisions for a treaty with Japan was as "satisfactory as Hamlet without the Prince of Denmark." The State

Department revision would show that "economic warfare" against China would actually undermine the "possibility of Japan's achieving economic self-sufficiency in the foreseeable future." The addition of Japan, not China, to the Soviet bloc, represented the real danger to American interests, the one development in Asia "capable of shifting the balance of world power to the disadvantage of the United States."[24]

By late December, the State Department committees reworked the original draft of NSC 48 into a curious hybrid. At one level, it called on American policy to "contain and, where feasible, reduce the power and influence of the U.S.S.R." Yet, it also pointed out Japanese dependence on China for short-term recovery. The paper warned that additional meddling on Taiwan or support for anti-Communist forces on the mainland would only "rally all the anti-foreign sentiment in China" to the side of the Communists and the Soviets. Placing greater emphasis on Japan than China, the new draft directed attention away from Northeast Asia and toward the Great Crescent. As a long-term strategy, the United States would have to allow regulated Sino–Japanese trade while Japan developed new markets and sources of raw materials, particularly in Southeast Asia. Not surprisingly, this complete revision of NSC 48 elicited fierce opposition from the Defense Department, the JCS, and the congressional China bloc.[25]

Johnson, the JCS, and MacArthur all hoped that domestic political pressures would push Truman toward a more aggressive stance in Asia. While the NSC staff worked on the NSC paper, MacArthur and Pentagon planners pursued their own efforts to free up some of the MDAP money without restrictions imposed by the State Department. As early as October 1949, the Army Chief of Staff, Gen. J. Lawton Collins, asked the P&O Division to devise a "special operations" plan for spending the $75 million in the 303 fund. On November 10, Maj. Gen. Charles L. Bolte proposed to spend about half that sum supporting "legitimate governments or anti-communist groups" in Thailand, Burma, Indonesia, and China (including Tibet and Taiwan). The remainder would be kept in a contingency fund for Taiwan and Southeast Asia. However, these and similar air force proposals for covert military aid awaited the NSC's approval of either the Johnson or the Acheson version of NSC 48.[26]

Sen. H. Alexander Smith and William F. Knowland tried to generate enthusiasm for a renewed anti-Communist campaign by visiting the contested regions of Asia during September, October, and November. Smith's arrival in Tokyo (en route to Taiwan and Southeast Asia) coincided with a new SCAP campaign to highlight Taiwan's strategic value. Early in September, MacArthur told a visiting congressional delegation that the Soviet Union intended to conquer Europe through an Asian backdoor. To block this threat, he urged actions to weaken China and strengthen Taiwan. He would give Chennault a five-hundred-plane air force staffed by American "volunteers" and transfer enough ships to the Nationalist navy to shield Formosa and "blockade and destroy China's coastal cities."[27] At the same time (as noted earlier), MacArthur encouraged Sino–Japanese trade.

During October, MacArthur's deputies told State Department and Defense Department officials that any Japanese peace settlement must insure Taiwan remained in friendly hands. In Tokyo, meanwhile, Gen. Charles Willoughby, SCAP's intelligence chief, warned a visiting group of advisers to the JCS about future Communist plans to sever Japan's trade routes by using air and naval units operating on Taiwan. Once that island passed under enemy control, he predicted, the entire Pacific defense perimeter would become useless.[28]

Reports soon circulated in Washington and in Asian capitals that SCAP was encouraging skilled Japanese war veterans to assist Taiwan as the first stage in a plan to defend the island. The consul general in Taipei reported rumors that "SCAP will bring forces here on October 15 to thwart a Communist takeover." Prominent KMT officials both spread and believed the claim that MacArthur would pull hidden strings to block an invasion. The CIA (as noted earlier) reported that MacArthur was cooooperating with Chennault's scheme to patch together an air force and might transfer some equipment to the free-lance warrior. Senator Smith's well-publicized visits to Tokyo and Taipei also suggested that SCAP enjoyed some influential political backing for these activities in Washington.[29]

During November, Sen. William Knowland also beat a path through the Asian badlands with Claire Chennault as his guide. They visited the few remaining KMT strongpoints in China, adding an element of drama to the junket. Knowland's trip coincided with the arrest and threatened trial of Angus Ward by Communist authorities in Mukden (Shenyang). The two events generated renewed attention from some American journalist who had grown bored with reporting the nearly finished civil war. This flurry of interest caused General Bolte to suggest to his superiors that the time appeared "psychologically right for public opinion and the Congress to support positive measures with respect to Taiwan."[30]

By December, Defense Department officials were anxious to bring MacArthur into line on two outstanding Asian problems, the China–Taiwan issue and the Japanese treaty. Tracy Voorhees traveled to Tokyo in a vain effort to convince the general to soft pedal a treaty still opposed by the entire top echelon of the Defense Department. Although MacArthur refused to comply, he proved more than willing to cooperate with the effort of Johnson and the JCS on behalf of Taiwan. A Chinese Communist takeover of the island, he announced, would deal a "fatal" blow to American security in the Pacific. Even "Japan in enemy hands" was not "so dangerous as is Formosa in a like situation." MacArthur outlined a plan to safeguard the island by simply declaring it "neutral" and off limits to the Communists. Nor would he allow the Nationalists to launch attacks against the mainland. After stabilizing the situation, he would shore up an independent regime (whether or not under the current KMT leadership is unclear) by expending MDAP funds. Voorhees endorsed this proposal and sent it on to Louis Johnson in the form of a letter for the secretary to pass on to Truman.[31]

Based on these developments and on reports from the JCS intelligence staff that preserving a non-Communist Taiwan would at least delay international recognition of the PRC while deflecting Communist pressure from Southeast Asia, the JCS renewed a formal appeal for American protection of the island. Both the JCS and Louis Johnson realized that in making a case for Taiwan, they would simultaneously make a case to stiffen the terms of NSC 48, which was due for formal consideration shortly. On December 23, the JCS recommended that Johnson ask Truman to permit "limited military measures," including the stationing of fleet elements in Taiwanese waters to shield the island. As a step toward expanding military assistance, they also urged that MacArthur and the Seventh Fleet Commander, Adm. Russell S. Berkey, "make an immediate survey" of the island's defense requirements.[32]

The Nationalist regime learned of these proposals almost immediately from word leaked by sympathizers in the Defense Department and SCAP headquarters. Since August, Chinese Ambassador V. K. Wellington Koo had made the rounds of official Washington telling everyone that if his government survived, it could help shield Japan and Southeast Asia. This certainly had a more credible ring than trying to convince anyone that the KMT deserved help on its own merits. Now, it appeared, his own lobbying efforts dovetailed with proposals from the Defense Department.[33]

Buoyed by signs of renewed support, on December 23, Koo handed State Department officials a request for major new military assistance. The proposal outraged W. W. Butterworth who considered it a plan to "carry the war to the mainland." He found it even more disturbing that the request was nearly identical to the recommendations put forward by the Defense Department that same day. Butterworth alerted Acheson to the fact that the Pentagon and their Chinese allies really wanted to sabotage the State Department's moderate policy by underwriting the bellicose agenda of NSC 48. In essence, they wanted the United States actively back in the Chinese civil war. Johnson, Butterworth complained, would not rest until he saw American interests "nailed firmly to the mast of a discredited regime to the dismay of our friends in Asia and the delight of the Communists [who] would unite all mainland China on the issue of U.S. military intervention."[34]

State Department officials understood that this enthusiasm for Taiwan really aimed at making it impossible to achieve the goals of the "moderate" strategy in East Asia. Acheson's policy rested on dual pillars. He anticipated a reduction in Sino–American hostility once the KMT regime fell. Also, the American withdrawal from further involvement on Taiwan would free attention and resources for other, more important areas in Asia. Assuming the burden of defending Taiwan would not only outrage Peking— for no good purpose—but would tie the United States to a costly open-ended investment that starved more worthy projects.

Hoping to undermine this strategy on the eve of the crucial NSC meeting scheduled for late on December 29, Acheson confronted the JCS at a private morning session. He demanded that Gen. Omar Bradley explain why he and his colleagues had reversed their earlier positions to favor a direct commitment to Taiwan. Bradley replied that they had always "considered Formosa important" but had lacked enough funds to make it a priority. (Louis Johnson, ironically, had actually pledged to prune military spending.) Now, with the possibility of tapping into the $75 million MDAP 303 fund, the JCS had a source and a use for the money. Gen. J. Lawton Collins made another point. The Chinese Communist threat to Southeast Asia "might be deflected so long as they had Formosa to contend with or subdue."[35]

Acheson attacked these justifications as self-serving and primarily aimed at scaring Truman back into the Chinese struggle. The civil war was over, he insisted, lost because of KMT corruption and incompetence. If the military really wanted to contain communism, they ought to endorse the State Department's attempt to strengthen the "neighbors of China." Adventures and provocation in Taiwan or mainland China would only destroy Mao Zedong's core of independence from Moscow, America's "one important asset in China." Calls for economic warfare were equally dangerous because it would make Japan a "pensioner of the American taxpayer."

After raising some further half-hearted reasons for protecting the island, the JCS admitted that a communist Taiwan actually posed no special threat to Japan, Okinawa, or the Philippines—in contrast to what MacArthur claimed. Bradley conceded that Acheson's political considerations appeared to outweigh the military significance of what the JCS recommended. But he still tried to justify their position by reference to the MDAP Asia fund. Congress had "appropriated money to support these people who were resisting communism" and the JCS were simply trying to make good use of it.[36]

Temporarily, at least, the fight seemed to have gone out of the JCS and Louis Johnson. Acheson had lobbied successfully within the NSC and with the president to support the State Department's revision of the Asia policy paper. Once he realized NSC 48 would not mandate spending MDAP funds on a Defense Department controlled crusade, Johnson beat a tactical retreat. In fact, he arranged to leave Washington just before the critical NSC vote on December 29.

The NSC met on December 29 and 30 to pass judgment on the controversial Asia policy paper. The council easily approved the modified State Department draft, known as NSC 48/1. With President Truman presiding on December 30, the conclusions of the long document (under the heading NSC 48/2) were adopted as policy. The paper, replete with much anti-Communist rhetoric, basically sustained the "moderate" program of the last several months. Unless Asian states genuinely took the initiative, it did not even recommend formation of an American dominated Pacific military alliance. Although some "diplomatic and economic" aid to Taiwan might continue, NSC 48/2 placed the administration on record against defending the island or sustaining anti-Communist forces within China. Diplomatic ties with Taipei would be continued, but the Peking regime might be recognized when "it is clearly in the U.S. interest to do so." Meanwhile, Washington would not agitate against others recognizing the PRC nor would it forbid American or Japanese trade with the regime.

To protect regional American interests, NSC 48/2 called for greater pressure on France to transfer power to Bao Dai. Waffling on the thorny issue of the Japan treaty, nonetheless, the paper called for "improving" the American position in that nation, Okinawa, and the Philippines. Finally, to assuage both State Department and Defense Department planners, the document concluded with a recommendation that the $75 million available for the "general area of China" under Section 303 of the MDAP "be programmed as a matter of urgency."[37]

This admonition revealed how central the MDAP remained in the visions of both moderates and hard-liners at the close of 1949. Acheson would use the funds to begin assistance for Southeast Asian and Japanese development. Johnson and the JCS were eager to apply the funds toward military projects and adventures in Taiwan, China, and Southeast Asia. During the next six months, these two agencies fought constantly to control this money and the expanding MDAP. Their struggle had major implications for all the nations along the Great Crescent.

12

CONTAINMENT AND RECOVERY IN JAPAN AND SOUTHEAST ASIA

Early in 1950, Dean Acheson attempted to regain the policy-setting initiative by outlining a regional program for East and Southeast Asia. By assisting Japanese–Southeast Asian cooperation, he asserted, the United States could restrain further Communist expansion and insure political stability and economic progress. Although Acheson's many critics within the military establishment adopted the vocabulary of regional integration, they used it as a tool to undermine the State Department's influence over President Truman. Acheson and his advisers advocated selective military assistance, trade, and development as a key to containment. Military planners, in contrast, promoted several schemes for extensive military aid and for developing Japan as an arsenal supplying a coalition of anti-Communist regimes along China's periphery.

The secretary of state spoke of regional programs that spurred economic development, assisted moderate nationalism, and solidified the ties of East and Southeast Asia to the world economy. As stronger links developed between Japan and its non-Communist neighbors, China would diminish as a destabilizing factor. This should permit the United States and its regional allies to wait out the "radical" phase of China's revolution and its alliance with the Soviet Union. In contrast, most military planners rejected the premise and the conclusion of these assertions. After all, as the original drafters of NSC 48 declared, the United States should not await or reward Chinese "Titoism." Communism had to be opposed because of its "basic evil."

Like their State Department counterparts, Defense Secretary Johnson, Army Undersecretary Voorhees, and the JCS also favored expanding Japan's trade with Southeast Asia. However, this reduced dependence on China did not imply a willingness to tolerate or ignore the Communist regime. Freeing Japan from links to Northeast Asia, they argued, would permit a more active military stance against Peking. Eventually, Japan might coordinate a regional anti-Chinese alliance, linking Taiwan and Southeast Asia. For the first six months of 1950, up to the outbreak of the Korean War, these several factions jockeyed for control over the expanding MDAP budget, viewing that military and economic aid program as a vital lever in shifting American policy in their favored direction.

In January 1950, Harry Truman and Dean Acheson both publicized their determination to minimize further involvement in China's civil war. Instead, they sought to build new positions of strength outside China. Truman took the initiative at a news conference on January 5, announcing an end to "military aid or advice to Chinese forces" on Taiwan. The Nationalists would still be permitted to purchase arms with previously appropriated dollars and would continue to receive small amounts of nonmilitary aid, but the United States did not "desire to obtain special rights or privileges, or to establish military bases on Formosa at this time." Even though the president bowed to the pleas of Gen. Omar Bradley to insert the modifier "at this time" (implying that, in case of war, policy might change), Truman left little doubt that he intended to broaden the distance between his administration and the KMT remnants.[1]

Acheson offered a more comprehensive explanation of the administration's intentions during executive testimony to the Senate Foreign Relations Committee on January 10. Like Truman, he revealed the essence, if not the text, of the NSC 48/2 decision. Here, as in a subsequent public speech, Acheson distinguished between the Soviet threat and the more amorphous economic and political chaos sweeping the world. The Russians and their proxies might take opportunistic advantage of this disorder, he admitted, but Europe and Asia faced deep problems unrelated to Communist intrigue. For example, the nationalist revolts against colonialism sprang from indigenous roots. To deflect the appeal of communism, both American and European policy must soothe the underlying causes of conflict, not just counter Soviet ambitions. Similarly, the collapse of world trade, Acheson argued, stemmed more from the dislocations of the Second World War than from Moscow's disruptions. Current economic problems challenged America's ability to "incorporate" Germany and Japan "into something larger than themselves." Both former enemies required cheap raw materials and markets, problems that stretched back to even before the war.

The Chinese Revolution, too, stemmed largely from internal causes, the secretary told the senators. As had happened with Tito, he expected that Soviet pressure on China would provoke a sharp rift. The Chinese, however, were so unpredictable that they might compensate for losses to the Russians by expanding into Southeast Asia. In light of these uncertainties, he felt Washington would do best to avoid antagonizing China while building secure positions on its periphery.[2]

"The real center" of American interest, Acheson stressed, lay "in these other countries" along the "crescent or semi-circle which goes around . . . Japan, at one end, and India at the other." Although Japan comprised the anchor of this line, its economy still had to be reckoned a weak link. Because Japanese industry survived "on foreign trade," the United States could risk neither its dependence on, nor isolation from, China. The kind of blockade some officials and politicians favored, Acheson aserted, would make Tokyo's problems "quite insoluble." Japan would be reduced to an increasingly restive "pensioner of the U.S."

The secretary of state saw only one solution to the dilemma. Although permitting regulated Sino–Japanese trade, the United States could encourage alternative outlets for Japan. Dollars appropriated for the MDAP program, the $100 million remaining unexpended in the China Aid Act of 1948, and money that might become available under the (as yet unapproved) Point 4 development program might all be spent in "the Far East in such a way that we can get double benefits from them."

Rejecting the claims of Senators Arthur Vandenberg and H. Alexander Smith that more be done to save Taiwan, Acheson dismissed the Nationalist regime as a doomed anachronism. Instead, he repeated his reference to the "semi-circle of nations" anchored by Japan. If some way could be found to solve the "great question" of Tokyo's economic needs, he thought the entire region could be secured. If not, the Japanese might undertake their own expansion, seek a deal with the Soviets, or "ask for bids back and forth between the two sides."[3]

Although much of Southeast Asia remained in dreadful shape, Acheson portrayed Indonesia and French Indochina as the two most hopeful spots. Just a month before, the Dutch had finally relinquished power to the Indonesian Republic and now the French seemed ready to implement the March 8, 1949, agreement giving greater sovereignty to Bao Dai in Indochina. Acheson even felt the French had retaken the military initiative by constructing elevated blockhouses (resembling "the little forts we had in fighting the Indians") in contested areas. This, he expected, would rally more Vietnamese behind Bao Dai. Despite the expected collapse of Taiwan, then, progress in Indonesia and Indochina as well as Japan's gradual recovery promised to contain the spread of China's revolution.[4]

Acheson made these points publicly on January 12 in a speech to the National Press Club in Washington. He reaffirmed what he had said privately to the Senate, stressing the need to meet the "crisis in Asia" by accommodating the tide of nationalism. The people of Asia refused to accept any longer "misery and poverty as the normal condition of life." Even though Acheson doubted that colonialism bore much blame for underdevelopment, he acknowledged the power of this idea among most Asians. This explained why the Communists hitched their revolution to the nationalist banner and why the West must abandon efforts to maintain the status quo.

Speaking more specifically, the secretary of state called for standing aside and allowing China's wrath to be visited on Soviet, not American, interference in their affairs. Although the United States would provide military security for a defense perimeter including Japan, the Aleutians, the Ryukyus, and the Philippines, the greatest challenge lay in promoting stable regimes in Japan, Korea, and Southeast Asia. Japan required special help in regaining commercial access to the "mainland of Asia, in Southeast Asia and in other parts of the world." Along with this, Washington would push ahead with either a peace treaty or some "other mechanism" that would restore Japan's sovereignty. Over all, Acheson declared, the promotion of regional trade along the Great Crescent from Japan to India represented the wisest course in Asia.[5]

The successive statements by Truman and his secretary of state refocused, if only briefly, public discussion. Louis Johnson and Gen. Omar Bradley in Senate testimony of January 26 both obscured their former positions by denying they ever really favored an American defense of Taiwan. Sir Oliver Franks, the British ambassador to the United States, reported to London that the president and Acheson had resolved the policy debate definitively against the KMT. Eventually, he predicted, America would follow the British lead and recognize the PRC.

The British government's view of containment in Asia paralleled closely that articulated by Acheson. For two years, London had worried about American antagonism toward the Chinese Communists and feared that, in blocking Sino–Japanese trade, Washington would push Tokyo toward an exclusive economic relationship with Southeast Asia. Signs of a potential American accommodation with Peking promised to provide Japan diverse outlets and shelter the British sphere in Southeast Asia. Meanwhile, instead of its "fantastic" policy of tilting at Chinese windmills, the United States seemed ready to apply its great power at the "front line of the cold war in Asia . . . in Indochina."

The British were far more concerned about a Red advance south of China—into a vital economic zone—than over Mao's victory. If communism triumphed in Indochina, British diplomats believed, the Soviets would gain a "stranglehold on all Asia through control of their food supply." By abandoning the KMT and Taiwan, Ambassador Franks informed the British Foreign Office, the American government (or, at least, Truman and Acheson) had taken a giant stride in the direction of a rationale containment policy.[6]

Frank's description of unity in Washington, just as the professed moderation of Johnson and Bradley, proved to be temporary. Beneath the facade of cooperation, old rivalries and bureaucratic conflict simmered and intensified. Planners in the State and Defense departments, the Army, and SCAP as well as the ECA and the JCS all retained mutually exclusive designs on the money to be made available by Section 303 of the MDAP. Although the pot at first glance appeared quite meager (only $75 million), it represented only a down payment on a larger program. Slightly over $100 million remained unexpended from the China Aid Act of 1948 and Truman would probably request additional MAP money in the spring of 1950 (for fiscal 1951). In other words, about $200 to $300 million would soon be available, with few strings, for use in East and Southeast Asia. These stakes were certainly worth fighting for.

The JCS and the army (as mentioned before) had initiated studies of how to use MAP money as early as October 1949.* That same month, Acheson learned that Louis Johnson claimed to have reached an informal "understanding" with Truman securing Defense Department control over the fund. When the secretary of state questioned the president on this point, Truman did not explicitly deny a private arrangement with Johnson but assured Acheson he would honor only those requests coming jointly from the two departments via the Bureau of the Budget. Despite this reassurance, Acheson later discovered that Johnson continued to press schemes involving covert, MAP funded operations. During a trip to Paris in October, Johnson reportedly offered the French assistance in Indochina from the $75 million fund without bothering to inform the State Department.[7]

By January 1950, Johnson's efforts to control the MDAP program were rivaled by the other components of the Defense Department, the ECA, and, of course, the State Department. Each advocated a plan tailored to

---

* A small amount of money for covert activities in China was already being funneled by the CIA to Claire Chennault's airline, CAT. The State Department knew of this and, apparently, did not object to such limited operations.

its own needs and aspirations. New money and new programs promised something for everyone.

On January 10, Army Under Secretary Tracy Voorhees jumped into the competition by asking the NSC to undertake a study of how to coordinate assistance programs in Japan, China, and Southeast Asia. Voorhees declared:

> Continuing or even maintaining Japan's economic recovery depends upon keeping Communism out of Southeast Asia, promoting economic recovery there and in further developing those countries, together with Indonesia, the Philippines, Southern Korea and India as principal trading areas for Japan.

He also emphasized the importance of increasing the flow of Southeast Asian raw materials to Western Europe.[8]

Voorhees complained that a lack of coordination resulted in wasteful aid programs throughout Asia. He wanted existing agencies with overlapping jurisdictions replaced by a new agency making more efficient use of every aid dollar. This would permit assistance programs to be focused on the great "technical workshop" of Japan, with its nearly 50 percent unused capacity. Only if a new agency operated through this "central workshop" could every dollar be made to perform "double duty." Dollars, distributed through Japan, would finance exchanges of Southeast Asian raw materials for Japanese manufactured goods.

For example, Washington could provide financing and materials for the sale of Japanese irrigation equipment to Thailand. The increased rice production in Thailand would be sold to Japan as repayment. Soon, the United States would no longer have to expend dollars on food aid for Tokyo and Thailand would have a new outlet for commodities and an affordable source of consumer and light industrial products. As the exchanges grew to include more items, Japan's dependence on foreign assistance would diminish and the outflow of Southeast Asia raw materials would stimulate production both in Japan and the ERP countries.

Because manufactured products would yield greater profits, Japan could soon realize a hefty trade surplus with Southeast Asia and begin to perform regional credit functions. Although American seed money and some raw materials would still be needed to prime the pump, Voorhees argued, the trade relationship would quickly become self-sustaining, mutually beneficial, and an important basis of political stability.[9]

These proposals reflected, once again, the ideas of army economist Ralph Reid, adviser to Voorhees and Joseph Dodge. Reid emphasized Southeast Asia's future importance to Japan and warned that its loss would affect vital American interests. The Soviets and Chinese Communists supported nationalist insurgencies, Reid insisted, not so much to benefit themselves as to cripple American allies. The Kremlin leadership expected that Japan, "unless sustained indefinitely on an American dole, will be dependent upon Russia and her satellites for the bulk of her market and raw materials." Stalin assumed that Japan would "fall of its own weight once [the] [Communists] control the resources and markets of South and East Asia and U.S. aid to Japan comes to an inevitable end."[10]

At first glance, Voorhees and Reid appeared to make a fairly routine argument about integration speeding Japanese recovery, Southeast Asian development, and the saving of American-aid dollars. The army undersecretary had not yet included an anti-Communist military component in his proposal. However, as Voorhees revealed in the spring, he expected MDAP assistance actually to prime the pump of Japanese military production for export to Southeast Asia. This special trade would solve the lingering problem of what Japan would actually sell to whom. Although initiated with both American aid and American raw materials, the exchange would eventually become self-supporting through the provision of Southeast Asian industrial commodities to Japan. In the proces, Japan would become a "subcontractor" for containment and a military supplier, whatever the course of its own rearmament.

On the same day that Voorhees asked the NSC to begin a review of Asian economic policy, Defense Secretary Johnson ordered the JCS to formulate a new plan for spending the 303 fund. He intended to make certain that Acheson did not monopolize the MDAP program by submitting his own Defense Department agenda to Truman. Moreover, he encouraged the JCS to develop ideas for "covert assistance or operations" in China and Taiwan.[11] Although not opposed to Voorhees's long-range military-production scheme for MDAP, the defense secretary and the JCS wanted to make immediate use of the fund for supplying weapons.

Not surprisingly, in January 1950, the JCS appointed an ad hoc committee on aid to Southeast Asia that recommended that MAP money be spent almost exclusively on military rather than economic assistance. Its head, Maj. Gen. Robinson Duff supervised a report calling for creation of a special group to provide immediately $15 million for Indochina, $5 million for Indonesia, and $10 million for Thailand; also, $45 million would remain in reserve, for possible covert operations in China and Taiwan.[12]

Besides repeating much standard anti-Communist rhetoric, the report presented a new twist. Echoing an argument put forward by Acheson, the JCS planners emphasized Japan's vulnerability to Communist economic blackmail. Southeast Asia must be controlled by non-Communist governments to prevent Japan from "being drawn eventually into the Communist economic sphere," they wrote. Because Indochina represented the strategic center of the contest for power in Southeast Asia, the planning committee urged direct American support for the French military campaign there. By crushing the Vietminh, Washington would insure future access to the region's resources and materials. The "security interest of the United States" in Asia, the report held, hinged on "finding and securing an area to complement Japan as did Manchuria and Korea prior to World War II." Because China was likely to remain Communist for some time and any dependence on its resources could "draw Japan into the Communist orbit," the "urgency, strategically, of an arrangement with Southeast Asia" stood out "strongly." The "first priority for use of the President's emergency fund," the JCS staff concluded, should be for "stabilizing and securing Southeast Asia for its food and raw materials" so vital to America's allies.[13]

Although concerned with Southeast Asia's ultimate economic importance, the JCS and the Army and Defense departments still thought primarily in terms of using MAP to fund current military-assistance programs. Moreover, they wanted the control and distribution of this aid placed in the hands of a special agency rather than the Department of State. In early February, while Louis Johnson forwarded the JCS report to Dean Acheson (declaring it represented the "military point of view" that must be presented to Truman), Tracy Voorhees hurried to stake out the army's (and his own) position by organizing a special mission to Japan and Southeast Asia.[14]

Understandably, Acheson and Butterworth worried about losing the initiative to the Defense Department. To show Truman that they, too, had a plan for regional containment (although one not premised on covert military intervention in China and Southeast Asia), the two diplomats decided to field their own "experts." Acheson assigned Dean Rusk, who enjoyed good relations with many Defense Department officials, to discuss ideas for MAP with the Pentagon. Presumably, he could discover and short-circuit any particularly harebrained schemes. At the same time, the State Department dispatched its own experts to Southeast Asia, hoping to blunt the army's campaign. Early in January, Ambassador-at-Large Philip Jessup left for an extended tour of Asia, culminating in a security conference in Bangkok. Later that month, Acheson appointed R. Allen Griffin, a former deputy director of the ECA in China, to lead a special Southeast Asian mission. As a Republican from California on reasonably good terms with Senator Knowland, Butterworth and Acheson hoped his selection would demonstrate to the "Republicans in Congress that we were going to do something about Southeast Asia."[15]

From the perspectives of the rival bureaucracies, the access to additional money and control over new programs made MAP worth fighting for. Early in the year, it seemed clear that additional funds would soon flow into the unvouchered Asia account. In January, Acheson went before Congress to make the case for more aid to Korea and Southeast Asia. Owing to inadequate lobbying and Republican opposition, the House narrowly defeated an extension of the Korean aid bill that month. The clock was about to run out (in February) on the already extended China Aid Act, with nearly $105 million remaining in unexpended funds. The secretary of state now urged the Senate Foreign Relations Committee both to restore aid for Korea and to pass an amendment permitting funds from the original China Aid Act to be used in "the general area of China" through June 1951.

Of the $105 million in question, the administration intended to spend only some $28 million for economic assistance to Taiwan. It wanted the remainder of the money appropriated without strings. Acheson suggested it might be spent in Indochina, Indonesia, Thailand, and the Philippines for development projects. It might substitute for the president's Point 4 aid proposal mired in Congress. Although most senators endorsed this idea, Knowland continued to demand assurances of more aid for Taiwan. Fearing this dispute would delay the Korean aid portion of the bill, Acheson modified his original request.

The committee reported out a bill that extended the China Aid Act funds only until June 30, 1950 (instead of 1951) and deleted the "general area" clause. However, the State Department was relieved to win assistance for Korea, a six-month extension of the China Aid Act, and an informal assurance that it would get a favorable hearing in the future for a request to use the China Aid Act funds mostly in Southeast Asia. In May 1950, the department won approval on this point and also soon received fiscal 1951 MDAP funding as well.[16]

THE JESSUP MISSION

During the first two months of 1950, Ambassador-at-Large Phillip C. Jessup crisscrossed Asia on an extended tour. He had initially proposed the trip as a way of confirming American support for its nascent allies along the Great Crescent. Besides stops in Japan, South Korea, Indochina, Singapore, Thailand, Indonesia, and India, Jessup initially considered a visit with the new Communist leaders in Peking. In Bangkok, the ambassador planned to preside over a meeting of American diplomats from throughout Asia. Jessup hoped this itinerary would demonstrate the Truman administration's willingness to live with the Peking regime even as it worked to bolster Japan and Southeast Asia against communism.[17]

The prospects for a China visit, however, deteriorated as Sino–American tensions increased late in 1949. During the extended detention of Angus

Ward in Mukden (Shenyang), Truman considered some kind of military retaliation. Even after the diplomat's trial and expulsion in November, other incidents continued to plague the two nations. Early in January, for example, the Chinese government announced it would seize a portion of the American consular compound in Peking, ostensibly because the buildings were occupied as a result of an imperialist "unequal treaty imposed on the Ch'ing Dynasty." The real motive might have been to impress the Kremlin with Peking's militancy during the current Mao/Stalin negotiations in Moscow. Alternatively, the Chinese may have been applying crude pressure to force Washington to extend diplomatic recognition as the price of protection. In fact, the Chinese dropped earlier announced plans to seize British property after London recognized the PRC, even though the British decision was unrelated to the threat.

In any event, confiscation of the disputed property and subsequent interference with Consul General O. Edmund Clubb's radio communications prompted Dean Acheson to order the withdrawal of all diplomatic personnel. Even though he meant this partially as a temporary measure to avoid incidents, it placed a pall over relations. After the American departure, reestablishing contact would be far more difficult. Almost certainly, the administration could not move until after the 1950 elections. These incidents dashed any remaining possibility that Jessup might visit Peking. Ironically, he ended up calling on Jiang in Taiwan, a very bad omen.[18]

The roving ambassador conferred first with Douglas MacArthur at the beginning of January. The general proved unusually cordial, possibly because both he and Jessup shared their rage over the Defense Department's success in blocking a Japanese peace settlement. Instead of criticizing Acheson, MacArthur turned on the retired Gen. George Marshall. Had he, rather than Marshall, been sent to China during 1946, MacArthur claimed, "we would have made the military decision to meet [the Communist drive] and it would have been easily handled." In the interim, Jiang had botched things so badly that nothing could save the mainland.

Despite this complaint, the Supreme Commander appeared to agree with Acheson's emphasis on regional security rather than remilitarizing Japan. He told Jessup that there was "very little communism in Japan" and no threat of a takeover. MacArthur felt the "area approach" described by his visitor resembled the "basically sound concept behind the Japanese co-prosperity sphere," minus the misguided attempt by Tokyo at military domination. Both Jessup and his host agreed that a generous peace settlement that assigned Japan a central economic and political role in the region would prove to other Asians that "we were not imperialist but were ready to satisfy the legitimate desires of the people."[19]

Just like the State Department leadership, MacArthur blamed the Defense Department rather than the Russians for the failure to achieve a settlement with Tokyo. He believed the Soviets would agree to almost any reasonable terms, including provisions for a small post-Occupation American force. But the JCS, whom he characterized as ignorant and easily bullied by Louis Johnson, feared any change in the status quo.

Because the administration had overruled the military establishment on the China–Taiwan issue, MacArthur professed not to understand why Johnson and the JCS had been given a near veto on a peace treaty. Pledging to support Truman and Acheson if they defied the defense establishment, he declared that "when decisions were made by the Secretary of State," they were "decisions of the United States and he would loyally carry them out." MacArthur even implied that if the State Department could deliver a peace treaty, he would at least tone down his criticism of administration china policy.[20]

While in Tokyo, Jessup also met with Japanese political and business representatives to discuss their concerns. Although unable to offer much encouragement about the stalled treaty, he did lobby on behalf of Southeast Asia. The ambassador urged the Japanese to send technical specialists and trade representatives to the region and indicated that Washington would soon begin a major assistance program to confront the "immediate danger" confronting "vitally important" Indochina.[21]

From Japan, Jessup visited Taiwan briefly for courtesy talks with the Nationalist leadership. Jiang Jieshi described his island as the primary front of a global war and as one of the only anti-Communist bastions left in Asia. The ambassador, however, was unimpressed by Jiang's claim that "American aid to him was the only way in which the world could be saved." He departed more sure than before that the regime should be allowed to collapse.[22]

Late in January, Jessup reached Indochina. Traveling widely through the war-torn colony, he conducted extensive discussions both with Bao Dai and his French masters. The American's visit followed the long-delayed ratification in Paris of the March 8, 1949, agreement transferring nominal home rule to Vietnam. Jessup's arrival also coincided with a Soviet decision to formally recognize the government of Ho Chi Minh. The public and private endorsements lavished on Bao Dai's regime by Jessup served as the precursor of formal diplomatic recognition, which came a few weeks later.[23]

After conferring with British High Commissioner Sir Malcolm MacDonald in Singapore, the Ambassador-at-Large finally reached Bangkok. A large delegation of diplomats, ECA officials, Defense Department, and SCAP representatives had gathered there in mid-February for a security conference. Jessup and Butterworth attended as State Department delegates, presiding over discussions on how to counter Communist threats to the region while cultivating Southeast Asia as a Japanese economic zone. The two diplomats told the conference that in order for Japan to "regain its prewar trade position," the United States must provide both security assistance and invest in large-scale development projects. Because the Soviets were probing relentlessly for "soft spots," Jessup declared, greater American involvement would demonstrate that Southeast Asia was not ripe for Soviet harvesting.[24]

Both Army Department and State Department representatives came away enthusiastic about the consensus in favor of American support for Japanese links with Southeast Asia. For example, William Sebald returned to Tokyo and informed Sir Alvary Gascoigne that the Bangkok conference marked the first step in a real program to check Asian communism. The stress on Southeast Asia would help keep that area "out of the communist fold" and insure economic access for "the good of Japan." In his enthusiasm, Sebald sided with his military colleagues in urging that most MAP money be expended in defending Indochina, which he described as Japan's defense perimeter.[25]

THE ANDREWS/WEST MISSION

The Army Department mission dispatched in late January tried to capitalize on the momentum generated at Bangkok. Voorhees sent his Deputy Under Secretary, Robert West, and Stanley Andrews, Director of the Agriculture Department's Office of Foreign Agricultural Relations, to make a "broad appraisal of the food and trade situation" in Southeast Asia as it related to the "food and raw material supply for Japan in exchange for Japanese goods." The team was to explore how future regional assistance "might be pooled and administered under a coordinated arrangement" to improve efficiency and lower costs. They would determine the extent that "Japan, through development of trade, through extension of credit, supplying of materials, and the supply of technical knowledge and personnel" could assist the "improvement of the total economies and the total food supply and stability of Southeast and South Asia."[26]

The survey team worried that radical, anticolonial insurgencies, especially in Indochina, imperiled regional integration. Andrews and West considered it imperative for the United States to help restore "internal order" within the "rice bowl" of Southeast Asia. If the Indochina peninsula went the "way of China," they warned, Japan would be reduced to dependence on American charity or acceptance of a Communist offer for it to come "behind the iron curtain." Yet, with sufficient assistance, they believed, Southeast Asia could eventually supply "about two-thirds" or more of Japan's food imports and raw material requirements. The region would also become an "assured market" for Japanese "knick-knacks" and other products suitable for less developed peoples. Tokyo's influence, moreover, would promote political stability in the wake of the European exodus and Communist advance.[27]

In their reports to Voorhees, the army survey team recommended that the United States begin immediately to extend capital either directly to Japan or to Southeast Asian states. This ought to be done through the unification of all Asian assistance programs into a single agency concentrating on integrated trade. Dollars would initiate the Japan–Southeast Asia exchange, but it would become self-sustaining as commodity production increased and Japanese industry expanded. Describing the moment as "critical," Andrews and West urged expending the coveted MAP funds immediately under the aegis of a new "authoritative central" planning agency.[28]

THE GRIFFIN MISSION

Traipsing through Southeast Asia, Andrews and West crossed paths with what amounted to a rival mission sent by the State Department. Since his selection to lead that survey, R. Allen Griffin had spent weeks assembling a team of economic experts drawn from State, Treasury, and ECA ranks. Late in February, the Defense Department asked that an army and navy officer be included, to which Griffin reluctantly acceded. In an attmept to insure that this team buttressed the work of Andrews and West, Tracy Voorhees lectured the mission members on the eve of their departure.[29]

Griffin insisted that his first stop be Tokyo, explaining that it made no sense to send an "economic mission to that part of the world without communicating with the guy who is supreme commander." Good relations with MacArthur were important, he believed because a major purpose of the survey was to lay the groundwork for "an expanded trade between the countries visited and Japan." Besides this long-term strategy, Acheson and Butterworth expected Griffin to recommend emergency financing of selected projects in Southeast Asia to demonstrate the "immediate political significance" of the area.[30]

In Tokyo, Griffin conferred with Robert West who was then completing the army's survey. As had Voorhees, West harangued Griffin with justifications for channeling all MAP dollars for Southeast Asia first through Japan. Making each dollar "do the work of two," West said, would stimulate Japanese recovery even as it helped those Southeast Asian nations threatened by communism. MacArthur's intelligence chief, General Willoughby, made a related appeal. Recently, he had traveled throughout the region, conferring with colonial officials and local politicians. Vietnam represented the "strategic key" to Asian security, he told the group, comparing its importance to Greece in 1947. Willoughby urged that all available MAP funds be used to restore "law and order" in Indochina through the provision of military aid.[31]

Although Griffin agreed on Indochina's strategic importance, he felt strongly that his mission ought to concentrate on preparing an economic development agenda for the area. Although military assistance might come from other sources, he wanted MAP money used for a quick infusion of highly visible nonmilitary aid. Samuel Hayes, an economist with the group, recalled that the staff spent much of its time discussing Southeast Asia's role in the world economy. They predicted that Japan might eventually surpass Western Europe as the region's major trading partner. Assuming Japan sold "its services and capital goods in Southeast Asia, and if it could buy rice, coal and raw materials cheaply there, its dependence on American aid would be lessened," Hayes noted.[32]

In Saigon, however, Griffin discovered that his military colleagues, Col. E. A. Duff and Capt. Frederick Warder, had secretly conferred with Bao Dai and promised to provide him with extensive armaments through MAP. Also, units of the 7th fleet paid courtesy calls on the just recognized regime. Fearing these signs would undermine a more balanced program, Griffin ordered the two officers to quit the group and travel on their own. His concerns were justified because Duff and Warder promptly urged the Defense Department to restrict all MAP-funded assistance to military expenditures in Southeast Asia.[33] Warder even accompanied French forces in combat against the Vietminh.

The cables sent by Griffin and his aides during March radiated enthusiasm over the prospects for building a viable anti-Communist state in Vietnam. The Americans dismissed allegations that Bao Dai was a puppet, preferring to describe his government as "intensely nationalistic" and "struggling to secure more control and authority from the French." In this regard, a quick, well-publicized aid program, with grants made directly to Bao Dai rather than the French, would bolster his fledgling regime by providing the "appearance of independence" and help "win from Ho" the loyalty of non-communist nationalists and "fence-sitters." This infusion of aid ought to follow "closely in the wake of military operations," building support for Bao Dai on a village-by-village basis, Griffin argued.[34]

During the spring, Griffin submitted a series of tentative proposals totaling nearly $65 million for agricultural, health, educational, propaganda, and security programs. Of this, about a third would go to Indochina. However, he and his team opposed putting the American military in charge of the program or creating a new agency to administer it, as Tracy Voorhees urged. Griffin preferred to have the State Department and ECA along with the Defense Department create a series of STEMs, Special Technical and Economic Missions, attached to the U.S. Embassy in each Southeast Asian nation. These would provide expert advice on the need for, and utilization of, foreign economic and military assistance.[35]

Acheson applauded Griffin's preliminary recommendations because they reflected his own preferences about the need to balance military and civilian assistance. Not incidentally, they also stole some of the Defense Department's thunder. Furthermore, the mission provided highly visible evidence of an American commitment to what was seen as a vital and vulnerable area. During a major address before the San Francisco commonwealth Club on March 15, Acheson stressed all these points. In a significant toughening of his attitude toward Peking, the secretary of state accused the Chinese Communists of acting as Soviet puppets in a plan to initiate "adventures beyond their borders." He referred specifically to dangers confronting South Korea and the states of Southeast Asia, proclaiming that these nations were now protected by the umbrella of the Truman Doctrine. Griffin's reports, he explained, established the basis for American support of these "free peoples who are resisting attempted subjugation by armed minorities or by outside pressure."[36]

BUREAUCRATIC RESISTANCE TO INTEGRATION

By early 1950, a variety of sometimes-contradictory schemes huddled under the umbrella concept of regional integration. Tracy Voorhees and his aides spoke of utilizing MDAP and other aid sources to bind Japanese industry to Southeast Asian resources, with the goal of producing military equipment. This, he believed, would cut dollar costs, assure Japan export markets, and forge an active anti-Communist alliance. Others in the defense establishment and some of MacArthur's aides called for channeling all possible military assistance directly to Southeast Asia on an emergency basis. This, they argued, would provide an interim defense shield for Japan. The State Department's Griffin mission and the Far Eastern consultants regarded MDAP as an investment in long-term development for Southeast Asia. This would create a visible sign of American commitment and insure growth opportunities for Japan. Ultimately, Voorhees, Johnson, and the JCS envisioned integration as a military lever to maximize pressure against China at reduced cost and risk to the United States. Concerned about Communist pressures beyond China, State Department planners considered it feasible to construct a containment zone primarily through economic assistance.

Late in February, spurred by the initial findings of the Andrews/West mission, Tracy Voorhees convened a special interagency "working group" on aid to Far Eastern areas. Just before their February 28 meeting, delegates from the State, Treasury, Commerce, and Defense departments as well as from the NSC and the ECA received from Voorhees copies of the Reid memorandum warning that Japan would quickly succumb to communism following an insurgent victory in Indochina.

Dean Rusk, representing Secretary of State Acheson on the panel, opposed Voorhees's effort to have the working group recommend creation of a special agency to oversee Asian assistance. Speaking at length on the "possibility of developing trade between Japan and other parts of Asia and thereby cheapening the process of assisting" recovery, Voorhees emphasized the importance of preventing Japan from "being dependent on China." The only way to cut across bureaucratic lines in Washington and Tokyo, he insisted, was to appoint a "czar" in the Executive Office of the president to "control all of the programs for Asia."[37]

MacArthur, like Acheson, recognized Voorhees's new scheme as a bold attempt to cut both the State Department and SCAP out of formulating and implementing economic and security programs. In February, the general complained to W. W. Butterworth (then visiting Tokyo en route to Bangkok) that Voorhees imagined himself directing Japan's resurgence as a great regional military power. Presumably, he reached this judgment, in part, during the army undersecretary's December 1949 visit to Tokyo. The Defense Department leadership opposed a reasonable peace settlement, MacArthur charged, because it conflicted with Voorhees's "fantastic scheme for Asiatic trade which no doubt he conceived he would head."[38]

During March, the State Department, the Treasury Department, and ECA all joined forces in opposition to Voorhees's call for a new "super agency." They objected both to the army's attempt to dominate what had previously been a sphere reserved for civilian agencies as well as to the program's likely impact on overall policy. For example, ECA representatives on the working group complained that programs giving Japan special assistance and privileges in Southeast Asia would seriously hamper the access of the Western European nations to low-cost raw materials. Money saved in East Asia would only be added to the European dollar gap financed by the Marshall Plan.[39]

These criticisms forced Voorhees to drop his demands to appoint a White House-level coordinator for Japan–Southeast Asia assistance. Instead, he settled for an agreement to upgrade the status of the working group. Early in April, a new ad hoc Interdepartmental Committee on the Coordination of Far Eastern Programs met, only to bog down immediately in a dispute over preferential treatment for Japan. Voorhees's representatives urged that all procurements for Southeast Asia purchased with MDAP funds should be obtained in Japan, regardless of cost. In effect, this would partly transform MDAP into a financing program for Japanese industry. Harlan Cleveland of the ECA condemned this as both a violation of basic free trading principles and a direct threat to European recovery, if Southeast Asia became Japan's preserve.[40]

State Department officials, although enthusiastic about the concept of regional trade, believed such blatant favoritism would elicit a backlash against Washington and Tokyo. For example, during April, American diplomatic representatives from throughout Asia met in Tokyo and agreed that the wartime legacy of mistrust toward Japan made most Southeast Asian states reluctant to link, or subordinate, their economies with Tokyo. For the present, the Tokyo conference recommended education efforts to soften local resistance to a return of Japanese technical personnel and traders. The diplomats also suggested encouraging the Japanese government to begin granting yen credits to potential Southeast Asian customers in order to open markets.[41]

The Tokyo economic conference stimulated greater efforts among State Department personnel in Washington to devise an alternative program to that promoted by Voorhees. Both Japan and Southeast Asia specialists in the department had taken to ridiculing the army under secretary for his interest in recreating what they called Voorhees's Greater East Asia Co-Prosperity Sphere. Arm twisting the Southeast Asian states into economic dependence on Tokyo, they complained, would elicit "maximum ill will" and alienate, not integrate, the region. During March and April, William S. B. Lacy, C. H. Shohan, E. M. Doherty, John Allison, and Willard Thorp all explored methods for having Japan extend voluntary yen credits that would make trade attractive but not compulsory.[42]

State Department officials were attracted to the idea of a yen credit fund targeted especially on Southeast Asia. These credits could finance such things as textile sales and irrigation equipment needed by Japan's neighbors. Although Japan would still require some $200 million per year to finance food and commodity imports, Tokyo should be able to boost exports to Southeast Asia by at least that amount. In effect, the money owed to the United States could be paid out in yen and then used to establish the credit fund for Southeast Asia. As commodity production in the region increased, Japan would become less dependent on American financed raw materials, thus reducing the dollar deficit. Ideally, this coordinated approach would promote regional recovery and stability with minimal new dollar costs. It also avoided the appearance of the United States compelling Southeast Asia to subordinate itself to Japan.[43]

By the middle of April, the State Department circulated a proposal,

Utilization of Japanese Capacity to Promote Economic Development in South and Southeast Asia. Assistant Secretary for Economic Affairs Willard Thorp suggested that Japan be required to create a yen counterpart fund for investment in Southeast Asian food and mineral production as payment for some $200 million provided annually in the form of raw materials by the United States. Japan's growing investment in the region, Thorp argued, would reduce "potential undue dependence on Chinese sources of supply" and provide for the "stability and welfare of Southeast Asia."[44]

Even this modification of Voorhees's ideas still troubled ECA representatives. John Sumner of ECA, for example, told Harlan Cleveland that the yen credits proposal held "grave dangers along both economic and political lines" by giving Tokyo "terrific bargaining advantages" over European competitors. Southeast Asia could not be of much use to the ERP countries if Washington helped Japan to "restore a pre-war trading position" in the region.[45]

Despite ECA's opposition, SCAP officials expressed support for the State Department's new initiative. Although Voorhees's proposal threatened to monopolize virtually all GARIOA and other funds expended in Asia—leaving SCAP with little money or leverage—the yen-credits proposal neither reduced the flow of GARIOA dollars into Tokyo nor displaced SCAP's influence. Credits provided from a counterpart fund would tend to "establish an area economy in the Far East more nearly than any of the other alternatives" by giving Southeast Asian countries a positive incentive to trade with Japan. SCAP economic specialists in Washington and Tokyo clearly endorsed this approach as the one most likely to benefit Japan while leaving their organization intact.[46]

Japanese political and financial leaders also favored the idea of providing credits from counterpart funds. The severe economic contraction brought on by the Dodge austerity plan increased pressure to boost foreign sales. But Japan remained largely shut out of the Southeast Asia market as deteriorating Sino–American relations threatened to preclude commerce with China. Caught in this squeeze and with diminishing likelihood of a quick peace settlement, Prime Minister Yoshida sent his finance minister, Ikeda Hayato, on a mission to Washington.

Early in May, Ikeda conferred with Joseph Dodge and Ralph Reid about prospects for increased financial assistance and movement toward a treaty. He also transmitted a secret feeler from Yoshida that offered to provide post-Occupation bases for American forces. As will be discussed later, Yoshida hoped this offer might speed a settlement. But the appeal for economic assistance took priority.[47]

The finance minister wanted pledges for additional dollar aid and as-

sistance in promoting trade with Southeast Asia. As a result of discussions
with Dodge, Reid, and Treasury Department officials, Ikeda proposed that
the Japanese government create a new Export Finance Corporation cap-
italized at two billion yen. It would issue credits up to forty billion yen,
providing "export trades and manufacturers with long-term loans and also
extend credit to overseas importers and importing nations." Instead of
holding back the existing counterpart fund in Tokyo for debt retirement
(as Dodge originally proposed), Ikeda wanted to utilize it for this new
purpose. Later in May, Yoshida forwarded Ikeda's report to MacArthur
and asked that SCAP help campaign for Japanese and American approval
for the credits plan.[48]

Nearly all the concerned officials of the State and Treasury departments
as well as SCAP expressed support for the credit proposal. This proposal
would block the Army Department's power grab and it would still generate
increased trade and other ties on a regional basis. By the middle of June,
the Department of State notified Joseph Dodge it had tentatively approved
the "yen fund proposal" as the best way to coordinate Japan's new relationship with Southeast Asia.[49]

Tracy Voorhees reacted to these developments with mounting frustration. By April, he decided to resign as army under secretary, although he
continued to badger the State Department and ECA with additional proposals for channeling Southeast Asian assistance through Japan. Before
leaving office, he circulated a proposal to "coordinate" the cold war by
"modernizing", or militarizing, the Marshall Plan. Although his opponents
could not guess so at the time, this report foretold developments brought
about by the Korean War.[50]

Voorhees's report noted that although the ERP would end in less than
two years and despite its success in restoring production, both Europe and
Japan continued to labor under a chronic dollar gap. Abundant productive
capacity now existed in these formerly war-ravaged economies, but they
still lacked sufficient export markets and access to secure sources of non-
dollar raw materials. Voorhees proposed supplanting the Marshall Plan
with a program to encourage the "production of defensive weapons." Dollars given to Europe and Japan for arms production (or the dollars earned
by the sale of weapons) would then "purchase our wheat, cotton and
tobacco," making each dollar do the work of two. The army under secretary
predicted this military aid scheme would find more support in Congress
than mere proposals to extend the Marshall Plan.[51]

This program might operate by assisting the expansion of German steel
production, with the product sold to other Western Europeans for fabri-
cation into weapons. In effect, ECA and MDAP funds would be combined
into one pool, providing dollars and raw materials for military production

among American allies. If the United States expected to sustain foreign demand for its own exports, it must realize that military and economic aid "were now obviously inextricably interrelated," Voorhees asserted. Although focused primarily on Europe, the new program would supercede all assistance plans in Asia, as well. The Japanese would be expected to "earn their dollars by agreeing to provide most of the economic assistance required for Southeast Asia." As the price for receiving dollar assistance, Tokyo would become the supplier of low-cost military equipment to Southeast Asia, meeting the region's defense needs at little direct expense to Washington while developing a new line of exports for Japan. To a great extent, the Off-Shore Procurement Program begun during the Korean War met these specifications.[52]

Even though Voorhees was departing (temporarily, it developed) from the administration, Joseph Dodge presented a similar message to both Congress and ECA. In April, he told a congressional committee that Washington must inevitably rely on Japan as a "springboard" supplying the "material goods required for American aid to the Far East." Later that month, he explained his belief that Japan would serve as the "bulwark" protecting the "states newly created in Southeast Asia" and beset by "economic problems and political stability" from "communist expansion." The United States could, in one sweep, restore the "natural workshop of the East," get the Japanese "off our shoulder," and restrain Communist expansion—if it coordinated aid to Japan and Southeast Asia.[53]

Suggestions by Voorhees and Dodge about merging economic assistance with military production in Europe and Japan coincided with other trends in the Truman administration. During April, a special State Department/ Defense Department draft study of national security requirements in light of the Soviet atomic bomb and Chinese Revolution (NSC 68) revealed parallel concerns. Under the guiding influence of the new PPS head, Paul Nitze, the NSC 68 draft urged vastly increased defense spending both to counter Soviet power and to stimulate the troubled economies of America's allies. Also, that spring, Truman appointed former Army Secretary Gordon Gray to study the persistent dollar-gap crisis, with a view toward forging a foreign economic program to supplant the Marshall Plan. American support of European and Japanese military production, Voorhees believed, would sustain foreign economies, earn dollars for the purchase of American exports, and solidify the strength of the non-communist camp.

The Voorhees plan found public expression in the writings of journalist Stewart Alsop. Returning from another Asian tour, he published an article in the *Saturday Evening Post* with the pessimistic title, "We Are Losing Asia Fast." In the working draft (more clearly than in the printed version), Alsop revealed his debt to Voorhees and Louis Johnson.

The loss of China, he warned, placed a dagger at the throat of Southeast Asia. As the world's "greatest reservoir of untapped natural wealth," it could become the catalyst to mobilize Asia's "unlimited manpower." Just as Japan, in 1941, risked everything to seize control of its Co-Prosperity Sphere, Alsop explained, the Kremlin had resolved to "organize another, infinitely vaster Asiatic Co-Prosperity Sphere." In an ironic reversal of the earlier adventure, the Soviets intended to move from China through mainland and island Southeast Asia to Formosa, South Korea, and, finally, Japan.

The whole process, Alsop explained, had an analogy with bowling. What would happen in Asia occurred when "a good bowler hit the head pin hard."

> The head pin was China. It is down already. The two pins in the second row are Burma and Indo-China. If they go, the three pins in the third row, Siam, Malaya and Indonesia, are pretty sure to topple in their turn. And if all the rest of Asia goes, the resulting psychological, political and economic magnetism will almost certainly drag down the four pins of the fourth row, India, Pakistan, Japan and the Philippines.

Only two hopeful signs appeared in Southeast Asia, Alsop wrote. The unexpected courage of Bao Dai and evidence of his complete support by Washington had delayed Ho Chi Minh's anticipated victory in Vietnam. The emperor had emerged as the "Indo-Chinese hope of the Western World." Similarly, in Indonesia, adroit support for the Republicans had convinced Sukarno and Hatta to cast their lot with the West. When the Communist insurgent, Musso, led a revolt late in 1948, Hatta and Sukarno, Alsop reported with glee, immediately had the rebels "stood up against a wall and shot."

The journalist then came around to his major point, Japan's vulnerability to the Red Conquest of Asia. Stewart Alsop recounted a discussion with Nozaka Sanzo, Japan's Communist party head, "intimate" of Mao, and a leader reputedly so powerful he could defy Stalin's criticism of his political line (an interesting point, although one contradicting Alsop's argument). In the version of the meeting with Nozaka that appeared in his notes (different only in a few details from the published account), Alsop described the lifelong revolutionary as "probably the most interesting political figure in Japan" and a politician who exercised more power there "than any other single individual" except MacArthur.

Nozaka, Alsop claimed, boasted about the Communist master plan. Making a curving gesture, he outlined a giant crescent of Soviet power, extending from "Northern Siberia all the way to New Guinea, surrounding Japan and embracing all its natural trading area." With a "shrug of his shoulders," Nozaka implied that this "immense new Russian empire in Asia" along with other pressures" would drive Japan into the Kremlin's corner. With a "broad, cheerful grin," the diminutive conspirator remarked, "It won't be long now."

The loss of Southeast Asia, Alsop concluded, made Japan's loss inevitable. Americans, both in the government and private life, must mobilize their energies to develop immediately an Asiatic Recovery Administration with "authority to employ the full strategic, political and economic weight of this country in Asia as each local situation may demand." A lesser response, or toleration of the loss of Southeast Asia, would create the "nightmare of Japanese industry married to the raw material wealth of Asia and the growing power of the existing Soviet empire in Europe."[54]

Alsop's awkward conjuring of a "bowling pin theory" gave birth, of course, to the fabled domino theory of the 1950s. Terminology aside, the events of the spring of 1950 eroded the pillars of a moderate foreign policy. The deterioration of Sino–American relations, the critical military situation in French Indochina, the inability among Americans to agree on terms of a Japanese settlement, and disputes over the nature of assistance to East and Southeast Asia all diminished Acheson's leverage. The resurgence of Defense Department influence over Truman and widespread fears of a Communist breakthrough in Asia pushed policy into ever more militarized channels. Actions taken all along the Great Crescent confirmed this dangerous trend.

13

A COMMITMENT TO VIETNAM

Despite the later tragic results of the decisions taken in 1950, the most thoughtful and moderate as well as the most bellicose foreign policy experts in the American government considered aid to Vietnam the centerpiece of constructive policy. Although the State and Defense departments quibbled endlessly over the details of involvement in Indochina, both agencies embraced the troubled colony and emerging nation as a testing ground where the United States could employ new techniques to restrain communism, promote moderate nationalism, and lay the foundation for regional stability. For many in the State Department, involvement in Vietnam seemed the ideal way both to contain Chinese pressure while deflecting American military power away from a direct confrontation with Peking. Defense officials, stymied in their efforts to shield Taiwan and fight communism inside China, saw the new policy as a way to sustain American military pressure on China's threshold. After Taiwan fell and Japan recovered its sovereignty, Vietnam might serve as an important lever to apply pressure against Peking.

Late in 1949, an intelligence report circulated by the CIA warned of an imminent Communist victory in Indochina unless the United States became more directly involved in the conflict. In about six months, the report predicted, the Chinese Communists would begin furnishing extensive assistance to the Vietminh guerrillas, making the French position hopeless. Inevitably, a French defeat would weaken the Western European containment barrier. In Asia, a victory by Ho's guerrillas would lead quickly to Communist takeovers in Burma, Thailand, and Indonesia. To reverse this slide, the French had no choice but to grant moderate Vietnamese nationalists partial independence, American analysts concluded. Once local support was assured, providing "U.S. military assistance" might then stem the tide. But even this policy represented a "calculated risk with only a moderate chance of success." Unfortunately, about 80 percent of the Vietnamese, the CIA estimated, professed loyalty to Ho Chi Minh and viewed Bao Dai as an unworthy puppet. Given the dangers of a Communist victory, however, the intelligence staff felt Washington had little choice but to commit itself to the French cause.[1]

Although American estimates of the Vietnamese internal situation remained pretty grim, international developments pushed the United States ever closer to a direct commitment. Early in 1950, the French government ratified the March 8, 1949, agreements transferring nominal sovereignty to Bao Dai's regime. When the Soviet block responded by recognizing Ho's Democratic Republic of Vietnam (DRV), Dean Acheson issued a statement claiming this act removed "any illusions as to the 'nationalist' nature of Ho Chi Minh's aims and reveals Ho in his true colors as the mortal enemy of native independence in Indochina." In contrast, the secretary of state lavished praise on French moves to transfer power to the governments of Laos, Cambodia, and Vietnam. He also instructed Philip Jessup to pledge American support during his upcoming meeting with Bao Dai. On February 2, Acheson urged Truman to recognize formally the new Vietnamese regime, an action taken by the president on February 7.[2]

During February and March, of course, Jessup, the Andrews/West mission, units of the 7th Fleet, and the Griffin mission all visited Vietnam, discussing with Bao Dai various options for American military and economic assistance. While attending the Bangkok regional conference in mid-February, Jessup cabled Acheson with the advice that he make a well-publicized speech outlining the importance of Vietnam. Such a declaration, Jessup felt, should emphasize America's commitment to the security of all the nations on China's periphery.

As noted earlier, the JCS and Louis Johnson had, in January, proposed immediate allocation of $15 million from the MAP fund for military aid to Indochina. The Defense Department also insisted on its right to codetermine with the State Department the contours of any future aid program. Although the two agencies quickly reached agreement to spend about $5 million arming the Indonesian police and for expenditures of some $6 million on improving Japanese airfields for heavy bombers, they parted ways on the question of assistance for Indochina. The State Department did not quibble over the importance of underwriting Bao Dai, but it felt the United States had to supply more than weapons.

Within the State Department, a special working group of officers from the Western European division, the Office of Philippine and Southeast Asian Affairs and the MDAP outlined their concerns in a paper shared with their Defense Department counterparts. Revising previous assumptions, they now dismissed the likelihood of "an effective split between the USSR and Communist China within the next three years." In light of this, they predicted, Moscow would utilize Chinese and "indigenous communists" to seize power in Vietnam. Although acknowledging the shallow local support for Bao Dai, the State Department experts vehemently opposed any accommodation with Ho Chi Minh. Ho's taking power, whatever the circumstances, would quickly "open the door to complete communist domination of Southeast Asia," with "severe repercussions" throughout the "non-communist world." Because a failure to support the French and their puppet would bring about a Communist triumph over the "remainder of the continental area of Southeast Asia, and possibly further westward," the United States would have to make "staggering investments" to hold a "much protracted" Pacific line. Denying support to the French and Bao Dai because of their shortcomings would seem a case of "Penny wise, pound foolish," they declared. Accordingly, even the State Department study group recommended extending part of the 303 fund for military aid to the French and their "French Union" Vietnamese allies.[3]

Early in March, Acheson and Johnson jointly recommended that Truman respond favorably to a renewed French request for assistance. They urged the president to authorize expenditures of about $15 million for Indochina and $10 million for Thailand. Truman responded almost immediately to their appeal (which echoed the report of the special working group), instructing the two secretaries to submit specific allocation requests to him through the Bureau of the Budget. Over the next three months, they called on Truman to release funds for a variety of overt and covert projects totaling some $50 million. Of this, nearly $21 million went to Indochina. Meanwhile, of course, the Griffin and Andrews/West missions recommended a variety of assistance projects for funding by MDAP, the China Aid Act, or Point 4.[4]

Having crossed the threshold of direct aid, State Department and Defense Department planners now hastened to develop formal justifications for the strategic significance of Southeast Asia. On February 27, the State Department submitted a brief report on Indochina for consideration by the NSC. Enlisting a view originating with PPS 51 the year before, Acheson hoped that swift acceptance by the NSC would provide additional leverage in upcoming negotiations with the military. NSC 64, as the draft was known, declared that a Communist victory in Indochina would threaten vital American interests throughout Southeast Asia. This challenge demanded full civilian-military cooperation to develop a program to protect Indochina "as a matter or priority."[5]

Acheson also appointed Under Secretary of State Dean Rusk (soon named assistant secretary for the Far East) as a liaison to the Defense Department. Rusk, he hoped, would coordinate the State Department's economic aid programs with military projects favored by the Pentagon. Although pleased by this gesture, Defense Department officials planned to extract maximum benefits as their price for cooperation. Essentially, they wanted to insure that as much of the MDAP fund as possible went for military rather than economic assistance.[6]

Following recognition of the Bao Dai regime, Acheson undertook a variety of other initiatives to emphasize the administration's interest in Vietnam and to strengthen the State Department's grip over policy formulation. On March 15 (as mentioned earlier), he publicly warned China and the Soviet Union against threatening the non-Communist states of East and Southeast Asia by declaring them under the umbrella of the Truman Doctrine. In the same speech, he announced tentative acceptance of the Griffin mission's agenda, for future assistance to Southeast Asia. Two weeks later, he, Jessup, and Butterworth appeared before an executive session of the Senate Foreign Relations Committee where they described Southeast Asia as an area of "key importance." The pro-American regimes in Korea, the Philippines, Burma, and Vietnam already faced a "hot war" against communism, the diplomats noted. Jessup made an especially strong plea for additional economic and military assistance as well as for congressional support in speeding a Japanese peace settlement.[7]

Acheson explained that much of the money destined for Southeast Asia would come out of current or future MDAP funds. Many of these projects were so secret that he declined to provide details, although he did state that a portion would go toward providing military hardware to Vietnam. When Sen. Theorodore Green (D–Vermont) disputed the wisdom of supporting what still amounted to a colonial war, Acheson insisted America had no alternative. If the United States imposed strict political conditions, the French might say, "All right, take over the damned country. We don't want it" and put their soldiers on ships and send them back to France. Then, the United States would either have to intervene directly or risk a terrible loss, Acheson retorted.[8]

The three ranking diplomatic officials agreed that a peace treaty with Japan still remained the "number one problem" of Asia. Normalizing

Japan's status would do more to stabilize the region, they insisted, than futile attacks on China or harping on the Taiwan issue. They also described the security of Japan and Southeast Asia as interdependent. Butterworth remarked that Japan desperately required an Asian trading zone to complement Northeast Asia, and most of the Senators appeared to share his concern. Even Republican Sen. Henry Cabot Lodge remarked that the larger Communist plan probably placed a lower value on the conquest of Formosa as compared to the domination of Japan through economic blackmail. When Jessup interjected that Tokyo's plight justified permitting some Sino–Japanese trade, Lodge felt this made assistance to Southeast Asia even more imperative. Both agreed that "the importance of keeping the Chinese Communists out of the Southeast" was more important than "holding a little island like Formosa."⁹

Over the following months, Congress proved sympathetic toward this strategy, as shown by a new willingness to reprogram the $100 million remaining in the old China Aid Act. The administration wanted modifications to extend the bill through June 30, 1951. Under pressure from its China bloc, the Senate Foreign Relations Committee reported out a bill providing about $50 million for non-Communist areas of China (i.e., Taiwan) if the president deemed such aid "practicable." But the Senate finally accepted a modified House version, appropriating $40 million for Taiwan, $40 million for the "general area of China" (meaning anywhere in Asia), $6 million for educating Chinese in America, and $8 million for famine relief in China. But now the president retained discretionary authority over Taiwan aid, as the State Department desired. This law, the China Area Aid Act, passed Congress on June 5 and Truman signed it quickly. As a result, an additional $40 million became available immediately for Southeast Asia, beyond the already appropriated $75 million in the 1949 MDAP account. More could be expected shortly for technical aid to underdeveloped countries, such as in Southeast Asia, from the 1950 MDAP request and from pending Point 4 legislation.¹⁰*

Even though this growing stream of money pleased members of the administration, they continually differed on its intended use. The JCS and Louis Johnson, especially, still hoped to use MDAP as a means of increasing military aid to Southeast Asia and, if possible, as a wedge to reenter the Chinese civil war. Commenting on the State Department's Vietnam proposal (NSC 64) the JCS emphasized that a communist victory in Indochina would destroy the integrity of the "offshore island chain from

---

* The omnibus Foreign Economic Assistance Act of 1950 included the China area bill and, as Title IV, the Act for International Development. The latter, derived form Truman's Point 4 proposal in his 1949 inaugural speech, appropriated about $27 million for technological assistance to less developed regions, including Southeast Asia.

Japan to Indonesia." A Communist Vietnam, they warned, would soon dominate all Southeast Asia, "affecting the balance of power between the United States and the U.S.S.R." Soviet domination of the region would imperil Japan "since that country could thereby be denied its Asian markets, sources of food and other raw materials." This prospect so troubled the JCS that they wanted the NSC to expedite aid to all Southeast Asia on a priority basis, including an expected $100 million from the extension of the MDAP into fiscal 1951 (July 1950–June 1951). The military also insisted that the Defense Department representatives be included in a series of upcoming missions scheduled to report on security needs in Southeast Asia.[11]

After appending these demands to the State Department's Vietnam policy paper before the NSC, Johnson and the JCS upped the ante further. Although agreeing to the importance of blocking a Communist victory in Vietnam, they also asserted that China still remained the "vital strategic area in Asia." Protecting Southeast Asia really depended on "prompt and continuing measures . . . to reduce the pressure from Communist China." As a first step, Johnson and the JCS urged Truman to reconsider protecting Taiwan, resuming military and economic assistance to the KMT regime and, possibly, assisting the Nationalists' blockade of Chinese ports. To assure Japan access to food, raw materials, and markets while the campaign against China proceeded, the JCS recommended "long-term measures" to secure these items from "non-communist held areas in the Far East." The Andrews/West mission, of course, represented a move in this direction.[12]

Johnson's subordinates hoped to take advantage of the State Department's eagerness to assist Vietnam by demanding greater license to oppose China. On April 6, for example, John Magruder urged Johnson to insist on creation of a special executive agency to conduct warfare throughout the Far East. He felt a defense of Southeast Asia must be coupled with "establishment in China of a non-communist regime or at least a regime free from dominance by the Kremlin." So long as "China remained a base for Soviet-inspired imperialism," there was little point in defending Indochina. If the "cold war in China" was lost, he told Johnson, all Asia was in jeopardy. He recommended a well-planned campaign employing covert military, political, and economic sabotage to paralyze China. The executive agency could bring about "decisive results," Magruder assured his boss.[13]

In a compromise resembling the way NSC 48 had been finessed the previous December, the NSC and Truman approved on April 18 the essence of the State Department's Indochina paper. To assuage the Defense Department planners, the NSC included part of their flamboyant anti-China rhetoric, noting, however, that the proposals for widening the campaign against China should be employed for "advisory purposes" rather than for immediate implementation. In any case, the president signed the document on April 24, thus confirming the decision to expedite aid to Indochina as a vital American interest. This action cleared the way for a May 1 presidential authorization to release $13 million to the Defense Department and $5 million to the State Department from Section 303 funds.[14]

Few voices within or outside the administration questioned the basic wisdom or necessity of the path being undertaken in Vietnam. Southeast Asia, even more than China, remained nearly a total mystery to Americans, with few journalists, missionaries, diplomats, soldiers, or entrepreneurs knowing the region. The handful of State Department officers concerned with Southeast Asia usually had professional training as Europeanists, whereas those with actual field expertise were dismissed as "junior" or "too close to the natives."

One of the few "private sector" specialists on Southeast Asia, *Newsweek* reporter Harold Isaacs, presented a unique challenge to the administration's policy. More prescient than influential, he pled, in vain, for a halt to involvement. A veteran of both the China and Indochina struggles, Isaacs had traveled with Viet Minh guerrillas and interviewed their leaders, including Ho Chi Minh. In mid-April, when he learned that American military aid would go to Bao Dai and the French, the journalist made a pilgrimage to the State Department.

Rebuffed in his attempt to speak with "important" officials, he was received by a relatively junior Southeast Asia specialist, Charlton Ogburn. Although Isaacs did not know it, Ogburn secretly shared many of his doubts about the wisdom of supporting the Bao Dai regime. Nevertheless, the diplomat doggedly defended the official line and served as a foil to Isaacs's critique.

Bao Dai, Isaacs declared, symbolized the problem in Vietnam, not the solution. He asked, rhetorically, if American diplomacy was really so obtuse that it failed to understand that support of a colonial puppet would backfire and "lead to the alienation of the entire region and its loss to communism." During a ninety-minute diatribe, the reporter characterized Bao Dai (and his regime) as a "figure deserving of the ridicule and contempt with which he is generally regarded by the Vietnamese." Only foreign fools, totally "ignorant of Asian realties," could imagine this regime would survive, no less thrive, as an American asset.[15]

Isaacs dismissed Ogburn's rehashing of American efforts to contain Sino–Soviet expansion and support true nationalism as nothing but five years of American "ineptitude." No one really familiar with Asian nationalism would reduce the struggle in Vietnam to a stepchild of the cold war. The American mind set, the jouranlist insisted, reflected the views of "officers on the European desk who had no knowledge or understanding of what was going on in Asia and did not really care what happened there."

If Washington went ahead with its plan to subsidize the French and their puppets, Isaacs prophesied, the "best" outcome would be an "unlimited military commitment," the eventual dispatch of an "American army of occupation," and the devastation of Indochina as the United States sought to control a "bitterly hostile and vengeful population." Before too long, he warned, some "madman" in Washington would see no alternative to sending "American bombers over Saigon." Ultimately, all Asians would look on the United States (rather than Russia or China) as the true threat to their independence.[16]

Ogburn hushed his own doubts about Acheson's policy and fell back on a reference to congressional demands that the administration block Asian communism. Redbaiting, Isaacs retorted, was no substitute for policy. A somewhat dejected Ogburn did try to arrange a subsequent meeting between Isaacs and senior diplomats, but the latter refused. No one in a position of authority wanted to hear this Cassandra.

With supplies and money in the pipeline and a consensus within the administration, Acheson had no time to entertain critics from the Left. By late April, he concerned himself most with opening up formal discussion with the French and British, an opportunity provided by the upcoming foreign ministers' meeting in London. Immediately before departing for Europe, the secretary briefed an executive session of the Senate Foreign Relations Committee. After providing a standard litany about the Soviet military threat, he discussed the equally stubborn economic danger faced by America's allies. Acheson noted that the Marshall Plan had succeeded almost too well in restoring production, thus "more productive power" existed today "than there are markets to buy the stuff." The Europeans desperately required new markets and cheap sources of raw material, perhaps by "opening up" Africa, the Middle East, and Southeast Asia. Unless new sources for the "raw materials to keep you going—food and otherwise" were found, the foundations of Western stability would crumble through "lack of a broad enough economic base."[17]

Although Europe always remained the major focus of his remarks, Acheson also stressed the importance of assisting the French in Indochina. To forestall a Communist victory, he told the senators, the United States must temper its traditional support for nationalism and do anything necessary to "keep the French in there." Admitting that this made American policy appear "quite inconsistent," Acheson justified temporary support for colonialism because Washington needed "the French to stay until this crisis is in better shape than it is now." Meanwhile, the United States must try to "convince the French they should go forward and play with this nationalist movement and give Bao Dai a chance, really, to get the nationalists on his side." Although he acknowledged the risks in relying on Bao Dai, Acheson considered it a necessary gamble "because Ho Chi Minh, who is the other possibility, is a very clear enemy of ours and we can't expect anything from him except to go along with Moscow." He concluded, "Those are our choices," with no alternative in sight.[18]

Acheson and many of his aides later complained that the French "blackmailed" the United States—by insisting on aid for Indochina as the price of French support for a unified European force and possible German rearmament. However, the contemporary record suggests that although American policymakers were eager to win French support for European military reorganization, virtually all top diplomatic and military officials cooperated enthusiastically with the French and considered their Indochinese war effort vital. Americans frequently quibbled about French reluctance to devolve power quickly enough on the Bao Dai regime and their hesitation in following outside advice, but the United States was as eager to provide assistance as their ally was to receive it.

Even when American diplomats differed with their Anglo–French counterparts over the Europeans' desire to improve relations with China, they generally found common ground on the issue of Vietnam. In March, for example, Philip Jessup urged British and French representatives to press the Vatican to "exert its influence on the Catholic area of Indochina with a view to winning over the Catholics to Bao Dai," an idea that appealed to French Foreign Minister Robert Schuman. In May, Jessup and other State Department officials reached quick agreement with their Western European counterparts on preparing an agenda on Southeast Asia for a foreign ministers' conference.[19]

Acheson met with Schuman in Paris before reaching London and praised effusively the "wise and progressive" actions taken by the French in transferring sovereignty to Bao Dai. The secretary of state took the occasion to inform Schuman, "on a confidential basis," that about $20 million of aid would become available for Indochina during the next two months. If Congress modified the China Aid Act and extended MDAP as expected, the amount should grow larger. Acheson did implore the French to accelerate the transfer of power to Bao Dai, warning that unless the native regime acquired greater legitimacy, Ho Chi Minh would capture the halo of Vietnamese nationalism. Speaking emotionally, the secretary of state declared that the moment of truth in Vietnam had entered a "critical period which must be measured in weeks, not months."[20]*

---

* After two months in the pipeline, the first military equipment, eight C-47 cargo planes, were transferred to Saigon on June 29, 1950.

On the American side, the State and Defense departments along with the ECA moved to expedite current and projected assistance. The new Assistant Secretary of State for Far Eastern Affairs, Dean Rusk, worked closely with his Defense Department counterpart, Gen. James Burns, on the Vietnam program. They lobbied jointly for an augmented MDAP Asia program and to establish a special Southeast Asia Aid Committee chaired by Rusk. They also agreed to invite the ECA to join representatives of their two departments on a series of MDAP survey teams scheduled to tour Southeast Asia in preparation for expanded aid requests to Congress.[21]

Because all this depended on additional congressional funding, the group began pressing an augmented $1.25 billion MDAP appropriation on June 1. The proposal included an additional $75 million for the East Asia 303 fund. Rusk, John Ohly (an MDAP specialist with the State Department), and Gen. Lyman Lemnitzer (of the Defense Department), all praised the 303 fund as a vital element in stemming the Communist tide menacing Southeast Asia. To assuage both the Defense Department and the congressional China bloc, Rusk promised to consider spending some MDAP money in Formosa if Congress agreed to renew the fund on an unvouchered basis.[22]

During previous, informal testimony before members of the Senate Foreign Relations Committee, Rusk, Ohly, and Lemnitzer were even more emphatic about uses of the MDAP fund. The unvouchered appropriation, Rusk declared, provided an "extremely useful" tool in the American effort to halt Chinese penetration of Southeast Asia. The nature of guerrilla warfare required just this type of flexible, unvouchered account to support overt and covert operations. Rusk told the senators that it played an especially important part in operations against China, the details of which he declined to reveal. About $50 million of the 1949 appropriations had already been allocated with almost $21 million slated for Indochina, $10 million for Thailand, $3.5 million for Burma, $6.5 million for airfields in Japan, about $5 million for Indonesia, "and an unstated amount for covered [*sic*] activity in and around China." These totals suggested that $6 or $7 million had been spent on undercover operations, possibly intelligence-gathering missions in China and that about $25 million remained unexpended. The administration, Rusk indicated, wanted an additional $40 million for secret operations in the upcoming year.[23]

Sen. Elbert Thomas (D–Utah) explained that if the administration wanted permission to carry over the approximately $25 million remaining from 1949–50 in addition to new appropriations for 1950–51, it must convince the Senate that Southeast Asian operations were really vital. Except for the small group committed to Taiwan, Thomas and the other senators stressed the need to correlate Southeast Asian assistance with the security of Japan and the Philippines. Those nations, he insisted, were of primary importance to the United States. "Our interest in the rest of Southeast Asia was secondary, and important only as it contributed to the performance of our primary obligations in the Philippines and Japan." Thomas even coached Rusk on how to persuade the full committee to grant the desired discretionary control over MDAP funds:

> Build your strategy around the Philippines and Japan and show how Indochina and the other areas would threaten the Philippines and Japan if they were subjected to communist conquest—Relate what you are trying to do in the Southeast Asia area to what you have to do in the Philippines and Japan—just to try to stop communism in Southeast Asia is merely putting your finger in the dike—We have only relative obligations in Southeast Asia, but in the Philippines and Japan we have direct and primary obligations which must be protected and which must be discharged.[24]

John Ohly and General Lemnitzer quickly took the bait, telling Senator Thomas that they shared his judgment. Ohly declared that "Southeast Asia is, of course, the ricebowl and breadbasket of Japan." Lemnitzer emphasized "the importance of Southeast Asia as the principal market for Japanese finished products and, of course, its principal source of the raw materials." Although neither of these assertions were true in 1950, they indicated the direction of American hopes as well as the eagerness of Ohly and Lemnitzer to stroke a friendly senator whose support they counted on.

Further negotiations led to an agreement between Rusk and the senators over how to camouflage funds for covert activities under Section 303. Thomas and his colleagues made it easy, admitting they did not really want to know details of the secret expenditures. But all agreed that even if Japan were not specifically named as the intended recipient of the 303 fund, the administration should specify informally that aid for the "general area of China" primarily meant protecting Japan and the Philippines by drawing the line in Indochina.[25]

After perfunctory hearings in June, the Mutual Defense Assistance Act of 1950 sailed through the upper chamber. At the insistence of Sen. H. Alexander Smith and William Knowland, the administration accepted a partial-reporting formula (in contrast to the wholly unvouchered 1949 provision) in the 1950 act. Hoping to insure that at least something went to Taiwan, the two senators convinced their colleagues to specify that of the $75 million total, $40 million must be publicly accounted for. The use of the remaining $35 million need only be reported to the Senate Foreign Relations and Armed Services committees as well as to the House Foreign

Affairs Committee. However, if the president desired, $7.5 million of the $35 million could be spent on an entirely unvouchered basis.*

The Foreign Relations Committee reported the bill on June 21, four days before the clash in Korea. The full Senate passed it without dissent on June 30, followed by the House on July 19. With the Korean crisis as a backdrop, only one member of Congress opposed the legislation. The president signed the bill, PL621, on July 26. He thereby formalized actions already taken by administrative fiat because a month before, in response to the North Korean attack, Truman had issued emergency orders to augment assistance to Southeast Asia. The president called for an "acceleration in the furnishing of military assistance to the forces of France and the Associated States in Indochina and the dispatch of a military mission to provide close working relations with these forces." Still the basic decision to expand aid and send an advisory team had been reached long before North Korean forces crossed the thirty-eighth parallel.[26]

The decision to support directly the French war effort in Vietnam reflected a broad consensus within the Truman administration and Congress. Any misgivings about French policy paled in comparison to the value placed on Southeast Asia by both civilian and military experts. Tactically, Dean Acheson hoped that the commitment would deflect the attention of military officials away from China and toward support of a nascent Japan–Southeast Asia partnership. Although he succeeded only too well in cultivating interest in Vietnam's vital importance, Acheson failed dismally to bury the China issue or to enlist Defense Department support behind a Japanese settlement. Only a military crisis proved capable of unifying American policy, and then largely on the Defense Department's terms.

---

* Actually, more than the $75 million allotted in Section 303 of MDAP was potentially available for the "general area of China." The MDAP bill allowed the administration to transfer a small percentage of funds among the various provisions of the billion-dollar MDAP program. Thus, some money initially scheduled for Europe could be reallocated for Asia at a later time.

14
JAPAN
AND THE REKINDLED
CRISIS WITH CHINA

Although in retrospect quite peculiar, during the spring of 1950, Vietnam appeared almost a bright spot on the Great Crescent. In contrast to their disputes over China and Japan, the administration's feuding factions co-operated, more or less, in support of France's anti–Vietminh struggle. With most progress toward a Japanese settlement stalled and Sino–American relations steadily deteriorating, moderates in the American government reluctantly concluded that only a militarized policy toward China, Japan, and Southeast Asia might salvage some form of regional integration.

On the final day of 1949, at an NSC meeting that confirmed NSC 48/2, President Truman made one of his infrequent comments about Japan. Debunking the Defense Department's claim that Washington must win both Chinese and Soviet backing before formally offering a peace treaty, he stressed the nearly exclusive American character of the Occupation. Although the Soviets might eventually be invited to endorse a settlement, Truman had "no doubt the United States and the United Kingdom could negotiate a treaty with Japan whether the USSR participated or not."[1]

Although the president's comment did not comprise a definite program of action, it was welcome news to the secretary of state. If nothing else, Truman had undercut a major objection to a treaty touted by the Pentagon.

For some time, the JCS, Louis Johnson, and Tracy Voorhees had all insisted that a treaty must both grant American forces nearly unlimited use of Japan *and* be acceptable to Moscow and Peking. The extent of the military's appetite, of course, made the demands mutually exclusive. Yet, military spokesmen warned that a settlement not approved and signed by the Soviet Union would lack legal validity and provide some justification for a Russian attempt to garrison the islands themselves. However, the United States could choose simply to return "home rule" to the Japanese through a limited settlement that preserved SCAP on a standby basis and left American forces intact. Technically, no change would have occurred in Japan's status, thus preventing Moscow from charging a violation of international accords. Besides preserving unimpeded military use and freezing out the Soviet Union, Defense Department officials believed this partial restoration of sovereignty would assuage Japanese opinion.

During months of debate, Acheson, supported by General MacArthur, refuted these contentions. State Department specialists insisted that although the Soviets should be invited to sign an American-authored treaty, their approval was not a prerequisite for the restoration of full Japanese sovereignty. As for defense, a peace settlement could easily be coupled to a pair of security pacts. One would give the United States specified, and exclusive, base rights, whereas another bound the non-Communist states of the Pacific region to a pact barring aggression by or against Japan.[2]

By early 1950, the range of differences between the State and Defense departments (MacArthur, broadly speaking, stood in the diplomat's corner on this issue) regarding a treaty with Japan had, in fact, narrowed considerably. Both agencies agreed to several important questions of principle. Neither thought a direct Soviet military assault on Japan likely. They accepted the need for limited rearmament of Japan, the restoration of some military production, and the retention of American bases and troops in the post-Occupation period. Security would be maintained through a special bilateral defense arrangement accompanying a treaty as well as through the promotion of some form of defense arrangement with regional non-Communist states.

However, the two groups continued to dispute important questions of quantity (as compared to quality) and the timing of any settlement. The military establishment insisted on explicit assurances of speedy Japanese rearmament, greater emphasis on industrial rearmament, and guarantees of extensive American base and troop dispositions throughout Japan. The military voiced more concern with using Japan as a forward base in a war with the Soviet Union than in merely protecting it from conquest by an enemy. A case in point, defense planners favored a Pacific pact as an active, anti-Communist mechanism to ally friendly nations with the United

States and Japan against China and the Soviet Union. When State Department officials considered this arrangement, they described it as a method to stabilize the region by assuaging fears of both Communist and future Japanese expansion among those nations with whom a revived Japan must trade.

Finally, the positions of the two departments reflected a different assessment of the political psychology within Japan. The Defense Department and the JCS retained a deep suspicion about Japanese loyalties and feared that Tokyo might take advantage of its sovereignty by becoming neutral or even reaching an accord with the Soviet bloc. Hence, a treaty ought to be postponed as long as possible and must include ironclad provisions for keeping Japan in the Western camp. Acheson and his advisers shared some doubts about Tokyo's inclinations, but they argued that a prolonged Occupation would only undermine the still predominant pro-American, anti-Communist consensus. Thus, a "reasonable" treaty providing for limited bases and a general commitment to limited rearmament represented the surest way to affirm Japanese–American ties.

In light of Truman's expression of support for this position, Acheson and his under secretary, Dean Rusk, presented a fuller case to the president on February 20. They ridiculed the military's concept of a partial or postponed treaty and insisted that unless Japan achieved full sovereignty, its alliance with the United States would count for little. The Soviet Union, Acheson claimed, had slight interest in reaching a settlement. Instead, Moscow intended to "concentrate its attention on China and Southeast Asia," creating a puppet empire from which to blackmail Japan. Nothing Washington did would "materially alter Soviet actions with respect to Japan or the Soviet timetable in Southeast Asia," he added, fatalistically. Consequently, Acheson asked that Truman and the NSC approve, as a "matter of urgency," discussions with friendly governments leading toward a peace treaty and a "Pacific collective security arrangement." Together, these pacts would enhance the security of, and economic cooperation among, "individual countries such as Korea, the Philippines, Indonesia and Indochina."[3] The briefing papers for Acheson's meeting with Truman also emphasized the belief that a Japanese security pact with Canada, the Philippines, Australia, and New Zealand would provide a psychological "backstop" for Indochina and all Southeast Asia in its struggle against "Soviet expansion." In seed form, here were the inspirations for the half-dozen Pacific security pacts implemented during and after the Korean War.

Despite Truman's encouragement and Acheson's drive, the Pentagon maintained a nearly solid wall of opposition. In February, the JCS returned from a tour of Japan and told the president that they "were still strongly of the opinion that it is premature to make a treaty at this time. . . ." If the United States ignored the Soviets and pushed through a treaty with provisions for American bases, they warned, the "Russians could make the same claim to bases that we make." This might even precipitate a Soviet blockade or invasion in retaliation. The *New York Times* quoted one of the chiefs as remarking that "the former enemy appeared to be not only the strongest bastion but about the only tangible thing left of the fruits of victory in the Pacific."[4]

Tracy Voorhees again played a leading role in these deliberations. Since the previous December, he had been attempting, without success, to win MacArthur's support for the Defense Department's no-treaty position. MacArthur, of course, objected violently to this stance and considered Voorhees an especially obnoxious individual. The general denounced him in conversation with State Department officials, such as W. W. Butterworth, during a February 1950 discussion. MacArthur criticized Voorhees as the greatest single impediment to a treaty and a man who intended to use American bases in Japan for future "forward air operations against Russia in time of war." (JCS policy, of course, specified this.) He thought Voorhees would resign rather than "be party to a treaty." About the only thing that the army under secretary really cared about, MacArthur charged, was his "fantastic scheme for Asiatic trade," through which he expected to manipulate the administration's entire Asia policy.[5]

As if to confirm this assessment, Voorhees met with Dean Acheson late in March to deliver a proposal endorsed by himself, Louis Johnson, and the JCS. The army under secretary recommended that instead of a normal treaty, the United States merely invite friendly nations to approve a document returning nonsecurity functions to Japanese control. The administrative aspects of SCAP would be maintained on a standby basis (thus fulfilling international obligations) and the American military presence would continue largely as before. Voorhees claimed this arrangement would both appease Japanese opinion and safeguard American security requirements. He seemed oblivious to the months of debate over the question of Japan's true value to the United States. Most of the military establishment still perceived the island nation as primarily a giant forward base. Voorhees's interest in its economic future seemed confined to his scheme to develop Japan as a regional producer and exporter of military items for Southeast Asian clients.[6]

Unfortunately for Acheson, the impasse over Japan coincided with an erosion of the State Department's moderate approach in Asia. More important, Acheson had begun to lose his paramount influence over Truman. A series of disputes with China and developments within the United States that started in mid-January undercut the secretary of state's strategy of waiting for the "dust to settle" in East Asia. In fact, only days after he and the president had publicly repudiated the KMT in January 1950, relations with the PRC deteriorated. The seizure of American consular property, followed by the departure of American diplomatic personnel, closed nearly all channels of direct communication. Other problems followed quickly.

Amidst renewed verbal assaults on the State Department by Sens. William Knowland and H. Alexander Smith, the little-known Republican junior senator from Wisconsin, Joseph McCarthy, launched a sensational attack on the administration's policy. In a February 9, 1950, speech in Wheeling, West Virginia, McCarthy accused a large subversive clique in the State Department of responsibility for selling out China to communism. He singled out Ambassador Philip C. Jessup and a foreign service officer, John Service, as particularly culpable. Although the State Department leadership first considered these boorish slurs only a minor irritant, McCarthy's subsequent accusations and deft manipulation of Senate investigations during the following months, soon polarized China policy along intensely partisan lines.[7]

On February 14, as newspaper headlines reported McCarthy's charges, the Soviet Union and the PRC signed a thirty-year treaty of friendship. The pact pledged Soviet economic assistance and the eventual return of property and territory extracted from the Nationalist regime by the Sino–Soviet treaty of 1945. The agreement also highlighted the potential threat posed by the United States and Japan to Moscow and Peking. The two signatories pledged cooperation to prevent "aggressive action on the part of Japan or any other state which should unite with Japan, directly or indirectly, in acts of aggression."[8]

Both hardliners and moderates in the administration worried that this security clause masked a secret threat to Japan. It might indicate a Communist drive to scare Tokyo away from signing a separate peace and an alliance with the United States, or could presage a separate Chinese–Soviet peace offer designed to undermine the American treaty effort. In any case, the Stalin/Mao pact stunned officials who had anticipated an imminent Sino–Soviet split. Virtually all Acheson's advisers on China policy had predicted such a quick break, so long as America minimized support for Taiwan, permitted private trade with China, and held the door open for an eventual accommodation with Peking. They had assumed that Russian pressure on Manchuria and Sinkiang, along with traditional xenophobia, would stimulate Chinese "Titoism." The friendship treaty appeared to dash all hopes for a rapid break and severely reduced the leverage of moderates over a naturally more bellicose president.

These domestic and international developments only whetted the appetites of those eager to tighten the noose around China. In mid-February,

Louis Johnson began to test the limits of the president's January ban on further military aid to Taiwan. After making several requests, he gradually won permission to deliver military supplies already funded under the China Aid Act or in the supply pipeline at the time Truman imposed the ban. Even though these deliveries were not, technically, "new" aid, they bolstered Nationalist morale and outranged the Communists.[9]

Private interest groups, some linked at least indirectly to the government, also worked to rekindle the China crisis. Late in 1949 and early in 1950, for example, a complicated legal fight erupted in Hong Kong over possession of a fleet of transport planes owned by the China National Aircraft Corporation (CNAC). Shortly before the Communist takeover, Nationalist authorities ordered the planes flown to Hong Kong and sold to "private" investors, who included Claire Chennault, former Flying Tiger and KMT protégé. When the new Chinese government and some of the flight crews disputed this sale, British courts became involved. Chennault and one of his partners, former OSS head William (Wild Bill) Donovan, fought vigorously to keep control of the aircraft. Traveling to London, Hong Kong, and Tokyo on behalf of the case, Donovan also labored to instigate attacks against China.[10]

In London in December, Donovan told Air Chief Marshall Sir John C. Slessor that the JCS favored creation of an Anglo–American "resistance force inside China" and spoke of organizing a "government in exile with someone like Chennault as Minister of Defense." Presumably, the CNAC aircraft would comprise part of Chennault's arsenal. By the time Donovan reached Tokyo in February 1950, he had grown disillusioned with British efforts to accomodate Peking through diplomatic recognition. In a discussion with Brig. Gen. Fergusson, the British military adviser in Japan and an old friend, the former OSS leader fumed about his inability "to get a judge" to fix the case in Hong Kong. Later, both men met with Gen. Charles Willoughby, MacArthurs' intelligence chief, who raised the possibility of establishing joint spy networks inside China. Donovan boasted that he and his group soon planned to initiate a guerrilla war aimed at unseating the Peking regime. In reporting these discussions, Fergusson concluded that SCAP leaders were eager and willing to support some sort of campaign against the Chinese Communists and might cooperate with Donovan, regardless of official American policy.[11]

By late March, the impact of the Sino–Soviet Pact, Senator McCarthy's charges, Defense Department pressure, and Chinese harrassment of O. Edmund Clubb when the consul general sought to leave Peking toughened even the State Department moderates. On March 15 (as noted earlier), Acheson issued a public warning to China against any "adventures beyond [its] borders" that threatened "American interests" in Asia. He also promised substantial assistance to anti-Communist regimes in Korea and Southeast Asia. Moreover, the secretary of state extended an olive branch to Senate Republicans in the form of a shake-up among his staff.

Aware that President Truman and Sen. Arthur Vandenberg (R–Michigan) had recently exchanged public pledges to resume a bipartisan foreign policy, Acheson reshuffled his top Asia advisers in a way certain to please conservative critics. On March 28, the secretary of state transferred his outspoken friend, W. W. Butterworth, from the sensitive position of assistant secretary for Far Eastern affairs to the amorphous post of "adviser" on the Japanese treaty. Six weeks later, he nominated Butterworth as ambassador to Sweden, removing him entirely from East Asian affairs. Acheson selected another friend, Deputy Under Secretary Dean Rusk, to fill the FE position. Rusk was widely regarded as more tolerant of the Nationalists than his predecessor and was certainly more diplomatic in his dealing with both Senate Republicans and Defense Department officials. At the same time, Acheson selected John Sherman Cooper, a liberal Republican from Kentucky, for another advisory post in the State Department.[12]

These changes, however, failed to satisfy Vandenberg, as the administration had passed over the "leading" Republican foreign policy spokesman, John Foster Dulles. When filling a vacant Senate seat from New York, and then during an unsuccessful 1950 election campaign, Dulles had fiercely criticized Truman's domestic program. But in response to Vandenburg's pressure, Truman and Acheson swallowed their distaste and named Dulles as a "top adviser" in the State Department. On May 18, he assumed primary responsibility for the Japanese treaty, in a move Rusk admitted was designed to blunt additional Republican attacks on Far Eastern policy. Although the Japanese treaty had not yet become a "bone of partisan contention," Acheson guessed the Pentagon would try to link it to the sensitive Taiwan and China issues. Having someone like Dulles lined up with the moderates might nip a Republican-Defense Department offensive in the bud.[13]

In his new post, Dean Rusk quickly pressed for a reconsideration of the administration's policy toward Taiwan. Although not especially eager to confront the Communists on the mainland, he believed that the Nationalist-held island should and could be kept out of Peking's control through indirect intervention. Late in April, he forwarded numerous reports to Acheson containing new reasons for assisting Taiwan. Based on intelligence information, Rusk argued that the Soviet military presence in China had grown larger than predicted. He also claimed that the longer the Nationalists held out, Taiwan rather than Southeast Asia would attract the "major attention and efforts of the Communists' military forces." Fortunately,

Rusk asserted, the KMT regime had lately showed a renewed vigor, justifying new assistance.[14]

During the spring, other important State Department moderates changed their minds about China. On April 25, shortly after finally closing the Peking Consulate, O. Edmund Clubb informed George Kennan of his own revised opinion. In a highly emotional style, Clubb admitted that he now despaired of any accommodation with Peking. The CCP had "oriented its own program to Moscow's and attached China to the Soviet chariot, for better or worse." The Chinese leadership, like the Russians, he warned, "do not think like other men," and were prepared to risk world destruction in pursuit of their goals. Clubb described China's political frenzy as being "as perverted in some respects as that of Hitlerite Germany, but is less intelligent in even a Machiavellian sense." There was simply "no reasoning" with that "madness born of xenophobia" and subordination to the Soviets.

Dismissing the likelihood for improving relations, Clubb urged that Washington prepare for a "shooting war." Although he opposed any return to a policy favoring the KMT, the diplomat supported an American buildup in Southeast Asia and, especially, Japan. Japanese nationalism, he wrote Kennan, ought to be encouraged as the leading anti-Communist force in Asia, both to contain China and to eliminate the possibility of a future deal between Tokyo and the Kremlin. Meanwhile, because he now considered America "at war," Clubb recommended imposing harsh trade sanctions against Peking, assisting anti-Communist elements on the mainland, and utilizing Japanese agents for covert military actions inside China. The Japanese were "ready to go to work," he said, "if we can show them the profit." Only by taking "the fight to the enemy," Clubb concluded, could an atomic war be avoided, "or if not avoided, won."[15]

By early June, another leading moderate also spoke of "taking the war to the enemy." John P. Davies, in a PPS report influenced by Clubb, spoke of Peking's emergence as a Soviet puppet regime. To win the "minds, emotions and loyalties" of the Asian peasantry, the United States must rally non-Communist forces and produce a "dramatic success—either in the form of creating a situation of strength or causing a communist defeat." Specifically, Davies recommended assisting anti-Communist forces in China and North Korea with the interim objective of splitting these areas from the Soviet Union and with the ultimate goal of overthrowing the Communist system. In the case of China, he thought it advisable to begin a campaign to "split-off Southern China as a regional government" with the "next logical objective" support for "revolution from the ground up against the unified strength of the whole communist apparatus." All of this, he declared, required that, from "Pakistan to the Philippines," the United

States be prepared to equip security forces and supervise "political organization extending down into the villages and hamlets."[16]

The sentiments voiced by Clubb and Davies revealed how militarized even the moderate position had become. These men now viewed Southeast Asia and Japan not only as barriers to Chinese expansion but as possible spearheads to confront China. Yet, the supposed anchor of American policy in East Asia, Japan, still dangled in political and military limbo. Certainly, so far as the State Department leadership saw events, containment in Asia had no base so long as neither a peace settlement nor a security treaty with Japan existed.

Along with Dean Rusk, John Foster Dulles worked tirelessly to redirect the administration's policy in East Asia. His attacks on Truman while in the Senate seemed forgotten by both sides once he joined the State Department in April 1950. Dulles saw his role as bringing together the administration and Republican critics by nudging both toward a compromise of earlier positions. In a checklist he prepared right after his appointment, the new adviser described his interest in knitting together a consensus on the Far East, "perhaps to include all the area from Japan through Pakistan, inclusive." He intended to prepare an agenda for Congress erring "on the side of oversimplification," listing basic objectives, plus and minus factors, and the "action we should take to repair the minus factors." Like Rusk, Dulles planned to appease the China bloc whenever possible by conveying at least the impression that the State Department had taken "a new look at the whole Formosa situation." Even such a pro-KMT senator as H. Alexander Smith came away from a series of meetings with the new team agreeing to "start no fireworks until Dulles has a chance to move in on this with Acheson." In fact, Acheson named Dulles as the top Japan treaty architect largely because of the support he elicited from normally critical Republican senators.[17]

During his first meetings with Acheson's top assistants in April, Dulles centered the discussion around the Japanese settlement. To the delight of the State Department professionals, he dismissed most of the Defense Department's case against a treaty. Dulles asserted that the Occupation could be ended swiftly and that security matters and the question of post-treaty bases could be resolved through bilateral Japanese–American agreement. He considered it vital to maintain Japan's good will and feared that further delays might undermine, fatally, Tokyo's willingness and ability to ally with the United States. Should Japan become anti-American, no number of foreign troops or bases would make a difference. Dulles especially objected to Voorhees's contention that unless the Soviets and Chinese agreed to all American terms it was better to maintain the status quo. He considered Voorhees a fool who had mucked up previous international negotiations with similar sophistry. Dulles felt the United States had both the right and ability to enact a treaty and form a security alliance with or without Soviet support. Although he would not offer Japan guarantees quite so firm as given the NATO allies, Dulles saw no problem in linking the United States, Japan, and friendly Pacific countries in some sort of mutual defense arrangement.[18]

Like his State Department colleagues, Dulles considered it reasonable to insist that Japan provide selected and limited post-Occupation military facilities to the United States. This, he believed, should suffice to appease the Pentagon and provide the navy and air force adequate staging areas for defensive operations. Yet, the JCS continued to insist on virtually unlimited military access, a position that offended the Japanese, Soviets, Chinese, and most Pacific nations. MacArthur, as usual, took varying positions on this, depending on his audience. In April, he told William Sebald that "95% of the Japanese people are opposed to American bases" and that unless Tokyo made a "whole-hearted request for American troops and bases," the "entire proposition should be abandoned." However, at other times, he indicated support for including some post-Occupation bases as one provision of a bilateral security agreement.[19]

The situation became even more confusing when the JCS and Tracy Voorhees hardened their opposition still further, claiming that overall Asian conditions were so unstable that no settlement at all should be considered. Voorhees, just in advance of his retirement, got in some parting shots by leaking derogatory stories to the press concerning Butterworth. He charged the former assistant secretary for Far Eastern affairs with sole blame for the impasse over Japan.[20]

Disgusted with this backstabbing and troubled by the fact that in three weeks he was scheduled to confer with the French and British foreign ministers whose support he needed, Acheson decided to arrange a personal meeting with his rival, Louis Johnson. The two secretaries met on April 24 for what proved an extremely tense discussion. Acheson immediately attacked the Pentagon's notion that the Occupation could continue indefinitely or that the Japanese would settle for a partial return of sovereignty. He also dismissed the contention that a settlement must await Soviet and Chinese approval and warned that Moscow might actually offer a liberal treaty of its own to Tokyo. If Washington expected to win any British, French, and Japanese support for its China and Southeast Asia policies, Acheson insisted, the United States should immediately offer Tokyo a treaty accompanied by a security pact permitting the retention of some American bases.[21]

Louis Johnson, flanked by the JCS, disputed all these points. He accused Acheson and his aides of distorting the facts and leaking embarrassing information to the press. The Defense chief even claimed that "the only propaganda for a peace treaty . . . came out of the Department of State." Gen. Omar Bradley agreed, adding that the political-military balance in Asia was so unstable that nothing should be done to upset the status quo. Adm. Forrest Sherman warned that any reduction of American forces in Japan would appear an invitation for Communist meddling. Gens. Hoyt Vandenberg and J. Lawton Collins claimed that even MacArthur, secretly, opposed a treaty. They believed the Supreme Commander only wanted to stage a peace conference where he would hand the Soviets a treaty they could not accept and then force them to walk out. In light of this, Johnson and the military chiefs insisted that talk of a settlement be deferred at least until they returned from a June visit to Tokyo.[22]

Acheson appeared startled both by their overall objections and the news of the intended Far Eastern tour. He and Butterworth repeated stories of growing resentment among the Japanese and the erosion of support for Yoshida's pro-American policy. Given all the talk of military requirements, Butterworth wondered just how the JCS intended to use Japan, for defense purposes or for "offensive operations against the Soviets in the event war should break out in Europe." The military commanders made no direct response, and Johnson snapped that he failed to see "what difference the answer to his question might make." Butterworth pointed out that from the perspective of the Japanese, it made a tremendous difference if they were to become "a magnet to draw upon them the consequences of any military operations between the United States and the U.S.S.R."[23]

With no common ground between them, Acheson achieved neither a meeting of the minds nor agreement over what he should tell the European allies about American policy. Subsequent meetings between State and Defense officials also failed to reach any concensus about what Acheson might tell Bevin and Schuman of Washington's policy toward Japan. Dean Rusk angrily accused Johnson of trying to make Acheson "play the role of village idiot" at the upcoming London conference.[24]

About the only hopeful sign, as Acheson prepared to depart for Europe, came from Tokyo. Fearful that the dispute among Americans might prolong the Occupation indefinitely, the Japanese government sought to break the deadlock. Prime Minister Yoshida and his aides felt that if they demonstrated their willingness to accept a so-called separate treaty, which both excluded the Soviets and provided for American bases, the Defense Department might soften its resistance. In a conversation with American Embassy counselor in Tokyo, Cloyce Huston, for example, Yoshida noted that Japan would have to remain dependent on American protection long after the Occupation ended. Although some of his countrymen spoke of neutrality and objected to subordinating Tokyo to Washington, he "humorously" recalled the relationship between the American colonies and Britain before the revolution. Just as the Americans later assumed dominance in the Atlantic community, Yoshida quipped, "if Japan becomes a colony of the United States, it will also eventually become the stronger." Although not specifically promising to request posttreaty bases, the prime minister indicated acceptance of "whatever practical arrangements the United States might consider necessary."

The prime minister's historical license even extended to the emerging Sino–Soviet relationship that so frightened Washington. Dismissing the American view, Yoshida insisted "China would never become a slave of the Kremlin." He predicted that, as in the past, it would frustrate all foreign "efforts at domination and absorbtion." Given time, the Chinese would simply prove "too much for the Russians," as they had for others.[25]

Yoshida followed up these hints by sending two of his aides to Washington. Early in May, Shirasu Jiro, a personal assistant, called on W. W. Butterworth and Marshall Green at the State Department. He warned that the indefinite continuation of the Occupation enraged many Japanese and had begun to undermine Yoshida's governing coalition. Still, Shirasu acknowledged, "permanent neutrality" was clearly impossible and his government wanted protection from "Soviet intimidation." Although not favoring rearmament, he suggested that the United States at least restore home rule in Tokyo and, perhaps, retain armed forces on the islands under some special security arrangement.[26]

At the same time, Finance Minister Ikeda Hayato also visited Joseph Dodge and his assistant, Ralph W. E. Reid. The envoy came to plead for a relaxation of the tight money policies imposed on Tokyo by the Dodge plan and for permission to divert the yen counterpart fund from debt repayment to financing credit sales to Southeast Asia. Besides these economic issues, Ikeda discussed the domestic political effects of the stalled peace treaty. A growing coalition of Japanese political interests now accused Yoshida of being an American toady with no results to show for it. This same opposition group called for a treaty acceptable to Moscow and Peking as well as one that forbade post-Occupation foreign bases. Yoshida, for his part, preferred to sign a treaty with "all interested parties included," but would accept the "other kind of treaty" (i.e., without Communist participation and permitting bases) if Washington moved quickly. As Dodge and Reid interpreted Ikeda's message, the Japanese government wanted the "best they can get under the circumstances and as quickly as possible," whether or not China and the Soviet Union participated.[27]

After warning of growing leftist and even centrist opposition to the Occupation, Ikeda conveyed a secret message from Yoshida to the effect that if Washington insisted on the "maintenance of U.S. forces to secure the treaty" and if the "U.S. Government hesitates to make these conditions [public, the] Japanese Government will try to find a way to offer them [freely]." He hoped, apparently, that this sign of good faith would bridge the differences between the State and Defense departments.

At the same time, however, Ikeda warned that Japan wanted to see real evidence of American strength in East Asia. He recalled Kenneth Royall's comments about his nations' strategic irrelevance and worried that the administration had "written off" not only Formosa but Indochina as well. South Korea also was "not strong and could, perhaps, easily be abandoned." Even in Europe, American diplomacy seemed bent on making concessions, he complained. Moscow, Ikeda asserted, might capitalize on these trends by offering Japan "a peace treaty in advance of the United States and might include in that offer the return of Sakhalin and the Kuriles." Such a move might impress the Japanese greatly, given America's determination to hold Okinawa and its delay in offering a treaty, and erode the anti-Communist consensus prevailing since 1945.

If the United States really wanted to regain the initiative, Ikeda advised, it must move at once to wind down the Occupation. While Washington negotiated the details of a settlement, it should give Tokyo the "effect of a treaty" by creating a "de facto treaty situation." By this he meant returning to the Japanese control of their "own domestic and political affairs." In any case, he stressed, the Communist advance in Asia left his countrymen "desperately looking for firm ground." They were extremely "skeptical on just what and when and where the United States would stand firm, and particularly with respect to Japan." On June 1, the Japanese government issued a White Paper declaring its willingness to sign a peace treaty with any nation that recognized its independence. Its phrasing signified Tokyo would sign a "separate" treaty with the United States.[28]

Butterworth (then serving out his last days as treaty coordinator), Rusk, and Dulles recognized at once the importance of Ikeda's remarks. They represented, Butterworth told his superiors, the first "official" evidence that Yoshida's government would not only accept but, if need be, request a treaty shunning the Soviet Union and providing for American bases. At the same time, the Japanese were clearly restive and even threatening to cut their own deal with the Soviet bloc unless the United States rationalized its policy throughout the region.[29]

Unfortunately, these signs of Japanese flexibility were of little immediate help to Dean Acheson and his aides in London. There, during early May, the American delegates (led by Livingston Merchant and Philip Jessup) met with the British Assistant Under Secretary, now titled Sir Esler Dening, to prepare the agenda for higher level discussions. Although both sides reached speedy agreement regarding the need to assist Indochina and

Southeast Asia, generally, they found little common ground regarding China and Japan. Dening complained that Washington's policy had done little more than to drive the Chinese closer to Moscow while alienating the Japanese. Americans, the British clucked, seemed to rely on a hope "that some miracle will occur." When he requested some indication of when Japan might regain its sovereignty, Dening found "[the Americans'] lips sealed." His warnings to the State Department delegation about Soviet inroads in the wake of antagonizing Peking and ignoring Tokyo elicited no substantive response. In disgust, Dening informed Bevin that, because of American blunders, "China will be irretrievably lost for a long time" and Japan "may eventually follow suit." To make matters even worse, the United States now wanted Britain to sever its diplomatic ties with Peking and help keep China out of the United Nations. Even the more cosmopolitan members of the Truman administration, it seemed, failed to see London was "performing a service, not only for ourselves, but for the United States and the Western powers in general by our endeavor to maintain contacts and to prevent the final and irrevocable severance of China from the West." Similarly, Washington's inertia and refusal to provide the British with "any idea" of what it intended to do with Japan risked "driving" Tokyo "into the Soviet Camp."[30]

As Dening predicted, Acheson was no more forthcoming with Bevin than Jessup or Merchant had been. The foreign secretary explained that American stalling regarding Japan had placed the British in a "position of extreme difficulty," had embarrassed London with its Commonwealth partners, and had provided the Soviet Union with a golden opportunity to "take the initiative" and "write a peace treaty" of its own. Acheson apologized but admitted that the impasse within the administration made it impossible to tell Bevin anything about the American position.[31]

The tension during the London talks over the Western approach toward China and Japan foreshadowed the increasing "hardening" or militarization of East Asia policy during the late spring. For example, on May 18, the new Japan treaty coordinator, John Foster Dulles, circulated a paper that linked Japan's security to a renewed defense of Taiwan. Written in response to Ikeda's comments of May 2, Dulles also worried that Communist pressures on Indochina, Taiwan, and Korea made leaders in Tokyo question whether the United States intended to "stand firm" with "respect to Japan." The Japanese, like most of the world, Dulles argued, believed the Communist victory in China heralded a global "shift in the balance of power in favor of Soviet Russia and to the disfavor of the United States." They now searched desperately for a sign revealing either America's determination to stand firm or to "fall back and allow doubtful areas to fall under Soviet Communist control." Especially in the Middle and Far East, he felt, once local populations decided that the United States had retreated behind the NATO and Western Hemisphere defense shields, these outlying areas would be impossible to defend.[32]

Somewhat like Kennan, Dulles downplayed the likelihood of a Soviet–American war. Instead, he considered the Communist threat to countries like Japan largely psychological. Rather than risking a general offensive, Moscow would rely on a few symbolic victories to spread fear and panic. However, if "at some doubtful point we quickly take a dramatic and strong stand that shows our confidence and resolution," the United States could still prevent this "series of disasters." Formosa, he maintained, was exactly the kind of "doubtful" area where a "stand must be taken." Whatever the KMT's political defects, Dulles insisted, the island could and should be defended.

With little risk of war with Russia, Dulles believed, the United States could "neutralize Formosa" and impress the "eyes of the world." A failure to act would convince fence sitters in the developing world that Washington refused to oppose communism outside Europe and the Western Hemisphere. The small danger of war or political embarrassment that might result from intervention on behalf of the Nationalist regime, he argued, faded in importance when measured against the "national prestige required if we are to play our indispensible part in sustaining the free world."[33]

Dulles's memorandum opened a new front in the campaign to commit the United States to salvage the KMT. Along with Dean Rusk and their Defense Department allies, he pursued the argument that Taiwan's defense really represented a commitment to protect Japan and Southeast Asia from communism. Maintaining any sort of non-Communist regime on the island, they insisted, would deflect Peking's power away from North and Southeast Asia, rally the anti-Communist sentiments of millions of overseas Chinese, and, most important, assure wavering allies in Japan and Indochina that America stood by them.

Paul Nitze, Kennan's recent successor as head of the PPS, anticipated many of these points in the highly classified security study, NSC 68, of which he was chief architect. This draft, completed in April, called for massive rearmament coupled with a global resistance to revolutionary movements regardless of their "objective" importance to American security. It scuttled the implicit limits of Kennan's containment doctrine, acknowledging few geographic, political, or military boundaries to the cold war. Dulles circulated his Formosa recommendations to Nitze and Dean Rusk, relying on their influence over the secretary of state to change Acheson's thinking about the connection between Japan and Taiwan.[34]

Rusk was particularly effective in working with Dulles for a reversal of administration policy. In addition to his State Department position and close liaison with members of Congress and the Defense Department, he chaired two special interdepartmental committees overseeing the development of aid programs in Southeast Asia. His amiable relations with both Acheson and the secretary's critics provided a powerful, if informal, basis for redirecting policy.

As soon as he received Dulles's May 18 memorandum, Rusk took it as his cue to lobby within the department and among other agencies for a new agenda in East Asia. On May 25, he and Johnson's special assistant, Gen. John H. Burns, reached an informal agreement to provide maximum assistance to the "Chinese Nationalist Government on Formosa" within "existing United States policy." This involved broadening the types of weapons that might be delivered to Taiwan, expediting military cash sales, and lobbying to eliminate existing restrictions on military aid. They also decided that limited "covert action in support of resistance on Formosa" was permissible and desirable under current circumstances. Rusk promised to try to win release of additional MDAP 303 funds for certain secret "projects."[35]

Encouraged by Dulles, Rusk convened a special meeting on May 31, bringing together Philip C. Jessup, Livingston Merchant, Philip Sprouse, Fisher Howe (deputy special assistant for intelligence), and the new head of the PPS, Paul Nitze. The PPS had by now gained a measure of control over the dispersal of secret MAP funds. At the meeting, Rusk delivered a vigorous argument on behalf of reversing East Asia policy and submitted extensive reports he had prepared on the subject. Both "world opinion and U.S. opinion," he insisted, demanded that America dig in its heels and "draw the line" in Asia. Rusk wanted the group's support for a recommendation to Acheson that the United States use force to defend Taiwan while (perhaps) combining that move with a "package" solution for the entire region. This "package" might include admitting the PRC to the United Nations, increasing aid to Southeast Asia and South Korea, and speeding a Japanese peace settlement.[36]

To begin with, Rusk, like many others, felt the time had come to dispose of Jiang Jieshi. He suggested that when John Foster Dulles embarked for Japan in a few weeks, he also carry a secret ultimatum to Taipei. It would inform the venerable KMT leader that Washington would not defend Taiwan so long as he remained in power. But if Jiang requested that the United Nations assume a "trusteeship" over the island, the United States would use its navy to "prevent any armed attack while the move for trusteeship was pending." In effect, this would both neutralize the island indefinitely and eliminate the contentious Nationalist leader. Although most of the group thought the idea worth pursuing, Fisher Howe predicted the Soviets might actually welcome a "partial commitment of U.S. forces" to

Formosa because it would provide a golden opportunity to push the "Chinese Communists into a clash with us" and thereby make them more dependent on Moscow.[37]

Rusk's highly classified memorandum "U.S. Policy toward Formosa" actually went much further than merely protecting the island, however. This report for Acheson (it is unclear whether the secretary of state saw the report in this written form or whether Rusk delivered it verbally), called for reversing the assumptions that limited American support for, and involvement in, Taiwan. Rusk noted that current policy permitted the Nationalists to receive a small amount of military assistance from old funds, some economic aid from the ECA, and some help with "covert activities directed against the Communists on the mainland and directed to support certain elements on Formosa, including the possibility of some armed assistance on a covert basis." All this, however, was a stopgap because Acheson and Truman felt the island was doomed and not worth defending.[38]*

But since the implementation of the new U.S. policy on Formosa in January, Rusk asserted, significant "new elements" had come into play. In effect, he argued, the "moderates" agenda had either failed or had been superceded by events. The Sino–Soviet treaty, for example, had led to Soviet "dismemberment designs" on China and a growing Russian military presence south of Siberia. The Communist bloc's recognition of Ho Chi Minh's regime provided further evidence of "increasing aggressiveness toward other countries of Southeast Asia." Anziety about China's future behavior and the unresolved status of Taiwan (along with the other factors), created "uncertainty regarding U.S. policy in such key areas as Japan, the Philippines, Indo-China and other threatened countries where 'fence-sitting' is assuming greater proportions pending clarification" as to "who will 'win' in the Struggle of the Pacific," Rusk wrote.

Leaning heavily on Dulles's arguments (he included a copy of the May 18 memorandum), Rusk warned that a strategy based on a "holding operation" in Asia made sense only "if we do in fact hold." Once the United States permitted any violent change in the status quo, not even a redeployment of "major forces for the purposes of recapture" might prove adequate. The ripple effects of any new Communist advance would be felt globally, not just regionally.[39]

Rusk piled report on report to the effect that the Soviets, through their

---

* Although concerned with keeping Taiwan in non-Communist hands, Rusk was quite prepared to eliminate its current rulers. His proposal included lengthy and detailed assessments of how Jiang might be eased out of power or overthrown, depending on circumstances. These contingency studies were probably prepared by Philip Sprouse and W. W. Stuart of the Office of China Affairs.

new Chinese puppets, had begun a coordinated offensive against all their neighbors. They expected to soften up strong points like Japan and Southeast Asia by first knocking off such weak spots as Formosa. At the same time, he alleged, they had begun to provide substantial support for such Communist guerrilla groups as the Huks in the Philippines, the Vietminh in Vietnam, and armed elements in Malaya. Peking also placed special emphasis on recruiting supporters among the millions of overseas Chinese scattered throughout Southeast Asia.

But among all the "new elements" cited, Rusk placed the strongest emphasis on the "basic questions arising in Japan about its own future orientation." Both the delay in signing a treaty and the "consolidation of the Communist position in Siberia, north Korea and Manchuria" resulted in "active public discussion in Japan" about the value of an alliance with the United States. He cited from Ikeda's remarks to Dodge, especially noting Yoshida's anxiety about the American commitments to Formosa, Indochina, South Korea, and India. If the Japanese were to be counted on in the future, they must know immediately "just what and when and where the United States would stand firm," Rusk emphasized.[40]

The assistant secretary outlined a procedure for enhancing American credibility, beginning with Jiang Jieshi's "retirement." Once a "government of Formosa" initiated a request for UN protection, the United States should deploy the Seventh Fleet in the Taiwan Strait to prevent further fighting. The flotilla, he said, would "prevent action by or against Formosa which would disturb the peace" pending an international resolution of the island's status. Rusk even drafted a speech for the president to issue that closely resembled the text of Truman's June 27 statement regarding the outbreak of Korean hostilities.

The draft asserted that recent developments had "clearly revealed" a new phase in Soviet and Chinese intentions to "dominate and use China in their program of world revolution and aggression by subversive means." The Communist regime, it declared, was a complete satellite of the Kremlin, a base for Russian military power, and Moscow's agent in "aggression against the independent nations of Southeast Asia and the Pacific. . . ." Because the Chinese Communist puppets could speak neither for the mainland nor Taiwan, the United States would defend the principles of the UN charter by sending the "United States Navy to visit Formosan waters and to prevent armed action by or against Formosa." In an aside, Rusk urged that this act be coupled with a substantial increase in American assistance to Vietnam and the Philippines.[41]

During the following three weeks, Rusk worked tirelessly to generate wider support within the administration and Congress for what he called the "new packaging" of the China problem. During May and early June (as noted earlier), he had lobbied the Senate Foreign Relations Committee on behalf of extending MDAP, arguing that unvouchered funds were vital for operations in Southeast Asia, Japan, and China. He also suggested that Acheson approach Senate Republicans with a deal, trading American protection for Taiwan with their acceptance of de facto recognition and UN membership for Peking.

Rusk thought it might be possible for himself and Dulles to get the Republicans, the Defense Department, and, implicitly, both Chinese factions to accept a "single package" in East Asia. In essence, Washington would replace the old guard KMT on Taiwan and then inform the Chinese government that America would not permit "hostile acts between Formosa and the mainland." Chinese Communist outrage at Washington's sponsorship of a separatist regime might be mitigated by extending some form of de facto recognition to the PRC and permitting the United Nations to seat the regime by a simple majority vote. Although satisfying no one completely, Rusk imagined the China bloc, the Defense and State departments, the Chinese Communists, the population of Taiwan, and America's allies would all accept portions of the compromise. In one stroke, the bipartisan basis of policy would be enhanced and the anti-Communist perimeter in Asia strengthened.[42]

Rusk's willingness to extend a limited "feeler" to the PRC, should it accept this "one China, one Formosa policy," did not mitigate or slow his campaign to accelerate military and economic aid to Taiwan. Prompted by Rusk, Dean Acheson had by June 8 eliminated almost all remaining limits on Nationalist purchases of arms from previously appropriated funds. Because this involved only small deliveries, Rusk sought cooperation from other agencies in boosting aid levels.[43]

On June 14, Rusk and his deputy, Livingston Merchant, conferred with ECA personnel who administered the remnants of the China Aid Act program on Taiwan. These officials, Harlan Cleveland, John Nason, and Shanon McCune listened as Rusk urged immediate action to "bolster the economy" of Taiwan by releasing nearly all remaining China Aid Act funds over the next ninety days. The Communists, he argued, were waiting for the Nationalists' morale to crack before moving against the island, something that would happen by September unless new assistance arrived. If the island were stabilized until early autumn, Rusk claimed, "the weather conditions prevailing in the Strait of Formosa during the fall and winter" made an invasion extremely unlikely. Thus, a fast infusion of aid would provide "an opportunity to see whether something might not be worked out which would deny Formosa to the Communists permanently."[44]

Rusk went on to imply, without revealing specifics, that his request coincided with a new approach toward overt and covert assistance. Currently, he noted, the ECA provided about $2 million per month in economic aid to Taiwan. Although the delays inherent in any delivery schedule meant that ECA could not really telescope its remaining aid dollars into a crash, three-month effort, Rusk pounded away on the theme of the "immediate psychological benefits that could be obtained from announcements of authorization, especially if they were publicized in such fashion as to indicate an increased U.S. interest in the Formosa situation."[45]

Harlan Cleveland and his colleagues doubted whether the Nationalists would make good use of accelerated aid. More significant, however, was the fact that they pondered the deeper meaning of Rusk's plea. For a year, the administration had gone out of its way to deemphasize the importance of the small ECA program on Taiwan, hoping to minimize the loss of prestige once the KMT collapsed. Now, Rusk wanted a high-profile declaration from the ECA promising to accelerate assistance. Rusk and Merchant implied that the "new look" in policy meant that all agencies must work "more vigorously" to protect Taiwan. If these hints were correct, Cleveland wrote his bosses, the "ECA should certainly not be among the laggards, indeed, we should not hesitate to get out ahead of the parade if that seems to be the most sensible tactic." However, he urged the ECA leadership to exercise "elementary self-protection" by finding out whether "there is in fact going to be a parade—that more vigorous military steps are in fact contemplated."[46]

Rusk also helped catalyze sentiment within the Defense Department to pursue the "new look." As evidence of the State Department's hardening line was transmitted from Rusk to Gen. John Burns, Defense Department planners offered their own policy recommendations in line with the suggestions of Dulles and Rusk. On June 19, one of Burns's civilian advisers on Far Eastern affairs, Kenneth T. Young, prepared a study of open and secret measures that could be initiated quickly. Like Rusk, Young doubted that the Communists would assault Taiwan before an internal political collapse. Thus, by fortifying the overall "combat morale" of Nationalist forces, the United States could prevent the fall of the island indefinitely. As soon as the president approved a "reversal of his January policy," Young wrote, the Defense and State departments ought to be ready with a three-phase "integrated" program of action.[47]

The immediate appointment of a senior American military or naval officer to Taiwan, Young felt, would bolster the Nationalists and enhance Washington's control of the military situation. He particularly favored appointment to that post of Adm. Milton Miles, a notoriously reactionary, pro-KMT officer who had cooperated with Jiang's secret police in a wartime organization known as the Sino-American Cooperative Organization (SACO). In addition, Young advocated dispatch of nine field-grade officers, naval visits to the island, allocation of at least $10 million from the MDAP fund for military aid and a "public announcement" by the State Department declaring a "shift in U.S. policy." After taking these actions, the NSC should revise NSC 48/2 to permit the use of military force in defending Taiwan. This would involve deployment of the Seventh Fleet, having American agents undertake "covert means to insure silver to the [KMT] troops," and support of a "voluntary American group of fliers to help defend Formosa."[48]

Many of Young's suggestions paralleled Rusk's view, including his contention that the long-term viability of a non-Communist Taiwan required the elimination of the unpopular Jiang Jieshi. He urged that American agents on the island prepare the ground for a successor regime and that Washington insure its speedy recognition by "Japan, the Philippines and Vietnam." This would also facilitate the development of security and commercial ties among the non-Communist states on China's periphery. Eventually, as the situation stabilized, all these nations might become sites of "guerrilla training schools" for "tactical, political and military training for operations in China and each country of Southeast Asia.[49]

During May and early June, the activities of Rusk, Dulles, and their Defense Department counterparts were given added support by Douglas MacArthur. Since the previous January, when he spoke with Philip Jessup, MacArthur had been rather reserved on the China–Taiwan issue. Probably, he hoped that his silence might assist Acheson's pursuit of a peace settlement with Japan. Now that the treaty languished and the influence of the State Department moderates had dissipated, the general saw the Taiwan bandwagon as a winning issue that might allow him to regain attention and initiative. It also might provide him with new leverage over the JCS and the defense secretary, who opposed a Japan treaty but favored defending Taiwan.

During the spring, both MacArthur and the JCS received detailed reports on the Formosan situation from retired Adm. Charles M. Cooke, former commander of the Seventh Fleet and KMT confidant. Since retiring, he had worked as a "correspondent" for the International News Service on Taiwan and acted as an informal liaison between the Nationalists regime and SCAP. Early in May, he spent a week conferring with MacArthur in Tokyo, providing a most positive account of the situation in Taiwan. He insisted that Jiang still ruled a united and determined army on his island fortress and also controlled a force of "500,000 Nationalist guerrillas on the mainland" as well. At little cost, Cooke wrote, the United States could "match and counter" Russian penetration of China. By transferring to the Nationalists a large assortment of "surplus" ships and planes in Japan, the KMT could hold Taiwan, frighten the Soviets out of China, and cross over the "threshold of a vital doorway into the future of the world." Cooke concluded his appeal to the JCS by emphasizing that MacArthur endorsed his recommendation.[50]

When he circulated this information among his fellow commanders, Adm. Forrest Sherman added one major point. One of the "best methods" of deflecting communism from Southeast Asia, he wrote, was to sustain anti-Communist resistance forces on "the mainland of China, in Formosa," and on nearby offshore islands. However, when they met a few days later, the JCS still hesitated to endorse the direct use of American forces to defend Taiwan. MacArthur, in contrast, made a stronger pitch than ever for intervention.

Should Taiwan come under Communist control, he notified the JCS on May 20, the entire Pacific defense perimeter would be placed in jeopardy. He compared Formosa to an "unsinkable aircraft carrier and submarine tender, ideally located to accomplish Soviet strategy" and to "checkmate" American forces. General Bradley considered this message so important that he asked it to be "brought to the personal attention of the President."[51]

MacArthur also circulated these warnings among British diplomatic and military representatives in Tokyo. For example, he told Sir Alvary Gascoigne and Adm. Sir Patrick Brand that control of Formosa dictated the future security of Japan and Southeast Asia. In writing off the island, he complained, the Truman administration had thrown open these vital areas to eventual Communist control. The situation appeared so desperate, he explained to these two men, that he no longer felt an "urgent need" to conclude a peace treaty with Japan unless Washington made a greater military commitment to both Taiwan and French Indochina.[52]

Within Japan, SCAP noticeably hardened its attitude toward opposition on the Left. Previously, MacArthur had claimed that any effort to retain bases would elicit overwhelming disapproval among the Japanese. By late May, however, he concluded that regional developments as well as the insistence of the Defense Department required a more substantial post-Occupation American presence. The general told William Sebald that a plebiscite should be held in which an end to the Occupation would be made conditional on Japan providing bases "reserved to United States troops. . . ."[53]

MacArthur also ordered a crackdown against the Japan Communist Party (JCP), long a thorn in his side. Alleging that the JCP had recently undertaken or advocated violent opposition to Occupation forces, SCAP began a purge of the party leadership. A hard-line faction, led by Gen. Charles Willoughby, demanded the immediate suppression of the JCP, Government Section, however, argued such a total ban would be counterproductive and tarnish the image of SCAP. MacArthur took a middle approach, instructing Prime Minister Yoshida on June 6 to purge the JCP's executive committee and the staff of its daily paper, *Akahata*. Utilizing regulations originally designed to suppress ultra-Right militarists, this order forbade the party's leadership from carrying out any political activities.[54]

The broad drift within the administration and SCAP toward a harder, or more militarized, position further limited Acheson's ability to keep President Truman on the moderate course mapped out in January 1950. The pressure for a change in policy grew even stronger as a result of fierce lobbying by Chinese Nationalist representatives in Washington. For at least six months, both Louis Johnson and his assistant, Paul Griffith, had shared sensitive information with the Chinese ambassador, Wellington Koo. As Koo realized that the balance of forces within the administration had begun to shift in Taiwan's favor, he redoubled his efforts to influence Defense and State department officials.

Through contacts with Congressman Walter Judd and Assistant Secretary of Defense Griffith, Koo understood the need to rephrase his usual pitch. Judd noted that although Acheson still opposed substantial help for Taiwan, the secretary of state had worked hard to convince Congress to recognize "Indochina as a focal point for aid to resist the spread of Communism in Asia." Similarly, Griffith mentioned that although Truman had told Louis Johnson to "keep out of the China question," the Defense Department had much leverage over Japan and Southeast Asia. Once pointed in this direction, Koo began telling all who would listen that Taiwan actually represented the defense shield around Japan and Vietnam. He asked Griffith to help convince Johnson and Bradley to cooperate with MacArthur on a plan to transfer military supplies from SCAP stocks to the Nationalists without going through regular channels. (Admiral Cooke had recommended this in May.) Koo obviously had indications of MacArthur's support for this scheme and felt the details could be worked out when Bradley and Johnson visited Tokyo. The ambassador even suggested the possibility of bringing this group together with Jiang.[55]

Ironically, John Foster Dulles proved a far less sympathetic audience to the peripatetic ambassador. When Koo called on Dulles shortly before the latter's departure for Tokyo, the diplomat dismissed Koo's effusive flattery. Despite Dulles's efforts within the administration on behalf of the KMT regime, he chose to recount to Koo the miserable record of Jiang's government. Instead of providing for their own defense, he complained, the Nationalists threw themselves on America's mercy. To make matters worse, even while pleading for aid, rumors circulated that Jiang intended to flee Taiwan and leave America holding the bag. Dulles, presumably, felt a need to mobilize Nationalist resolve by warning Koo not to sit back and rely on salvation by the United States. He noted that although Taiwan was important to regional security, it was not vitally important. In any case, Washington could do nothing so long as Nationalists failed to place their own affairs in order. In fact, Dulles's reference to Jiang fleeing may have been a subtle hint that the Generalissimo should depart in a timely manner, placing the reigns of power in more competent hands. The State Department had already made discreet inquiries about a foreign haven for him.[56]

Koo wanted promises of aid from Dulles, not suggestions on how to reorganize the KMT. As he had with Griffith, the ambassador asked Dulles to prod MacArthur to release aircraft from Japan for Taiwan. "If the general, who understands the Far Eastern situation and its implications for the defense of the U.S. very well, could agree to such a suggestion," Koo stated, "it would be easier to arrange for making such equipment and supplies available to Formosa without necessarily obtaining the formal approval of Washington." The ambassador also requested that covert funds might be drawn from the MDAP account, further minimizing the need for any accounting. Yet, Dulles made only noncommittal responses to all these appeals.[57]

Dulles did, however, reveal something of great potential value. In discussing his imminent mission to Tokyo, he noted Washington's determination to move ahead with a Japanese peace settlement, regardless of the attitude of the Soviet Union or China. If they balked at accepting a settlement composed by the United States, it was unlikely that Washington would agree in writing to return Taiwan to the control of a Communist Chinese government. The hiatus provided by this unresolved status could provide an opportunity for extending some form of American or UN protection over the island during an interim period.

On the eve of the departure to Tokyo of two important delegations, Taiwan had assumed a central place among American concerns. As a symbolic and material bastion, it might deflect Chinese power away from more important nation's on China's periphery. At another level, Dean Rusk and John Foster Dulles hoped that by recommitting the United States to the island's defense, the State Department could placate the Defense Department, the Congressional China bloc, and MacArthur, thus speeding a Japanese peace treaty and clearing the decks for more assistance to Southeast Asia.

But even if the contending factions in the administration could resolve the question of whether to defend Taiwan, they still disagreed on whether this represented a last stand or merely the opening phase for the quickening militarization of containment in East Asia. As they prepared to embark for Tokyo, Louis Johnson and Omar Bradley reviewed a briefing paper prepared for them by Gen. Carter B. Magruder, then a special assistant for Occupied areas. Essentially, it provided a checklist for rebuffing all proposals from MacArthur and Acheson, starting with the allegation that the Japanese had grown weary of, and frustrated with, the Occupation. Ironically, Magruder agreed that the Soviet Union might eagerly accept and honor a treaty that both insured Japanese neutrality and even permitted the retention of a small American garrison. But, he asserted, this "trip wire" defense was really the essential reason the JCS and Johnson should oppose the proposals of SCAP and the State Department. Japan must not be permitted to sit out the cold war or a hot conflict as a spectator. Should war erupt with the Soviet bloc, Japan had to be enlisted as an "active ally." It would be a "great disadvantage" if Japan "could not be utilized to assist in ending Russian domination of Manchuria and China" or in helping "Manchuria and China win their freedom" from the Communists. Even if no war occurred, Magruder emphasized, neutrality must be shunned as an arrangement that would, inevitably, push Japan toward an accommodation with its Communist neighbors. Accordingly, he recommended that the defense secretary and JCS continue to resist all proposals for a treaty, delaying consideration at least until "Japan has her own armed forces or until the world situation radically changes."[58]

Dulles and his advisers (John Allison, Maxwell Hamilton, John Howard, and Robert Feary) reached a very different conclusion based on the same evidence. As they prepared to visit Tokyo, the State Department planners continued to downplay the direct Soviet threat to Japan or even Japan's primary utility as a military ally. Dulles told Acheson that Japan's importance lay in its ability to serve as an "example" to the peoples of "Asia and the Pacific Islands" of the rewards that followed a pro-Western orientation. Its success and progress, he believed would "help in the effort to resist and throw back communism in this part of the world." Dismissing the dangers of a physical threat from Russia or China, Dulles worried that the "natural sources of raw material" and the Asian markets vital for recovery all lay in the "communized parts of Asia." This economic encirclement, he feared, could not be overcome by a "defensive policy" or simply by garrisoning Japan with excessive forces. Only if the United States began a "counteroffensive" designed to "prevent the easy and quick consolidation by Soviet-inspired Communists of these recently won areas" could Japan be "saved from communism."

On the eve of his mission to Tokyo, Dulles recommended to Acheson that the United States avoid turning Japan into a fortress (which he believed the Defense Department had in mind) but rather undertake a dynamic program on Japan's behalf. This might entail covert attacks aimed at destabilizing Communist control of China and North Korea and action to develop "outside of the communised area, adequate sources of raw materials and markets for Japanese industry. . . ." Although even Dulles acknowledged that short-term recovery required some Sino–Japanese trade, he considered it vital to provide alternatives to any "dangerous dependence on Communist-controlled areas . . . which would expose Japan to successful Communist blackmail at a subsequent date."[59]

As Dulles and his staff formulated an agenda, , they described certain requirements. Any international arrangement must assure Japan commercial access to non-Communist Asian states. Thus, South Korea, Taiwan, Indochina, Thailand, and Indonesia should all be prodded to sign peace and security pacts with Japan. Dulles also resolved to accommodate, to a degree, the Defense Department's demands. He informed Acheson that he accepted the principle of maintaining selective American bases and troop garrisons after a treaty. As for rearmament, the documents prepared for Dulles urged the Japanese to augment their police, constabulary, and coast guard to deal with "indirect aggression." Personally, however, the emissary must have favored creation of a small de facto army because he raised this issue on his arrival in Tokyo. In any case, Acheson discussed these points before the mission departed and voiced his overall approval of the agenda.[60]

Despite Dulles's later reputation as an extreme "cold warrior," he was more flexible than Acheson about some terms of a settlement. Initially, at least, Dulles considered it preferable to seek Chinese and Soviet participation at a peace conference. After hearing Acheson's objections, however, he appeared to drop the idea in favor of a unilateral approach. While en route to Tokyo on June 15 he clarified his thoughts further. Instead of worrying about Soviet-bloc reaction to his mission, Dulles pondered how to resolve contradictions within the American government. Two basic questions, he wrote, remained in dispute. The JCS seemed determined to "use Japan generally as a major advanced *offensive* air base," a policy Dulles feared would only destabilize the region. He also worried about how the administration would handle the problems of "South Korea and Formosa."

He perceived these two issues as interrelated in a fundamental way. The JCS, for example, justified demands for utilizing Japan as an offensive base because of Communist pressure along the periphery of China. However, if Washington demonstrated to the Soviets and the non-Communist Asians a determination to "stand fast" in Korea and Taiwan, it should be possible to protect Japan with only a "*defensive* guarantee, stiffened by a continuing presence of some skeleton U.S. force." A sufficient show of strength in the "environs of Japan," Dulles wrote, might resolve the administration's fundamental problem—deterring the Soviet Union while persuading the Defense Department not to attempt the "overmilitarization" of Japan.[61]

Many points made by Dulles appear cryptic and somewhat sinister in light of the Korean War, but he seemed to believe that a demonstration of American resolve along the periphery of China would deter Communist threats, satisfy Japanese desires for a show of strength, and convince the American military to settle for something less than a fortress Japan. He, at least, believed his approach entailed fewer provocations against China and the Soviet Union than did that of the JCS and Louis Johnson. They appeared content to leave Japan in political limbo as they built up American regional strength in a haphazard manner. The military spoke of protecting Taiwan but ignored Japanese economic security and demands for an end to the Occupation. Also, Dulles noted, the JCS cared little about how the Japanese saw the relative importance of Communist threats to Korea, Southeast Asia, and Taiwan. On the eve of his arrival in Tokyo, the State Department envoy hoped to find a path out of this thicket of contradictions.

15
AT WAR IN ASIA

On June 17, 1950, in a duet characteristic of the contradictions afflicting the Truman administration's Asia policy, not one but two delegations from Washington arrived in Japan. John Foster Dulles and a small group of State Department aides landed in Tokyo only long enough to hold a brief press conference before departing for South Korea. Dulles returned to Tokyo on June 21 and remained there until June 27. Also on June 17, a separate plane brought Defense Secretary Louis Johnson and JCS chairman, Gen. Omar Bradley to Japan. Neither delegation had coordinated their itinerary nor even bothered to inform the other of their purpose. Not only could casual observers detect tensions between them, but the State Department's representative in Tokyo, William Sebald, did not even think that Dulles spoke with Bradley and Johnson.[1]

Almost as soon as he arrived, Louis Johnson got into a public row by taking over the rostrum at a SCAP briefing. In the "course of a fifteen minute harangue," Sebald reported, Johnson denounced the "State Department crowd" in terms that the diplomat considered "shocking." He also voiced doubts regarding the true nature of Japan's inclinations in the cold war. The defense secretary first condemned the Japanese for allegedly not fulfilling their obligations under the Potsdam Declaration and also questioned whether they could really be trusted to grant the United States effective military access to Japan after the Occupation. Johnson then disparaged Dulles as an "impractical man who approached the world's problems with a religious, moral and pacifistic attitude," unsuited for the real world.[2] His words could hardly encourage the State Department mission, MacArthur, or the Yoshida government.

Dulles could not counter these charges, as he had already departed for Korea. During the following three days, he toured the thirty-eighth parallel, conferred with South Korean leaders, and gave a rousing anti-Communist speech to the legislature in Seoul. On June 19, he listened as President Syngman Rhee implored the Americans to take "positive action" to make the task of the "Communists in North Korea . . . more difficult." He asked for promises of support should he strike north across the thirty-eighth parallel in the coming months. Rhee stressed the importance of acting quickly, before the Chinese Communists consolidated their position. The South Korean leader also tied his nation's fate to that of Taiwan, arguing that the longer the Nationalist stronghold remained severed from the mainland, the longer Chinese power would be deflected away from other targets—like South Korea.[3]

William R. Mathews, an Arizona newspaper editor and friend of Dulles, heard even more ominous rumblings as he toured Korea and Japan just in advance of the State Department envoy. Mathews predicted a quick crisis because Rhee "as much as said" to him that within one year the South would "take the offensive and take over North Korea." In fact, he reported, numerous aides to Rhee described their plan to take "early action" against the North. Mathews also met in Seoul an old American friend "lately come from Formosa" who predicted that South Korea and Taiwan would coordinate an anti-Communist strategy. According to the anonymous friend, the KMT would not only hold Taiwan but, within a year, planned to reinvade the Chinese mainland. The regimes in Seoul and Taipei, he explained, would coordinate their actions in an effort to create conditions that would elicit at least expanded military assistance from the United States. On the basis of these bits of evidence, Mathews reported to Dulles his fear that "within months we are going to have a couple of hot potatoes on our hands." The United States would have to demonstrate "firm determined action" if it expected to secure Japan and surrounding areas, Mathews wrote.[4]

While Dulles and his party visited Korea, Johnson and Bradley tried to persuade Douglas MacArthur to abandon support for a peace treaty. The Supreme Commander, however, refused to relent. He showed his visitors (first Bradley and Johnson, then on June 22, Dulles) two lengthy memoranda he had prepared on June 14 in anticipation of their arrival. To seize the offensive in East Asia, MacArthur explained, America must both offer Japan a settlement and shield Taiwan from invasion. Each act would complement and give meaning to the other. Should the Chinese Communists take Formosa, he warned, it would represent a "disaster of utmost importance to the U.S." Washington had tolerated the Communist advance so long that now only one island province remained a free bastion. If Soviet air and naval forces used it as a base to mount operations, they could easily isolate and control both Japan and Southeast Asia. Even Europe would soon feel the pinch of economic blackmail from the loss of Southeast Asia, MacArthur predicted.[5]

Taiwan's symbolic political importance, he declared, surpassed even its military significance. It stood as a beacon to the "other endangered peoples on and near the periphery of China" who saw its fate linked to their own. Whatever happened there would determine the "political alignment of those national groups who have or must soon make a choice between communism and the West." Unless a "line" were "drawn beyond which Communist expansion will be stopped," MacArthur stated, the United States would soon have to "abandon" all of Asia. Still, the general described a road to salvation. He could snatch a victory from the string of defeats if permitted to visit Taiwan and make a survey of the "military, economic and political requirements to prevent" a Communist takeover. If Washington only accepted his recommendations as the "basis for United States national policy," success was certain.[6]

MacArthur obviously hoped his rousing declaration on behalf of defending Taiwan would soften Defense Department opposition to his plan for a Japan treaty. After all, he reasoned, if Chinese and Soviet power were deflected by an anti-Communist bastion in the South, the danger to Japan and the importance of American bases there might be reduced proportionately. Abandoning plans for a treaty or insisting that Japan serve as a forward base against China and the Soviet Union, he complained, would needlessly provoke the Communist powers and alienate millions of Japanese who had faithfully carried out surrender terms. MacArthur denounced Voorhees's plan for a halfway settlement and implored Johnson and Bradley to support a "normal treaty" that included a "security reservation" granting the United States exclusive, but limited, rights for post-Occupation bases in Japan. Partially abandoning his earlier opposition to *any* bases, MacArthur agreed on the need to maintain a small American "trip wire" force so long as "irresponsible militarism" existed in the world. Besides its other virtues, the general insisted, retaining limited forces would not unduly trouble the Soviet Union.[7]

Unfortunately, neither MacArthur's invocation of Japanese loyalty nor his estimate of the sufficiency of minimal bases persuaded his two visitors.

From the moment he landed in Tokyo, Johnson had indicated how little faith he possessed in Japan's allegiance to the American camp. Nursing memories of the Second World War and fears caused by Japanese interest in developing a relationship with China, the defense secretary insisted that only a prolonged Occupation could affirm the former enemy's transformation. Despite all evidence to the contrary, Johnson even claimed that most Japanese had little interest in securing an immediate return of sovereignty. Bradley appeared to share these suspicions and certainly recoiled at the prospect of a treaty that required the military to abandon any of its prerogatives.

Nor were military planners impressed by MacArthur's contention that a neutralization scheme and a "trip wire" defense would shield Japan from a Soviet onslaught. This was, in fact, largely beside the point. Internal Japanese forces and a small American garrison, they conceded, could probably ward off or suppress domestic and foreign threats. The real problem stemmed from the fact that American war planning counted on using Japan as an offensive springboard in case of conflict with the Soviet Union. Thus, they feared, Moscow would have every incentive to accept and honor an international arrangement guaranteeing a neutral Japan. Because Mac-Arthur's proposals fundamentally contradicted these strategic assumptions, Bradley and Johnson rejected his recommendations. They agreed only to carry the general's plea on behalf of Taiwan back to Truman because it so closely resembled their own.

Fortunately for the Supreme Commander, John Foster Dulles proved a far more sympathetic audience than his immediate predecessors. As soon as Dulles returned to Tokyo from Seoul on June 21, he and MacArthur went into conference. The general presented his two memoranda and found that both conformed to Dulles's preconceptions. Unlike the visiting military delegation that had had little interest in meeting Japanese, MacArthur found Dulles eager to contact a "large cross section of Japanese leaders, foreign diplomats, businessmen, and others with views about the treaty." Even the emperor secretly contacted the envoy, urging him to consult with influential Japanese, including some in disgrace "because of their alleged former militaristic outlook." In his message (given to Dulles after fighting erupted in Korea), the emperor indicated that certain "older people, the majority of whom have been purged," would now be important as sources of "valuable advice and assistance to Americans. . . ."[8]

During his round of meetings in Tokyo, Dulles expressed particular interest in Japan's future contributions to American defense requirements. This emerged most clearly in conversation with Prime Minister Yoshida. When they met, according to William Sebald, the Japanese leader was in a "puckish" mood, speaking in "parables" and refusing to "talk sense."

Dulles asked whether the Japanese might be willing to placate the United States by agreeing, as part of a treaty, to rebuild a small national army. (The JCS had urged this since 1948.) Yoshida retorted that the "peace constitution" and public opinion barred any such move. Instead, Japan relied for security on American protection (he had already indicated approval for post-Occupation bases) and world opinion.

When Yoshida asked that the rearmament issue be put to MacArthur, the general supported the prime minister's position, emphasizing his belief that Japan could neither politically nor economically tolerate an army large enough to be of military value. However, MacArthur suggested that Japan contribute to the Western alliance in other ways, such as by reactivating the factories for military production needed in the "reconstruction of American armaments." This would help stimulate economic recovery in Japan and allow Japan to contribute to an anti-Communist program. These somewhat vague exchanges took on added meaning when MacArthur spoke privately with Johnson and Bradley and then later with Dulles.

The strident opposition voiced by Bradley and Johnson to any peace settlement prompted MacArthur to submit a new compromise proposal. During a three-hour conversation with the visiting Defense Department officials and in later talks with Dulles on June 23, the Supreme Commander tried to reconcile the views of the two departments. Abandoning the concept of a limited post-Occupation military presence, MacArthur suddenly declared that the "entire area" of Japan must "be regarded as a potential base for defensive maneuver with unrestricted freedom reserved to the United States as the protecting power through her local commander, acting in the normal chain of command to the Department of Defense." Contradicting his statements of the previous four years, MacArthur claimed this "unrestricted" base plan would actually prove less offensive to Japanese sensibilities than taking specific territory for military use. In fact, the Supreme Commander knew most Japanese would be outraged at this limitation of their national sovereignty. But, he predicted, Washington could assuage their feelings by implementing a new "pay-as-you-go" aid program providing an additional $300 million per year to Tokyo in exchange for unrestricted base rights. This amount, he pointed out to Johnson and Bradley, would bridge the gap between "the existing deficit economy and a completely self-sustaining economy."

To win Defense Department support, MacArthur even relented on one of his deepest convictions—that Japan be permanently disarmed. He agreed to discard the concept of "neutrality" and promise to support a plan encouraging a sovereign Japan to rebuild its own defense capability. In effect, this meant rebuilding at least modest armed forces. But so long as Japan remained dependent on American arms, the Supreme Commander agreed that U.S. forces would operate solely under Defense Department command, subject neither to State Department nor Japanese control. In his almost desperate desire to pull some sort of treaty out of his hat, MacArthur consented to nearly every principle sought by Johnson and Bradley. He verbally committed himself to support a comprehensive military alliance, unlimited bases on Japanese soil, industrial rearmament and, possibly, building a new army. Yet, even when he agreed to pay this price, Johnson and Bradley departed Tokyo still opposed to a peace settlement.[9]

Not surprisingly, MacArthur had better luck with his "Formosa Memorandum" than with his appeal for a treaty. Bradley and Johnson considered it useful leverage in their campaign to move Truman. When they returned to Washington, they presented it to the president as one of his options in response to the Korean fighting. Dulles acted even more quickly, however, sending the document to the State Department on June 22 or 23. On receiving it, Acheson conferred with his top Asia policy advisers, minus Dean Rusk, then out of Washington. Rusk's deputy, Livingston Merchant, notified his boss of the group's concern that the intense focus placed on the island by Dulles and MacArthur increased the "incentive for the Russians to make some surprise move for purposes of embarrassment or propaganda." Sending MacArthur to Taipei would symbolize a major policy shift and vastly increase the attention paid to the island's fate. The "moment General MacArthur debarks on Formosa," Merchant informed Rusk, "we will be committed." If the United States accepted this commitment, it should, simultaneously replace Jiang with a less discredited leader. Summarizing the inconclusive discussion of MacArthur's proposal, Merchant declared that if and when the administration followed the general's scheme, it had better be prepared to "go the whole hog if required."[10]

The tone of the group's deliberation revealed their shared interest in somehow preventing a Communist seizure of Taiwan. However, Acheson and his advisers still hesitated to commit an act certain to drive Peking closer to Moscow. Nor were they eager to do anything likely to save Jiang Jieshi from the fate they felt he deserved. Yet, if some way could be found to finesse these problems, Acheson seemed willing to do more to keep the Communists off the island. In fact, the Korean struggle that began a few days later prompted the secretary of state to advocate extending protection over Taiwan without, he hoped, saving Jiang's rule.

The North Korean assault across the thirty-eighth parallel on June 25, 1950 (June 24 Washington time) became the catalyst transforming American policy throughout Asia. It provided the momentum that carried the United States more fully into the Chinese civil war, into the Indochina war, and toward a separate peace settlement with Japan. Within a few days of the attack, the Truman administration committed American ground forces to the defense of the Korean Peninsula, dispatched naval units to protect Taiwan, and greatly accelerated assistance to French Indochina and the Philippines. Ironically, the Korean conflict and the militarization of Asia policy cleared away the bureaucratic roadblocks hampering a settlement with Japan and helped fund that nation's economic recovery. In a very real sense, Japan arose from the ashes of the Second World War largely on the crest of an expanded American military crusade in Asia.

The outbreak of large-scale fighting on the Korean Peninsula in June climaxed a long period of guerrilla warfare, peasant revolts, provocations by the regimes on either side of the thirty-eighth parallel, and the creation of a pair of antagonistic clients by the Soviet Union and the United States. Although the exact circumstances of the events of June 24 (local time) remain uncertain, both Washington and Moscow had become deeply involved in the fate of their Korean proxies. Almost certainly, the North Koreans struck first on the day in question. Yet, many American observers had long feared a similar cross-border attack by the Rhee regime in the South. As a recent major study of the war's origins by Bruce Cumings has demonstrated, the United States and the Soviet Union each bore responsibility for the permanent division of the Korean nation. American occupation forces also directly assisted the creation of a militant, repressive South Korean government that was committed to unification by force.[11]

Historians have long noticed the glaring contradiction in American Korean policy on the eve of the war. Most military planners (including MacArthur) had minimized the value of holding the southern half of the peninsula. During the period of the occupation (1945 to 1948) they considered it an expensive drain on scarce resources and a superfluous position in light of the Communist advance in China. Civilian planners, especially in the State Department, expressed greater concern with supporting the Republic of Korea after 1948, arguing that, as an American offspring, its survival symbolized the credibility of U.S. support. To abandon it might both encourage Communist aggression in more vital areas and frighten the Japanese and Western Europeans.[12]

Despite the American role in creating the repressive Rhee regime, assistance to Korea was relatively limited before 1950. The Seoul regime received some aid from GARIOA, EROA, MDAP, and from some additional funds that Congress voted in 1949 and 1950. But Korea had few enthusiastic supporters in Congress. Even members of the China bloc had voted against spending additional money in Korea early in 1950, arguing that, after China's "loss," it made no sense to try to salvage the Seoul regime. Yet, Secretary of State Dean Acheson and his advisers insisted that the United States must respond to an outside attack on South Korea, especially because they viewed North Korea as a Soviet puppet. Although

Acheson excluded Korea from the most vital category in his "defense perimeter" speech of January 1950, he had pledged then that America would utilize the United Nations to defend Korea. In March, he went further, declaring that Korea now fell under the protective umbrella of an Asian "Truman Doctrine." In any case, whatever misgivings existed in the State Department about the peninsula's strategic importance or Rhee's tattered government paled in the face of an actual attack by Communist forces across an "international frontier."[13]

Not exactly pleased by the North Korean attack, nevertheless, many diplomatic officials imagined positive results from an engagement of American power. Rusk and Dulles, of course, had spent the previous month arguing the need to make a military demonstration in East Asia, in large part to shore up Japanese resolve. Although they had assumed a crisis would come first in Taiwan, both men (as well as Japanese envoys) had emphasized the symbolic value of defending South Korea. The fear that unopposed aggression might unravel NATO and undermine Japan found expression within hours of the attack. Charles Bohlen wrote George Kennan on June 26 that "all Europeans to say nothing of Asiatics are watching to see what the United States will do." Kennan, although he had no illusions about Korea's strategic value, prepared a memorandum for Acheson that same day warning that if the United States did not resist North Korea, "there will scarcely be any theater of the east-west conflict which will not be adversely affected thereby from our standpoint." Still other administration officials viewed the attack as a direct challenge to the United Nations, prompting President Truman (as recalled by Ambassador Philip Jessup) to exclaim "We can't let the UN down!"[14]

Besides considerations of global strategy and alliance relations, committing American forces to the defense of South Korea might also rectify contradictions within the administration. Engaging American power and prestige on China's periphery would almost certainly lead to a reversal of policy toward Taiwan. This, in turn, might convince the Defense Department and JCS to accept the State Department's plan for a treaty with Japan whose terms would now surely include more generous provisions for post-Occupation military facilities. Finally, even a limited war would galvanize public and congressional opinion to support defense spending far in excess of the relatively small figure approved for 1950. This made it possible, finally, for the administration to initiate the massive rearmament proposed months earlier in NSC 68.

Within seventy-two hours of the attack, intelligence planners in both the State Department and the army reached nearly identical evaluations of the situation. The North Korean assault, they concluded, had been planned by Moscow to destabilize anti-Communist governments throughout Europe and Asia. By destroying an American-sponsored regime, the Soviets hoped to shock the Japanese out of signing a military pact with Washington, weaken KMT resolve on Formosa, boost the prospects of the Vietminh in Indochina, and undermine faith among the NATO allies. The army intelligence staff provided several justifications for a counteroffensive that matched perfectly the fears voiced by State Department analysts. By successfully repulsing North Korea, Washington would enhance its own prestige, bolster Japanese resolve to accept American bases, stiffen West Germany's bond to the West, make NATO a more effective alliance, possibly drive a wedge between the British and the Chinese Communists, and inspire the French to fight harder in Indochina.[15]

The Truman administration developed its response to the Korean conflict during two meetings at Blair House (the presidential residence during White House renovations) on the evenings of June 25 and June 26. However, as soon as word arrived of the fighting in Korea, the State Department called for a UN Security Council meeting. Taking advantage of an ongoing Soviet boycott (in response to China's being unrepresented), the American delegation pushed a resolution through the council on the evening of June 25. It condemned North Korean aggression, demanded the immediate cessation of fighting, withdrawal of forces to the thirty-eighth parallel, and called for member states to assist the South Korean regime.

The most striking feature of all this as well as the discussions at Blair House was the enthusiastically aggressive tone struck by Dean Acheson, Truman's receptiveness for direct action, and the comparatively reserved stance of Louis Johnson and the JCS. As the meetings proceeded, State Department representatives took the offensive in urging military aid to Seoul; the use of American air, sea, and ground forces; potential operations against North Korea; protection of Taiwan from a Chinese assault; and the escalation of aid to Indochina and the Philippines.

All this reflected several bureaucratic and political factors. Already under mounting attack by Republicans for their alleged "appeasement" in East Asia, both Truman and Acheson probably feared that any reserve, hesitation, or moderation might fuel greater attacks by McCarthy and his ilk. Within the administration, Acheson probably wanted to seize the initiative (and Truman's trust) by demonstrating his forcefulness in responding to what he judged as a clear-cut act of aggression by a Soviet satellite state. In addition, the State Department had always placed greater stock in the symbolic political importance of South Korea than had the Defense Department, which saw the tiny state as a strategic backwater and drain on scarce resources. Johnson and the JCS had long insisted that Taiwan and the southeastern Asian states comprised far more important positions for American security. As events developed, Acheson not only urged the defense of Korea, but he now endorsed most of the military's earlier contentions. As for fighting a war on the Asiatic mainland, the generals, admirals, and defense secretary were perfectly happy to let the secretary of state urge the president to place American lives in jeopardy.

As it turned out, Acheson rightly feared Johnson would try to make him the fall guy in the entire episode. The secretary of defense, in the wake of the administration's decision to intervene in Korea, spread stories blaming his colleague first for inviting the attack and then for alleged softness in meeting it. When Truman committed the United States to Korea, Taiwan, and Indochina, Johnson sought to vault onto the bandwagon by tossing Acheson off.[16]

Two other supposed hard-liners, John Foster Dulles and Douglas MacArthur, also had reservations about committing American forces directly to the Korean Peninsula. MacArthur initially downplayed the significance of the attack, the possibility of Soviet involvement, or even the danger of the North Koreans overrunning the South. Although ordering logistic and air support for the Koreans almost at once, the general hesitated to propose the engagement of American ground forces on the Asian mainland. Only after he found Truman and Acheson eagerly supporting intervention did MacArthur come out strongly in favor. This reserve, some have speculated, revealed the general's confusion and lack of preparation at the moment of crisis. Alternatively, he may have preferred not to show his hand or reveal his intentions until the civilian and military leadership in Washington had done so. Dulles, too, early voiced private doubts (although public approval) about intervention on the ground. Like Army Secretary Frank Pace, he worried about the ability of China and the Soviet Union to overwhelm American land forces on "the continent of Asia. . . ."[17]

At the first Blair House meeting on June 25, Acheson took the initiative in urging that the president authorize General MacArthur to provide arms, ammunition, and air cover to South Korea. He "next suggested that the President should order the Seventh Fleet to proceed to Formosa and prevent an attack on Formosa from the mainland." This idea flowed naturally from MacArthur's June 14 memorandum that Omar Bradley had read to the group before dinner. Acheson, as noted earlier, had received the report on June 23 and discussed it in some detail with his staff. The secretary of state now argued that the fleet should prevent attacks in either direction across the Taiwan Strait, thus preventing Nationalist forays against the mainland. He also urged that no commitments be given Jiang Jieshi about the island's future so that its status might eventually "be determined by the UN." Truman interjected that the island's fate might eventually be resolved as part of a Japanese treaty. In either case, it appeared, Acheson and Truman hoped to foster a Taiwan independent of the Communists and old-guard Nationalists. The secretary of state concluded his assessment of the crisis by recommending that "aid to Indochina should be stepped up."

The military establishment in attendance seemed pleased by Acheson's stance. They, however, stressed the strategic importance to Japan of both Korea and Taiwan. Adm. Forrest Sherman, for example, urged augmenting MacArthur's authority as SCAP to include Formosa, a proposal strongly opposed by Acheson. Ironically, Louis Johnson (who suddenly professed agreement with Acheson) similarly urged that Truman limit what he called MacArthur's "discretion." He opposed too great a delegation of "presidential authority" to the field commander, especially one so frequently at odds with the Pentagon. Johnson also voiced misgivings over Acheson's eagerness to commit ground combat troops.

Acheson's strategy (if that is what it was) worked as he hoped. Truman came down closest to his secretary of state's hard-line during the discussions. He interpreted the Korean attack as a challenge to the United Nations, a test of American credibility, and, probably, a Soviet probe of Western resolve. Fearful of additional Russian moves, the president even ordered the military to prepare contingency plans to "wipe out all Soviet air bases in the Far East."[18]

The JCS appeared mildly startled with the positions taken by Acheson and Truman. They had, of course, long pressed for action to protect Taiwan, only to be rebuffed by the president and the secretary of state. Earlier in the meeting, JCS Chairman, Gen. Omar Bradley, not only presented MacArthur's plea on behalf of the island but carried a message of his own. He described Taiwan's security as vital to the American positions in Japan, Okinawa, and the Philippines. In light of this, Bradley recommended that Truman dispatch MacArthur to survey Taiwan's defense needs.[19] Although Acheson still opposed sending MacArthur or making political commitments to the KMT, he had already acceded to the military logic behind Bradley's appeal.

Despite this fact, Dean Acheson had his own agenda regarding Taiwan. Acknowledging its new importance, he still hoped to prevent the Korean crisis from saving Jiang's despised regime. By having the Seventh Fleet "neutralize" the Taiwan Strait in both directions, Acheson thought it might be possible to separate the island from the mainland, place it under temporary American or UN authority, and, eventually, provide for home rule by a native regime. In effect, he accepted the ideas advanced earlier by Dean Rusk and John Foster Dulles.[20]

Over the next twenty-four hours, Truman pondered the recommendations made to him at the June 25 meeting, especially those from Acheson. The Defense Department officials, clearly, had greater interest in the implications of the attack for Taiwan and Southeast Asia than in the fate of South Korea. Gen. Omar Bradley used the interval between the first and second Blair House conferences to revise the JCS's formal recommendation to the president. On June 26, he informed Truman of his own conviction that "Korea, Japan, Okinawa, Formosa, the Philippines and Southeast Asia are all part of the same problem." Because their positions were "interdependent," there was "an urgent need for a coordinated overall policy in the Far East." Bradley sought to insure that if the president accepted Acheson's commitment to South Korea, he would also adopt the military's view on Taiwan, Southeast Asia, and the Japanese settlement.[21]

Soon after the meeting of June 26 convened, Acheson again assumed a highly belligerent tone, urging that an "all out order be issued to the Navy and Air Force to waive all restrictions on their operations in Korea. . . ." Both he and the president indicated that future developments might even require attacks north of the thirty-eighth parallel. Acheson then pressed for a decision on his proposals of the day before. Besides interposing the fleet in the Taiwan Strait, he now recommended that assistance to both the Philippines and Indochina be increased and that a "strong military mission should be sent" to the latter. These commitments, he emphasized, should be undertaken within a day.[22]

Still, Acheson hoped to distinguish between preventing a Communist conquest of Taiwan, rescuing the Nationalists, and cutting all lines to China. Truman obviously sympathized with his purpose, suggesting, somewhat crudely, that the island be again declared "part of Japan" and placed "under MacArthur's command." The president surprised everyone by claiming that a month earlier Jiang had written him a secret letter offering to "step out of the situation" if that would alter American policy. Now, he thought, the Generalissimo might "step out if MacArthur were put in." Acheson prevailed on Truman to defer such a move, arguing that the immediate priority was to prevent a Chinese Communist or Soviet occupation, not to get "mixed up in the question of the Chinese administration of the island." This led both the president and, curiously, Louis Johnson to agree that the Nationalists were all swindlers who had misappropriated aid funds into "United States real estate" and "banks in the Philippine Islands."[23]

Ultimately, the President opted to follow Acheson's suggestions as bolstered and endorsed by Defense Secretary Johnson and the JCS. Although the administration would seek additional UN authorization for its actions, the possibility of a Soviet veto (should their delegate return to the Security Council) required a prior American declaration of intent. Also, mostly for cosmetic reasons, the president agreed to brief congressional leaders on his decisions, but he declined to ask Congress for any formal approval.[24]

The next morning, June 27, the White House issued a statement confirming that American air and sea forces would assist fully the South Korean government. (The decision to send ground forces came three days later). Truman's text echoed the consensus of the Blair House meetings, but it also followed closely the speech drafted by Dean Rusk late in May. The attack by the North, he declared, proved that "Communism has passed beyond the use of subversion to conquer independent nations and will now use armed invasion and war." He tied this broad indictment of communism (rather than of North Korea) to the Formosan question, asserting that the island, in enemy hands, would be a "direct threat to the security of the Pacific area and to United States forces performing their lawful and necessary functions in that area." As a result, he had ordered the Seventh Fleet to interpose itself between Taiwan and the mainland and had authorized it to prevent military moves by either side. Any determination of the island's future status "must await the restoration of security in the Pacific, a peace settlement with Japan, or consideration by the United Nations." In effect, the United States interceded to prevent the conclusion of the Chinese civil war, making itself the real arbiter of Taiwan's sovereignty.[25]*

Extending American intervention still further, the president announced that aid to both the Philippines and the "forces of France and the Associated States in Indochina" would be accelerated. A "military mission" would also be sent to Indochina to provide "close working relations" with anti-Communist elements. Justifying these actions as a commitment to the "rule of law" against the "rule of force," Truman quickly cleared the way for participation in three Asian wars.[26]

Continuing until the summer of 1953, the Korean War promoted a version of Asian integration, although hardly in a format predicted by its initial sponsors. The deepening American military, political, and economic involvement in East and Southeast Asia provided an unexpected solution to Japan's postwar economic crisis. Japan was spared the devastation that the conflict brought on Korea, China, and Indochina; on the other hand, the conflict contributed immeasurably to the "economic miracle" that became that nation's hallmark in the subsequent three decades.

The Korean decision also proved the salvation of the floundering Chinese Nationalists on Taiwan. Despite Acheson's determined effort to keep the KMT at arm's length, inevitably, American strategy, MacArthur's tactics, and China's entry into the war forged a new bond to the Nationalists. In

---

* As few American ships or planes were available to patrol the Taiwan Strait, this comprised a largely paper blockade for two months. Because most observers expected a Communist occupation of Taiwan only in the wake of an internal collapse, its purpose was as much to bolster KMT morale as to deter the Communists.

the opinion of Sen. H. Alexander Smith, "It was all very wonderful and an answer to prayer." The "saving of Formosa," he felt certain, "was clearly God guided."[27]

Divine intervention or not, Defense Secretary Louis Johnson and his assistant, Paul Griffith, were both eager to take much of the credit. On June 30, Johnson met with the Chinese Nationalist Ambassador, Wellington Koo, to hear himself praised as Taiwan's savior. It had been a "hard struggle in the face of determined opposition from the State Department," Johnson boasted, "but in the end he had won his fight." In truth, of course, Dean Acheson had finally convinced Truman to protect the orphaned island. Nevertheless, the Defense Department chief bragged that his trip to Japan in June and great clout within the administration had turned the Korean crisis into a "change of policy vis-à-vis Formosa." Cryptically, Johnson asked Koo to "tell Madame Chiang and Dr. Kung he had kept his promise." In an expansive mood, the ambassador responded with an offer to send KMT troops to Korea to fight under MacArthur, exactly as Acheson had feared.[28]

Later that day, Koo met with Assistant Defense Secretary Griffith, both men congratulating each other for Johnson's supposed triumph over Dean Acheson. Griffith expressed particular pleasure at the offer to send troops from Taiwan to the Korean battlefront. He also criticized the secretary of state for ignoring his earlier advice about keeping the one-hundred thousand Dutch troops from the East Indies armed, supplied, and ready for action in Asia. Had they been on station, Griffith claimed, it would have made "a very great difference in a critical situation."[29]

During July, the Nationalists on Taiwan pushed hard to establish ties between MacArthur, the war effort in Korea, and their own pretensions to reconquer the mainland. On July 31, MacArthur, who had just been appointed UN commander, suddenly flew to the beleaguered island for two days of secret talks with Jiang Jieshi. He returned to Tokyo and released a statement (despite the fact he had neither cleared the trip with the State Department nor formally reported on it to Washington) about having made plans for coordinating an American–KMT military defense of the island in case of Chinese attack. Celebrating Jiang's "indomitable determination to resist Communist domination," MacArthur spoke of their "common interests" that "all people in the Pacific should be free—not slaves." Jiang, in turn, announced new accords for "Sino–American military cooperation." The support promised by his "old comrade in arms" now made victory certain. Reports even circulated that MacArthur intended to transfer aircraft to Taiwan for use in attacking the mainland.

Concern in Washington and foreign capitals that MacArthur planned to commit the United States to the KMT's goal of reconquest led Truman to chastise the general by dispatching Averell Harriman to Tokyo for consultations. The president also reassured the Western Europeans about America's limited objectives. Although MacArthur told Harriman he understood the administration's policy, he soon made well-publicized statements about the need to seize the political and military initiative throughout Asia. The ambivalence of the administration's own policy became clear as it approved the resumption of military assistance to Taiwan and dispatched a high-level survey team to report on future defense requirements. All of these moves allowed Jiang to rally his dispirited supporters and suppress the long-rumored coup to depose him. Within four months, the American juggernaut north of the thirty-eighth parallel provoked Chinese intervention in Korea, elevating Taiwan to a de facto ally and pillar of the Pacific defense perimeter.[30]

Indochina also "benefited" from the Korean conflict. The June 27 pronouncement pledged an expanded American commitment to the French campaign against the Vietminh. This involved increased economic and military aid as well as a willingness to cooperate with "unofficial" anti-Communist groups, such as the Cao Dai religious sect and the Catholic Church. A joint State Department/Defense Department MDAP mission visited Vietnam from July 15 to August 7 to survey immediate needs. Its head, John Melby, had opposed further intervention in China. But like many "moderates," he described Indochina as the "keystone of [the] SEA defense arch." A failure there would "inevitably precipitate" all of the "SEA mainland into [the] Communist orbit with excellent prospect of [a] similar eventuality in Indonesia and [the] Philippines, barring American occupation of [the] latter." Melby and his mission colleague, Gen. G. B. Erskine, recommended additional military aid to the French in order to "hold the lid on the Indochinese kettle for the predictable, if relatively limited future." For the long run, France must be induced to turn the war over to indigenous anti-Communist Vietnamese, the "U.S. would as usual pay most of the bills."[31]

Fearful of both a Communist victory in Indochina as well as the perils of association with French colonialism, American policy remained mired in contradictions. Charlton Ogburn, a seasoned diplomat with extensive experience in the region, warned Dean Rusk of the "two ghastly choices" confronting America. We could, he wrote:

1. wash our hands of the country and allow the Communists to overrun it; or,
2. . . . continue to pour treasure (and perhaps eventually lives) into a hopeless cause in which the French have already expended about a billion and a half dollars and about fifty thousand lives—and this at a cost of alienating vital segments of Asian public opinion.

Although it might please certain segments of the public and Congress to give the impression "that we are confronted with a clear case of Communist aggression in Indochina and that we are meeting it in a hard-hitting, two-fisted manner," Ogburn cautioned, such propaganda risked "sowing the whirlwind— . . . unless of course we intend when the time comes to commit American ground forces in Indochina and thus throw all Asia to the wolves. . . ."[32]

Ogburn's anguished cry had little impact on policy. Rather, the JCS set the future agenda in a report they prepared for the Defense Department and the NSC in November 1950. Drawing on the recommendations of the JSSC, the JCS urged that the United States "as a matter of urgency" do everything short of deploying its own forces to "deny Indochina to Communism." In practical terms, this meant increased military aid to the French, an accelerated program to recruit an anti-Communist Vietnamese army, and constant pressure on Paris to grant the Vietnamese greater self-rule.[33]

The military planners explained why they considered Indochina a strategic point. In the event of global war, of course, areas like Vietnam were irrelevant. However, assuming that future confrontations between the American and Soviet blocs remained a "cold war," then communist control of the disputed colony

> [would] bring about almost immediately a dangerous condition with respect to the internal security of all of the other countries of Southeast Asia, as well as the Philippines and Indonesia, and would contribute to their probable eventual fall to communism. Even India and Pakistan would be threatened.

The fall of Southeast Asian dominoes would have "political and psychological repercussions . . . throughout the world."[34]

Besides paving the way for a peace treaty, the most telling impact of the Korean War on Japan came in the economic sphere. As MacArthur and Yoshida had suggested to Dulles in June 1950, harnessing Japan's industrial potential rather than its soldiers would make the greatest contribution to America's aims in East Asia. In drawing on Japanese industry for a host of military supplies, the United States both solved its own logistic problems and gave a tremendous boost to the stalled recovery program. During 1951–52, American military orders, known as off-shore procurements, reached nearly $800 million per year. Even accounting for the slowed pace of dollar aid during the 1953 battlefield lull, nearly $3 billion flowed into Japan by the end of 1954. During the remainder of the decade funds from the new Mutual Security Program and, later, the Foreign Operations Administration continued the stream of support. These expenditures not only helped balance the still chronic dollar gap and compensated for the barriers imposed on trade with China, but they created for the first time since 1945 an assured foreign market for heavy-industrial and high-technology exports for which no other customer existed. Special procurements subsidized industrial rearmament and linked Japanese prosperity to American security policy in ways far more profound than the tentative steps taken in July 1950 to establish a small army or National Police Reserve.[35]

American officials, and nearly all Japanese, realized the benefits Tokyo reaped from the carnage in Korea. In a letter to President Truman, Joseph Dodge described Japan as the "one nation receiving substantial benefits from the Korean War." Nearly every sector of the economy, from electronics to construction, to textiles, to the numerous small workshops that performed piecework for the *zaibatsu* experienced a rebirth. With orders and technological assistance from the United States, owners, managers, and workers learned new techniques and procedures that eventually found application in nonmilitary production.

The experience of the Toyota Motor Sales Company resembled that of many other businesses. On the day the Korean War began, company president Kamiya Shotaro had arrived in the United States in hopes of salvaging his foundering firm by negotiating a tie-up with the powerful Ford Motor Company of Detroit. Ford expressed only moderate interest in the offer, and the Defense Department opposed cooperation as a diversion from domestic production. However, the flood of American orders for Toyota trucks, which began in July, quickly lifted the spirits of the despondent executive and his company. Kamiya later described these orders as "Toyota's salvation," despite his sense of guilt that "I was rejoicing over another country's war." The company's profits from truck orders and development of new production techniques allowed it to resume profitable passenger-car production on a national and then international basis.[36]

Japanese journalists, writing in the 1970s, emphasized how "even today Japanese businessmen shudder at the thought of what might have happened if there had been no war in Korea at that time." The war-related orders stimulated a "boom" critical for subsequent growth and prosperity. The governor of the Bank of Japan captured the sense best by describing the procurement program simply as "Divine Aid."[37]

16
AFTERWARD:
THE WORKSHOP
OF ASIA

The onset of the Korean War, ironically, set the stage for the termination of the Occupation. Although the spectacular series of victories and reverses on the battlefield during the first year of fighting gave the military establishment second thoughts, the momentum for a treaty proved irreversible. Even before MacArthur's mid-September successful landing at Inchon, the Defense Department and the JCS modified their opposition to a settlement. In a neat twist of logic, Louis Johnson and Omar Bradley now argued that the outbreak of war had actually clarified positively the balance of forces in East Asia, resolving the uncertainties that had made it unwise to end the Occupation. On August 22, 1950, the JCS informed Johnson that current circumstances justified a peace settlement with Japan. If, pending success on the Korean battlefront, Washington could obtain a treaty retaining American forces and bases and committing Japan to rearm, the military would no longer oppose ratification.[1]

During a hurried few weeks of high level State Department Defense Department negotiations, the two agencies finally reached an accord on the preconditions for a treaty. In an unusual joint memorandum for the president, Acheson and Johnson sealed their agreement. Once the "situation in Korea" had been fovorably resolved, a settlement should take effect. Through informal negotiations with Japan and other nations, the State Department would prepare a treaty meeting the security criteria long demanded by the military. When agreement on these provisions was assured, the terms would be presented at a formal conference for ratification.[2]

Although the shock of Chinese intervention in Korea during November briefly delayed this timetable, Acheson still managed to move forward with a treaty. In January 1951, he dispatched John Foster Dulles on a second mission to Tokyo to clarify details with both the Japanese government and MacArthur. Neither the bloody seesaw on the Korean Peninsula nor the subsequent recall of MacArthur stemmed the momentum toward a settlement. By September 1951, at a carefully orchestrated conference in San Francisco, the acceptance of a prearranged text restored Japan's sovereignty effective the following April.

Just as the Korean War facilitated a peace settlement, it shaped Japan's long-term diplomatic and economic orientation. Together, the war and American policy resulted in an "area approach" to Asia that included various, if distorted, elements of the integrationist schemes previously discussed. However, the actual direction of integration defied almost all pre-1950 predictions.

Even after June 25, 1950, most Japanese still anticipated the revival of large-scale trade with China. Exchanges had increased early in the year and continued to grow until the Chinese intervention of November led to an embargo. Subsequently, the United States levied a variety of restrictions on Sino–Japanese trade that remained in effect until the early 1970's. In 1952, Washington insisted on imposing even tighter restrictions on Japanese sales to China than those applied to its European allies or on Western sales to the Soviets. This bitterly disappointed Japanese political and business leaders, resulting in nearly two decades of squabbling between Tokyo and Washington.

Besides immediate concerns during the Korean War that Japanese trade would benefit China's military sector, American policymakers worried about the long-term political implications of this commerce. Any substantial economic relationship between the two Asian powers they feared, would expose Tokyo to Communist blackmail and ideological contamination. Given the increased reluctance of Congress to ease tariff restrictions or appropriate nonmilitary economic aid (with the exception of surplus grains later in the 1950s), Japan faced, at best, a clouded future.

This anxiety surfaced in the thoughts of John Foster Dulles and others even in October 1950 when the fighting in Korea seemed decisively to America's advantage. Late in that month, the Council on Foreign Relations invited Dulles to lead a discussion on the Japanese treaty among a group that included such notables as Hugh Borton, who drafted the abortive 1947 treaty; Everett Case, one of Acheson's Far Eastern consultants; John Allison, the director of the Office of Northeast Asian Affairs in the State Department; Charles L. Kades, former SCAP official; and William H. Draper, Jr., former under secretary of the army and coauthor of the "reverse course." All agreed that the ultimate goal of a treaty was to keep Japan out of Soviet hands lest its industrial potential tip the balance of power.

Dulles echoed George Kennan's argument that the "future of the world depends largely on whether the Soviet Union will be able to get control over West Germany and Japan by means short of war." By preventing their conquest, he asserted, the risk of war would be reduced greatly. In light of this, Dulles reasoned (forgetting his earlier misgivings about Korea's significance), the attack in Korea was "probably aimed at getting control over Japan, for had Korea been conquered Japan would have fallen without an open struggle." The loss of American credibility in the face of Soviet power would have persuaded Japan to switch its allegiance. Ironically, the solution to Japan's security was now possible "only because of Korea" and the resulting demonstration of American determination. If given a pledge of American protection, acceptance of its "approximate equality" with the West, and an opportunity to support itself, Dulles declared, Japan could be kept within the orbit of the free world.[3]

Yet, no matter how farsighted or generous an eventual peace treaty, Japan faced a fundamental problem that the formal settlement could not resolve. The nation must be assured a "satisfactory livelihood" without placing it "in a position of dependence upon the Communist-dominated mainland of Asia." The difficulites of resolving this problem were "enormous," Dulles confessed. But unless overcome, the peace treaty would be a "failure." The United States, he believed, had no choice but to try to enlarge markets for Japanese exports "in the underdeveloped areas of Southeast Asia.

The entire group supported this line of argument. John Allison noted that the North Korean attack had been tremendously helpful in convincing Japan to abandon illusions of neutrality in the cold war. It also displaced British Commonwealth fears of future Japanese aggression. William Draper worried whether Communist control of Manchuria would become an impossibly seductive attraction. At the "right moment," the Soviet Union might offer it "as an outlet" for Japan's "surplus population." Eugene Dooman, a former diplomat closely tied to Ambassador Joseph C. Grew, doubted that it was even realistic to ponder a viable Japanese economy "disassociated from the mainland of Eastern Asia." Percy Bidwell feared that Germany and Japan in a desperate competition for trade outlets among the poorest lands might be drawn into hostilities with each other.[4]

Dulles, nevertheless, continued to assure the group that the United

States could develop a Japanese–Southeast Asian economic link to substitute for dependence on China. This might require post-Occupation aid, American investments, and convincing Southeast Asians they could not "develop their economies unless they are willing to regard Japan as the natural workshop of Asia and to trade with it." By relying on some Western trade and newly opened Asian markets, Tokyo eventually could prosper without China. For the moment, however, the Korean War boom must serve as the catalyst for economic revival. During at least the next five years, Dulles predicted, American military spending would give Japan a chance to find its footing. "Indeed, its position may become almost too good," he speculated.[5]

As preparations continued for a peace conference, the United States labored to forge a framework of overlapping military, diplomatic, and trade mechanisms that would both buttress Japan and ensure its ties to an anticommunist alliance. Some of these policies proved quite successful, whereas others failed to achieve the desired results. In the case of American support for the French colonial war effort in Indochina, the commitment mutated into a seemingly endless struggle.

In July 1950, the Japanese reluctantly agreed to Washington's demand that they begin raising a small army, or National Police Reserve, of some three hundred to three hundred fifty thousand troops. While Dulles and the Defense Department placed great emphasis on this, Yoshida worked to sabotage the program. Even Japanese conservatives cited economic, political, and philosophical objections to direct rearmament. It would, they feared, elicit tremendous opposition at home, rekindle anxiety among Japan's wartime victims, isolate the nation from its Asian neighbors, and defy the letter and spirit of Article 9 of the new constitution. The antiwar clause, initiated by MacArthur, was now treasured by most Japanese. Amending or defying the constitution would incur political risks for the ruling party. Besides these concerns, many Japanese wordered what the Americans would want this new army to do. So long as the Korean War continued, the United States would probably press Japan to send troops to that battlefront. Yoshida used these broadly shared objections to slow down the creation of the army for the duration of the Occupation and even after.

However, both Washington and Tokyo pushed forward rapidly toward a formal peace settlement despite the fighting in Korea. By September 1951, after months of preparation, the United States presented a treaty to an international conference in San Francisco. The text had been carefully prepared in advance, and the procedural rules allowed delegates little opportunity to comment or criticize. Even Prime Minister Yoshida found himself censored when the U.S. delegation forced him to dispose of his prepared speech and substitute one written by American diplomats. The simple and generous terms of the treaty (in most instances it followed the State Department drafts dating from 1949) mollified Yoshida while upsetting many Asian and Soviet bloc nations.

Simultaneously with the approval of the treaty, the United States concluded a security pact with Japan granting American forces extensive base rights in the post-Occupation period. Washington also signed a series of security pacts with the Philippines, New Zealand, and Australia, assuaging their fears of both Communist and Japanese aggression. These arrangements also established the framework for later defense treaties with the Republic of Korea (1953), Nationalist China (1954), and the Southeast Asia Treaty Organization (SEATO 1954), composed of the non-Communist states in that region.

The Soviet Union, to the surprise of the United States, had attended the deliberations at San Francisco. However, the refusal of the American hosts to entertain any serious debate or amendments to the text, as well as the conclusion of the several military alliances, prompted the Soviets to balk at signing. The intention of Washington to isolate the Chinese Communist regime from the conference as well as from future relations with Japan proved a stickier issue. Both the British and the Japanese hoped to resume trade with Peking after hostilities ceased in Korea. Snubbing the PRC or signing a treaty with Taiwan, they feared, would dash any possibility for improved relations.

The American government, however, intended to minimize, if not smash, these prospects. Washington finessed the question of Chinese representation in San Francisco by inviting neither the Communist nor the Nationalist governments to attend. Dulles reassured both London and Tokyo by giving them the impression that they could deal freely with either Chinese regime in subsequent bilateral negotiations. Despite this professed flexibility on the issue of Sino–Japanese ties, Dulles and the Senate Foreign Relations Committee later compelled the Japanese government to step into line. Influential senators insisted that Dulles convey a warning to Prime Minister Yoshida that unless he pledged to deal only with Taipei, the Senate would reject the peace treaty and extend the Occupation. In a letter Dulles then ghosted for Yoshida, the harried prime minister made the required promise. In the spring of 1952, Tokyo and Taipei signed a peace treaty and established diplomatic and trade relations.[6]

To further insure Japan's alienation from China, the United States created a special oversight organization to impose strict limitations on any sales to China. It drafted Japan into the China Subcommittee of the Paris-based Coordinating Committee on Export Controls (CHINCOM/COCOM) to the Soviet bloc. In addition to restrictions placed on the Europeans, Japan had to abide by a special list of some four hundred embargoed products.

With China closed for the immediate future, the Southeast Asia issue resurfaced as quite critical. While the Occupation remained in place, SCAP and planners in Washington attempted to stimulate integrated regional trade under the dubious label of U.S.–Japan Economic Cooperation. This involved dispatching a Japanese trade mission to Southeast Asia in mid-1951 and, curiously, an American proposal to assess additional reparations. At the San Francisco conference, John Foster Dulles urged Japan to pay reparations to its Southeast Asian wartime victims out of current production (in contrast to industrial plant transfers) as a way of reentering closed markets. Reparations, he hoped, would both assuage the recipients and "hook" them into an ongoing relationship.

Despite great hopes, Southeast Asia proved no quick panacea for the Japanese economy and certainly no substitute for Northeast Asian markets and raw materials. Improverished, underdeveloped, and extremely anti-Japanese, most Southeast Asian states rejected these inducements during the 1950s. Yet, American concern about Chinese expansion, the continued crisis in Korea, and fears over the impact of a Communist victory in Southeast Asia did result in policies that created a wholly new Asian economy.

The Special Procurements program, which flooded Japan with war orders in 1950, was followed by the New Special Procurements program in 1951, aid from the Mutual Security Program in 1952–53, and subsequent assistance from the Foreign Operations Administration and the PL 480 surplus food program during the remainder of the decade. This influx of orders, cash, and technology, historian William Borden has shown, played a pivotal role in reintegrating Japan with the world economy. Dollars placed for military orders filled the shortfall, or dollar gap, in current trade accounts and financed the purchase of industrial raw materials from abroad. But of much greater importance was that these orders created a large stable demand for high-technology, and heavy-export goods, thereby subsidizing the expansion and modernization of Japanese industry. This was of fundamental importance during the 1950s, because few "normal" foreign market outlets existed for these exports. Moreover, the bulk of these military orders were for "nonlethal" equipment, such as clothing, electronics, transportation vehicles, and so on. Unlike weapons, these had direct consumer counterparts. Thus, the factories, techniques, and labor skills involved in production could, eventually, be utilized in the consumer and export sectors.

Most Japanese manufactured products had difficulty competing in the world market during the 1950s. High tariffs and low demand limited sales to the United States and Western Europe. Stringent American regulations (many retained until the early 1970s) restricted trade with China in most categories. Southeast Asia remained too poor and undeveloped (in many cases, too anti-Japanese) to supply sufficient raw materials or absorb large quantities of manufactured exports. Although all of these regions would later blossom as major trading partners, this change occurred in large part because of a major transformation of Japan's economy. American military orders throughout the decade played a critical role in supplying the dollars, demand, technology, and market for the modernization of the industrial base.

Between 1945 and 1955, the cumulative dollar gap totaled some $6.2 billion, balanced by $2 billion in economic aid and $4 billion in military expenditures. During the next decade, military procurements increased by about $3.2 billion. As American spending for the Vietnam War accelerated from 1965 to 1970, military orders placed in Japan rose by nearly another $3 billion. The total of about $10 billion worked out to an average annual American military subsidy for Japan of some $500 million per year over twenty years. These expenditures cemented the relationship between Japanese recovery and American security policy throughout Asia.[7]

In the early 1950s, of course, no one prophesied these developments. Japan's obvious dependence on American aid appeared as a long-term drain on both economies. The perceived weakness of its major Asian ally only enhanced Washington's grave concern about the mounting crisis in Vietnam and its potential impact on the regional power balance.

Within a week of succeeding Dean Acheson as Secretary of State, President Dwight D. Eisenhower's appointee, John Foster Dulles, addressed these dilemmas in both public and private forums. In a national radio and television broadcast on January 27, 1953, he discussed several pressing foreign policy issues. Speaking of East Asia, Dulles observed:

> The Soviet Russians are making a drive to get Japan, not only through what they are doing in the northern areas of the islands and in Korea but also through what they are doing in Indochina. If they could get this peninsula of Indochina, Siam, Burma, Malaya, they would have what is called the rice bowl of Asia. That's the area from which the great peoples' of Asia, great countries of Asia such as Japan and India get a large measure of their food. And you can see that, if the Soviet Union had control of the rice bowl of Asia, that would be another weapon which would tend to expand their control into Japan and into India. That is a growing danger.

Relating this threat also to Europe, the secretary of state warned that the bleeding of French forces in Southeast Asia seriously hampered their contributions to a "European Army" arrayed against the Soviets.[8]

The next day, Dulles chaired a meeting of leading diplomatic, intelligence, and military officials convened to discuss the implications of this public talk. The new director of the Mutual Security Program, Harold Stassen, questioned the impact of a French defeat in Indochina. Gen. Omar Bradley predicted this would "lead to the loss of all Southeast Asia." "If Southeast Asia were lost," Dulles added, "this would lead to the loss of Japan." The outlook was sufficiently bleak with "China being Commie," the secretary lamented. Further Communist expansion might not cause the loss of Japan "immediately," but "from there on out the Japs would be thinking on how to get on the other side." Having established these truths, the group went on to discuss possible means for holding at least some anti-Communist enclave in Vietnam should the French abandon, or be thrown out of, Indochina.[9]

Clearly, the restoration of Japanese sovereignty in 1952 and the approaching armistice in Korea had not resolved the crisis of American policy in postwar East Asia. Ever fearful that an independent Japan might, through blackmail or free will, reestablish close links to China, the United States threw a military cordon around the PRC. The military alliances with Southeast Asia, Taiwan, Korea, Australia, and New Zealand, the Truman and Eisenhower administrations hoped, would buttress Japan psychologically and preserve these areas as future U.S. partners.

This policy, of course, proved one of the postwar epoch's cruelest ironies. American policymakers held themselves on a course of action that almost no one else found credible. Both the Europeans and Japanese resented bitterly American-imposed restrictions on trade with China. The Japanese, at least through the 1960s, were far more interested in commerce with China and with the West (for which they needed hard currencies) than in the barterlike arrangements Washington hoped to foster with Southeast Asia. To assuage Japanese resentment and to meet their dollar needs, the United States had to continue a variety of expensive military procurement programs for many years. This helped, simultaneously, to modernize Japan's high-technology and extremely competitive export sector. In effect, American defense procurements abroad provided a catalyst for the "economic miracle" in unarmed Japan.

Beyond the balance sheet that testifies to the role played by American military expenditures in Japan's recovery, we must also acknowledge the tragic dimensions of these events. The protracted effort to assure Japan access to Southeast Asia, and to isolate China trapped the United States in a "dead end alley" of its own device in Vietnam. Justified initially as an inexpensive, low-risk commitment, the suppression of communism in Indochina seemed critical to nearly all calculations of how to achieve containment and assure the stability and prosperity of America's Asian allies. Unable or unwilling to fathom the power of Vietnamese and Chinese nationalism, American leaders gradually committed their nation to a contest the United States could neither win, nor once joined, apparently abandon.

For its part, Japan, spurred on by technical innovations, finally cracked the lucrative consumer markets of the West. America's huge escalation of the Vietnam War during the 1960s abetted this process and actually helped Japan reenter the Southeast Asian economy. Ironically, when the consensus supporting the war eroded, forcing the Nixon administration to withdraw from Vietnam, this region emerged as a major Japanese trading partner. By the early 1970s, the United States abandoned its twenty-year effort to isolate China, hoping to gain for its own troubled economy a portion of the China market so long denied Japan. Tokyo, needless to say, took full advantage of this opening, as well. With access to China, Southeast Asia, and the West, Japan seemed to "have it all."

In retrospect, one is reminded of the prophetic remarks cited at the beginning of this study. The exchange between John Emmerson and the Mitsui executive regarding America's future management of the Co-Prosperity Sphere revealed a sophisticated insight into the coming era. As heir to an empire, the United States assumed not only the military mantle previously shouldered by Japan but also the added responsibility of integrating the humbled imperial power into the postwar world. The emerging Soviet–American confrontation and the world economic crisis coupled with Washington's growing fear of Asian revolution transformed the problem of Japan in the minds of American leaders. The Great Crescent, it seemed, could be secured by Japan; in addition, Japan could not survive without a vibrant, industrial economy tied to a pliable, non-Communist Southeast Asian base. Fearful that either an economic collapse or Communist blandishments might suck Japan into the Soviet orbit, American policy sought to provide its former enemy a new, if much modified, Co-Prosperity Sphere.

For their part, Japan's business and political leaders held fast to an economic strategy first developed in the 1930s. They encouraged and abetted the United States in its eagerness to restore Japan as a great trading nation. Although the fruits of this labor were not harvested until a decade after the Occupation ended, the course was charted by 1947. The Korean War accelerated many trends, yet the outline of American policy toward Japan, China, Korea, and Vietnam for the next twenty years was set even before the fighting began. Perhaps Yoshida Shigeru spoke a truth (if not *the* truth) when he predicted, in 1950, that, like the changing balance between the American colonies and imperial Britain more than a century before, if Japan temporarily became a "colony of the United States, it [would] also eventually become the stronger."

ABBREVIATIONS
AND ACRONYMS

ABC	American-British Conversation File
ACJ	Allied Council for Japan
AEC	Atomic Energy Commission
AFL-CIO	American Federation of Labor—Congress of Industrial Relations
CAD	Civil Affairs Division
CCP	Chinese Communist party
CCS	Combined Chiefs of Staff
CFM	Council of Foreign Ministers
CHINCOM/COCOM	China Subcommitte of the Coordinating Committee on Export Controls
CIA	Central Intelligence Agency
CIC	Counter-Intelligence Corps
CINFE	Commander-in-Chief, Far East
CJCS	Combined Joint Chiefs of Staff
CNAC	China National Aircraft Corporation
DOS	Department of State
DRB	Deconcentration Review Board
DRV	Democratic Republic of Vietnam
ECA	Economic Cooperation Administration
EROA	Economic Recovery in Occupied Areas

ERP	European Recovery Program
ESS	Economic-Scientific Section
FE	Office of Far Eastern Affairs
FEAC	Far Eastern Advisory Commission
FO	Foreign Office
FOIA	Freedom of Information Act
FRUS	Foreign Relations of the United States
GARIOA	Government and Relief in Occupied Areas
HCLC	Holding Company Liquidation Commission
INR	Intelligence and Research, Department of State
IPCOG	Informal Policy Committee on Germany
JCP	Japan Communist party
JCS	Joint Chiefs of Staff
JIS	Joint Intelligence Staff
JPS	Joint Planning Staff
JSSC	Joint Strategic Survey Committee
JWPC	Joint War Plans Committee
KMT	Kuomintang
MAP	Military Assistance Program
MDAP	Mutual Defense Assistance Program
MITI	Ministry of International Trade and Industry
MMR	Modern Military Records Branch, National Archives
NATO	North Atlantic Treaty Organization
NSC	National Security Council
OASIA	Office of the Assistant Secretary for International Affairs
OCI	Overseas Consultants Incorporated
OIR	Office of Intelligence and Research
OPD	Operations Division
ORE	Office of Regional Estimates, CIA
OSS	Office of Strategic Services
P&O	Plans and Operations
POW	prisoner of war
PPS	Policy Planning Staff
PRC	People's Republic of China
PRJ	Political Reorientation of Japan
PRO	Public Record Office
PSA	Philippine/Southeast Asian Affairs
PSF	President's Secretaries File
R&A	Research and Analgris
SACO	Sino-American Cooperative Organization
SAOUS	Secretary of the Army, Office of the Undersecretary

SCAP	Supreme Commander for the Allied Powers
SEA	Southeast Asia
SEATO	Southeast Asia Treaty Organization
SS	*Schutzstaffel* (Black Shirts)
STEM	Special Technical and Economic Mission
SWNCC	State–War–Navy Coordinating Committee
UNRRA	United Nations Relief and Rehabilitation Administration
WNRC	Washington National Records Center

NOTES

CHAPTER 1

1. The British embassy in Washington closely monitored expressions of public opinion during 1944. See FO 371/41793, Public Record Office, London (hereafter cited as PRO with file number); John Morton Blum, ed., *The Price of Vision: The Diary of Henry A. Wallace, 1942–46* (Boston, 1973), 448; Bilbo to MacArthur, September 14, 1945, VIP File, RG 10, Douglas MacArthur Papers. For other statements, see Roger Buckley, *Occupation Diplomacy: Britain, the United States and Japan, 1942–45* (Cambridge, 1982), 15; Roosevelt's extensive correspondence with Arleš Hrdlička is detailed in Christopher Thorne, *Allies of a Kind: The United States, Britain and the War against Japan, 1941–1945* (New York, 1978), 158–59, 167–68.
2. Memorandum by Grew, July 31, 1945, V 7, 46, Joseph C. Grew Papers.
3. Quoted in John D. Montgomery, *Forced to Be Free: The Artificial Revolution in Germany and Japan* (Chicago, 1957), 106–7.
4. See Akira Iriye, *Power and Culture: The Japanese–American War, 1941–1945* (Cambridge, Mass., 1981).
5. John W. Dower, *Empire and Aftermath: Yoshida Shigeru and the Japanese Experience, 1878–1954* (Cambridge, Mass., 1979), 258–59.
6. Ibid., 264.
7. Hugh Borton, *American Presurrender Planning for Postwar Japan* (New York, 1967), 12; Hilldring and Pence to Dunn, February 18, 1944, *Foreign Relations of the United States* (Washington, 1965), Vol. 5, 1190–94 (hereafter abbreviated as FRUS, with appropriate volume and page).

8. PWC 111, March 13, 1944, FRUS 19, Vol. 5, 1202–5; PWC 116d, May 9, 1944, ibid., 1250–55; Borton, *Presurrender Planning*, 17.

9. Borton, *Presurrender Planning*, 20.

10. Record of conversation with MacArthur, February 1945, U.S. Department of Defense, *The Entry of the Soviet Union into the War against Japan: Military Plans 1941–45* (Washington, 1955), 51–52; Forrestal diary, February 28, 1945, James Forrestal Papers; D. Clayton James, *The Years of MacArthur, Vol. 2, 1941–1945* (Boston, 1975), 763–65.

11. Grew to Stimson, May 12, 1945, ABC 336, "Russia in the Far East," Department of the Army Records, RG 165.

12. Memorandum by Grew May 19, 1945, quoted in Waldo Heinrichs, *American Ambassador: Joseph C. Grew and the Development of the United States Diplomatic Tradition* (Boston, 1966), 374.

13. Heinrichs, American Ambassador, 365–73; Donovan to Truman, May 12, 1945, President's Secretaries File (hereafter cited as PSF), Harry S. Truman Papers. Japanese peacefeelers are discussed at length in FRUS 1945, Vol. 6, 478 and passim.

14. Memorandum by Grew of conversation with Truman, May 28, 1945, FRUS 1945, Vol. 6, 545–47; Heinrichs, *American Ambassador*, 374–78.

15. Memorandum by Stimson of conversation with Truman, June 6, 1945, folder 18, box 172, Henry L. Stimson Papers.

16. On the role of the atomic bomb in relation to the war in China and against Japan, see Michael Schaller, *The U.S. Crusade in China, 1938–45* (New York, 1979), passim; and Martin Sherwin, *A World Destroyed: The Atomic Bomb and the Grand Alliance* (New York, 1977), passim.

17. Stimson to Truman, June 26, 1945, "Proposed Program for Japan," second draft, Japan box, Stimson Safe File, July 1940–September 1945, Department of the Army Records, RG 107.

18. Ibid.

19. Memoranda by Hoover, June 4, 9, 1945, "Stimson Top Secret Safe File," Japan after December 7, 1941, Department of the Army Records, RG 107.

20. Stimson to Grew, May 21, 1945, ABC 336, "Russia in the Far East," Department of the Army Records, RG 165.

21. Marshall and Handy to Stimson, July 7, 1945, "Stimson Top Secret Safe File," Japan after December 7, 1941, Department of the Army Records, RG 107; Conference of Berlin, FRUS 1945, Vol. 1, 905. Despite this rebuff, Hoover later played a major role in setting policy for Japan.

22. Truman quoted in Daniel Yergin, *Shattered Peace: The Origins of the Cold War and the National Security State* (Boston, 1977), 113.

23. W. Averell Harriman and Ellie Abel, *Special Envoy to Churchill and Stalin, 1941–1946* (New York, 1975), 488; Stimson diary, July 14, 1945, Stimson Papers. On the relationships at Potsdam, see also Robert Messer, *The End of an Alliance: James F. Byrnes, Roosevelt, Truman and the Origins of the Cold War* (Chapel Hill, N.C., 1982), passim.

24. Walter Brown diary, July 18, 1945, James F. Byrnes Papers.

25. Ibid., July 20 and 24, 1945.

26. Notes, July 24, 1945, folder 18, box 172, Stimson Papers; undated notes on Potsdam Conference, folder 19, ibid. See also Sherwin, *A World Destroyed*, 234–37; Gregg Herken, *The Winning Weapon: The Atomic Bomb and the*

Cold War, 1945-50 (New York, 1982), 20; Henry Stimson with McGeorge Bundy, *On Active Service in Peace and War* (New York, 1948), 612-56.
27. Harriman and Abel, *Special Envoy*, 486.
28. Walter Brown diary, August 3, 1945, Byrnes Papers; Stimson diary, July 30, 1945, Stimson Papers.
29. Marshall to MacArthur, July 25, 1945, and H. A. Craig to John E. Hull, July 25, 1945, OPD 014.1 TS, sec. 3, Records of the U.S. Army Staff; James Matray, "Captive of the Cold War: The Decision to Divide Korea at the 38th Parallel," *Pacific Historical Review* (Vol. 50, no. 2, May 1981), 145-68.
30. Harriman to Byrnes, August 7 and 8, 1945, FRUS 1945, Vol. 7, 957-58; Memorandum by Harriman of conversation with Stalin, August 8, 1945, ibid., 960-65; Byrnes to Harriman, August 9, 1945, ibid., 965-66; Harriman to Truman and Byrnes, August 10, 1945, ibid., 967; Harriman and Abel, *Special Envoy*, 495-97; Matray, "Captive of the Cold War"; Bruce Cumings, *The Origins of the Korean War: Liberation and the Emergence of Separate Regimes, 1945-1947* (Princeton, N.J., 1981), 114, 120.
31. Schaller, *The U.S. Crusade in China*, 259-61.
32. Blum, *The Price of Vision*, 470; Stimson-Grew discussions of proposed "Post Hostilities Policy toward Japan," August 4 and 6, 1945, FRUS 1945, Vol. 6, 584-90; "National Composition of Forces," SWNCC 70/5, August 11, 1945, ibid., 603; "U.S. Initial Post-Defeat Policy Relating to Japan," SWNCC 150/2, ibid., 609; Paper on Composition of Forces, signed by Truman, August 19, 1945, PSF, Truman Papers.
33. Blum, *The Price of Vision*, 473-75.
34. Harriman and Abel, *Special Envoy*, 499-500.
35. Ibid., 501; FRUS 1945, Vol. 6, 628-31.
36. Harriman and Abel, *Special Envoy*, 501.

CHAPTER 2
1. Douglas MacArthur, *Reminiscences* (New York, 1964), 322-23; the most compelling study of the general's career during the 1930s and the war years is D. Clayton James, *The Years of MacArthur*, 2 vols. (Boston, 1970-75). Ickes's quotes appear in his diary, June 9 and August 26, 1945. See also Carol M. Petillo, *Douglas MacArthur: The Philippine Years* (Bloomington, Ind., 1981), 238, which explores the psychological ramifications of the general's service in the Philippines in relation to later duties. For Truman's views, see Robert Ferrell, *Off The Record: The Private Papers of Harry S. Truman* (New York, 1980), 47.
2. John K. Emmerson, *The Japanese Thread: A Life in the Foreign Service* (New York, 1978), 256.
3. John Gunther, *The Riddle of MacArthur: Japan, Korea, and the Far East* (New York, 1951), 8; *New York Times*, August 29, 1945; James, *Years of MacArthur, Vol. 2*, 778-81.
4. Courtney Whitney, *MacArthur: His Rendezvous with History* (New York, 1956), 213. For a perceptive analysis of the "heroic" literature surrounding MacArthur and the Occupation, see Carol Gluck's analysis of both English and Japanese language sources: "Entangling Illusions—Japanese and American Views of the Occupation" in Warren I. Cohen, ed., *New Frontiers in American–East Asian Relations* (New York, 1983), 169-236.

5. See JCS 1380/5, November 3, 1945, SCAP, *The Political Reorientation of Japan, September 1945–September 1948. Report of the Governmental Section of SCAP* (Washington, 1948), Vol. 2, 428 (hereafter this collection of SCAP documents cited as PRJ.)

6. Otis Cary, ed., *War Wasted Asia: Letters, 1945–46* (Tokyo, 1975), 48.

7. Harry Emerson Wildes, *Typhoon in Tokyo: The Occupation and Its Aftermath* (New York, 1954), 8–9.

8. John R. Stewart, *Notes on the Economic Aspects of the Allied Occupation of Japan* (New York, 1947). Prepared by Stewart, a SCAP veteran, for the Institute of Pacific Relations.

9. Atcheson to Dean Acheson, November 7, 1945, FRUS 1945, Vol. 6, 838–41.

10. Dower, *Empire and Aftermath*, 296.

11. JCS to MacArthur, "Basic Directive for Post-Surrender Military Government in Japan Proper," November 3, 1945, PRJ, Vol. 2, 428–39.

12. The bureaucratic debate over economic policy toward the conclusion of the war is analyzed carefully by Marlene Mayo, "American Economic Planning for Occupied Japan: The Issue of Zaibatsu Dissolution, 1942–45," in *Proceedings of a Symposium Sponsored by the MacArthur Memorial* (Norfolk, Va., 1978), 205–8.

13. Thomas A. Bisson, *Japan's War Economy* (New York, 1945). By the same author: "Increase of Zaibatsu Predominance in Wartime Japan," *Pacific Affairs* (Vol. 18, no. 1, March 1945), 55–61; "The Zaibatsu's Wartime Role," *Pacific Affairs* (Vol. 18, no. 4, December 1945), 355–68; *Prospects for Democracy in Japan* (New York, 1949); *Zaibatsu Dissolution in Japan* (Berkeley, Calif., 1954). For a thoughtful analysis of Bisson's life and work, see Howard Schonberger, "T. A. Bisson and the Limits of Reform in Occupied Japan," *Bulletin of Concerned Asian Scholars* (Vol. 14, no. 4, October–December 1980), 26–37.

14. Bisson, *Japan's War Economy*, 198–205; Jerome Cohen, *Japan's Economy in War and Reconstruction* (Minneapolis, Minn., 1949), 1–22.

15. Eleanor Hadley, "Trust Busting in Japan," *Harvard Business Review* (Vol. 26, no. 4, July 1948, 425–40.

16. Bisson, *Zaibatsu Dissolution in Japan*; Eleanor Hadley, *Anti-Trust in Japan* (Princeton, N.J., 1970).

17. E. A. Locke (presidential adviser) to Truman, October 19, 1945, PSF, Truman Papers.

18. Yoshida quoted in Bisson, *Zaibatsu Dissolution in Japan*, 70.

19. Cary, ed., *War Wasted Asia*, 57, 83.

20. SCAPIN 244, PRJ, Vol. 2, app. B, 565.

21. *Report of the Mission on Japanese Combines* (Washington, 1946), Publication 2628, Far Eastern Series.

22. Edwin Pauley, "U.S. Reparations Policy—Preliminary Statement," October 31, 1945, box 21, Records of the U.S. Mission on Reparations, RG 59, National Archives (hereafter cited as Pauley Mission Records).

23. Lattimore to H. D. Maxwell, November 6, 1945, box 24, ibid.

24. Lattimore to H. D. Maxwell, November 10, 1945, box 22, ibid.

25. Draft report by Lattimore, November 12, 1945, box 21, ibid.; notes of staff discussion by Lattimore for Pauley, November 15, 1945, box 21, ibid.

26. Lattimore diary, December 4, 1945, staff diaries, ibid.

27. Pauley to MacArthur, December 5 and 6, 1945, box 21, ibid.; press release, December 6, 1945, box 24, ibid.
28. Pauley report for President Truman, "Reparations from Japan—Immediate Program," December 8, 1945, ibid.; Pauley report, May 10, 1946, ibid.
29. Truman to Byrnes, December 21, 1945, and JCS to MacArthur, January 26, 1946, both in SWNCC 236/3/D, SWNCC 236 File, SWNCC Records, RG 353.
30. *Report of the Mission on Japanese Combines*, see note 21 above; Corwin Edwards, "The Dissolution of the Japanese Combines," *Pacific Affairs* (Vol. 19, no. 3, September 1946), 227–40.
31. Edwards, "The Dissolution of Japanese Combines."
32. "Reform of Business Enterprise: Elimination of Zaibatsu Control, 1945–50," Pt. A, Vol. 10, Center for Military History, SCAP Monograph Series.
33. SWNCC 302/4 and FEC 230 are reprinted in Hadley, *Anti-Trust in Japan*, 495–515.
34. Whitney, *MacArthur*, 251.
35. PRJ, Vol. 2, app. B, 470–71.
36. Ronald P. Dore, *Land Reform in Japan* (London, 1959), passim.
37. PRJ, Vol. 1, 14.
38. Hans Baerwald, *The Purge of Japanese Leaders under the Occupation* (Berkeley, Calif., 1959), passim.
39. Kurt Steiner, *Local Government in Japan* (Stanford, Calif., 1965), passim.
40. Miriam S. Farley, *Aspects of Japan's Labor Problems* (New York, 1950), passim; Howard Schonberger, "American Labor's Cold War in Occupied Japan," *Diplomatic History* (Vol. 3, no. 3, Summer 1979), 249–72.
41. I. F. Stone, "Behind the MacArthur Row," *Nation* (Vol. 161, no.13, September 29, 1945), 297–99.
42. McCloy Memorandum for Gen. George Lincoln, "Visit to Japan," February 17, 1946, box 222, Records of the Far Eastern Commission, RG 43.
43. John Maki, "Japan: Political Reconstruction," *Far Eastern Survey* (Vol. 1, no. 7, April 9, 1947), 73–77.
44. Memorandum, December 12, 1947, in William F. Draper to Gordon Gray, December 14, 1947, Under Secretary of the Army, General Correspondence—Security Classified, August 1947–January 1949, SAOUS, 004 Japan, Records of the Office of the Secretary of the Army, RG 335.
45. For an analysis of the evolution of Japanese conservative politics after 1945, see Dower, *Empire and Aftermath*, 312–13.
46. Ibid.; Bisson, *Prospects for Democracy in Japan*, passim; Allan B. Cole, George Totten, and Cecil Uyehara, *Socialist Parties in Postwar Japan* (New Haven, Conn., 1966), passim.
47. Farley, *Aspects of Labor Passion*; Mark Gayn, *Japan Diary* (New York, 1948); Joe Moore, *Japanese Workers and the Struggle for Power, 1945–1947* (Madison, Wis., 1983), 3–31. Moore examines the radical struggle of labor unions and the conservative reaction by the Japanese government and SCAP.
48. MacArthur statement, May 20, 1946, PRJ, Vol. 2, app. F, 750.
49. Gayn, *Japan Diary*, 231–32.
50. Ibid., 263–65; Farley, *Aspects of Labor*, 44–50; MacArthur statement, September 2, 1946, PRJ, Vol. 2, app. F, 756–57.

51. MacArthur statement calling off general strike, January 31, 1947, PRJ, Vol. 2, app. F, 762.

CHAPTER 3
1. "Notes on Meeting in the Pacific of Sherman and MacArthur," November 9, 1944, box 5, Adm. Forrest Sherman Papers, Operational Archives.
2. "Strategic Interests in the Far East," Report by the Joint Planning Staff of the War Cabinet, January 1, 1945, FO 371/46336, PRO; JCS 698/1, March 4, 1944, JCS Records, RG 218; JCS Memorandum for Information no. 374, February 5, 1945, CCS 000.1, USSR (10–2–44), ibid.
3. Policy paper forwarded by Joseph Grew to Henry Stimson, June 28, 1945, FRUS 1945, Vol. 6, 556–79.
4. Melvyn P. Leffler, "The American Conception of National Security and the Beginnings of the Cold War, 1945–48," *American Historical Review* (Vol. 89, no. 2, April 1984), 346–81.
5. Ibid. For treatment of the immensely complex negotiations regarding the disposition of Pacific islands and European colonies, see Thorne, *Allies of a Kind*; William Roger Louis, *Imperialism at Bay* (New York, 1978); Michael Sherry, *Planning for the Next War* (New Haven, Conn., 1977); Lester J. Foltos, "The Bulwark of Freedom: American Security Policy for East Asia, 1945–50," Ph.D. diss., University of Illinois, 1980.
6. Roger Dingman, "Strategic Planning and the Policy Process: American Plans for War in East Asia, 1945–50," *Naval War College Review* (Vol. 32, no. 6, November–December, 1979), 4–21; Stephen Pelz, "U.S. Decisions on Korean Policy, 1943–50: Some Hypotheses" in Bruce Cumings, ed., *Child of Conflict: The Korean–American Relationship, 1943–53* (Seattle, 1983), 93–132.
7. JIS 80/7, October 23, 1945, CCS 092, USSR (3–27–43), JCS Records, RG 218; JIS 80/9, October 26, 1945, ibid.; JCS 570/40, October 25, 1945, CCS 360 (12–9–42), ibid. Military strategy for the Pacific and war plans, such as War Plan Broiler, are described in: JPS 789/1, April 13, 1946, CCS 381, USSR (3–2–46), ibid.; JWPC, 432/7, June 18, 1946, ibid.; JWPC 476/2, August 28, 1947, ibid.; and JSC Memorandum for Truman, September 9, 1947, FRUS 1947, Vol. 1, 766–67. See also Dingman, "Strategic Planning" and Foltos, "Bulwark of Freedom"; JCS Report to Army Secretary Royall and the Secretary of Defense, mid-1947, 091 Japan 1947, General Correspondence— Security Classified, July 1947–December 1950, Records of the Office of the Secretary of the Army, RG 335; MacArthur and the JCS to State and War departments, September 1, 1947, Records of the Office of the Secretary of Defense, July–December 1950, 091 Japan, 1948–49, RG 330.
8. The State Department expressed its views in SWNCC 59/1, June 24, 1946, SWNCC 59 File, SWNCC Records, RF 353. For JCS position, see SWNCC 59/2, June 28, 1946, ibid. For Truman's decision, see Acting Secretary of State to U.S. Representative to the UN, November 6, 1946, FRUS 1946, Vol. 1, 674–75. See also Foltos, "Bulwark of Freedom," 30–38.
9. Stalin to Truman, August 16, 1945, FRUS 1945, Vol. 6, 667–68.
10. Ibid. For more detailed records of the Truman-Stalin exchanges on occupation and landing rights, see Truman to Stalin, August 18, 1945; Stalin to Truman, August 22, 1945; Truman to Stalin, August 27, 1945; and Stalin to Truman,

August 30, 1945—all in "Stalin-Truman Messages, 1944–46" File 94, Leahy File, JCS Records, RG 218.

11. Harriman to Byrnes, August 23, 1945, FRUS 1945, Vol. 6, 689; Harriman and Abel, *Special Envoy*, 504.

12. British Embassy to Department of State, August 20, 1945, FRUS 1945, Vol. 6, 678–80; Brynes to United Kingdom and USSR, August 21, 1945, ibid., 683–85. See also "Establishment of a Far Eastern Advisory Commission," April 30, 1945, ibid., 529–35.

13. Dunn to Byrnes, August 30, 1945, ibid., 697–98; Ernest Bevin to Byrnes, September 12, 1945, ibid., 713–15; Byrnes to Molotov, September 19, 1945, ibid., 726–27. Discussion between Dean Acheson and George Atcheson, Jr., October 22, 1945, ibid., 708–12.

14. Harriman and Abel, *Special Envoy*, 509.

15. Byrnes quoted by Theodore Achilles in Yergin, *Shattered Peace*, 132; Harriman and Abel, *Special Envoy*, 508–9; Messer, *End of an Alliance*, 115–35.

16. Leahy diary, September 12, 1945; *New York Times*, September 25, 1945; Walter Brown diary, September 27, 1945, Byrnes Papers; Yergin, *Shattered Peace*, 131–32; Messer, *End of an Alliance*, 130.

17. Harriman and Abel, *Special Envoy*, 508–9; Messer, *End of an Alliance*, 139.

18. Leahy diary, October 24, 1945; E. A. Locke to Truman, October 19, 1945, PSF, Truman Papers.

19. Harriman and Abel, *Special Envoy*, 511; Harriman to Byrnes, October 16, 1945, FRUS 1945, Vol. 6, 754–56.

20. Harriman-Stalin conversation, October 24, 1945, ibid., 782–85.

21. Harriman and Abel, *Special Envoy*, 515–16; Harriman-Stalin conversation, October 25, 1945, FRUS 1945, Vol. 6, 787–95.

22. Harriman to Byrnes, November 2, 1945, FRUS 1945, Vol. 6, 815–17; Harriman to Byrnes, November 6, 1945, ibid., 831–32; Byrnes to Harriman, November 7, 1945, ibid., 834–36.

23. For the substance of the discussions at Moscow, see transcripts of Byrnes conversations with Molotov and Stalin, in FRUS 1945, Vol. 7, 835–50; Messer, *End of an Alliance*, 150.

24. Ibid.; Ferrell, *Off the Record*, 80. For background on Truman's decision to send Marshall to China, see Schaller, *U.S. Crusade in China*, 280–300.

25. MacArthur, *Reminiscences*, 293; William Macmahon Ball, *Japan Enemy or Ally?* (New York, 1949), 27–35.

26. Harriman and Abel, *Special Envoy*, 531–33.

27. Ibid., 540–41.

28. Ibid., 541–45.

29. Statement by SCAP, September 17, 1945, FRUS 1945, Vol. 6, 715.

30. Truman-Acheson conversation, September 17, 1945, ibid., 716–17; Harry S. Truman, *Memoirs, Vol. 1, Year of Decisions* (New York, 1955), 520–21; Robert J. Donovan, *Conflict and Crisis: The Presidency of Harry S. Truman, 1945–1948* (New York, 1977), 127–28.

31. E. A. Locke to Truman, October 19, 1945, PSF, Truman Papers.

32. Report by D. R. Jenkins to Treasury Department, February 21, 1946, box 23, Office of the Assistant Secretary for International Affairs File, Records of the Department of the Treasury, FOIA (hereafter cited as OASIA File);

Butterworth to Stuart and Byrnes, August 20, 1946, FRUS 1946, Vol. 8, 303–304.

33. Forrestal diary, July 10, 1946, Forrestal Papers.

34. MacArthur statement of September 2, 1946, PRJ, Vol. 2, app. F, 756–57; MacArthur message to Congress, February 20, 1947, ibid., 763–64.

35. MacArthur statement on the selection of Katayama Tetsu as prime minister, May 24, 1947, ibid., 770. MacArthur encouraged many missionary groups and bible societies; presumably, he envisioned them as potential political supporters in an American election campaign. He often boasted of his own missionary efforts in talks with visiting officials. For a discussion of this, see Lawrence S. Wittner, "MacArthur and the Missionaries: God and Man in Occupied Japan," *Pacific Historical Review*, (Vol. 40, no. 1, February 1971), 77–97.

36. Memorandum of conversation between Kennan and MacArthur, March 1, 1948, FRUS 1948, Vol. 6, 697–99.

37. Gascoigne to British Under Secretary for Foreign Affairs, M. E. Dening, December 2, 1946, FO 371/54335, PRO.

38. Lt. Gen. Charles Gairdner to Gascoigne, December 2, 1946, ibid.

39. Gascoigne to Prime Minister Clement Attlee, December 26, 1947, FO 371/63830, PRO.

40. Gascoigne to Dening, February 28, 1948, FO 371/69818, PRO.

41. MacArthur statement to Eaton Committee, March 3, 1948, CCS 383.21, Japan (3–13–45), sec. 20, JCS Records, RG 218.

42. MacArthur to Department of the Army for Wedemeyer, November 20, 1948, ibid.

43. Marshall to Leahy, November 30, 1945, FRUS 1945, Vol. 7, 748; notes by Marshall of meeting with Truman, December 11 and 14, 1945, ibid., 767–70.

44. John F. Melby, *The Mandate of Heaven: Record of a Civil War in China, 1945–49* (Toronto, 1968); James Reardon-Anderson, *Yenan and the Great Powers* (New York, 1980); Suzanne Pepper, *Civil War in China: The Political Struggle, 1945–49* (Berkeley, Calif., 1978); Steven I. Levine, "A New Look at American Mediation in the Chinese Civil War: The Marshall Mission in Manchuria," *Diplomatic History* (Vol. 3 no. 2, Fall 1979), 349–75.

45. Marshall to Truman, November 28, 1946, FRUS 1946, Vol. 10, 661–65; Minutes of meeting between Marshall and John Leighton Stuart, American ambassador in China December 9, 1946, ibid., 599–602; Marshall to John Carter Vincent, February 27, 1947, FRUS 1947, Vol. 7, 803–4; Marshall to Robert Patterson, March 4, 1947, ibid., 805–8. Despite reservations, aid to the Nationalists totaled some $3 billion during the civil war, including lend-lease and surplus transfers, loans, and assistance under the China Aid Act.

46. Marshall at meeting of the Secretaries of State, War, and Navy, June 26, 1947, FRUS 1947, Vol. 7, 850–51; Marshall's comment to James Forrestal, Forrestal diary, February 12, 1948, Forrestal Papers; Marshall testimony, House Foreign Affairs Committee, February 20, 1948, in Committee on International Relations, Selected Executive Session Hearings of the Committee, 1943–50, *U.S. Policy in the Far East, Pt. 1* (Washington, 1976), Vol. 7, 159–69. On the role of the congressional China bloc, see Robert M. Blum, *Drawing the Line: The Origin of American Containment Policy in East Asia* (New York, 1982); William W. Stueck, *The Road to Confrontation* (Chapel Hill,

N.C., 1981); Nancy B. Tucker, *Patterns in the Dust: Chinese-American Relations and the Recognition Controversy, 1949–50* (New York, 1983).

47. The most authoritative history of the early occupation of Korea and the emergence of separate regimes is, Bruce Cumings, *The Origins of the Korean War* (Princeton, N.J., 1981). Also see, Stueck, *The Road to Confrontation* and James Matray, "An End to Indifference: America's Korea Policy during World War II," *Diplomatic History* (Vol. 2, no. 2, 1978), 181–96. See also the collection of essays in Cumings, ed., *Child of Conflict.*

48. Matray, "Captive of the Cold War."

49. Pauley to Truman, June 22, 1946, FRUS 1946, Vol. 8, 706–9; Truman to Pauley, July 16, 1946, ibid., 714–15; Truman to Secretary of War, July 29, 1946, ibid., 721.

50. The evolution of American military strategy in Korea is discussed in John L. Gaddis, "Korea in American Politics, Strategy and Diplomacy, 1945–50," in Nagai Yonosuke and Akira Iriye, eds., *The Origins of the Cold War in Asia* (New York, 1977), 277–8. See also Gaddis, "The Strategic Perspective: The Rise and Fall of the Defensive Perimeter Concept, 1947–1951," in Dorothy Borg and Waldo Heinrichs, eds., *Uncertain Years: Chinese–American Relations, 1947–50* (New York, 1980), 61–118. See also essays by Cumings, Matray, and Pelz in Cumings, ed., *Child of Conflict.*

CHAPTER 4

1. Truman quoted in memorandum of February 25, 1947, SWNCC 360 File, March 1947, SWNCC Records, RG 353.

2. Forrestal diary, March 3, 1947, Forrestal Papers.

3. Ibid., March 13 and April 18, 1947.

4. Ibid., April 16, 1947; Minutes of the meeting of the Secretaries of State, War, and Navy, April 16, 1947, Forrestal Papers.

5. Jerome Cohen, *Japan's Economy in War and Reconstruction*, 493–94; SCAP, Occupation History, "Foreign Trade," Center for Military History.

6. Ibid.; William S. Borden, *The Pacific Alliance: United States Foreign Economic Policy and Japanese Trade Recovery, 1947–55* (Madison, Wis., 1984), 3–43.

7. FRUS 1946, Vol. 6, 696–706. The most thorough analysis of Kennan's ideas and their impact is presented by John L. Gaddis, *Strategies of Containment* (New York, 1982), passim.

8. National War College lecture, October 6, 1947, "Soviet Diplomacy," box 17, George F. Kennan Papers; "Talk on Russian–American Relations" to Board of Governors of the Federal Reserve System and the Secretary of the Navy's Council, December 3, 1947, ibid.; PPS 13, November 6, 1947, FRUS 1947, Vol. 1, 771; PPS 1, "Policy with Respect to American Aid to Western Europe," May 23, 1947, ibid., Vol. 3, 225.

9. "Contemporary Problems of Foreign Policy," National War College lecture, September 17, 1948, box 17, Kennan Papers.

10. PPS 13, November 6, 1947, FRUS 1947, Vol. 1, 771; PPS 23, February 24, 1948, FRUS 1948, Vol. 1, 515–18.

11. Talk to Board of Governors of the Federal Reserve System and the Secretary of the Navy's Council, December 3, 1947, box 17, Kennan Papers.

12. Kennan quoted in Gaddis, *Strategies of Containment*, 41; Kennan to R. A.

Winnacker of the National War College, December 8, 1948, box 13, PPS Records, RG 59.

13. Kennan to Lovett, June 23, 1947, Gaddis, *Strategies of Containment,* 41; Kennan to Marshall, "The Situation in China and U.S. Policy," November 4, 1947, ibid.; PPS 13, November 5, 1947, FRUS 1947, Vol. 1, 772–7; PPS 23, February 24, 1948, FRUS 1948, Vol. 1, pt. 2, 523–6; NSC 34, October 13, 1948, FRUS 1948, Vol. 8, 146–55; PPS 39/1, November 23, 1948, ibid., 208–11

14. JCS 1769/1, April 29, 1947, FRUS 1947, Vol. 1, 738–50.

15. See Reports on Japan in SWNCC 360, April 21, 1947; SWNCC 360/1, May 12, 1947; SWNCC 360/2, June 3, 1947; SWNCC 360/3, October 11, 1947— all in SWNCC 360 Series, RG 353.

16. Martin to Hilldring, February 26, 1947, box 222, Records of the Far Eastern Commission, RG 43, National Archives; Martin to Hilldring, March 5, 1947, ibid.

17. Ibid.; Martin to Hilldring, March 12, 1947, FRUS 1947, Vol. 6, 184–86.

18. Hoover to Patterson, May 7, 1947, box 222, FEC Records, RG 43; Hoover to Marshall, May 14, 1947, ibid.

19. Harold Lavine (formerly of *Newsweek*) to Michael Schaller, November 19, 1982. For additional information on Kern and *Newsweek*, see Howard Schonberger, "The Japan Lobby in American Diplomacy, 1947–1952," *Pacific Historical Review* (Vol. 416, no. 3, August 1977), 327–59.

20. Schonberger, "The Japan Lobby in American Diplomacy"; Joyce Kolko and Gabriel Kolko, *The Limits of Power: The World and United States Foreign Policy, 1945–1954* (New York, 1972), 323–25.

21. *Newsweek*, Vol. 29, no.4, January 27, 1947, 40. In fact, after review, fewer than five hundred executives were removed from their positions, see Baerwald, *Purge of Japanese Leaders.*

22. *Newsweek*, Vol. 29, no. 5, June 23, 1947, 37–43; Vol. 30, no. 5, August 4, 1947, 38.

23. Minutes of the meeting of the Secretaries of State, War, and Navy, April 16, 1947, in Forrestal diary, Forrestal Papers; Acheson to Patterson, April 14, 1947, filed with 740.00119 Control (Japan) 9–1347, RG 59; Patterson to Acheson, April 21, 1947, ibid.

24. Note to E.A. Locke, April 18, 1947, filed with Patterson to Acheson, ibid.

25. Record of conversation with MacArthur, Gascoigne to Foreign Office, March 4, 1947, FO 371/63766, PRO.

26. MacArthur interview with press correspondents, March 17, 1947, PRJ, Vol. 2, app. F, 765–67.

27. Dean Acheson, "The Requirements of Reconstruction," speech of May 8, 1947, *Department of State Bulletin*, (Vol. 16, no. 411, May 18, 1947), 991–94.

CHAPTER 5

1. Frederick S. Dunn, *Peacemaking and the Settlement with Japan*, (Princeton, N.J., 1963), 53–69; Memorandum by Edwin F. Martin, October 3, 1946, FRUS 1946, Vol. 8, 326–29; Memorandum by Ruth Bacon, October 25, 1946, ibid., 348–49.

2. Memorandum by MacArthur, March 21, 1947, FRUS 1947, Vol. 6, 454–56; MacArthur to Secretary of State, September 1, 1947, ibid., 512–15; Mac-Arthur statement to the *Economist*, Vol. 153, July 5, 1947.
3. See JCS Report to Army Sec. Royall and to the Secretary of Defense, mid 1947, 091 Japan 1947, General Correspondence—Security Classified, July 1947–December 1950, Records of the Office of the Secretary of the Army, RG 335; Memorandum by Admiral Wooldridge to Hugh Borton, August 18, 1947, FRUS 1947, Vol. 6, 494–96; Adm. Forrest Sherman to George Kennan, September 24, 1947, PPS Records, FOIA; Col. S. F. Giffin, "The Japanese Peace Treaty," August 14, 1947, ibid.
4. British Embassy to the Department of State, July 15, 1947, Vol. 6, 471–72; internal British Foreign Office discussion about the invitation is contained in file FO 371/63772, PRO.
5. The most thorough analysis of British policy toward the Occupation is contained in Buckley, *Occupation Diplomacy*.
6. "British Foreign Policy in the Far East," April 16, 1946, prepared by Cabinet Committee, FO 371/54052, PRO; F. K. Roberts to Bevin, September 5, 1946, FO 371/54335; British Chiefs of Staff to the JCS, October 17, 1946, in JIC Memorandum for Information no. 234, ABC 336, Russia (22 August 1943), sec. 1c, RG 165; Gascoigne to Foreign Office, March 4, 1947, FO 371/63766, PRO.
7. Extensive documentation on this topic appears in FRUS 1947, Vol. 6, 469–522.
8. Col. S. F. Giffin to PPS, August 14, 1947, PPS Records, FOIA.
9. Minutes of meeting of August 7, 1947, box 32, PPS Records, RG 59.
10. Davies to Kennan, August 11, 1947, FRUS 1947, Vol. 6, 485–86.
11. Kennan to Lovett and Lovett to Kennan, August 12, 1947, ibid., 486–87.
12. Colonel S. F. Giffin to PPS, August 14, 1947, PPS Records, FOIA.
13. Butterworth to Secretary of State, August 20, 1946, FRUS 1946, Vol. 8, 301–304.
14. Butterworth to Marshall, September 22, 1947, FRUS 1947, Vol. 6, 523–25.
15. Minutes of discussion of treaty draft, Meeting 48, August 25, 1947, box 32, PPS Records, RG 59.
16. Meeting 54, September 4, 1947, ibid.
17. Meeting 65, September 22, 1947, ibid.
18. Ibid.
19. (?) Rudlin to Charles Saltzman, October 6, 1947, 740.0019 Control (Japan)/10–647, Records of the Department of State, RG 59 (hereafter cited as DOS with date and decimal).
20. Borton to Maxwell Hamilton, September 29, 1947, 740.0011 PW (Peace) 9–2947, DOS, RG 59; Martin to Borton, September 26, 1947, attached ibid.
21. Schuyler to William Draper, October 20, 1947, ABC 388, Japan (1 September 1947), RG 165; Adm. Forrest Sherman to Kennan, September 24, 1947, PPS Records, FOIA; Sherman to Kennan, October 15, 1947, ibid.
22. Kennan to Lovett and Marshall, October 14, 1947, FRUS 1947, Vol. 6, 536–43; Memorandum by Carlisle Humelsine to Willard Thorp et al., October 29, 1947, PPS Records, FOIA; Humelsine to Gen. Marshall Carter, October 16, 1947, ibid.

23. Forrestal diary, October 31, 1947, Forrestal Papers.
24. Forrestal diary, November 7, 1947, ibid.

CHAPTER 6

1. F. C. Everson (British Embassy staff) to D. F. MacDermot (Foreign Office), February 24, 1947, FO 371/63643, PRO.
2. Strike report, cited in SCAP, Occupation Histories, Vol. 11, "Reparations and Property Administration," Center for Military History.
3. Pauley to Gen. John H. Hilldring, March 1947, box 4, Pauley Mission Records, RG 59; advanced transfer policy is discussed in chap. 2.
4. For an analysis of the evolution of FEC 230, see Hadley, *Anti-Trust in Japan*, 495–515.
5. SWNCC 381, July 22, 1947, SWNCC Records, RG 353.
6. Ibid.
7. SWNCC 360/1, 360/2, and 360/3—all prepared between May and December 1947 and derived from SWNCC 360, April 21, 1947, SWNCC Records, RG 353.
8. Discussion of July 22, 1947, in ABC 014, Japan (4-13-45), sec. 40, Department of the Army Records, RG 335.
9. File attached to Col. F. P. Munson to Charles Saltzman, September 13, 1947, DOS, 740.00119 Control (Japan) 9–1347, RG 59.
10. Kauffman report of September 6, 1947, excerpted in *Newsweek*, Vol. 30, no. 22, December 1, 1947.
11. Forrestal to Royall, October 15, 1947, Forrestal Papers.
12. Forrestal diary, October 31, 1947, ibid.
13. Kennan quoted in Forrestal diary, October 31, 1947, ibid.; Forrestal to Royall, November 1, 1947, ibid.
14. Saltzman memoranda for Marshall on SWNCC 384, October 9, 1947, DOS, 894.50/10–947, RG 59; Saltzman draft letter to Draper, November 11, 1947, SWNCC 384 File, SWNCC Records, RG 353; minutes of 61st meeting of SWNCC, October 23, 1947, ibid.
15. "Economic Rehabilitation for Japan, South Korea and the Ryukyu Islands," ESS, box 7692, Records of the Supreme Commander for the Allied Powers, RG 331, Washington National Records Center.
16. Memorandum by O. J. McDiarmid to Roswell H. Whitman, January 7, 1948, PU 894.50/1–848, DOS, RG 59.
17. Department of the Army to MacArthur, October 20 and 21, 1947; SCAP to Department of the Army, October 25, 1947—all in memorandum of December 9, 1947, by Robert Blum, CD 3–1–9, Records of the Office of the Secretary of Defense, RG 330. Blum, then an aide to Forrestal, compiled an extensive file on the disputes between SCAP and authorities in Washington. Defense Department officials passed on MacArthur's cable to former Secretary of War Henry Stimson, hoping that he would press the general to curtail the anti-*zaibatsu* campaign. Stimson informed the administration he opposed deconcentration, but he declined to enter the fray.
18. Royall to MacArthur, December 6, 1947, CD 3–1–9, ibid.
19. Telephone transcript of Forrestal-John Biggers conversation, December 5, 1947, ibid.
20. Memorandum, December 12, 1947, in Draper to Gray, December 14, 1947,

Under Secretary of the Army, General Correspondence—Security Classified, August 1947–January 1949, SAOUS 004, Japan, Records of the Office of the Secretary of the Army, RG 335.

21. Gascoigne to British Prime Minister Clement Atlee, December 26, 1947, FO 371/63830, PRO.

22. Draper to Gray, see note 20 above.

23. *Congressional Record*, December 19, 1947, Vol. 11, 686–88; Knowland to Royall, December 29, 1947, and Royall to Knowland, December 31, 1947, and January 10, 1948—all in Office of the Secretary of the Army, Unclassified General Correspondence, July 1947–December 1950, "Japan" Foreign Country File, Records of the Office of the Secretary of the Army, RG 335. During this period, the State Department's Office of Public Opinion Studies surveyed the large amount of published criticism of SCAP. See "U.S. Opinion on Japan and Korea," December 1947–January 1948, in Records of the Office of Public Opinion Studies, DOS, RG 59.

24. Speech by Kenneth Royall, January 5, 1948, printed in Jon Livingston et al., eds., *Postwar Japan: 1945 to the Present* (New York, 1973), 116–19; letter from Royall to Speaker of the House of Representatives, January 17, 1948, U.S. House of Representatives, Committee on International Relations, Selected Executive Session Hearings of the Committee, 1943–50, *U.S. Policy in the Far East, Pt. 1* (Washington, 1976), Vol. 6, 277–78.

25. MacArthur to Draper for House and Senate Appropriations Committees, January 18, 1948, PRJ, Vol. 2, 778–79.

26. *Congressional Record*, January 19, 1948, 298–99.

27. Memorandum from R. W. Barnett to E. F. Martin, January 8, 1948, 894.50/1–848, DOS, RG 59; Penfield to Butterworth, January 9, 1948, PW 894.50/1–848, ibid.

28. Discussions of January 15, 21, and 23, 1948—all in SWNCC 384 File, SWNCC Records, RG 53; statement to FEC, January 22, 1948, FRUS 1948, Vol. 6, 654–56.

29. Overseas Consultants, Inc., *Report on Industrial Reparations Survey of Japan to the United States of America* (New York, 1948), 223–24.

30. MacArthur to Sen. Brien McMahon, February 1, 1948, PRJ, Vol. 2, 783.

31. MacArthur to J. H. Gipson, February 1, 1948, ibid, 780–81.

CHAPTER 7

1. George F. Kennan, *Memoirs, 1925–50* (Boston, 1967), 393.

2. C. H. Hummelsine to Kennan, February 9, 1948, box 19, PPS Records, FOIA; Kennan memorandum of conversation with Marshall, February 19, 1948, ibid.

3. PPS 23, February 24, 1948, FRUS 1948, Vol. 1, pt. 2, 523–26; Kennan, *Memoirs*, 381.

4. Kennan to Lovett, February 24, 1948, box 45, PPS Records, FOIA; Frank Wisner to Gen. Frank McCoy, March 2, 1948, FRUS 1948, Vol. 6, 953; Wisner to McCoy, March 12, 1948, 091 Japan TS, sec. 1, P&O, Department of the Army Records, RG 165; George Butler to Lovett, March 8, 1948, box 45, PPS Records, FOIA.

5. Stewart Hensiey, February 27, 1948, United Press release; Theodore Koslow, February 26, 1948, International News Service release; SCAP ordered these

reports censored in the Japanese press, claiming they represented Draper's effort to undermine MacArthur. See, Sebald to Niles Bond (of the State Department), March 3, 1948, 740.00119 Control (Japan) 3–348, DOS, RG 59; Royall to Forrestal, May 18, 1948, 091 Japan TS, sec. 1A, P&O, Army Department Records, RG 319.

6. Kennan Report, FRUS 1948, Vol. 6, 697–99; Kennan, *Memoirs*, 384; Kennan to MacArthur, March 5, 1948, box 19, PPS Records, FOIA.

7. Kennan memorandum of conversation with MacArthur, March 5, 1948, FRUS 1948, Vol. 6, 699–706.

8. Ibid.

9. Kennan to Butterworth, March 9, 1948, box 19, PPS Records, FOIA.

10. Kennan to Butterworth, March 14, 1948, ibid.; Kennan to Butterworth, March 16, 1948, ibid.

11. PPS 28, March 25, 1948, PPS Records, RG 59; for an edited versison, see FRUS 1948, Vol. 6, 691–98.

12. Testimony of Draper, March 5, 1948, Committee on International Relations, *U.S. Policy in the Far East, Pt. 1* 187–203, 313–15.

13. William H. Draper, Jr. Oral History, Truman Library; Bisson, *Zaibatsu Dissolution*, 142–43.

14. Gascoigne to Foreign Office, April 6, 1948, FO 371/69886, PRO.

15. MacArthur, Draper, Kennan conversation transcript, March 21, 1948, FRUS 1948, Vol. 6, 706–12; Wedemeyer to Army Chief of Staff, April 27, 1948, 091 Japan TS, sec. 1A, P&O, Army Department Records, RG 319; Royall to Forrestal, May 18, 1948, ibid.

16. *Pacific Stars and Stripes*, April 12, 1948; *New York Times*, April 20, 1948; Memorandum by Draper aide, Col. T. N. Depuy, to Director, CAD, with enclosures of April 15, 1948, CAD 1948 Decimal File, CAD 014 Japan, sec. 2, March 1, 1948–May 31, 1948, Records of the War Department General and Special Staffs, RG 165; Memorandum for General Marquat in memorandum given to Paul G. Hoffman, April 13, 1948, box 6396, SCAP Records, RG 331; Memorandum on final reparations program for Japan, April 1, 1948, box 5977, ibid.; Report by General Schuyler on Economic Study of Japan by Civilian Advisory Group, April 1948, 091 Japan TS, sec. 1, case 4, P&O, Army Department Records, RG 319.

17. British Embassy Counselor H. A. Graves to D. F. MacDermot (Foreign Office), with enclosures, May 1, 1948, FO 371/69887, PRO. For additional reports regarding British concern with new policies, see files FO 371/69886 and 69887.

18. Percy Johnston et al., "Report on the Economic Position and Prospects of Japan and Korea and the Measures Required to Improve Them," Dodge Papers; Jerome Cohen, "Japan: Reform vs. Recovery," *Far Eastern Survey* (Vol. 17, no. 12, June 23, 1948), 137–42.

19. MacArthur to Department of the Army, January 26, 1948, cited in Hadley, *Anti-Trust in Japan*, 142–43; Royall to Forrestal, April 28, 1948, CD 3–1–9, Records of the Office of the Secretary of Defense, RG 330.

20. Welsch quoted in Hadley, *Anti-Trust in Japan*, 180.

21. Gunther, *Riddle of MacArthur*, 60–62; Howard Schonberger, "The General and the Presidency: Douglas MacArthur and the Election of 1948," *Wisconsin Magazine of History* (Vol. 57, no. 3, 1974), 201–19.

22. Guy Swope to Justin Williams (SCAP Government Section), letters of March 17, May 21, and September 13, 1948, file 106, Justin Williams Papers.
23. Draper to MacArthur, April 28, 1948, box 6721, SCAP Records, RG 331; Draper to MacArthur, May 23, 1948, ibid.; House of Representatives, Appropriations Committee, *Hearings on Foreign Aid Appropriations, 1949*, 80th Cong, 2d sess., May 11 and 13, 1948, 84–170.
24. Draper speech, "Japan's Key Position in the Far East," May 17, 1948, before Bay Area World Institute; copy furnished by John Dower.
25. For British reporting on EROA, see H. A. Graves to D. F. MacDermot, June 25, 1948, FO 371/F9139/1230/23, PRO. For the most astute analysis of Draper's role in arranging cotton credits and other aid, see Howard Schonberger, "General William F. Draper, the 80th Congress and the Origins of the Reverse Course," conference paper.
26. George Butler to Lovett, May 26, 1948, FRUS 1948, Vol. 6, 775–81; NSC 13 file, Modern Military Branch, National Archives. See also Wedemeyer to Army Chief of Staff, April 27, 1948, and Royall to Forrestal, May 18, 1948, both in 091 Japan TS, sec. 1A, P&O, Army Department Records, RG 319.
27. Memorandum by Marshall Green, Northeast Asia specialist, May 28, 1948, FRUS 1948, Vol. 6, 788–94.
28. Memorandum by Marshall Green, June 2, 1948, ibid., 796–99; M. E. Dening to Michael Wright, June 1, 1948, FO 371/69926, PRO; Sir Oliver Franks to Foreign Office, May 31, 1948, ibid.; Graves to Dening, Oct. 6 and 20, 1948, FO 371/69887, PRO.
29. Draper speech to Council on Foreign Relations, October 21, 1948, quoted in John C. Perry, *Beneath the Eagles Wing: Americans in Occupied Japan* (Boston, 1981), 128; Draper speech to National Foreign Trade Council Convention, November 9, 1948, Dodge Papers.
30. See memorandum of conversation by G. W. Lewis, "Economic Aspects of the Japanese Occupation," July 27, 1948, 894.50/7–2748, DOS, RG 59.
31. Draper to MacArthur, June 7, 1948, PPS Records, FOIA; MacArthur to Draper, June 12, 1948, FRUS 1948, Vol. 6, 819–23.
32. Ivan Pink to Foreign Office, August 26, 1948, FO 371/69823, PRO.
33. Ibid.
34. MacArthur to Prime Minister Ashida, July 22, 1948, PRJ, Vol. 2, 581. This order resulted in the resignation of Killen and several other Labor Division aides.
35. Gascoigne to Foreign Office, September 1, 1948, FO 371/69823, PRO.
36. Sebald to Secretary of State, December 9, 1948, FRUS 1948, Vol. 6, 916–21; Sebald to Lovett, January 3, 1949, FRUS 1949, Vol. 7, 601–3; Farley, *Aspects of Labor in Japan*, 189–207.
37. Thorp to Butterworth, April 6, 1948, FRUS 1948, Vol. 6, 964–65; Saltzman to Marshall, June 5, 1948, ibid., 973–77; Highlights of State-Army meeting on new Japanese policy paper, May 24, 1948, 091 Japan TS, sec. 1A, P&O, Army Department Records, RG 319; Royall to Marshall, July 28, 1948, ibid.
38. Marshall to Royall, August 26, 1948, FRUS 1948, Vol. 6, 996–1000; Royall to Marshall, August 31, 1948, ibid., 1001–5; Draper memorandum for Royall meeting with Marshall, September 14, 1948, 091 Japan TS, sec. 1B, pt. 2, P&O, Department of the Army Records, RG 319; Memoranda on Draper-Kennan discussions, October 14, 15, 1948, P&O, 091 Japan TS, 1B, pt. 3,

ibid.; Saltzman to Marshall, September 15, 1948, FRUS 1948, Vol. 6, 1015–16; Lovett to Royall, October 28, 1948, ibid., 1035–40.

39. Memorandum for the record by Ralph W. E. Reid, November 19, 1948, Under Secretary of the Army, General Correspondence—Security Classified, August 1947–January 1949, SAOUS 091, Japan, Records of the Office of the Secretary of the Army, RG 335; Reid memorandum for the record, December 9, 1948, ibid.

40. "Informal memorandum of understanding between State and Army departments concerning implementation of NSC 13, December 7, 1948, Under Secretary of the Army, Draper/Voorhees Project Decimal File, 1947–50, 091 Japan, Records of the Department of the Army, RG 335; Draper-Lovett exchange, December 13, 1948, FRUS 1948, Vol. 6, 1060.

41. Draper Oral History, 56–57, Truman Library; statement on economic stabilization of Japan, December 10, 1948, FRUS 1948, Vol. 6, 1059–60.

42. Sebald to John Allison, November 29, 1948, 820.02, Records of the Foreign Service Posts of the Department of State, 59 A 543, pt. 9, RG 84, Washington National Records Center; MacArthur to Army Department, December 4, 1948, Draper/Voorhees Project File, RG 335; Draper to SCAP, December 10, 1948, and SCAP to Draper, December 12, 1948, both in "Japan—1947–48: MacArthur Communications," File 42, Leahy Files, JCS Records, RG 218.

43. MacArthur to Draper, December 18, 1948, P&O, 091 Japan TS, sec. 1B, pt. 2, Records of the Department of the Army, RG 319.

44. Max Bishop to Butterworth, December 28, 1948, PPS Records, FOIA; Lovett to National Security Council, December 29, 1948, ibid.

45. MacArthur to Yoshida, December 19, 1948, FRUS 1948, Vol. 6, 1066–67.

46. Kern to Draper, July 25, 1948, CAD 1948 Decimal File, CAD 014, Japan, sec. 3, June 1, 1948, to August 31, 1948, RG 165. The origins and activities of the council are discussed in Howard Schonberger, "The Japan Lobby in American Diplomacy, 1947–52," *Pacific Historical Review* (Vol. 46, no. 3, August 1977), 327–59.

47. Harry F. Kern to Joseph Dodge, January 24, 1949, cover letter and report by the American Council on Japan, copy in Dodge Papers.

48. For Eichelberger's criticism, see Memorandum by Rear Adm. H. H. McLean, "Aspects of the Occupation of Japan, presented by Lt. General Eichelberger," September 23, 1948, Strategic Plan EF 37, Japan, Operational Archives, Center for Naval History; Schonberger, "The Japan Lobby in American Diplomacy."

49. Kern to Draper, February 5, 1949, 091 Japan, Records of the Office of the Secretary of the Army, RG 335; Memorandum by Draper for Royall, February 10, 1949, ibid.

50. R. W. Barnett to Paul Nitze, notes on "American Council for Japan Dinner for Mr. Royall's Mission," February 23, 1949, 740.00119 Control (Japan) 2–2349, DOS, RG 59.

CHAPTER 8

1. Roswell H. Whitman to Emmerson Ross, March 11, 1948, box 7688, SCAP Records, RG 331; Memorandum by Emmerson Ross, March 31, 1948, "State Department Program for Economic Recovery in Japan," ibid. See also Ken-

neth Landon to Butterworth, November 19, 1947, "Problem of a Unified Policy for the Far East," box 10, Chinese Affairs Lot File, DOS, RG 59.

2. Robert W. Barnett to Edwin F. Martin, "Memorandum Regarding Cranking-Up," September 8, 1947, box 222, FEC Records, RG 43; Barnett to Martin, "Your Comment on Expansion of Crank-Up," September 10, 1947, ibid.

3. Joseph Jones to Tyler Wood (ECA official), "Suggested Speech for Mr. Hoffman," October 14, 1948, box 32, 53 A 405, Records of the ECA, RG 286, Washington National Records Center.

4. Col. R. W. Porter, Jr., to Chief, Civil Affairs Division, October 13, 1948, CAD 014, Japan, sec. 4, September 1948–December 31, 1948, Civil Affairs Division Decimal File, RG 165; Ralph W. E. Reid to Draper and Dodge, October 18, 1948, box 222, FEC Records, RG 43.

5. Memorandum for the record by Reid, November 19, 1948, Under Secretary of the Army, General Correspondence, Security Classified, August 1947–January 1949, SAOUS 091, Japan, RG 335; Memorandum for the record by Reid, December 9, 1948, 091.3, Japan, ibid.; "Program for a Self-Supporting Economy," ESS, November 1948, box 8361, SCAP Records, RG 331.

6. Ibid.

7. Draper to Lovett, December 14, 1948, FRUS 1948, Vol. 6, 1062–63.

8. "Study of a U.S. Aid Program for the Far East," February 14, 1948, SAOUS, 400.3591, Draper/Voorhees Project Decimal File, RG 335.

9. Robert W. Barnett to Burke Knapp, "Far Eastern Recovery Program," October 14, 1948, box 222, FEC Records, RG 43; Joseph Carwell to Meville Walker, "Preliminary Proposals for an Economic Coordination Program for the Far East," October 14, 1948, ibid.; Paul Nitze to Butterworth, "A Coordinated Economic Policy for the Far East," October 26, 1948, ibid.; Memorandum for circulation within the Department of State, "The Japanese Recovery Program in Relation to Economic Conditions in the Far East," December 1948, 890.50/4–749, DOS, RG 59; "Economic Aspects of U.S. Policy with Respect to South and Southeast Asia," May 25, 1949, 890.50/7–1149, ibid.; Butterworth to Lovett, October 27, 1948, 890.50/10–2748, ibid.; Butterworth Oral History, Truman Library.

10. Lovett to Draper, December 28, 1948, FRUS 1948, Vol. 6, 1073–75.

11. Joseph Dodge, "The Role of Japan in Our Relations with the Orient," July 7, 1949, Memorandum to the Division of Northeast Asian Affairs, Department of State, copy in Dodge Papers; Statement by Dodge to the National Advisory Council, January 12, 1950, ibid.; Dodge quoted in Jon Halliday, *A Political History of Japanese Capitalism* (New York, 1967), 197.

12. Dodge to Hoffman in Draper to Hoffman, February 25, 1949, box 19, Draper/Voorhees Project File, RG 335.

13. Cleveland to Hoffman, "Coordination of Far Eastern Programs," April 11, 1949, box 32, 53A 405, ECA Records, RG 286.

14. For descriptions of the role of Southeast Asia in the world economy, see "Economic Colonialism in Southeast Asia," R&A Report no. 5036, August 26, 1949, DOS, RG 59; "Far Eastern Economic Aspects: The Postwar Pattern of Far Eastern Foreign Trade," OIR Report no. 4526.1, January 1, 1949, ibid.; "Strategic Importance of Japan," May 24, 1948, CIA, ORE 43–48, FOIA; "The Place of Foreign Trade in the Japanese Economy," INR Report OCL 2815, August 29, 1946, DOS, RG 59; "Southeast Asia Regional

Conference Folder," box 3, Philippines–Southeast Asia Lot File, DOS, RG 59.

15. Edwin Stanton to James C. Dunn, April 21, 1945, 851g.00/4–2845, DOS, RG 59; Walter LaFeber, "Roosevelt, Churchill and Indochina, 1942–45," *American Historical Review* (Vol. 80, no. 5, December 1975), 1277–95; Gary R. Hess, "Franklin D. Roosevelt and Indochina," *Journal of American History* (Vol. 59, no. 2, September 1972) 353–68; Christopher Thorne, *Allies of a Kind*; Robert J. McMahon, *Colonialism and Cold War: The United States and the Struggle for Indonesian Independence, 1945–49* (Ithaca, N.Y., 1982); William Rogers Louis, *Imperialism at Bay*.

16. OSS report on "Problems and Objectives of United States Policy," April 2, 1945, Rose Conway file, box 15, Truman Papers; Policy paper forwarded by Grew to Stimson, June 28, 1945, FRUS 1945, Vol. 6, 556–70; Preliminary report by SWNCC, "Basic Policies and Objectives of the U.S. in the Pacific and Far East," August 31, 1945, box 99, SWNCC Records, RG 353.

17. Department of State Policy Statement on Indochina, September 27, 1948, FRUS 1948, Vol. 6, 43–49; Lovett to Frank Graham, December 31, 1947, FRUS 1947, Vol. 6, 1099–1101.

18. Testimony of Dean Acheson, January 29, 1948, U.S. Congress, House Committee on Foreign Affairs, *Hearings: U.S. Foreign Policy for a Postwar Recovery Program*, 80th Congress, 2d sess., 1948, pt. 1 (Washington, 1948), 739; Testimony of Richard Bissell, January 12, 1948, U.S. Congress, Senate Committee on Foreign Relations, *Hearings: European Recovery Program*, 80th Congress, 2d sess., 1948, pt. 1, (Washington, 1948), 273.

19. Robert M. Blum, "Ho Chi Minh and the United States, 1944–46," in U.S. Senate, Committee on Foreign Relations, *The United States and Vietnam, 1944–47* (Washington, 1972), 13; Archimedes Patti, *Why Vietnam: The Road to America's Albatross* (Berkeley, Calif., 1981); Jefferson Caffery to State Department, September 11, 1946, 851g.00/9–1146, DOS, RG 59; Memorandum by George Abbott, September 12, 1946, 851g.00/9–1246, ibid.; Caffery to State Department, September 16, 1946, 851g.00/9–1646, ibid.

20. Acheson (probably written by John Carter Vincent) to Saigon, December 5, 1946, 851g.00/12–346, ibid.

21. Byrnes to Certain American Missions, "Basic French-Vietnamese Differences," December 17, 1946, 851g.00/12–1747, ibid; Moffat to Byrnes, January 7, 1947, 851g.00/1–747, ibid.

22. Marshall to American Embassy in Paris, February 3, 1947, 851g.00/2–347; Marshall to American Embassy in Paris, May 13, 1947, FRUS 1947, Vol. 6, 95–97.

23. Marshall to American Embassy in Paris, May 13, 1947, ibid; Charles Reed to Secretary of State, July 11, 1947, ibid., 110–16; Moffat to Penfield, July 23, 1947, 851g.00/6–1447, DOS, RG 59; Memorandum of conversation by Arthur Ringwalt, October 20, 1949, 851g.00/10–2049, ibid.

24. James O'Sullivan to John Melby, June 9, 1948, John F. Melby Papers.

25. Minutes of talks between Dening and U.S. officials on Southeast Asia, June 7, 1948, FO 371/69927, PRO.

26. O'Sullivan to Melby, June 9, 1948, Melby Papers.

27. Edwin F. Stanton to Department of State, June 29, 1948, 890.00 SEA Area/6–2948, DOS, RG 59.

28. Reports of discussions in "Southeast Asia Regional Folder," June 21–26, 1948, box 3, PSA Lot File, DOS, RG 59.
29. Charles Reed to Benninghoff, August 27, 1948, 865D.00/8–2748, DOS, RG 59.
30. Marhsall to Cochran, August 31, 1948, FRUS 1948, Vol. 6, 312; Marhsall to Cochran, September 1, 1948, ibid., 314; Memorandum by James W. Barco to Dean Rusk, September 3, 1948, ibid., 318–22; Marshall to Cochran, September 9, 1948, ibid., 327–28; Memorandum of conversation by Lovett, September 17, 1948, ibid., 345–47; Report to General Wedemeyer, September 14, 1948, P&O 092, RG 335. For a broad analysis of American policy, see McMahon, *Colonialism and Cold War*, 235–40.
31. Livengood to Marshall, September 20, 1948, FRUS 1948, Vol. 6, 356–57; Cochran to Marshall, September 20, 1948, ibid., 357–58.
32. Rusk to Ambassador-at-large Jessup, December 23, 1948, ibid., 597–600.
33. Lovett to American Embassy in the Soviet Union, December 30, 1948, ibid., 613–16; Lovett to Certain Diplomatic and Consular Offices Abroad, December 31, 1948, ibid., 617–18.
34. McMahon, *Colonialism and Cold War*, 267–95.
35. Memorandum on "U.S. Policy in Indonesia," probably May 1949, box 12, PSA Lot File, DOS, RG 59. See also, CIA, "Review of the World Situation as it Relates to the Security of the United States," CIA 1–49, PSF, Truman Papers.
36. McMahon, *Colonialism and Cold War*, 287–303.
37. Memorandum by Davies, "U.S. Policy with Respect to the Far East," December 6, 1948, box 222, FEC Records, RG 43.
38. Acheson testimony of February 15, 1949, "Extension of the ERP," House of Representatives, Committee on International Relations, *Selected Executive Session Hearings of the Committee, 1943–50*, Vol. 4, *Foreign Economic Assistance Programs, Pt. 2* (Washington, 1976), 38–43.
39. PPS 51, March 29, 1949, in NSC 51, "U.S. Policy toward Southeast Asia," July 1, 1949, NSC files, MMR. An excerpt appears in FRUS 1949, Vol. 7, 1128–33.
40. Minutes of Under Secretaries Meeting, "To Define U.S. Policy towards Southeast Asia," April 6, 1949, PPS Records, FOIA.
41. Dening for Bevin, "Southeast Asia," March 23, 1949, FO 371/76023, PRO; Bevin presented this paper to Acheson on or about April 4, 1949. See FRUS 1949, Vol. 7, 1135–37.
42. Memorandum of conversation with Ernest Bevin by Jacob Beam, April 4, 1949, FRUS 1949, Vol. 7, pt. 2, 1138–41.
43. Memorandum of conference in State Department, by Charlton Ogburn, May 17, 1949, FRUS 1949, Vol. 7, pt. 1, 27; Acheson to Consulate General at Saigon, May 20, 1949, ibid., 28–29; Acheson to Consulate at Hanoi, May 20, 1949, ibid., 29–30.
44. David Bruce to Acheson, June 2, 1949, ibid., 36–38; Memorandum by the Department of State to French Foreign Office, June 6, 1949, ibid., 39–45; Bruce to Acheson, June 13, 1945, ibid., 45–46.
45. Acting Secretary of State to Certain Diplomatic and Consular Offices Abroad, June 14, 21, 1949, ibid., 53–54; Department of State *Bulletin*, press release, June 21, 1949 (Vol. 21, July 18, 1949), 75.

46. PPS 51, submitted as NSC 51, July 1, 1949, NSC files, Modern Military Branch, National Archives.

CHAPTER 9

1. See Report of "Secretary of the Army's Off-the-Record Press Conference," in Sebald to Secretary of State, February 15, 1949, 740.00119 Control (Japan) 2–1549, DOS, RG 59.
2. Ibid.; Memorandum by Butterworth of a conversation with H.A. Graves, February 11, 1949, 740.00119 Control (Japan) 2–1149, ibid.; Statement by Acheson, February 19, 1949, FRUS 1949, Vol. 7, pt. 2, 664.
3. Memorandum by Gen. Omar Bradley to Secretary of Defense, March 1, 1949, in NSC 44, March 11, 1949, Modern Military Branch.
4. NSC 13/3, May 6, 1949, FRUS 1949, Vol. 7, pt. 2, 730–36; Acheson to Certain Diplomatic Officials, May 8, 1949, ibid., 736–37.
5. JCS, "Strategic Evaluation of U.S. Security Needs in Japan," June 9, 1949, enclosed in NSC 49, June 15, 1949, ibid., 773–77
6. MacArthur to Acheson, June 16, 1949, ibid., 778–81; Acheson, of course, dismissed MacArthur's contention regarding SCAP's status. Acheson to MacArthur, September 9, 1949, ibid., 850–52; Cloyce Huston (American diplomatic counselor in Tokyo) to Acheson, July 21, 1949, ibid., 803–07.
7. Sebald to Butterworth, July 26, 1949, ibid., 808–12; Sebald to Acheson, August 20, 1949, ibid., 830–40.
8. Sebald memorandum of conversation with MacArthur, September 21, 1949, ibid., 862–64.
9. Memorandum by Marshall Green, Northeast Asia specialist, "Views of Other Countries Toward a Japanese Peace Settlement," July 29, 1949, ibid., 819–25.
10. Memorandum of conversation with Dening, by Marshall Green, September 9, 1949, ibid., 853–56; Memorandum of conversation among Dening, Butterworth, Allison, Marshall Green, and Livingston Merchant on Japanese Peace Treaty, September 9, 1949, FO 371/76212, PRO.
11. Conversation with Mr. Bevin on the Far East, minutes by L. L. Satterthwaite, September 13, 1949, PPS Records, FOIA; Extracts in FRUS 1949, Vol. 7, pt. 2, 858–59.
12. Memorandum by Acheson of discussion with the president, September 16, 1949, ibid., 860.
13. NSC 49/1, Department of State Comments on NSC 49, September 30, 1949, ibid., 871–73. See Davies's draft of this document, September 29, 1949, PPS Records, FOIA; Acheson testimony of October 12, 1949, U.S. Congress, Senate, Committee on Foreign Relations, *Reviews of the World Situation: 1949–50, Hearings held in Executive Session on the World Situation*, 81st Congress, 1st and 2d sess. (Washington, 1974), 102 (hereafter, cited as "Reviews of the World Situation").
14. See Memorandum by Butterworth to Acheson, November 30, 1949, FRUS 1949, Vol. 7, pt. 2, 907–08.
15. Treaty draft of October 13, 1949, in Feary to Allison, October 14, 1949, 740.0011 PW (Peace) 10–1449, DOS, RG 59; "Notes on Discussion of Peace with Japan," October 21, 1949, 740.0011 PW (Peace) 10–2149, ibid.
16. Kennan Oral History, remark of August 30, 1949, George F. Kennan Papers.

17. Memorandum of conversation by Feary, "MacArthur's Views on a Japanese Peace Treaty," November 2, 1949, FRUS 1949, Vol. 7, pt. 2, 890–94; Transcript of a meeting with Col. Babcock, JSSC 388.1 Japan, sec. 1 (9–1–47), JCS Records, RG 218.
18. Sebald to Acheson, September 9, 1949, FRUS 1949, Vol. 7, pt. 2. 857; MacDonald to Gascoigne, December 15, 1949, FO 371/84531, PRO.
19. The evolution and debate over Taiwan policy is discussed most authoritatively in Blum, *Drawing the Line*, and Tucker, *Patterns in the Dust*.
20. Transcript of a meeting with Col. Babcock, November 10, 1949 JSSC 388.1, Japan, sec. 1, (9–1–47), JCS Records, RG 218; Report by the JSSC to the JCS on "Impact of an Early Peace Treaty with Japan on U.S. Strategic Requirements," "November 30, 1949, JCS 1380/75, ibid.
21. Ibid.
22. Memorandum by Allison of conversation with H. A. Graves, November 30, 1949, 740.0011 PW (Peace) 11–3049, DOS, RG 59; Notes on a memorandum of conversation with Goldthwaite Dorr by John Howard, December 8, 1949, FRUS 1949, Vol. 6, 1128.
23. Voorhees notes of summary of General MacArthur's opinions on a Japanese Peace Treaty, December 14, 1949, CJCS 092.2 Japanese Peace Treaty 1950, JCS Records, RG 218.
24. Deputy Assistant Secretary of the Army Robert West told this to Hubert A. Graves. See Graves to Dening, December 2, 1949, FO 371/76214, PRO.
25. Gen. Carter B. Magruder to JCS, December 3, 1949, enclosed in JCS 1380/76, CCS 388.1, Japan, sec. 1 (9–1–47); JCS 1380/77, December 10, 1949, ibid.; Johnson to Acheson, December 23, 1949, with enclosure of memorandum by the JCS to the Secretary of Defense, December 22, 1949, FRUS 1949, Vol. 7, pt. 2, 922–23—circulated as NSC 60, December 27, 1949.
26. Memorandum of conversation by Maxwell Hamilton of meeting with Gens. Bradley and Burns, December 24, 1949, ibid., 924–26; Informal memorandum by Acheson to the British Ambassador (Sir Oliver Franks), December 24, 1949, ibid., 927–29.
27. Ibid.
28. Memorandum by Rusk of statement by Truman, January 24, 1950, FRUS 1950, Vol. 6, 1131.
29. Notes of a discussion with Sir Oliver Franks, February 8, 1950, FO 371/84528, PRO.

CHAPTER 10

1. The most persusasive analysis of the "moderate" approach of Dean Acheson and the Department of State appears in Tucker, *Patterns in the Dust*.
2. The remarks by Kennan and Philip Taylor appear in "Department of State Conference on Problems of U.S. Policy in China," October 6–8, 1949, copy in OASIA File 69–A–4707–71, Department of the Treasury Records, FOIA. See also, box 174, PSF, Truman Papers.
3. H. A. Graves to Dening, October 27, 1949, FO 371/76213, PRO.
4. *Washington Post*, August 22, 1949.
5. Ibid., August 24, 1949.
6. Ibid., August 29, 1949.
7. Ibid., September 18, 1949.

8. Memorandum by George Kennan to Dean Rusk and Philip Jessup, September 8, 1949, under cover letter of Kennan to Rusk, October 6, 1949, box 13, PPS Records, RG 59.

9. *New York Times*, March 11, 1949. For an evaluation of the limited influence of the China Lobby, see Tucker, *Patterns in the Dust*; Blum, *Drawing the Line*; and Stueck, *The Road to Confrontation*.

10. *New York Times*, May 4, 1949; Stueck, *The Road to Confrontation*, 126–30.

11. Stueck, ibid.; Blum, *Drawing the Line*, 97–102.

12. Wedemeyer to Forrestal, March 29, 1949, in NSC 6 File, March 26, 1948, "The Position of the U.S. Regarding Short-term Assistance to China," NSC files, Modern Military Branch.

13. Military aid policy can be traced in the following documents: NSC 22, July 26, 1948; NSC 22/1, August 6, 1948; NSC 22/3, February 2, 1949; NSC Action Memorandum no. 180, February 8, 1949—all in NSC 22 file, Modern Military Branch; See also, NSC 34, October 13, 1948, which details the amounts of aid given China after 1945, Modern Military Branch.

14. Blum, *Drawing the Line*, 26–28, 35.

15. Acheson to Stuart, March 24, 1949, FRUS 1949, Vol. 9, 304; Stueck, *The Road to Confrontation*, 120; Blum, *Drawing the Line*, 24–80.

16. JCS to Forrestal, November 24, 1948, FRUS 1949, Vol. 9, 261–62; JCS to Forrestal, February 10, 1949, ibid., 284–86.

17. Bishop memorandum of conversation with General MacArthur, February 16, 1949, ibid., Vol. 7, pt. 2, 656–57; Report of meeting between General MacArthur and Chennault, November 21, 1949, NLT–12, CIA, FOIA; Memorandum of conversation: MacArthur briefing to Huber Subcommittee, September 5, 1949, CCS 452, China (4–3–43), sec. 7, pt. 5, JCS Records, RG 218.

18. Warren Cohen, "Acheson, His Advisers and China, 1949–50," in Borg and Heinrichs, eds., *Uncertain Years*, 13–52. See also John Lewis Gaddis, "The Strategic Perspective: The Rise and Fall of the Defensive Perimeter Concept, 1947–51," ibid., 61–118; See also, Tucker, *Patterns in the Dust*; Stueck, *The Road to Confrontation*; and Blum, *Drawing the Line*.

19. NSC 34/2, "U.S. Policy Toward China," February 28, 1949, approved by Truman on March 3, 1949, NSC 34 File, Modern Military Branch; FRUS 1949, Vol. 9, 499.

20. NSC 11/2, December 14, 1948, FRUS 1948, Vol. 8, 341; Acheson statement to the NSC, March 1, 1949, FRUS 1949, Vol. 9, 295; NSC 37/1, January 19, 1949, ibid., 272–73; Livingston Merchant to Acheson, March 23, 1949, ibid., 280–82; Acheson to Merchant, February 14, 1949, ibid., 287–88; NSC 37/4, February 18, 1949, ibid., 288–89; NSC 37/5, March 1, 1949, ibid., 296–97; Truman approved NSC 37/5 on March 3, 1949.

21. Butterworth to Acting Secretary of State, (December 13, 1948), box 13, PPS Records, RG 59.

22. For a thoughtful analysis of the great concern in Tokyo and Washington regarding trade with China, see Nancy Bernkopf Tucker, "American Policy toward Sino–Japanese Trade in the Postwar Years: Politics and Prosperity," *Diplomatic History* (Vol. 8, no 3, Summer 1984), 183–208.

23. Clubb to Acheson, April 30, 1949, FRUS 1949, Vol. 9, 974–76; OIR Report no. 4867, January 24, 1949, "The Effect of a Communist Dominated China on Other Areas of the Far East," DOS, RG 59.

24. Ibid.; William Costello, "Could Japan Go Communist?" *Nation* (Vol. 168,

no. 20, May 14, 1949), 554; Allison to Butterworth, 693.9431/12–1949, DOS, RG 59.

25. OIR Report no. 4867 and no. 5063, October 14, 1949, "Japan's Reaction to Sino–Soviet Trade Problems," DOS, RG 54;. *New York Times*, November 25, 1949.

26. Col. R. W. Porter for Under Secretary of the Army to Civil Affairs Division, January 10, 1949, "Trade between Japan and Communist Areas of the Far East," Under Secretary of the Army, General Correspondence—Security Classified, August 1947–January 1949, folder 091.31, Japan, Records of the Office of the Secretary of the Army, RG 335; Gen. G. L. Eberlie to Gen. E. M. Almond, "Trade between Japan and Communist Areas in the Far East," January 12, 1949, ibid.

27. Royall's statement is with enclosures of William Sebald to Acheson, February 15, 1949, 740.00119 Control (Japan) 2–1549, DOS, RG 59.

28. OIR Reort no. 4867; see note 23 above.

29. Ibid.

30. NSC 41, "U.S. Policy Regarding Trade with China," February 28, 1949, NSC Files, Modern Military Branch, National Archives. Approved by the NSC and Truman on March 3, 1949. See also, Tucker, "American Policy toward Sino–Japanese Trade."

31. West to SCAP, May 7, 1949, FRUS 1949, Vol. 9, 977–79.

32. Memorandum by R. Magill to Philip Sprouse, May 20, 1949, box 15, Chinese Affairs Lot File, DOS, RG 59. For MacArthur's simultaneous endorsement of trade with China and a blockade, see MacArthur to Huber Subcommittee Memorandum, September 5, 1949, P&O, 091 Formosa TS, Department of the Army Records, RG 319. See also MacArthur's statements favoring a blockade to Sir Alvary Gascoigne in Tucker, "American Policy Toward Sino–Japanese Trade."

33. Acheson to Executive Secretary, NSC, November 4, 1949; NSC 41/1, November 7, 1949, NSC files, Modern Military Branch, National Archives.

34. Acheson's testimony of January 10, 1950, in U.S. Senate, *Reviews of the World Situation*, 105–71.

35. Ibid.

CHAPTER 11

1. This point is made most persuasively by John L. Gaddis, "The Strategic Perspective: The Rise and Fall of the 'Defensive Perimeter' Concept, 1947–51," in Borg and Heinrichs, eds., *Uncertain Years*.

2. Blum, *Drawing the Line*, 17; David E. Lilienthal, *The Journals of David E. Lilienthal*, Vol. 2, *The Atomic Energy Years, 1945–50* (New York, 1964), 508–9.

3. Louis Johnson to Executive Secretary, NSC, June 10, 1949, NSC 48 File, Modern Military Branch.

4. U.S. Senate, Committee on Foreign Relations, *Military Assistance Program: 1949, Joint Hearings Held in Executive Session before the Committee on Foreign-Relations and the Committee on Armed Services*, 81st Cong., 1st sess. (1974), 35, 48 (hereafter Senate MAP Hearings). The most thorough study of the Mutual Defense Assistance Act's impact on Asia in 1949–50 is Blum, *Drawing the Line*.

5. Smith to H. Kenaston Twitchell, August 15, 1949, H. Alexander Smith Papers.

6. Ibid.
7. Senate MAP hearings, 117–20, 172–84, 371–72.
8. U.S. Congress, House of Representatives, Committee on International Relations, *Selected Executive Session Hearings of the Committee, 1943–50*, Vol. 5, *Military Assistance Programs, pt. 1, Mutual Defense Assistance Act of 1949* (Washington, 1976), 25, 230–31 (Hereafter House MAP Hearings).
9. House MAP Hearings, 231, 348–50; Senate MAP Hearings, 473–77.
10. Senate MAP Hearings, 614–15, 582–97, 628.
11. Report no. 1068 in Senate MAP Hearings, 699–736.
12. Acheson Memorandum for Jessup, July 18, 1949, box 14, Chinese Affairs Lot File, DOS, RG 59.
13. For the impact and confusion surrounding the White Paper, see Tucker, *Patterns in the Dust* and Blum, *Drawing the Line*.
14. The drafts of NSC 48, prepared during the summer and fall of 1949, were obtained from the NSC through a FOIA request. See drafts of August 16, August 31, and September 9, 1949. FOIA.
15. NSC 48 drafts of October 7 and October 14, 1949, ibid.
16. NSC 48 drafts of October 4, October 7, and October 14, 1949, ibid.
17. Points for consideration by the Far Eastern Consultants, August 17, 1949, 890.00/8-1749, DOS, RG 59; Memorandum from Fosdick, Case, and Jessup for Acheson, August 29, 1949, 890.00/8-2949, ibid.; discussion of Far Eastern Affairs held in the Secretary's Office, September 13, 1949, FRUS 1949, Vol. 7, 1204–8.
18. Meeting of the Secretary and the Far Eastern Consultants, October 27, 1949, PPS Records, box 722, Asia, FOIA; decision reached by consensus at the meeting with the Secretary and the Far Eastern Consultants, November 2, 1949, box 14, Chinese Affairs Lot File, DOS, RG 59.
19. Memorandum by Merchant for Sprouse, August 24, 1949, FRUS 1949, Vol. 9, 870–71; Memorandum by Acheson of conversation with Truman, September 16, 1949, ibid., 878; Memoranda by Webb of conversations with Truman, October 1 and 31, 1949, ibid., 1141, 1335; Memorandum by Webb of conversation with Truman, October 3, 1949, box 13, China File, PPS Records, RG 59; Memorandum of conversation with the president, November 17, 1949, FRUS 1949, Vol. 8, 1008; "Memorandum," ibid., Vol. 9, 582–88. See, also, Blum, *Drawing the Line*, 162–63.
20. Mr. Jessup's statement of consultants' views on area approach to the Far East, November 3, 1949, box 846, 890.00, DOS, RG 59.
21. Outline of Far Eastern and Asian policy for review with the president, November 14, 1949, FRUS 1949, Vol. 7, 1210–14; Memorandum by Acheson of conversation with Truman, November 17, 1949, box 13, PPS Records, RG 59.
22. Cover letter and memorandum in Walter Wilds to Livingston Merchant, October 19, 1949, included with NSC 48 drafts, FOIA.
23. Ibid.; Stephen Brown to Philip Sprouse, October 24, 1949, box 15, Chinese Affairs Lot File, DOS, RG 59; John Allison to Butterworth, comment on third draft of NSC policy paper on Asia, October 19, 1949, NSC 48 drafts, FOIA.
24. Butterworth to Rusk, November 28, 1949, UM d–69, Records of the Executive Secretariat, DOS, RG 59; Allison to Rusk, December 5, 1949, ibid.

25. NSC 48/1, December 23, 1949, NSC files, Modern Military Branch.
26. Memorandum by Gen. L. L. Lemnitzer to JCS, September 13, 1949, JCS 1868/107, P&O, 091 China, sec 2a, case 27, RG 319; Bolte to Collins, November 10, 1949, 091 China TS, ibid.; Report by JSSC on military aid to China, October 6, 1949, JCS 1721/37, CCS 45d, China (4–3–45), sec. 7, pt. 5, JCS Records, RG 218.
27. Memorandum of MacArthur briefing of Huber Subcommittee, September 5, 1949, P&O, 091 Formosa TS, RG 319.
28. Paper no. 21, GHO seminar for JCS representatives, "Relation of World-Wide Political Situation to CINFE Mission," October 1, 1949, ibid.
29. Consul General at Taipei to Acheson, September 7 and 8, 1949, FRUS 1949, Vol. 9, 385–86. On Smith's trip, see Stueck, *Road to Confrontation*, 138–39.
30. *New York Times*, November 28 and 29, 1949; Bolte to Collins, December 1, 1949, P&O, 091 Formosa TS, RG 319.
31. Voorhees's notes of meetings with MacArthur, December 14, 1949, ibid.
32. JSSC report of December 16, 1949, CCS 381, Formosa (11–8–48), sec. 2, JCS Records, RG 218; Gruenther to JCS, December 22, 1949, P&O, 091 Formosa TS, RG 319; JCS to Johnson, December 23, 1949, FRUS 1949, Vol. 9, 460–61.
33. On Koo's lobbying, see transcripts of his meetings with Philip Jessup, August 26, 1949; Dean Rusk, September 21, 1949; W.W. Butterworth, November 9, 1949; James Webb, December 21, 1949; Paul Griffith, December 29, 1949—all in box 130, Wellington Koo Papers. In all likelihood, Assistant Defense Secretary Griffith served as the conduit between the Defense Department and Koo.
34. Memorandum by Butterworth of conversation with Koo, December 23, 1949, FRUS 1949, Vol. 9, 456–57; Butterworth Memorandum for Acheson, December 28, 1949, ibid., 461–62.
35. memorandum by Acheson of conversation, December 28, 1949, FRUS 1949, Vol. 9, 463–67.
36. Ibid.
37. NSC 48/2, December 30, 1949, NSC File, Modern Military Branch.

CHAPTER 12
1. Truman statement reprinted in Department of State *Bulletin* (Vol. 22, January 16, 1950), 79.
2. Acheson's testimony of January 10, 1950, *Reviews of the World Situation*, 113–17, 134.
3. Ibid., 135, 154.
4. Ibid., 159–70; Graham Greene's classic novel, *The Quiet American*, presents a rather harrowing account of the "little forts" that impressed Acheson.
5. Acheson's statement as reported in Department of State *Bulletin* (Vol. 22, January 22, 1950), 114–15.
6. Franks to Bevin, January 16, 1950, FO 371/83113, PRO. See also, "Notes on Far Eastern Policy," November 24, 1949, FO 371/83012, ibid.
7. Blum, *Drawing the Line*, 160–61; Secretary's Daily Meeting, October 13, 1949, Records of the Executive Secretariat, DOS, RG 59; Memorandum by Acheson of conversation with Truman, October 13, 1949, "Memoranda of Conversations" folder, Acheson Papers; Johnson's approach to the French is

noted in "Top secret Daily Staff Summary," December 21, 1949, Records of the Executive Secretariat, DOS, RG 59.

8. Tracy Voorhees to NSC, January 10, 1950, in NSC 61 File, January 27, 1950, NSC Files, Modern Military Branch, National Archives.
9. Ibid.
10. Ralph Reid to Voorhees, "Aid Program for Southeast Asia," February 27, 1950, Dodge Papers.
11. Johnson to JCS, January 10, 1950, JCS 1721/43, JCS Records, RG 218.
12. "Program of Assistance to General Area of China," January 16, 1950, ibid.
13. Ibid.
14. A sanitized, much abridged version of the January 16 report, JCS 1721/43 along with Johnson's cover letter to Acheson of February 1, 1950, appears in FRUS 1950, Vol. 6, 5–9.
15. Minutes of meetings of January 23, 24, and 26, 1950, Summaries of the Secretary's Daily Meetings, Records of the Executive Secretariat, DOS, RG 59; W. W. Butterworth Oral History, Truman Library; R. Allen Griffin Oral History, ibid.
16. Blum, *Drawing the Line*, 184–87; Acheson testimony, January 24, 1950, U.S. Senate, Committee on Foreign Relations, *Economic Assistance to China and Korea: 1949–50, Hearings Held in Executive Session before the Committee on Foreign Relations of the U.S. Senate, 81st Cong., 1st and 2nd sess.* (Washington, 1974), 193–99.
17. "Checklist for Southeast Asia," Fall 1949, prepared by Southeast Asia specialist W. S. B. Lacy, box 18, Chinese Affairs Lot File, DOS, RG 59.
18. Clubb to Acheson, January 10, 1950, FRUS 1950, Vol. 6, 273–75; Memorandum by Acting Secretary of State to Truman, January 10, 1950, ibid., 270–72; State Department press release of January 14, 1950, ibid., 278.
19. Memoranda by Jessup of conversations with MacArthur, January 5, 8, and 9, 1950, 694.001/1–1050, DOS, RG 59, a sanitized version of this appears in FRUS 1950, Vol. 6, 1114–15
20. Ibid.; Jessup to Acheson, January 10, 1950, ibid., 1114–15; Memorandum by Lucius Battle to William McWilliams, February 10, 1950, ibid.
21. Gascoigne to Foreign Office, "Jessup's Tour of Southeast Asia," January 17, 1950, FO 371/84514, PRO; Gascoigne to Foreign Office, January 18, 1950, FO 371/83840, PRO.
22. Memorandum of conversation by Jessup, January 16, 1950, FRUS 1950, Vol. 6, 280–83.
23. FRUS 1950, Vol. 6, 690–706.
24. Notes on conferences at office of the Commissioner General, February 6, 1950, ibid., 11–17; Ambassador Stanton to Secretary of State, February 17, 1950, ibid., 18–19; Stanton to Secretary of State, February 27, 1950, ibid., 28–29; Jessup's Report to Department, March 23, 1950, ibid., 69–70.
25. Gascoigne to Dening, February 27, 1950, FO 371/84514, PRO; See also, Voorhees to MacArthur, OAS Japan, February 22, 1950, box 18, Draper/ Voorhees Project Decimal File, 1947–50, Records of the Under Secretary of the Army, RG 335.
26. Memorandum by Andrews and West, for MacArthur, March 13, 1950, box 6365, SCAP Records, RG 331.
27. Ibid.

28. Andrews and West to Voorhees, April 22, 1950, box 5976, ibid.; West to Voorhees, March 22, 1950, DA CX, March 1950, RG 9, MacArthur Papers.
29. R. Allen Griffin, Oral History, Truman Library; Samuel P. Hayes, *The Beginning of American Aid to Southeast Asia: The Griffin Mission of 1950* (Lexington, Mass., 1971), 6–12.
30. Memorandum by Merrill C. Gay, February 7, 1950, cited in Hayes, 12.
31. Report of participation in the Griffin Mission, February 1950, CD–6–5–36, Records of the Office of the Secretary of Defense, RG 330; Hayes, *Beginning of American Aid*, 12.
32. Ibid., 22.
33. Report of participation in the Griffin Mission, see note 31; Griffin, Oral History, Truman Library.
34. Griffin mission cables, March 9, 13, and 18, 1950, box 7, Philippine/Southeast Asia Lot File, DOS, RG 59.
35. The formal report of the Griffin mission is printed in Hayes, *Beginning of American Aid*, app.; draft memorandum by ECA official Harlan Cleveland, May 13, 1950, box 55, 53–A–405, ECA Records, RG 286.
36. Dean Acheson, speech of March 15, 1950, Department of State *Bulletin* (Vol. 22, March 27, 1950), 467–72.
37. Cleveland report for ECA officials Richard Bissell and William C. Foster, "NSC Working Group on U.S. Economic Aid to Far Eastern Areas—NSC 61," March 1, 1950, box 55, 53–A–405, ECA Records, RG 286.
38. Memorandum by Butterworth of conversation with MacArthur, February 5, 1950, FRUS 1950, Vol. 6, 1133–35.
39. Cleveland to Foster and Bissell, March 2, 1950, box 55, 53–A–405, ECA Records, RG 286.
40. Ibid.; Cleveland to ECA official E. T. Dickinson et al., "Procurement Sources for Military Assistance to Far Eastern Area," April 6, 1950, box 144, 53–A–441, ibid.
41. For information on the conference held April 17–22, 1950, see Shaw to White, December 28, 1949, and White to Shaw, December 30, 1949, box 3, Philippine/Southeast Asia Lot File, DOS, RG 59; SCAP memorandum of March 31, 1950, box 5977, SCAP Records, RG 331; Allison to Merchant, April 5, 1950, box 3, Philippine/Southeast Asia Lot File, DOS, RG 59; "Possible Methods of Increasing Intra-Regional Trade and Commerce among Countries of South and East Asia," April 1945, box 3, Tokyo Economic Conference File, ibid.
42. Lacy to Merchant (drafted by Shohan), "Voorhees Greater East Asia Co-Prosperity Sphere," March 8, 1950, box 1, Philippine/Southeast Asia Lot File; Doherty to Allison, "Far Eastern Development Proposal," March 20, 1950, box 2, ibid.
43. Ibid.
44. Thorp to William McC. Martin, June 21, 1950, with memorandum of April 1950, "Proposed Utilization of Japanese Capacity to Promote Economic Development in South and Southeast Asia," box 23, 67–A–245, OASIA Files, Treasury Department Records.
45. John Sumner to Harlan Cleveland, April 22, 1950, box 7, John Sumner Papers. Additional reasons for opposing Voorhees's proposals are discussed in "Coordination of U.S. Assistance Programs in the Far East," May 23, 1950, box 32, 53–A–405, ECA Records, RG 286.

46. W. J. Garvin, Chief, Budget Group, to Marquat, May 29, 1950, box 8355, SCAP Records, RG 331; Memorandum by W. C. French to Morrow, ibid.

47. Reid to Butterworth, "Discussion of Japanese Peace Treaty with Mr. Ikeda, May 2, 1950," May 10, 1950, FRUS 1950, Vol. 6, 1193–98.

48. Recommendations by Ikeda in Yoshida to MacArthur, May 22, 1950, File 128, Justin Williams Papers.

49. Allison to Butterworth, March 14, 1950, and Doherty to Dodge, June 16, 1950, FRUS 1950, Vol. 6, 1223; Treasury officials Arthur Stewart to George Willis, May 18, 1950, "Proposals for Financing Japanese Exports," box 20, OASIA Files, Treasury Department Records; Willard Thorp to William McC. Martin, June 21, 1950, ibid. W. W. Diehl, financial attache in Tokyo, opposed this proposal in a memorandum to Sebald and Allison, June 20, 1950, FRUS 1950, Vol.6, 1223–27.

50. Voorhees Memorandum to Executive Secretary, NSC, "Coordination of U.S. Aid Programs for Far Eastern Areas," April 5, 1950, Dodge Papers; NSC 61/1, May 16, 1950, NSC files, Modern Military Branch; Memoranda by Cleveland for Bissell March 16, May 3, and May 4, 1950, box 55, 53–A–405, ECA Records, RG 286.

51. Voorhees Report of May 27, 1950, "A Proposal to Correlate Economic Aid to Europe with Military Defense," Cold War Coordination Staff memoranda, 39.32, box 62, Bureau of the Budget Records, RG 51, National Archives.

52. Ibid. See also, Borden, *The Pacific Alliance*, 47–49.

53. Dodge quoted in Halliday, *A Political History of Japanese Capitalism*, 197; Dodge testimony during meeting of ECA Advisory Committee on Fiscal and Monetary Problems, April 28, 1950, Dodge Papers.

54. Stewart Alsop, "We Are Losing Asia Fast," *Saturday Evening Post* (Vol. 222, no. 37, March 11, 1950), 29ff.—see draft mss. in Alsop Papers.

CHAPTER 13

1. "Consequences of Communist Control of French Indochina," Intelligence Memorandum no. 231, October 7, 1949, PSF, Truman Papers.

2. Acheson statement of February 1, 1950, FRUS 1950, Vol. 6, 711; Acheson Memorandum for Truman, February 2, 1950, ibid., 716–17; Memorandum of conversation by Acheson, February 3, 1950, ibid., 719.

3. "Problem Paper Prepared by a Working Group in the Department of State," February 1, 1950, ibid., 711–15.

4. Bohlen to Acheson, February 16, 1950, ibid., 734–35; Acheson to Truman, March 9, 1950, ibid., 40–44; Truman to Acheson, March 10, 1950, ibid.; Acheson to Truman, April 17, 1950, ibid., 785–86; Truman to Acheson, May 1, 1950, ibid., 791; Memorandum, Maj. Gen. J. F. Burns to Johnson, April 6, 1950, 091 French Indochina 1950, JCS Records, RG 218; Burns to Nolting, April 7, 1950, ibid. For estimates of funding, see Blum's analysis based on executive hearings of the Senate Foreign Relations Committee and House Foreign Affairs Committee, *Drawing the Line*, 202–4.

5. NSC 64, "The Position of the U.S. with Respect to Indochina," February 27, 1950, NSC files, Modern Military Branch.

6. Rusk to Maj. Gen. James H. Burns, March 7, 1950, CCS 092, Asia (5–25–48), sec. 3, JCS Records, RG 218; Burns to Louis Johnson, April 6, 1950, Indochina File, box 1, Bradley File, 1949–53, ibid.

7. Jessup testimony of March 29, 1950, in *Reviews of the World Situation*, 253–65.
8. Ibid., 266–67.
9. Ibid., 278–79.
10. U.S. Congress, Senate Committee on Foreign Relations, *Executive Sessions of the Senate Foreign Relations Committee* Vol. 2, *81st Cong., 1st and 2nd sess., 1949–50* (Washington, 1976), 297–302. See, also, U.S. Congress, Senate, Committee on Foreign Relations, *Legislative History of Committee on Foreign Relations, 81st Cong, 1st and 2nd sess., 1949–50* (Washington, 1950).
11. JCS report of April 10, 1950, in Johnson to Acheson, April 14, 1950, FRUS 1950, Vol. 6, 780–85.
12. Ibid.
13. John Magruder to Louis Johnson, "Suggested Organization for the Conduct of the Cold War in China," April 6, 1950, CD–3–30, Records of the Office of the Secretary of Defense, RG 330.
14. Record of Action by the NSC, Action no. 288, April 18, 1950, FRUS 1950, Vol. 6, 786–87; Memorandum by NSC secretary James S. Lay to NSC, April 24, 1950, ibid.; Memorandum by Acheson to Truman, April 17, 1950, ibid., 785–86; Memorandum by Gen. L. L. Lemnitzer to Bruce, April 19, 1950, ibid., 787–89; Truman to Acheson, May 1, 1950, ibid., 791.
15. Memorandum of conversation with Harold Isaacs, by Charlton Ogburn, April 17, 1950, box 9, PSA Lot File, RG 59.
16. Ibid.
17. Acheson testimony of May 1, 1950, *Reviews of the World Situation*, 287–90.
18. Ibid., 306.
19. Record of conversation between Jessup and representatives of the British Foreign Office, March 11, 1950, FRUS 1950, Vol. 6, 46–51; Memorandum of conversation at the Quai d'Orsay, Paris, March 13, 1950, ibid., 754–57; FRUS 1950, Vol. 3, 941–46, 994–96.
20. Acheson to Acting Secretary of State, May 8, 1950, ibid., 1010–12; statement by Acheson, May 8, 1950, ibid., Vol. 4, 812; Acting Secretary of State to American Embassy in France, May 25, 1950, ibid., 817–18.
21. Memorandum by Louis Johnson for the JCS, June 6, 1950, CCS 092, Asia (6–25–48), JCS Records, RG 218; Acting Secretary of State to Louis Johnson, May 16, 1950, FRUS 1950, Vol. 6, 816–17; Memorandum by John Ohly, June 1, 1950, ibid., 98–100.
22. Testimony of Rusk, Ohly, and Lemnitzer, June 20, 1950, in U.S. Congress, House Committee on International Relations, *Executive Session Hearings of the Committee*, Vol. 8, *United States Policy in the Far East, pt. 2: Korean Assistance and the Far Eastern Portion of the Mutual Defense Assistance Act of 1950* (Washington, 1976), 464–93.
23. "Preliminary Informal Discussion with Far Eastern Subcommittee of the Senate Foreign Relations Committee," May 25, 1950, CD–6–2–46, Records of the Office of the Secretary of Defense, RG 330.
24. Ibid.
25. Ibid.
26. The legislative history of the 1950 MDAP appears in *Executive Session Hearings*, see note 22; Senate Foreign Relations Committee, *Executive Sessions*, Vol. 2, 455–58, 523–25. See, also, Senate Foreign Relations Committee, *Leg-

islative History, 8–9. Truman's order of June 27, 1950, appears in FRUS 1950, Vol. 6, 831.

CHAPTER 14

1. Truman quoted in memorandum by Rusk, January 24, 1950, FRUS 1950, Vol. 6, 1131.
2. Memorandum by Butterworth for Acheson, "Outline for Meeting with Secretary on Japanese Peace Settlement," prepared by John B. Howard, January 18, 1950, ibid., 1117–19; Memorandum by Butterworth of conversation with MacArthur, February 5, 1950, ibid., 1133–35; Memorandum by Howard for Bohlen, March 31, 1950, ibid., 1157–59.
3. Memoranda and summary of discussion with Truman, in John Howard to Butterworth, "Japanese Peace and Security Settlement," March 9, 1950, ibid., 1138–49.
4. The views of the JCS are noted in Howard to Butterworth, ibid., 1133. I am grateful to John Dower for showing me this account of the JCS visit to Tokyo.
5. Memorandum by Butterworth of conversation with MacArthur, February 5, 1950, ibid., 1133–35.
6. Memorandum by Voorhees for Acheson in Howard to Jessup, March 24, 1950, ibid., 1150–53; Memorandum by Howard for Bohlen, March 31, 1950, ibid., 1157–60.
7. The attack on administration policy by McCarthy and his supporters is analyzed by Blum, *Drawing the Line*, 187–91; and Stueck, *Road to Confrontation*, 143–46. A broad analysis of McCarthy's assault on the State Department is found in two recent biographies, Thomas C. Reeves, *The Life and Times of Joe McCarthy* (New York, 1982); and David Oshinsky, *A Conspiracy So Immense* (New York, 1983). During the spring of 1950, Acheson and his aides frequently discussed the senator's charges. See Minutes of Secretary's Daily Meetings, February–June, 1950, Records of the Executive Secretariat, DOS, RG 59.
8. Note on Treaty, FRUS 1950, Vol. 6, 311.
9. Acheson to Johnson, March 7, 1950, ibid., 16–17; Acheson to Johnson, April 14, 1950, ibid., 325–26; Johnson to Acheson, May 6, 1950, ibid., 339; Acheson to Johnson, June 1, 1950, ibid., 351–53.
10. William M. Leary, Jr., "Aircraft and Anti-Communists: CAT in Action, 1949–52," *China Quarterly*, no. 52, (October–December 1972), 654–69. See also by the same author: *Perilous Missions: Civil Air Transport and CIA Covert Operations in Asia* (University of Alabama Press, 1984). Leary discusses the deep involvement of the American government in the effort to keep the disputed aircraft out of Chinese Communist control.
11. Slessor to P. Reilly, December 30, 1949, FO 371/83012, PRO; Fergusson to Gascoigne, February 11, 1950, FO 371/83013, PRO.
12. *New York Times*, March 28, 1950. On Rusk's career, see, Warren Cohen, *Dean Rusk* (Totawa, N.J., 1980).
13. Acheson, *Present at the Creation*, 337, 432–32; Vandenberg to Acheson, March 31, 1950, and Acheson memorandum of conversation with Dulles, April 5, 1950, box 65, Acheson Papers; "Appointment of JFD as Consultant to Acheson," April 6, 1950, box 47, Dulles Papers; FRUS 1950, Vol. 6, 1160–61.
14. Memorandum by Rusk for Acheson, April 26, 1950, ibid., 333–35.

15. O. Edmund Clubb to George F. Kennan, April 25, 1950, PPS Records, FOIA.
16. "East and Southeast Asia," study by John P. Davies, June 6, 1950, ibid.
17. Dulles's memorandum, "RE: Appointment of JFD Consultant to Acheson," April 5, 1950, box 47, Dulles Papers; Smith diary, May 14 and 24, 1950, H. Alexander Smith Papers.
18. Memorandum of conversation by John Howard, "Japanese Peace Settlement," April 7, 1950, FRUS 1950, Vol. 6, 1161–66.
19. Memorandum by Allison to Butterworth, April 11, 1950, ibid., 1167–71.
20. JCS 1380/87, April 19, 1950, CCS 388.4, Japan (10–1–47), sec. 2, JCS Records, RG 218; Voorhees Memorandum for Johnson, April 11, 1950, Japan, Records of the Office of the Secretary of Defense, RG 330; Voorhees Memorandum for Chairman of the JCS, April 22, 1950, ibid.
21. Memorandum by John Howard of conversation, "Japanese Peace Treaty," April 24, 1950, FRUS 1950, Vol. 6, 1175–82.
22. Ibid.
23. Ibid.
24. Memorandum by Rusk of conversation with Gens. Burns and Magruder, May 5, 1950, ibid., 1186–88; Memorandum by Butterworth for Acheson, May 5, 1950, ibid., 1191–94.
25. Memorandum by Huston, "American Military Bases in Japan," April 8, 1950, ibid., 1166–67.
26. Butterworth to Acheson, May 3, 1950, 694.001/5-350, DOS, RG 59; Memorandum by Green for Allison, August 2, 1950, 1262–63.
27. Ikeda's statement of May 2, 1950, in Reid to Butterworth, May 10, 1950, ibid., 1194–98.
28. Ibid.
29. Memorandum by Butterworth for Acting Secretary Webb, May 12, 1950, ibid., 1198; Butterworth sent copies of the Ikeda interview to Acheson (in Europe) as well as to Dulles and Rusk.
30. "Record of a Bipartite Sub-Committee Meeting held in Mr. Dening's Room," May 3, 1950, FO 371/83018, PRO; Dening to British diplomat Sir. W. W. Strang, May 3, 1950, FO 371/83013, PRO; Dening's notes for Bevin talks with Acheson, May 6, 1950, ibid.
31. Memorandum of conversation by Acheson, May 11, 1950, FRUS 1950, Vol. 6, 1199–1200.
32. Memorandum by Dulles for Dean Rusk, Paul Nitze, and Under Secretary Webb, May 18, 1950, ibid., Vol. 1, 314–16.
33. Ibid.
34. NSC 68, "United States Objectives and Programs for National Security," April 14, 1950, ibid., 237-92.
35. Memorandum by Burns to Rusk, May 29, 1950, ibid., Vol. 6, 346–47.
36. For a partial record of Rusk's presentation, see Memorandum by Acheson's aides Fisher Howe to W. Park Armstrong, May 31, 1950, ibid., 347–49.
37. Ibid.
38. Rusk's report of May 31, 1950, with accompanying documents is found in box 18, Chinese Affairs Lot File, DOS, RG 59.
39. Ibid.
40. Ibid.
41. Ibid.

42. Rusk to Acheson, "Bi-Partisan Policy on China–Formosa Problems," June 9, 1950, PPS Records, FOIA.
43. Johnson to Acheson, June 1, 1950, FRUS 1950, Vol. 6, 351–52; Acheson to Johnson, June 8, 1950, ibid.
44. Harlan Cleveland to ECA officials Paul Hoffman, William Foster, and Richard Bissell, Jr., "Formosa Policy," June 23, 1950, box 32, ECA Records, 53–A–405, RG 286.
45. Ibid.
46. Ibid.
47. Kenneth T. Young to Gen. Burns, "Action on Formosa," June 19, 1950, CD–6–4–6, Records of the Office of the Secretary of Defense, RG 330.
48. Ibid.
49. Ibid.
50. Cooke's letter and estimates are contained in a memorandum by the Chief of Naval Operations to the JCS, May 1, 1950, JCS 1966/27, CCS 381, Formosa (11–8–48), sec. 3, JCS Records, RG 218.
51. MacArthur to Department of the Army, C 56410, May 20, 1950, Formosa folder, box 2, RG 6, MacArthur Papers; Bradley to Johnson, May 31, 1950, CCS 381, Formosa (11–8–48), JCS Records, RG 218.
52. Memorandum of conversation between MacArthur and Adm. Sir Patrick Brand, in Gascoigne to Foreign Office, June 3, 1950, FO 371/83008, PRO.
53. Sebald to Butterworth, May 25, 1950, FRUS 1950, Vol. 6, 1205–7.
54. Memorandum by Marshall Green (Northeast Asia specialist) of conversation with Nicholas Cottrell (State Department), June 15, 1950, ibid., 1221–22.
55. Memorandum of Koo conversation with Judd, May 2, 1950, box 217, Koo Papers; Koo conversations with Griffith, June 3 and 7, 1950, box 180, ibid.
56. Koo conversation with Dulles, June 12, 1950, ibid. Also see Dulles's Memorandum of conversation with KMT official Hollington Tong, May 25, 1950, FRUS 1950, Vol. 6, 343–44. In this latter conversation, as with Koo, Dulles lambasted the Nationalists' performance. For references to American attempts to prepare a haven for Jiang, see FRUS 1950, Vol. 6, 346n.
57. Koo conversation with Dulles, June 12, 1950, box 180, Koo Papers.
58. Maj. Gen. Carter B. Magruder, Acting Special Assistant for Occupied Areas, to Gen. Omar Bradley and Defense Secretary Louis Johnson, June 5, 1950, CJCS 092.2, Japanese Peace Treaty—1950, JCS Records, RG 218.
59. Memorandum by Dulles for Acheson, June 6, 1950, FRUS 1950, Vol. 6, 1207–12.
60. Memorandum by Allison for Sebald, June 14, 1950, ibid., 1212–13.
61. Memorandum by Dulles, June 15, 1950, ibid., 1222–23.

CHAPTER 15
1. Although no written record appears to exist that contains the text of a meeting between the two delegations, both Dean Acheson and Dulles later made reference to some contact in Tokyo. See, FRUS 1950, Vol. 6, 1229, 1260.
2. William Sebald, *With MacArthur in Japan* (New York, 1965), 252–53.
3. Memorandum of conversation by John Allison, June 19, 1950, FRUS 1950, Vol. 7, 107–9.
4. William R. Mathews to Dulles, June 20, 1950, Dulles Papers.
5. MacArthur, Memorandum on Formosa, June 14, 1950, FRUS 1950, Vol. 7, 161–65.

6. Ibid.
7. MacArthur, Memorandum on peace treaty problem, ibid., Vol. 6, 1213–21.
8. Summary report by Dulles, July 3, 1950, ibid., 1230–37; Sebald, *With MacArthur*, 254.
9. Memorandum by Gen. Omar Bradley to the JCS, June 26, 1950, CJCS, 092.2 Japanese Peace Treaty, 1950, JCS Records, RG 218; Memorandum on the concept governing security in post-war Japan by MacArthur, June 23, 1950, FRUS 1950, Vol. 6, 1227–29; Memorandum by Dulles for Acheson, June 30, 1950, ibid., 1229–30.
10. Livingston Merchant to Dean Rusk, June 23, 1950, 694.001/6–2350, DOS, RG 59.
11. Bruce Cumings, *Origins of the Korean War*. This study examines the internal politics of North and South Korea and the American role in suppressing the Left after 1945. Cumings stresses the local origins of the conflict rather than its international causes.
12. Stueck, *Road to Confrontation*. This is the most complete analysis to date of how the State Department perceived the North Korean attack as a Soviet-inspired challenge to American "credibility." For a discussion of the political elements of Truman's decisionmaking, see, Pelz, "U.S. Decisions on Korean Policy" in Cumings, *Child of Conflict*, 93–132. For military considerations, see Gaddis, "The Strategic Perspective" in Borg and Heinrichs, eds., *Uncertain Years*, 61–118.
13. Ibid.
14. Ibid., 108; Bohlen to Kennan, June 26, 1950, FRUS 1950, Vol. 7, 174–75.
15. Intelligence estimate prepared by the estimates group, Office of Intelligence Research, June 25, 1950, ibid., 148–54; Maj. Gen. Charles A. Bolte to Army Secretary Frank Pace, June 28, 1950, 091 Korea TS, JCS Records, RG 218.
16. Stephen Pelz, "U.S. Decisions on Korean Policy" in Cumings, ed. *Child of Conflict*, 93–132; For U.N. resolution, see FRUS 1950, Vol. 7, 155–56.
17. See accounts of talks with MacArthur by John Allison, June 25 and 26, 1950, ibid., 140n, 141n; Dulles memorandum of conversation with Acheson, Pace, et al., July 1, 1950, box 47, Acheson folder, Dulles Papers; Dulles to Walter Lippmann, July 1, 1950, cited in Gaddis, "The Strategic Perspective,"; Stueck, *Road to Confrontation*, 177–180.
18. Memorandum of conversation by Jessup, June 25, 1950, FRUS 1950, Vol. 7, 157–61.
19. Memorandum by Gen. Omar Bradley for the president, June 25, 1950, CJCS 091 China, JCS Records, RG 218.
20. As early as May 30, 1950, Dean Rusk had prepared a memorandum for Acheson advising both use of the Seventh Fleet to "neutralize" Taiwan and increased aid to Southeast Asia. For a later elaboration of this theme, see discussion between Acheson and Dulles, October 23, 1950, FRUS 1950, Vol. 7, 534–36.
21. Memorandum by Gen. Omar Bradley for the president, June 26, 1950, CCS 381, Formosa (11–8–48), sec. 3, JCS Records, RG 218.
22. Memorandum of conversation by Jessup, June 26, 1950, FRUS 1950, Vol. 7, 178–83.
23. Ibid.
24. Ibid.
25. Statement issued by the president, June 27, 1950, ibid., 202–3.

26. Ibid.; Later the same day, June 27, the UN Security Council (with the U.S.S.R. still absent) approved an American resolution calling for member states to "furnish such assistance to the Republic of Korea as may be necessary to repel the armed attack and to restore international peace and security in the area," ibid., 211.

27. Smith diary, June 28, 1950, box 282, H. Alexander Smith Papers.

28. Memorandum of conversation with Johnson, June 30, 1950, box 180, Koo Papers.

29. Memorandum of conversation with Griffith, June 30, 1950, ibid.

30. Memoranda of conversation with Dean Rusk, July 3, 7, and 25, 1950, ibid.; NSC 37/10, August 3, 1950, FRUS 1950, Vol. 6, 413–14; Stueck, *Road to Confrontation*, 210–213.

31. Acheson to American Legation at Saigon, July 1, 1950, FRUS 1950, Vol. 6., 833–34; Acheson memorandum for Truman, July 3, 1950, ibid., 835–36; Report of MDAP Survey Mission to Foreign Military Assistance Coordinating Committee, August 6, 1950, ibid., 840–44; Melby to Rusk and Lacy, in Health to Acheson, August 7, 1950, ibid., 845–48.

32. Memorandum by Ogburn for Rusk, August 18, 1950, ibid., 862–64.

33. Memorandum by JCS to the Secretary of Defense, November 28, 1950, enclosure to NSC 64/1, December 21, 1950, ibid., 945–648.

34. Analysis prepared for the JCS by the JSSC, November 17, 1950, ibid., 949–53.

35. Dower, *Empire and Aftermath*, discusses the broader impact of the Korean War on Japanese life. For an accounting of military procurements after 1950, see Borden, *The Pacific Alliance*, 143–65.

36. Ibid., 146–47; Joseph Dodge to Truman, May 9, 1952, Dodge Papers; Asahi Shimbun, *The Pacific Rivals* (New York, 1972), 179, 193–95.

37. Ibid.

CHAPTER 16

1. Bradley to Secretary of Defense, August 22, 1950, FRUS 1950, Vol. 6, 1278–82.

2. For the record of State-Defense negotiations, see, ibid., 1278–1304.

3. "The Japanese Peace Treaty Problem," Minutes of Council of Foreign Relations Meeting, October 23, 1950, Dulles Papers.

4. Ibid.

5. Ibid.

6. For a detailed account of how Dulles manipulated both the Japanese and British into following the American lead on the China question, see Howard Schonberger, "John Foster Dulles and the China Question in the making of the Japanese Peace Treaty," in Thomas W. Burkman, ed., *The Occupation of Japan: The International Context* (Norfolk, Va., 1984), 229–54.

7. Borden, *The Pacific Alliance,* 220.

8. Address by John Foster Dulles, January 27, 1953, FRUS 1952-54, Vol. 13, 360.

9. "Substance of Discussions of State-DMS-JCS Meeting at the Pentagon Building," January 28, 1953, ibid., 361–63.

REFERENCES

OFFICIAL RECORDS

Unless otherwise indicated, all of the Record Groups are located in the National Archives, Washington, D.C. Records obtained from the Washington National Records Center, Suitland, Md., are noted as WNRC. Documents obtained as a result of Freedom of Information Act requests are noted as FOIA.

Allied Council for Japan, RG 43
Bureau of the Budget, RG 51
Department of Defense
    ABC File, RG 165
    Records of the Army Staff, RG 319
    Gen. Omar Bradley File, RG 218
    Army Civil Affairs Division, RG 165
    Draper/Voorhees Project Decimal File, RG 335
    Far Eastern Command, RG 332, WNRC
    Joint Chiefs of Staff, RG 218
    Adm. William Leahy File, RG 218
    Army Plans and Operations Division, RG 319
    Office of the Secretary of the Army and Under Secretary, RG 335
    Office of the Secretary of Defense, RG 330
    Secretary of War Files (including Henry L. Stimson and John J. McCloy files), RG 107
    Supreme Commander for the Allied Powers, RG 331, WNRC

Economic Cooperation Administration, RG 286, WNRC
Far Eastern Commission, RG 43
National Security Council
    Papers of the NSC in Modern Military Branch, National Archives
    NSC Documents, FOIA
Department of State
    Decimal Files, RG 59
    Tokyo Post Files, RG 84, WNRC
    Policy Planning Staff, RG 59
    Policy Planning Staff, FOIA
    U.S. Mission on Reparations, RG 59
    Executive Secretariat, RG 59
    Assistant Secretary for Occupied Areas, RG 59
    Philippine/Southeast Asia Lot File, RG 59
    Chinese Affairs Lot File, RG 59
    Research and Analysis Branch, OSS and Bureau of Intelligence and Research,
        RG 59
State-War-Navy Coordinating Committee, RG 353
Department of the Treasury
    Office of the Assistant Secretary for International Affairs, FOIA
British Foreign Office Records, FO 371, Public Record Office, London

MANUSCRIPT COLLECTIONS

Center for Military History
    History of the Nonmilitary Aspects of the Occupation of Japan, Unpublished
        Official Studies by SCAP
Center for Naval History
    Admiral Forrest Sherman Papers
Clemson University
    James F. Byrnes Papers
Columbia University
    Wellington Koo Papers
Detroit Public Library
    Joseph Dodge Papers
Harvard University
    Joseph C. Grew Papers
Library of Congress
    Joseph and Stewart Alsop Papers
    Claire Chennault Papers
    Philip C. Jessup Papers
    William Leahy Papers
MacArthur Memorial
    Douglas MacArthur Papers
University of Maryland
    Justin Williams Papers
Princeton University
    John Foster Dulles Papers
    James Forrestal Papers

George F. Kennan Papers
Karl Lott Rankin Papers
H. Alexander Smith Papers
Whiting Willauer Papers
Harry S. Truman Presidential Library
Dean Acheson Papers
Stanley Andrews Papers
Eben Ayers Diary
W. Walton Butterworth Oral History
Matthew Connelly Papers
George Elsey Papers
R. Allen Griffin Oral History
John F. Melby Papers
John Sumner Papers
Harry S. Truman Papers
Yale University
Henry L. Stimson Papers

PUBLISHED DOCUMENTS

Executive Branch
Department of State, *Bulletin*, 1945–50.
Department of State, *Foreign Relations of the United States*, Volumes for 1944–54 (Washington, 1966–1982).
Supreme Commander for the Allied Powers, *The Political Reorientation of Japan, September 1945–September 1948, Report of the Governmental Section of SCAP.* 2 vols. (Washington, 1948).
Congress
U.S. Congress, *Congressional Record,* 80th Cong. and 81st Cong. (Washington, 1948–50).
Senate Committee on Foreign Relations, *Executive Sessions of the Senate Foreign Relations Committee* (Historical Series), Vol. 1, 80th Cong., 1st and 2nd sess., 1947–48 (Washington, 1976); Vol. 2, 81st Cong., 1st and 2nd sess., 1949–50 (Washington, 1976).
Senate Committee on Foreign Relations, *Foreign Relief Assistance Act of 1948: Hearings Held in Executive Session on United States to Certain Countries* (Historical Series), 80th Cong., 2nd sess., 1949 (Washington, 1973).
Senate Committee on Foreign Relations, *Economic Assistance to China and Korea: 1949–50, Hearings Held in Executive Session on S. 1063, S. 2319 and S. 2845* (Historical Series), 81st Cong., 1st and 2nd sess. (Washington, 1974).
Senate Committee on Foreign Relations, *Reviews of the World Situation: 1949–50, Hearings Held in Executive Session on the World Situation,* 81st Cong., 1st and 2nd sess. (Washington, 1974).
Senate Committee on Foreign Relations, *The United States and Vietnam, 1944–47,* Staff Study no. 2 by Robert M. Blum (Washington, 1972).
Senate Committee on Foreign Relations, *The United States and Communist China in 1949 and 1950: The Question of Rapprochement and Recognition,* Staff Study by Robert M. Blum (Washington, 1973).
Senate Committee on Foreign Relations, *Hearings on the Causes, Origins and*

Lessons of the Vietnam War, 92nd Cong., 2nd sess. (Washington, 1973).
Senate Committee on Foreign Relations and Committee on Armed Services, *Military Assistance Program: 1949, Joint Hearings Held in Executive Session on S. 2388* (Historical Series), 81st Cong., 1st sess., 1949 (Washington, 1974).
Senate Committee on Foreign Relations and Committee on Armed Services, *Mutual Defense Assistance Program, 1950, Hearings on the Mutual Defense Assistance Program, 1950*, 81st Cong, 2nd sess., 1950 (Washington, 1950).
House Committee on International Relations, *Selected Executive Session Hearings of the Committee, 1943–1950*, Vols. 1–8 (Washington, 1976). (See, especially, vols. 7 and 8 for hearings on "Policy in the Far East" and the "Mutual Defense Assistance Program, 1950.")

BOOKS

This highly selective list should be supplemented by checking sources listed in the notes. The most important bibliography in English for the Occupation remains, Robert E. Ward and Frank Joseph Shulman, *The Allied Occupation of Japan, 1945–53: An Annotated Bibliography of Western-Language Materials* (Chicago, 1974). Readers should also utilize the excellent bibliography contained in John Dowers' *Empire and Aftermath*, listed below.

Acheson, Dean. *Present at the Creation: My Years in the State Department*. New York, 1969.
Asahi Shimbun. *The Pacific Rivals*. New York, 1972.
Ball, W. MacMahon. *Japan: Enemy or Ally?* New York, 1949.
Bisson, Thomas A. *Prospects for Democracy in Japan*. New York, 1949.
Bisson, Thomas A. *Zaibatsu Dissolution in Japan*. Berkeley, Calif., 1954.
Blum, Robert M. *Drawing the Line: The Origin of the American Containment Policy in East Asia*. New York, 1982.
Borden, William S. *The Pacific Alliance: United States Foreign Economic Policy and Japanese Trade Recovery, 1947–1955*. Madison, Wis., 1984.
Borg, Dorothy, and Heinrichs, Waldo, eds., *Uncertain Years: Chinese–American Relations, 1947–50*. New York, 1980.
Buhite, Russell D. *Soviet–American Relations, 1945–1954*. Norman, Okla., 1981.
Burkman, Thomas, ed. *The Occupation of Japan: The International Context*. Norfolk, Va., 1984.
Cohen, Jerome. *Japan's Economy in War and Reconstruction*. Minneapolis, Minn., 1949.
Cohen, Warren I., ed. *New Frontiers in American–East Asian Relations*. New York, 1983.
Cumings, Bruce, ed. *Child of Conflict: The Korean-American Relationship, 1943–53*. Seattle, 1983.
Cumings, Bruce. *The Origins of the Korean War: Liberation and the Emergence of Separate Regimes, 1945–1947*. Princeton, N.J., 1981.
Dower, John W. *Empire and Aftermath: Yoshida Shigeru and the Japanese Experience, 1878–1954*. Cambridge, 1979.
Dunn, Frederick S. *Peacemaking and the Settlement with Japan*. Princeton, N.J., 1973.
Gaddis, John L. *Strategies of Containment: A Critical Appraisal of Postwar National Security Policy*. New York, 1982.

Gayn, Mark. *Japan Diary*. New York, 1948.

Hadley, Eleanor. *Anti-Trust in Japan*. Princeton, N.J., 1974.

Harriman, W. Averell, and Abel, Ellie. *Special Envoy to Churchill and Stalin, 1941–1946*. New York, 1975.

Hayes, Samuel P. *The Beginning of American Aid to Southeast Asia: The Griffin Mission of 1950*. Lexington, Mass., 1971.

Iriye, Akira. *Power and Culture: The Japanese—American War, 1941–1945*. Cambridge, Mass., 1981.

James, D. Clayton. *The Years of MacArthur*, 2 vols. Boston, 1970–75. The third volume—*Triumph and Disaster, 1945–64* (Boston, 1985)—appeared as this book was going to press. Although its publication was too late to help with my work, readers will find it a great resource in interpreting the general's activities in Japan.

Kennan, George F. *Memoirs, 1925–50*. Boston, 1967.

Kolko, Joyce and Kolko, Gabriel. *The Limits of Power: The World and United States Foreign Policy, 1945–1954*. New York, 1972.

Louis, William R. *Imperialism at Bay*. New York, 1978.

MacArthur, Douglas. *Reminiscences*. New York, 1964.

McMahon, Robert J. *Colonialism and Cold War: The United States and the Struggle for Indonesian Independence, 1945–49*. Ithaca, N.Y. 1981.

Manchester, William. *American Caesar: Douglas MacArthur, 1880–1964*. New York, 1978.

Messer, Robert. *The End of an Alliance: James F. Byrnes, Roosevelt, Truman and the Origins of the Cold War*. Chapel Hill, N.C., 1982.

Moore, Joe. *Japanese Workers and the Struggle for Power, 1945–1947*. Madison, Wis., 1983.

Nagai, Yonosuke and Iriye, Akira, eds. *The Origins of the Cold War in Asia*. New York, 1977.

Petillo, Carol M. *Douglas MacArthur: The Philippine Years*. Bloomington, Ind., 1981.

Sebald, William, and Brines, Russell. *With MacArthur in Japan*. New York, 1965.

Stueck, William W. *The Road to Confrontation: American Policy toward China and Korea, 1947–1950*. Chapel Hill, N.C., 1981.

Thorne, Christopher. *Allies of a Kind: The United States, Britain and the War against Japan, 1941–1945*. New York, 1978.

Truman, Harry S. *Memoirs*, 2 vols. New York, 1955–56.

Tucker, Nancy B. *Patterns in the Dust: Chinese-American Relations and the Recognition Controversy, 1949–50*. New York, 1983.

Whitney, Courtney. *MacArthur: His Rendevous with History*. New York, 1956.

Willoughby, Charles A., and Chamberlain, John. *MacArthur, 1941–51*. New York, 1955.

Yoshida Shigeru. *The Yoshida Memoirs*. Cambridge, Mass., 1961.

ARTICLES

Dingman, Roger. "Strategic Planning and the Policy Process: American Plans for War in East Asia, 1945–50." *Naval War College Review*, Vol. 32, no. 6, November–December 1979, 4–21.

Leffler, Melvyn P. "The American Conception of National Security and the Beginnings of the Cold War, 1945–48." *American Historical Review*, Vol. 89, no. 2, April 1984, 346–81.

Schonberger, Howard. "American Labor's Cold War in Occupied Japan." *Diplomatic History*, Vol. 3, no 3, Summer 1979, 249–72.

Schonberger, Howard. "General William H. Draper, the 80th Congress and the Origins of the Reverse Course." Unpublished paper, Amherst Conference on Occupied Japan, 1980.

Schonberger, Howard. "The Japan Lobby in American Diplomacy, 1947–1952." *Pacific Historical Review*, Vol. 46, no. 3, August 1977, 327–59.

Tucker, Nancy Bernkopf. "American Policy toward Sino-Japanese Trade in the Postwar Years: Politics and Prosperity." *Diplomatic History*, Vol. 8, no 3, Summer 1984, 183–208.

UNPUBLISHED DOCTORAL DISSERTATIONS

Foltos, Lester J. "The Bulwark of Freedom: American Security Policy for East Asia, 1945–1950." Ph.D. diss., University of Illinois, 1980.

Rotter, Andrew J. "The Big Canvas: The United States, Southeast Asia and the World: 1948–50." Ph.D. diss., Stanford University, 1981.

APPENDIX

MacArthur's political agenda in the troop level episode and his antipathy toward FDR, the New Deal, and those associated with it are confirmed in several documents that were located as this study went to press.

On September 4, 1945, MacArthur's most intense political supporter, Sears Roebuck chairman Robert E. Wood, cautioned the general about sinister plans in Washington. According to Wood, the Truman administration expected to argue that a large-scale Japanese occupation requiring high troop levels necessitated continuation of the draft. In reality, Wood declared, this was only a "very clever ruse on the part of the politicians in Washington" to put the "burden of the blame on you [MacArthur]." Anyone deemed responsible for extending the unpopular draft would be "pilloried . . . in the eyes of the public."

MacArthur's military secretary, Gen. Bonner F. Fellers, thanked Wood for his advice and explained that he and MacArthur agreed that the State, War, and Navy departments had intended to use SCAP as the fall guy in their postwar planning. By proclaiming that he needed only 200,000 troops, MacArthur had foiled the plot.

The general's continued resentment of every person and every policy associated with Roosevelt is apparent in the record of a conversation he had with Herbert Hoover in May 1946. Hoover, then on a famine survey, spent the bulk of his time with MacArthur nursing old wounds about how FDR had abused them both. Roosevelt, MacArthur complained, had starved the Pacific theater of supplies, snubbed his advice, and "smeared" him in front of journalists by calling him "McClellan" and a "problem child." Later, FDR acceded to the plan to reconquer the Philippines, not because it was correct but because MacArthur "guaranteed to show great progress . . . before November 1944 if his plans were carried out." MacArthur told Hoover that "Roosevelt's whole interest was in the political possibilities for himself."

The general insisted that, following the liberation of the Philippines early in 1945, the "Jap military gang" wanted to surrender. But, Hoover and MacArthur maintained, neither FDR nor Truman had the sense to engineer a compromise peace "avoiding all of the losses, the atomic bomb, and the entry of Russia into Manchuria." In fact, they continued, this merely repeated FDR's pre-Pearl Harbor strategy which was designed to assure war, not peace, with Japan. MacArthur claimed to have proof that the emperor and Prince Konoe had "agreed to a complete withdrawal" from their conquests in the Pacific and mainland Asia when Roosevelt refused to meet Konoe.

As his anger mounted, MacArthur told Hoover that the "liberals" in Washington were "attempting to destroy Japan" through complex reparations and economic restructuring proposals. He urged that limits be placed on nothing besides munitions manufacturing. In the same vein, the general disparaged Marshall's mediation efforts in China. Although MacArthur denied to Hoover that he had future interest in the presidency, he agreed to consider a political speaking tour in the United States some time in 1947, or whenever the ex-president told him the "time was right."

Hoover noted that whenever he tried to speak with SCAP staff about "Asia, Japanese economics, the war and peace," the main response was a discussion of the "threat of Russia." Some even thought war might erupt within ninety days.

See Robert E. Wood to Douglas MacArthur, September 4, 1945, Wood Papers, MacArthur file; Bonner Fellers to Robert Wood, October 1, 1945, ibid.; memoranda of conversation with MacArthur by Herbert Hoover, May 4, 5, 6, 1946, Hoover Papers, Post-Presidential Subject file, "Famine Emergency Comm.—World Mission, Gen. H. H. Diary 1946, Journey." All documents are in the Herbert Hoover Presidential Library.

INDEX